Second Edition

Color
The Secret Influence

Kenneth R. Fehrman, Ed.D.

Cherie Fehrman

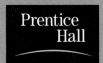
Prentice Hall

Upper Saddle River, NJ 07458

Library of Congress Cataloging-in-Publication Data

Fehrman, Kenneth.
    Color : the secret influence / Kenneth R. Fehrman, Cherie Fehrman.—2nd ed.
        p.   cm
    Includes bibliographical references and index.
    ISBN 0-13-035859-2
    1. Color. 2. Color—Psychological aspects.   I. Fehrman, Cherie, 1945-   II. Title.

QC495 .F43 2003
535.6—dc21   2002041040

Editor-in-Chief: Stephen Helba
Executive Assistant: Nancy Kesterson
Executive Editor: Vernon R. Anthony
Director of Manufacturing and Production: Bruce Johnson
Associate Editor: Marion Gottlieb
Editorial Assistant: Ann Brunner
Managing Editor: Mary Carnis
Production Liaison: Adele M. Kupchik
Marketing Manager: Ryan DeGrote
Production Management: UG/GGS Information Services, Inc.
Production Editor: Nancy Whelan
Manufacturing Manager: Ilene Sanford
Manufacturing Buyer: Cathleen Petersen
Creative Director: Cheryl Asherman
Senior Design Coordinator: Miguel Ortiz
Design Coordinator: Christopher Weigand
Interior Design: UG/GGS Information Services, Inc.
Printer/Binder: Banta Menasha
Cover Designer: Miguel Ortiz
Cover Image: Dorling Kindersley
Cover Printer: Phoenix Color

Pearson Education LTD.
Pearson Education Australia, PTY, Limited
Pearson Education Singapore, Pte. Ltd.
Pearson Education North Asia Ltd.
Pearson Education Canada Ltd.
Pearson Educación de Mexico, S.A. de C.V.
Pearson Education—Japan
Pearson Education Malaysia, Pte. Ltd.

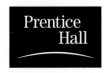

10 9 8 7 6 5 4 3 2 1
ISBN 0-13-035859-2

Contents

three

Color Myths and Biases   63

four

Color and Health   77

five

Color and Psychology   99

Workbook 299

Preface

Color: The Secret Influence—what does that title mean? In a nutshell, it means that color's effects on each of us are vast, but most of us don't have a clue that they are even happening. Color affects your health, your spending habits, your personal and professional image. Color and light are inextricably linked; you cannot have color without light. Yet, in our minds, we constantly separate the two and give little regard to the color/light that surrounds us, and even passes through us. In a very real sense, color/light affects every single aspect of our lives every day, and yet most of us go about our days without giving it a second thought or ever really understanding how we are being affected. Even artists and designers who have spent years working directly with color/light rarely know just how much it affects us physiologically, psychologically, and sociologically. But what if people did know? What if they better understood the possibilities and potential? What if they could recognize the many myths that circulate about color and focus on the facts? These were the questions that intrigued us enough to consider writing this book.

During our research, we often marveled at the information that we encountered—people who could "see" color with their skin, people who reported healing after exposure to color/light, people whose physiological readings were dramatically affected by being in rooms colored a certain way. We were equally mystified by the many myths we encountered that were accepted by the general population as truth without a shred of evidence to back them up. So often we heard people say "red excites you" or "blue is calming" without having any idea why they thought that. They had just heard it somewhere. They had no facts to support a statement, but they "knew" it was true—and they were often vehement about it. Our musings gradually took shape, and we realized that we wanted to write a book that would sort out the myths from the facts, that would show how color/light truly affects us, and that would help us improve our lives by gaining more knowledge about color. At least, those were our initial thoughts when we considered writing this book.

Later, other influences came into play. We knew there were already many color books on the market, so we asked ourselves how ours would be different. One thing we decided right off the bat was that we were not going to repeat the same old myths about color without having our facts in order. Searching through thousands and thousands of research documents for more than ten years, plus doing our own research, turned up some surprising information—sometimes just the opposite of what we expected. Next, we wanted to write a book that could have multiple uses: for the lay person, for the design professional, and for the student of color or design. Some of the books we encountered were so technical they were really physics manuals. Many were filled with pretty pictures and little information; others had a lot of information but little, if any, documentation supporting the "truths" that were set down. Frankly, what we found were the same myths repeated over and over again in book after book, and it seemed that no one had stopped to seek out the proof that should have accompanied the claims. We decided to take a different route and present the reader with facts based on scientific research rather than on hearsay or myth.

To meet our goal of a book that could serve the needs of different groups, we realized that a different kind of book on color/light was needed. We wanted to write an accessible book that presented color/light in an integrated way that not only incorporated the basics of color harmony and usage but also provided information about the vast and often hidden ways in which color affects our lives every day. *Color: The Secret Influence* is based on well-controlled scientific studies that dispel the misinformation about color that has become commonplace. It shows how color/light affects us, from our health to our spending habits, our perceived image, our communication, and even our weight, our sex lives, and why we choose one brand of laundry detergent over another. We wanted to reach a large population and present scientific facts without boring people into a coma, so we have tried to keep the writing lively and to personalize it from our own experience when appropriate. For serious students of design, we have included a workbook section at the end of the book that is filled with assignments, exercises, tests, and quizzes for classroom use. This book has been field-tested in university classrooms for several years, and a teacher's manual is available from the publisher to further aid in instruction of the subject.

Virtually everyone can benefit from a better knowledge of color/light, but it is essential for designers and design students. Designers affect people every day by the colors they choose in their work. Whether their work is interior design, fashion design, product design, graphic design, architecture, or any other related field, those color selections are having a marked influence on the population. It is therefore essential that designers should have a thorough understanding of the effects they produce. In today's competitive marketplace, a designer must have more than just the basic tools to survive. Savvy consumers want to get the most for their money, and designers must be armed with accurate information. Forward-thinking health care givers are beginning to realize the important effect that the color/light environment has on health. Similarly, consumers should be armed with knowledge that can help them make informed choices about purchasing, health and well-being, communication, and personal image. It is for these reasons that we wrote *Color: The Secret Influence*. We believe that color/light-related technologies will be a driving force in this new century and beyond. With this book, we hope to encourage others to seriously study and investigate this fascinating phenomenon. By the time you finish reading *Color: The Secret Influence*, you will find there's much more to color than meets the eye.

Acknowledgments

We are so grateful to everyone who helped to make *Color: The Secret Influence* a reality. We are thankful for your support, your willingness to share, and your dedication to creative learning. Specifically, we would like to thank Shirley P. Foster, Ph.D., University of Alabama; Diane Tepe, University of Memphis; and Katherine Thornhill, Scottsdale Community College, for reviewing the text. Many thanks also to Elizabeth Sugg and Vernon Anthony of Prentice Hall and to Nancy Whelan of UG / GGS Information Services, Inc.; also thanks to Ohlinger Publishing. Most of all, we thank Coco, who showed us with her life how important and effective color/light is. Coco, we will love you always.

Ken and Cherie Fehrman

About the Authors

Dr. Kenneth R. Fehrman earned his doctoral degree from the University of San Francisco, specializing in color and its effects. He is a professor of Interior Design at San Francisco State University and has been a color consultant and interior designer for the past twenty-five years. He has also taught graphic design, environmental design, textiles and aesthetics. Dr. Fehrman is a member of the International Interior Design Association (IIDA), the Interior Design Educators Council (IDEC) and the Inter-Society Color Council (ISCC).

Cherie Fehrman is an interior designer, color consultant, and writer. She has been Dr. Fehrman's color research assistant for many years. She has taught color and design courses at San Francisco State University, the Rudolph Schaeffer School of Design, and the Western Design Institute. She is a member of the Inter-Society Color Council (ISCC) and the Authors Guild. She is also founding President of STOLA—Saluki Tree of Life Alliance, Inc., a national nonprofit hound rescue and welfare group.

The Fehrmans founded PRISM (Photochromatic Research Institute for Science and Marketing) in 1990 to disseminate accurate information about color/light. Separately and together, they have written seven books and several hundred articles. Currently, they continue their color research in the area of color/light therapy and give seminars on the effects of color/light. They have been successful in reversing paralysis in one of their own dogs using color/light therapy and have also extended quality of life in cases of kidney failure in several other dogs using color/light therapy. They are now pursuing this avenue further with veterinarians and are beginning work on their next book.

Chapter one

The color connection

What Is Color?

Color affects every aspect of our lives every day. We take color for granted. It surrounds us. It penetrates our bodies as light waves. We eat it in fruits, vegetables, and artificial food colorings. Our lives depend on color. We rely on colored traffic lights to warn us of danger. We rely on color coding to separate beneficial medications from poisons. We buy products because color advertising appeals to us on a subliminal level. Yet, while color is a major part of our lives, most of us have only a vague awareness of what color is.

So, what is color? The answer may surprise you: Color is an illusion. Our environment only appears colored to us. When the eye sees color, it is being fooled because the world is completely colorless. The visible world consists of achromatic (colorless) substances and electromagnetic vibrations that are also achromatic and differ from one another only in their wavelengths. Color, light, brain waves, body heat, television and radio signals, and solar flares are all part of the same electromagnetic spectrum. The electromagnetic spectrum (Figure 1-1) is measured in meters. For example, radio waves are several hundred meters long, but visible light waves are so short they require their own measurement known as a nanometer. A nanometer is 1-millionth of a millimeter. Humans can perceive only a tiny amount of this spectrum with sensitivity from about 400 nanometers, which we see as deep blue, to about 700 nanometers, which we see as deep red. Even with our relatively limited ability to see color, we are still capable of distinguishing about ten million variations of color within this range. Below this range, there is a narrow band of energy that we perceive as body heat. Lower still is the energy used to transmit radio and television signals and the tiny amount of spectrum space we perceive as sound. At the other end of the human visual spectrum is ultraviolet light, the energy that causes suntanning and kills bacteria. Even further up and down the electromagnetic scale are molecular and radioactive energy, brain wave frequencies, electrical power, and so on.

So if we ask again, "What is color?" we can say that color is a small part of the vast electromagnetic band that encompasses and connects all things. Why did we previously call color an illusion? Because that's exactly what it is. The only distinctive features of electromagnetic energy vibrations are their wavelengths and their energy. They have no inherent color. The multicolored appearance of the environment is only the result of the **interactive visual process**. Color experience and color sensation exist only within the observer's brain (Figure 1-2). Yet, the wavelengths of energy that comprise color have a marked effect on our lives, our health, our behavior, our sexual preferences, and our spending habits.

Color and light are inseparable. In the absence of light, color cannot exist. In a completely dark room, a green carpet is as invisible as an orange or a tropical bird. Colored objects merely appear colored in relation to light. **The sensation of color depends solely on the brain's interpretation of signals coming from the eyes.** If sunlight falls on a field of wildflowers with no eyes and no brain to interpret the energy radiation, there is no color. **Color is not a tangible object. It is a vast interactive process.**

A major component of color is light. Sunlight is the ultimate natural light source, and it has become the standard by which colors are measured. Yet natural daylight is as changeable and ephemeral as color itself. If you are a woman, you have undoubtedly had the experience of buying a

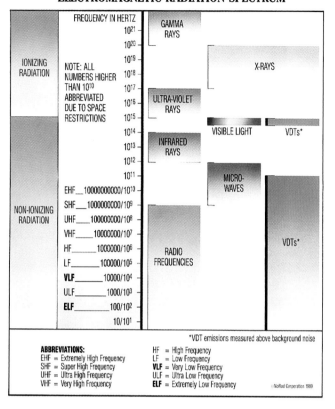

ELECTROMAGNETIC RADIATION SPECTRUM

figure 1-1

Electromagnetic Radiation Spectrum illustrating the small band of the spectrum that represents visible light. Electromagnetic radiation is composed of both electric and magnetic fields across all of the frequencies that make up the electromagnetic spectrum. The frequencies shown above can represent either electric or magnetic fields; in other words, ELF and VLF fields exist in the electric field and separately and simultaneously in the magnetic field. Above visible light and starting in the ultraviolet frequencies, ionizing radiation has sufficient capacity to break a chemical bond and destabilize an atom or molecule. Included in these frequencies are X-rays and gamma rays. Such ionizing radiation can cause genetic damage. Non-ionizing radiation starts at visible light and continues downward. It includes microwaves and radio frequencies (RF) with frequency ranges such as ultrahigh frequency (UHF), very high frequency (VHF), very low frequency (VLF), and extremely low frequency (ELF). Computer monitors and video display terminals emit frequencies beyond the ELF and VLF ranges into the microwave range. Low frequency fields induce electric currents in humans with the potential to cause biological harm. Magnetic fields in the ELF range are very difficult to shield, although technology is available to do so. *Reproduced with permission of Field Management Services (NoRAD)*

lipstick to go with a new dress. In the store the lipstick looked great, but when you get it home the lipstick and the dress look awful together. This happens because the condition of light has changed from the department store to your home. What is often forgotten is that the condition of light on a particular day and time will make colors appear one way, while later on that same day or on a different day they may appear dramatically different.

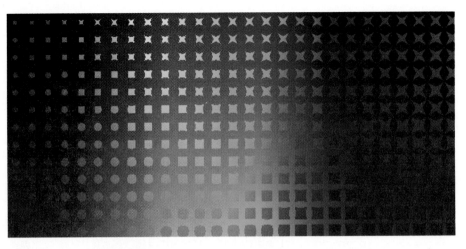

figure 1-2

The mind evaluates this pattern as foreground versus background, based on the grouping of lighter against darker elements. Where the foreground switches over from lighter to darker, the brain has trouble "seeing" this part of the pattern, even though the colors of foreground and background are, in fact, distinct. *Reprinted with permission of Edward S. May*

Because color is an individually perceived phenomenon, it is logical that it should be used to benefit the individual, not some preconceived set of standards. In the field of color, we all have a chance to express ourselves individually because the purchase of every object nearly always involves making a decision about color. From the choice of clothing, housewares, and furniture to the selection of a new car or the landscaping of a garden, color choice is always involved. But as anyone knows who has come home with an object that looks completely different from the way it looked in the store, color selection can be an extremely complex task.

Let's suppose a man wants to buy a pair of leather shoes to exactly match a navy blue suit. He goes into a store and picks out the shoes. To see the colors precisely, he steps outside the store entrance and compares the color of the shoes with his suit. While he is standing on the sidewalk making his choice, the sun is shining. He pays for his purchase, feeling pleased with himself that he was able to find the perfect match. By the time he reaches home, it has started raining. He unwraps his shoes and notes with a sinking feeling that they no longer match his suit. Like the woman with the lipstick, what seemed an identical match in the sunlight now looks totally wrong. This phenomenon is called **metamerism**. Two colors that are metameric look alike in sunlight, but once the light changes they no longer match.

In technology, the problem of metameric colors assumes great significance. For example, primary printing inks may appear exactly alike, but if made of different pigments they will appear completely different under different lighting conditions. The problem is basically the same in all fields of industry, whether in the manufacture of paint, textile printing, or cosmetics. Any interchange of color scales is possible only if the various primary inks or dyes made by different manufacturers contain pigments that are restricted to certain tolerance ranges. This is explained in detail in Chapter 11, Color Order Systems. For the moment it is enough to know that matching color accurately can be a very tricky business.

To assess colors accurately, a light source of equal, unvarying intensity is required. While natural sunlight is the ideal standard, even it cannot be trusted because of variances caused by weather conditions and shifting light conditions as day moves toward night. In an attempt to overcome this problem from an industrial point of view, light sources meeting the special demand of equal, unvarying intensity have been developed to emit a balanced spectral distribution. These are called color analysis lamps and are often used in color research and development.

In grade school we were taught that all the colors of the spectrum combined result in white light. White light, however, is not a homogeneous phenomenon. It does not consist of a large number of identical white light rays, but rather electromagnetic vibrations. The range of all the colors humans can perceive is contained in the white light of sunlight. If we isolate electromagnetic vibrations of only a single wavelength from the spectrum, we call this a **monochromatic color**. Even daylight is not always white. In daylight the ratios of the spectral colors change depending on the position of the sun in the sky, or whether the day is foggy, rainy, smoggy, or clear.

The effects of light on color are vast. For example, the yellow sodium light of a highway or parking lot causes color distortion, as do the greenish-white mercury lights that are often used in street lighting. Mercury light turns red objects a sickly brown. Orange-red incandescent light shows objects in closer conformity to daylight, but there are differences in color representation. Yellow lines on white paper are hard to see in incandescent light. Unfortunately, concerning artificial light sources, the most energy-efficient sources are also those that have the worst color-rendering capabilities. Low-pressure sodium lamps are extremely efficient in that they radiate only those wavelengths to which the eye is most sensitive—green and yellow. They provide great visibility for the least expenditure of energy, but their color distortion is so intense as to be disturbing, and negative health effects may be associated with them.

Sunlight or daylight remains the ideal lighting condition, allowing a great variety of color display. This is a major key in dealing with color because color is not static. **Color is constantly changing because light is constantly changing.** This is an essential fact to remember whenever color is being considered (Figure 1-3).

The color composition of natural light changes from dawn to dusk, from summer to winter, from north to south, and from east to west. California light is different from English light. Colors that look wonderful in the bright sunlight of California can be startling in the dimmer northern light of England. People in Mediterranean regions are accustomed to strong, mellow light, while the degree of cloud cover in northern Europe has conditioned the population to muted, grayed colors (Figure 1-4).

Even colors in a single room will appear different depending on the conditions of light. Walls opposite windows will be brighter than other walls. Ever-changing lighting conditions make it impossible to maintain the environment in a constant color. The point is not to try, but to use the ever-shifting interactive process of color/light to extend the range of visible color. We remember too well a client who had ordered white canvas blinds installed in her dining room. We received a frantic telephone call from her saying that her canvas blinds changed color to a peach tone at

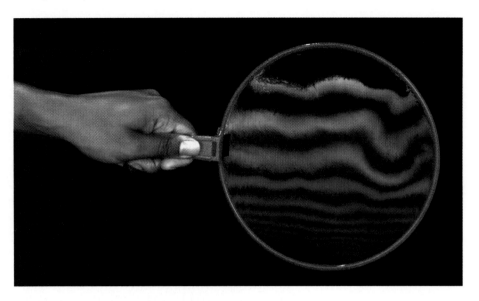

When light waves hit the soap film of this giant bubble maker, they reflect and interfere with each other. This interference causes the shimmering colors you see. White light is made of many different colors. When white light shines on the soap film, some light waves reflect from the front surface of the film, and some reflect from the back surface of the film. When these two sets of reflected waves meet, they can add together, cancel each other out, or partially cancel, depending on the thickness of the film and the initial color of the light. When light waves of a particular color meet and cancel each other, then that color is subtracted from white light. For example, if the red light waves cancel, then you see white light minus red light, which you perceive as blue-green light. *Reprinted with permission of Exploratorium, www.exploratorium.edu*

sunset, and for that fifteen-minute period each day they no longer matched her white sofa. Such unrealistic expectations occur because people do not really understand the nature of color and light.

Color Perception

In any serious discussion of color, the factor of color perception must be considered. Color perception varies greatly from person to person, depending on the individual brain's interpretation of color signals coming from the eye, on whether or not color vision is defective, and on our psychological and cultural biases toward color. Let's consider for the moment how most of us relate to color. The average person assumes that color is color. Red is always red. Blue is always blue. But color perception varies not only from person to person but from species to species, and the difference is often dramatic.

When we were doing the many years of research that led to a doctoral degree and, subsequently, to this book, we gathered masses of data. From all of it we found some of the most fascinating information related to how humans and other species see color differently. We found that stepping outside ourselves to view the world from a different vantage point somehow helped us gain a better understanding of our humanity. Let's take the common bee as our example, as described by Rivlin and Gravelle in their work on deciphering the senses. While human color vision is most sensitive to three areas of the spectrum—red, green, and

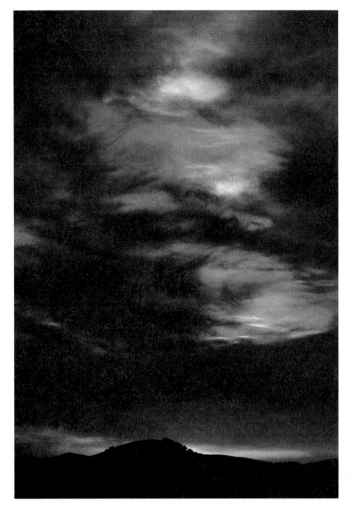

figure 1-4

We take the colors of a sunset for granted, yet to explain why the sky is blue, how a rainbow is formed, or why a spectrum can sometimes be seen through the mesh of a spider web involves the most complex physics and encompasses all that is known about the nature of light. *Reproduced by permission of Todd Pickering, photographer*

blue—bee vision is based on sensitivity to yellow, blue, and ultraviolet (which humans are unable to see). Bees are nearly unable to distinguish red as we know it. Since purple is a mixture of the two extremes of the visible spectrum (for humans, red and violet), "bee purple" is very different from "human purple" in that it is composed of yellow and ultraviolet. The neutral white is also perceived very differently by bees and humans. In human perception, white is a combination of all the visible spectral colors: red, orange, yellow, green, blue, and violet. Because bees have a different range of color perception, their concept of white is a mixture of yellow, blue, and ultraviolet, so a flower that looks white to a human would seem blue-green to a bee.

If we were temporarily able to see through a bee's eyes, the world would seem dramatically different. Flowers, for example, take on a completely different appearance once ultraviolet is included in the visible spectrum. Through bee eyes, red flowers are virtually invisible, but because different parts of a bloom may reflect ultraviolet light differently, most flowers also appear patterned to the bee. These patterns caused by ultraviolet reflections indicate to bees the presence of nectar. While humans see two red flowers as identical, they may appear as different to bees as red and green seem to us.

Another fascinating aspect of color takes place in the mind's eye. The eye's role is not just to transmit signals to the brain exactly as they enter the eye. To some extent the eye does a little editing on its own before the message is transmitted. It codes the information received from the external world in terms of texture, depth, shape, and color and then **the brain reconstructs, but does not exactly replicate, the image that originally entered the eye**. This means that what we think we see is not necessarily what's out there. Essentially, the external world is of our own creation.

The Language of Color

As is the case with any specialized field of study, color has its own vocabulary. In order to discuss color effectively, it is necessary to understand at least the basic terminology. The terms **color** and **hue** are synonyms that are often used interchangeably. **Hue** is an attribute by which one color is distinguished from another. All colors are considered to be similar to one or a portion of two of the spectral hues: red, orange, yellow, green, blue, and violet. Thus, crimson, vermilion, and pink, although different colors, are close in hue. Black, white, and gray lack hue and are considered **neutrals**. Physically, hue is determined by wavelength. The other two attributes of color are **saturation** and **value**. **Value** is the lightness or darkness of a surface color. It is measured by a comparative gray scale in which a series of grays is applied to a vertical axis with a perfect black (Value 0) at the bottom and a perfect white (Value 1) at the top. Colors of the same lightness as a given gray are assigned the same value and arranged on a corresponding horizontal axis. **Saturation** or **purity** is essentially the amount of pigment in a color and is defined as the strength or vividness of a hue. Red, for example, can increase in saturation from a pale pink to a vivid vermilion. Saturation is the amount of a particular color present in that color. The less white a pigment color contains, the more saturated it is. The **spectrum** is defined as the colored image formed when light is spread out according to its wavelength by being passed through a prism (Figure 1-5). The relative intensities of the

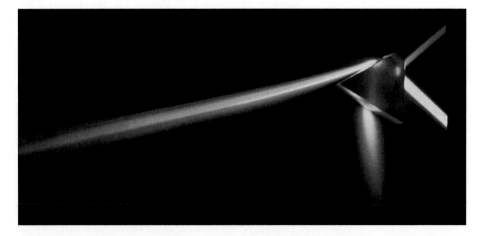

figure 1-5

Dispersion of light through this prism splits a beam of white light into its spectral colors, red, orange, yellow, green, blue, and violet. *Reprinted with permission of Exploratorium, www.exploratorium.edu*

colors in the spectrum of natural sunlight are different from their intensities in artificial light. **Spectral colors** are the colors that appear in the spectrum of sunlight, ranging from red through orange, yellow, green, blue, and violet. Spectral colors are perfectly saturated and do not contain contaminants in the form of brown, pink, purple, or gray. Other commonly used terms in the study of color are **tint** and **shade**. A **shade** occurs when a pure color is mixed with gray or black. A **tint** occurs when a pure color is mixed with white. Pastels are referred to as tints, while deeper tones are referred to as shades of a particular color. Other qualities of color are referred to as **flicker, glitter,** and **sheen**, which refer to variations in surface appearance in relation to lighting conditions. Additional color terms will be introduced in subsequent chapters as they relate to the area under discussion.

Color Conditioning

Color conditioning is an aspect of color that affects us in very subtle ways. We are all afflicted with color biases based on things we have been taught as children, based on our cultures, and based on misinformation that we have come to accept as fact. We are all particularly biased regarding color when it comes to food. Add a little blue food coloring to oatmeal and it becomes inedible to most people. On the other hand, a touch of red food coloring added to tofu makes it strongly resemble meat to vegetarians, even though it has virtually no flavor of its own. Most of our color biases are culturally learned rather than universal truths and, just as different countries attach different meanings to color, so their preferences for food colors differ. The British like green apples while Americans prefer red apples. West Indians like their bananas deep, ripe brown, while Europeans eat them when they are yellow and immature. Canned peas sold in France are a greenish gray color from blanching, but the British won't buy them that way so they are dyed green for the British market. The Danish like not only the peas but also the water in the can to be dyed green.

Color conditioning begins at birth. It has more to do with language than with color. Cultural background can affect color communication. In some cultures the language does not contain separate words for blue and green; in others yellow and orange are not distinguished. The linguistic basis of color symbolism is rooted in analogy. How often we have been told that red symbolizes fire. This symbolic connection presumably suggests itself because red and fire are alike in their redness. But the analogy *Red is like fire* tells us practically nothing about the color red. It does, however, present us with visual imagery that biases us to believe that red is warm, when there is absolutely no scientific basis for this claim.

Because of its past associations with fire and heat, red has become tangled in our minds with imagery that does nothing but confuse. The establishment of red as a "warm" color is so firmly entrenched in our culture that some people refuse to wear red in the summer, claiming that it is too hot. Such people are substituting their ideas of fire for their perceptions of red.

Color symbolism has been with us for centuries. Response to it is our response to color preconceptions and color biases. It is a predetermined response based on literary and psychological ideas about color rather than a response to the nature of color itself. In part, humans seem impelled to create symbols and to attach artificial significance to colors because our

feelings and emotions, our literary, psychological, and intellectual preconceptions interfere with our direct perception of the physical world.

Color in fashion and interiors, color traditions, and color conventions
are all specialized forms of transitory color conditioning and are determined by the traditional preconceptions of a society, not by its color perceptions. These fashions and fads are of varying duration. A color may
be "in fashion" for only a few months before it loses the connotations
that made it seem desirable. Other trends may last a few generations or
for centuries. The belief that only black was suitable for the clothing of
elderly women was furthered by the extended period of mourning practiced by Queen Victoria after the death of Prince Albert.

The Yezidi, a people who live in the Caucasus and in Armenia,
despise blue. They curse their enemies by saying, "May you die in blue
garments," because they have been conditioned to believe blue is an
undesirable color even though no one in their culture remembers why. If
their belief seems illogical or a trifle primitive, perhaps it is likely that
they would be equally amazed by some of our color prejudices.

We cast aspersions on a person's level of courage by calling him
yellow. We are *in the pink* when we feel good, *in the red* when we are in
debt, and *in the black* when we are solvent. We get *the blues* when we
are sad. We *talk a blue streak* when we are being wordy. We are *green
with envy* or we have a *purple fit* or *see red* or are in a *red rage* when we
are angry. *Scarlet women* always spell trouble.

Both in Imperial Rome and in China, white, rather than black, denoted
mourning. To the Maya, kings were not blue-blooded but white-blooded.
In the Hebrew Scriptures, red, blue, purple, and white respectively symbolized the elements of fire, air, water, and earth. Flames composed of
these four colors symbolized the presence of God. The Pueblo Indians of
the Southwest systematized color more than any other people. While the
colors used varied from tribe to tribe, the habit of assigning colors to various compass directions is common to all Pueblo tribes and finds no parallel in contemporary Western society. It is interesting to note that in
1922 the psychologist Rorschach's inkblot test associated green with
Russia, while later Russia and Communism were associated with red.
Rorschach suggested that green was associated with Russia because
Russia was usually colored green on maps at that time.

One of the clearest examples of bias occurs in black and white. In
Western culture they have always stood for good (white) and evil (black),
heaven versus hell, angel versus devil, and so on. But the ancient
Egyptians viewed black as the source of life, based on their perception of
the black mud of the life-giving Nile. To the ancient Egyptians, black had
positive rather than negative connotations. Japanese funeral garments
are made of white cloth and Japanese coffins are draped in white,
whereas in the West black is typically used at funerals except in the case
of infants or small children, when white is often used to denote purity.
In Buddhism, yellow is the color of death. In our culture, black is so
completely associated with heaviness that workers who were studied
with relation to lifting weight found black boxes far heavier to lift than
pale yellow boxes of exactly the same weight.

Is blue the sacred, tranquil color we think it to be in the West?
Americans prefer blue to every other color, according to a study done at

Western Washington University. In a cross-cultural test conducted at the Albert-Ludwigs University in Freiburg, Germany, the Spanish picked white as their first choice and tended to ignore blue. The so-called inherent emotional properties of color that we have been conditioned to accept are culturally biased also. Americans tend to think of greens and blues as soothing or calming, primarily because we have been taught to believe this without any scientific basis for the belief. Germans find clear, light colors stimulating, while the Spanish find them calming. Germans find dark blue calming but the Spanish do not.

In a study done at the University of Paris in which galvanic skin response was measured as an indication of excitement, French college students found purple to be the most arousing of the six colors being studied while green, violet, and yellow diminished arousal. However, similar studies in the United States have shown red to be more arousing and blue to be more calming and, contradictorily, that red and blue produce an equal effect. Our own studies showed no significant difference between red, blue, or yellow when subjects were tested for performance and emotional and physical stimulation. Studies among third-grade American children show yellow, orange, green, and blue to be "happy" colors. By the time Americans reach college level, however, blue has changed to a "sad" color. We will discuss these issues in greater detail in subsequent chapters. For the moment, the vital factors to consider in the discrepancies between these studies are **cultural bias** and **the control of color and light conditions** during the study.

Even the old myth that red appears to advance and is a warm color while blue appears to recede and is cool is nothing more than cultural bias and conditioned response. **The operative factor in advancing and receding colors appears to be the contrast between the colors and their backgrounds, rather than the colors themselves.** A study run at the University of Bologna, Italy, found that colors offering the most contrast appear to stand out or advance more than colors that blend with the background.

Many of our color taboos are relics from the 1940s, a decade notable for the dictatorial mandates of monochromatic living rooms, white kitchens, pastel nurseries, white shirts for men, and white Sunday dresses for young girls. Decorating books of a few decades past can provide a good chuckle in their presentation of the "proper" uses of color, "clashing" colors, and "tasteful" colors. In fact, colors are neither proper nor improper, colors do not clash, and tasteful colors are in the eye of the beholder. We continue to be burdened with far too many inaccurate and obsolete statements about color that have, unfortunately, become part of our culture. Statements such as "Black makes things seem smaller," "White makes things seem larger," "Old people and redheads shouldn't wear red," "Brunettes and blondes can't wear the same colors," "Red is a warm color," or "Blue is a cool color" should be banished from the vocabulary of any thinking person. All of these "rules" are based on nothing more than the personal whim of the individuals who initiated them. There is absolutely no scientific or rational basis for them, and yet they have entrenched themselves so firmly in our culture that they have spawned a public condition that we term chromophobia (fear of color), which is really a fear of appearing tasteless. Chromophobia is most often noted in the field of interior design. We wish we had a dollar for every time in our many years in the interior design business a client sheepishly said, "I've always secretly wanted to paint my living room red, but you know it's **red**, and I don't know what people might think." To our way of thinking, it's a sad state of affairs when people are so bound by irrelevant, outmoded color philosophies that they are afraid to do something as simple as paint a room in a color they really like. All these old "rules" serve to do is stifle individuality and creativity. In writing this book, we hope to defuse these bombs and to present readers with facts that will free them to make their own choices based on their individual preferences.

Color and Health

When discussing the effects of color on human health, it is important to consider that in this context color and light are synonymous. Color and light are inextricably linked. While we will go into this in greater detail in a later chapter, for this brief overview of color's effect on human biology we consider color and light as one linked phenomenon. Color/light affects our physical and psychological states both directly and indirectly. Different wavelengths (colors) of light entering the eye can directly affect the center of emotion in the brain (the hypothalamus), which, in turn, affects the pituitary gland, the "controller" gland of the entire endocrine system. The pituitary gland regulates the thyroid and sex glands, which, in turn, regulate hormone levels and the moods related to them.

Color/light not only affects us when entering through the eyes; it has the ability to penetrate our bodies and has a marked effect on biological systems. Some of the more commonly known effects include the synthesis of vitamin D through ultraviolet radiation acting on the skin, and the production of melanin pigment, which we know as tanning. Less known are the ability of photosensitive people to develop a skin rash as a result of chemical sensitizers in the blood interacting with sunlight, and the ability to treat various illnesses including herpes simplex and psoriasis with variations of color/light.

The chemical reaction involving light has been well known for centuries. Milk, beer, and many medicines change or develop strange flavors if exposed to light, so dark brown and green bottles were developed to screen out light. If potato chips or corn chips are left exposed under the glare of supermarket fluorescent lighting, they quickly turn rancid from the photooxidation of the cooking oils reacting with light. This is why they are usually packaged in opaque materials. Some pesticides become more toxic when exposed to sunlight. Yellow light has been introduced into the dairy sections of some supermarkets to retain the freshness of milk. While the effects of color/light have been noted for many years, it is only recently, through the relatively new scientific area of photobiology, that the ramifications of color/light for health and illness have been seriously considered.

One of the first widely accepted medical treatments with color/light began during the 1950s with the introduction of a radical new treatment for jaundice in newborns. The condition, called neonatal jaundice, stems from a buildup of incompatibilities between the mother's and the baby's blood, which results in a waste serum called bilirubin. The infant's immature liver is often incapable of filtering the wastes fast enough to prevent ensuing brain damage and death. Until the 1950s, blood transfusion was the only available treatment. Then a sharp-eyed British nurse noticed that when jaundiced babies in the hospital nursery were wheeled near windows and left in the sunlight, their jaundiced yellow skin color began to fade. Further research indicated that the sunlight had an effect on the babies that enabled them to excrete the toxic wastes that had been building up in them.

At first it was thought that the light broke down the bilirubin or stimulated the production of sluggish liver enzymes to speed up filtration of the toxins, but it has since been discovered that the sunlight penetrating the babies' skin produces a photon of visible blue light. When the blue light comes in contact with a molecule of bilirubin, it changes its physical structure in a way that makes the toxins water-soluble and easily excreted.

The antibacterial effects of sunlight were recognized during the nineteenth century and utilized in the treatment of diseases such as tuberculosis and strep and staph infections. More recent studies have shown that exposure to color/light in the form of ultraviolet light, a part of sunlight invisible to humans, increases the number of white blood cells in human blood, specifically the lymphocytes, which play an important role in immune defense systems. Continuing research is being conducted on color/light in relation to cancer, AIDS, and other immune system malfunctions.

In both popular and scientific areas, so much has been written about color that the distinction between fact and myth is easily blurred. Researchers have often focused their attention on physiological responses to color, but the results of these studies have subsequently been taken out of the context of the laboratory and applied indiscriminately to residences, workplaces, and institutions. An example of this is the belief that green in easy on the eyes. After spending hours in surgery visually focused on red blood, surgical staff would experience green flashes on the walls of the operating room, caused by the afterimage phenomenon. Hospitals replaced the white of operating room walls with light green to minimize these afterimages. It was then incorrectly inferred that a color used in hospitals as a visual aid must also be beneficial in other environments. Based on the false assumption that green is restful, it was selected for use in redecorating the main cell block and solitary confinement areas at Alcatraz Prison. From there it went on to coat the walls of libraries, classrooms, and public spaces. The indiscriminate use of green as a calming agent proliferated until the myth became established as fact.

"Pink is for girls, blue is for boys," says the old adage. We have come to accept with a benign smile the concept of dressing female infants in pink and male infants in blue to such an extent that some people even assume the gender of a strange child by the color of the clothes it is wearing. Pink is considered soft, feminine, and dainty while blue harbors the more masculine traits of sincerity, power, and assertiveness. Is this just sexist rhetoric or is there more behind pink and blue than meets the eye?

When giving color lectures we often begin by asking for a couple of volunteers—preferably a couple of large, athletic-looking males—to help us demonstrate the immediate physiological effects of color. The men in turn are asked to clasp their hands together and extend their arms out in front at shoulder level. One of us then applies pressure to their arms, asking them to resist. The men are able to resist the pressure and their arms remain straight out in front of them. We then apply the same pressure on their arms after covering each man's field of vision with a sheet of bubblegum pink construction paper (Figure 1-6). To the volunteers' amazement, they are totally unable to resist the pressure and their arms invariably fall limp. When the same pressure-resistance is tried with the volunteers' field of vision surrounded by blue construction paper (Figure 1-7) of the same value, their strength is restored and they are able to resist the pressure again. This demonstration is not scientific, but it does dramatically demonstrate before a group the immediate effects of color on the human body. The pink had made them weaker. The blue restored their strength. But what actually happened? How could simple sheets of pink or blue paper held before the eyes so drastically alter a person's strength? What might the ramifications be of the "pink for girls" influence? These questions, like most other things associated with color, cannot be answered in one simple sentence. First, we must look more closely at this pink-and-blue effect.

On March 1, 1979, based on the provocative results hinted at by studies investigating the effects of pink, a holding cell at the U.S. Naval Correctional Center, Naval Support Activity, in Seattle, Washington, was painted pink. The entire cell was painted pink except for the gray floor covering. Knowing that a new inmate is most prone to violence at initial intake, the holding cell was selected for the test to see if it could create a beneficial, calming effect. Each person about to be processed was held in the pink cell for ten to fifteen minutes while papers were being prepared. After 156 days of continuous use, the correctional center reported to the

figure 1-6

When doing color demonstrations, we have found that this "bubble gum pink" color has a physiological effect within an average of 2.7 seconds after exposure to it. It is thought that the color pink may act directly on the endocrine system to cause a change in the body's chemical balance that results in temporary muscle relaxation and weakness. Prolonged exposure to pink may cause aggression.

figure 1-7

This color blue restores the weakening effects of the pink in our color demonstrations. It is also the favorite color of the average American male.

Bureau of Naval Personnel, Law Enforcement and Corrections Division, Washington, D.C., that "since initiation of this procedure there have been no incidents of erratic or hostile behavior during the initial phase of confinement. Before painting the holding cell pink, duty intake officers remarked that hostile behavior by inmates was a 'whale of a problem.'"

These encouraging results prompted the commander of the Santa Clara County Jail in San Jose, California, to also try painting one of the holding cells pink. He even went a step further and painted a "fish tank" pink. A fish tank holds about fifteen inmates at a time until cell assignments have been made. Observers reported that the detainees were in a "humorous and restful mood" when in the pink rooms. Hopes were high that the color pink might hold the key to nonviolent behavior. This part of the study was much publicized and the initial impact of pink became known to the general public, but the full results of the study were not equally publicized. What seemed so promising at first did not continue to prove so promising in further studies.

Studies with animals found that pink light adversely affected their behavior, even causing some of them to become cannibalistic. At first this did not reconcile with the seemingly calming effects of pink, until an inmate was inadvertently left in a pink cell for about four hours. Nearing the four-hour mark, he went completely berserk, trying to destroy the cell and himself. This was in keeping with the animal studies. Further investigation disclosed that the relaxing effects of being in a pink room last about thirty minutes. If a person is exposed for longer than thirty minutes, a reversal tends to occur, causing hostility and increased strength. It appears that the calming effects of pink are only

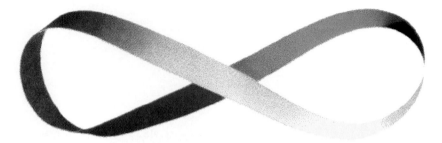

temporary. **What is significant is that these effects do occur.** Repeated testing found that the relaxing effects of pink occur in an average of 2.7 seconds after exposure. Why this occurs has yet to be explained, but it is thought that the color pink may act directly on the endocrine system, causing a change in the body's chemical balance that results in temporary muscle relaxation and weakness. Color, it seems, has astonishing power, a power that we are only just beginning to investigate and understand.

In this introductory chapter we have barely scratched the surface of color's effects. The color/light phenomenon forms a kind of invisible environment around us—invisible in the sense that humans can see only about 1 percent of the entire spectrum, and this is the part we call color. Yet, the electromagnetic waves of sunlight that we are unable to see with the naked eye have a marked effect on us. Life on earth depends on this radiant wavelength energy. It is as essential to life and health as are air and water. Without a sufficient and proper balance of color/light, we would grow sick and die.

Through relatively new areas of scientific study such as photobiology, we are beginning to discover in greater detail the links between color/light and human health and physiological processes. Researchers continue to investigate the psychological aspects of color that affect us in countless subtle ways. In this book we aspire to provide an overview of the importance of the interactive process of color (Figure 1-8), to aid readers in understanding it, and to show ways to use it advantageously in all aspects of your life.

REFERENCES

Bouma, P., *The Physical Aspects of Colour*, Macmillan, 1971.

Cimbalo, R., Beck, D., Sendziak, D., "Emotionally Toned Pictures and Color Selection for Children and College Students," *Journal of Genetic Psychology* 133 1978, (2) 303–304.

Colour, Marshall Editions Limited, Knapp Press, 1983, 37.

Darakis, L., "Influence of Five Stimulus Colors on GSR," *Bulletin de Psychologie* 30 1977, (14–16) 760–766.

Farne, M., Campione, F., "Color as an Indicator for Distance," *Giornale Italiano di Psicologia* 3 1976, (3) 415–420.

Fehrman, K. R., *The Effects of Interior Pigment Color on Task Performance Mediated by Arousal*, University of San Francisco, 1986, University Microfilms International, vol. 48, no. 4, 1987.

Felber, T. D., reported at American Medical Association Conference, June 1979, Atlantic City, NJ.

Knowles, P., "The Blue Seven Is Not a Phenomenon," *Perceptual and Motor Skills* 45 1944, (2) 648–650.

Maas, J., Jayson, J. K., Kleiber, D. A., "Effects of Spectral Differences in Illumination on Fatigue," *Journal of Applied Psychology* 59 1974, 524–526.

Nassau, K., *The Physics and Chemistry of Color*, John Wiley and Sons, 1983, 7.

Ott, J., *Light, Radiation and You*, Devin-Adair Company, 1982.

Rivlin, R., Gravelle, K., *Deciphering the Senses: The Expanding World of Human Perception*, Simon and Schuster, 1984, Ch. 3

Schickinger, P., "Intercultural Comparisons of Emotional Connotations of Colors in the Chromatic Pyramid Test, Using Factor Analysis," *Revista de Psicologia General y Applicada* 30 1975, (136) 781–808.

Van Essen, D., neurobiologist at Caltech, has suggested that there may be over 20 different processing centers for vision in the brain. Approximately 50 percent of a monkey's brain and 30 percent of the human brain appear to be involved in the visual process.

Wurtman, R. J., "Biological Implications of Artificial Illumination," National Technical Conference, Illuminating Engineering Society, Phoenix, Arizona, September 8–12, 1960.

Wurtman, R. J., "The Effects of Light and Visual Stimuli on Endocrine Function," *Neuroendocrinology* 12, 1967.

Wurtman, R. J., "The Pineal and Endocrine Function," *Hospital Practice* 4 1968, 32–37.

Wurtman, R. J., "The Effects of Light on the Human Body," *Scientific American*, July 1975.

Wurtman, R. J., Weisel, J., "Environmental Lighting and Neuroendocrine Function: Relationship between Spectrum of Light Source and Gonadal Growth," *Endocrinology* 85 1969, (6) 1218–1221.

Chapter two

Color: Pigment and light

This chapter covers the nuts and bolts of color and light. It contains a lot of information—much more, in fact, than the average person may ever want to know about color/light. It has been written with different readers in mind. If you are a serious student of color/light, you will need to read every word to gain a thorough understanding of the topic. If you are a reader who is more interested in quickly learning how to understand and use color in your own environment without delving into the subject in great depth, then you may want to skim for information pertinent to you.

The Nature of Color

Sensations of color do not exist without light. Even though a carrot may appear equally orange on the surface and in a cross-section, the color orange is not inherent in the carrot but in the conditions of light associated with it at a given time and place. Not until the development of quantum theory was this fully understood.

Einstein proved that light is composed of *quanta*, which he called *photons* from the Greek word *photos*, meaning "light." In motion as propagated light, photons behave as waves traveling with different frequencies or wavelengths. Different wavelengths of light, differently colored, are composed of photons of different energies. Those in the shortwave region of the spectrum have the most energy, and longwave photons have least energy. When light falls on an object, the photons behave not as waves but as particles, some of which are absorbed, some transmitted, and some reflected. The eye sees an object only by the light it reflects, so the wavelengths it reflects determine its color.

Some objects reflect or absorb light of all different wavelengths equally well. Black velvet absorbs nearly all light that falls on it (*incident light*). Snow reflects nearly all incident light. An object that absorbs some of each wavelength of incident light and reflects the rest appears gray—the actual shade of gray depending on the proportion reflected. Black, white, and gray are not considered colors, but *neutrals*.

Different objects are capable of selective absorption. They absorb photons of certain wavelengths from incident light and reflect the rest. In the carrot's case, most of the photons from the green, blue, and violet wavelengths are absorbed, and photons from the red, orange, and yellow regions of the wavelength spectrum are strongly reflected. To some degree, all matter absorbs and reflects light, but pigments are the most efficient agents of selective absorption. The carrot owes its orange color to pigments called carotenoids that absorb the shortwave light and reflect the long wavelengths (Figure 2-1).

Unabsorbed photons can be reflected in various ways. The ordered molecules in solid materials reflect them in a regular pattern, enabling the eye to see a sharp image of the objects of which they are composed. The disordered molecules in liquids and the sparse diffusions of gases can also react with light passing through them and reradiate at random in all directions. Instead of reflecting light, they scatter it.

Generally, the photons with the highest energies—the violet and blue—are scattered more easily than the lower energy photons such as red, yellow, or orange. This is why the sky looks blue during daylight. Milk has a blue tinge because particles of fat suspended in the liquid scatter photons of blue light.

TYPICAL SPECTRAL ENERGY DISTRIBUTION
400W, 4000K METAL HALIDE LAMP

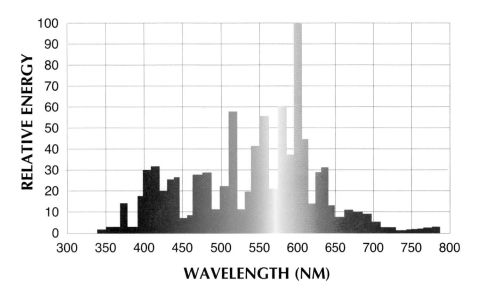

figure 2-1

SPECTRAL DISTRIBUTION CHART
When we look at a light source, we perceive a single color, but in actuality we are seeing literally thousands of colors and variations of colors. The combination of different wavelengths of light makes up the color we see. The different combinations and the relative intensity of various wavelengths of light can be used to determine a light source's Color Rendering Index (CRI). The CRI is an indication of a lamp's ability to show individual colors relative to a standard as indicated by the above chart showing the spectral energy distribution of a 400-watt metal halide lamp. *Reproduced by permission of Bright Ideas, an Advanced Lighting Technologies Company*

All of these reflection and scattering effects are caused by light being reradiated at the same frequency it had when it struck the object. Some materials can cause energy to reradiate at a lower frequency. This phenomenon of converting high-frequency radiation into visible light at a lower frequency is called *fluorescence.*

How the Human Eye Sees Color

At dawn, the world is gray (Figure 2-2). Irregularities in the landscape can barely be identified as the outlines of buildings, trees, or outcroppings of rock. Between five and ten photons of light (equivalent to a single candle flame burning ten miles away) are sufficient to produce the sensation of light in the human eye, so humans can orient themselves in very low levels of illumination.

Each rod and cone cell contains molecules of pigments that absorb light entering the eye. When light strikes a molecule of rod pigment called *rhodopsin,* the pigment bleaches as the molecule splits into its component parts, triggering the release of a chemical transmitter. This process initiates the electrical messages of the rods, which are ultimately conveyed to the brain, and special biochemical mechanisms continually regenerate bleached rhodopsin molecules to their native light-sensitive

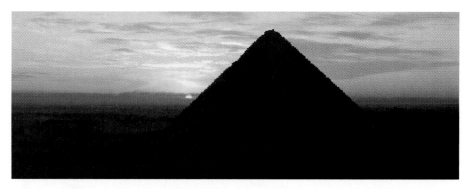

In dawn light, irregularities in the landscape can barely be identified as the outlines of buildings, trees, or outcroppings of rock, but even small amounts of light can be sufficient for humans to orient themselves. Although there is very little light in this dawn photograph, the outline of an Egyptian pyramid is clearly defined. © *Dorling Kindersley*

form. When the intensity of morning light increases, a level is reached that stimulates the cones, which then take over visual function from the rods, whose signal to the brain no longer "sees." Cones have pigments closely similar to the rhodopsin in rods, and these pigments go through similar cycles of bleaching and regeneration and cause the cone cells' electrical responses to light. Each time the level of illumination changes—for example, going into a dark theater from the daylight—the eye has to adapt. It takes twenty minutes for the bleached rhodopsin to fully regenerate, and more for the rods to regain maximum sensitivity.

There are three types of cones, each containing a different type of visual pigment like rhodopsin, although their exact chemical nature is still unknown. They regenerate much faster than rhodopsin and are sensitive in humans to three different ranges of the spectrum called for convenience red, blue, and green. In fact, the cones are most sensitive to yellow light of 575 nanometers, green light of 535 nanometers, and blue light of 444 nanometers. (A *nanometer* is one thousand-millionth of a meter, or one millionth of a millimeter.)

Light falling on the eye is refracted by the *cornea* and enters the eye chamber through the *pupil*, the circular opening in the colored iris (Figure 2-3). The iris dilates in bright light and constricts in the dark, altering the size of the pupil and controlling the amount of light admitted. The pupil is black because most of the light entering the eye is absorbed. The retina, only about 0.4 mm thick, contains about 120 million rods and about 6 million cones. Only when the light and color signals from the eye reach the visual cortex of the brain do we see color. Almost a third of the cerebral matter of the human brain is involved in processing visual information.

Problems with color vision range from a complete inability to see color to the inability to distinguish between particular hues. Many people are not aware until adulthood that their color vision is abnormal, but they may have suffered at school because of this. Learning involves color. It is used in teaching mathematics, geography, and the sciences and is playing an increasingly important role in modern teaching meth-

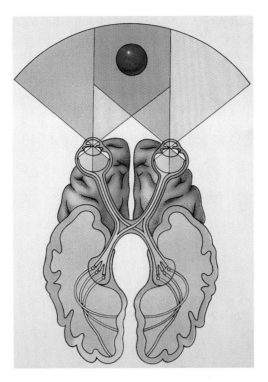

figure 2-3

Diagram of the human eye showing focus on nearby and distant objects. *Authors' collection*

ods. Since children can adapt if they know they are color-defective, and since education can be geared toward helping the visually disabled, children should be tested for color vision early in their school careers.

Color Vision

To gain a true understanding of color and be able to use it effectively in design or your daily life, you need to understand how people see color. Darwin believed that natural selection may have converted the simple apparatus of an optic nerve, coated with pigment and invested by transparent membrane, into an optical instrument. Creatures that first concentrated the light-absorbing carotenoid pigments present in their structure into specific light-sensitive areas developed an advantage in the struggle for survival.

There is a difference between light emitted from light sources and reflected light. The spectral composition of daylight has a relatively high content of short wavelengths because these are scattered by the atmosphere. Chlorophyll in plants absorbs both shortwave and longwave light, so the light reflected from them is dominated by green and yellow wavelengths.

Visual mechanisms able to distinguish different wavelengths can take advantage of the differences in spectral composition between direct and reflected light. Some frogs, for example, which have a primitive form of color vision, when startled will jump toward blue paper, which represents the safety of open water, but they will stay away from green paper, which represents the diffused light reflected by vegetation. The evolution of visual pigments sensitive to colors has helped in the fine discrimination of the visual field—of objects silhouetted against complex backgrounds. Backgrounds such as blue sky, green leaves, brown earth, and blue sea are fairly constant in their colors. If they change, the change is gradual from the green colors of summer to the reddish browns of autumn. The sharp contrasts between brightly colored plants and animals and the more uniform background of sky, sea, or forest facilitates recognition of friends and food—enemies are usually camouflaged. Color vision helps insects distinguish between edible and poisonous plants, between ripe and unripe fruit, and between flowers that contain nectar and those whose nectar has been exhausted.

To be able to image fine details precisely, an eye needs a single lens that can focus light onto a fine array of sensitive cells: a retina. Vertebrate animals have the most sophisticated eyes, in which a single lens directs light onto an array of photosensitive cells, just as the lens of a camera focuses light onto a film (Figure 2-4). The retina translates the elements of the picture into electrical impulses that are transmitted by nerve fibers to the brain. The retina's light-sensitive cells are of two types, called **rods** and **cones. Rods all contain the same visual pigment, rhodopsin, and work in dim light to produce the achromatic sensations of night vision. Cones contain pigments sensitive to the different spectral wavelengths, but they respond only in bright daylight**. The retinas of nocturnal animals such as rats and opossums, who are effectively color-blind, contain almost exclusively rods, while some diurnal birds have predominantly cones.

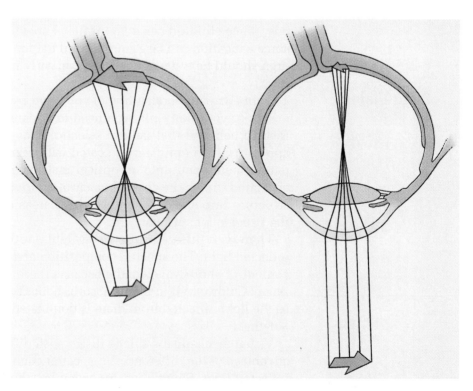

figure 2-4

Diagram of the primary visual pathways from the eye to the visual cortex. Keep in mind that what we see depends on the brain's interpretation of signals from the eye and involves complex interactions including personal and cultural biases. We see what we expect to see. © *Dorling Kindersley*

Many animals possess a more sophisticated retinal apparatus for color vision than humans. Birds and reptiles in particular often have differently colored oil droplets in front of some of their cones, making them effectively pentachromatic. These droplets filter all but one color out of the light and focus it accurately onto their associated cones in the retina. Normal human color vision is trichromatic, based on three colors.

Color vision probably originated some 400 million years ago in the ancestors of present-day fish, but eyes and vision evolved in the form best suited to the species' own special habitats and not in a linear evolutionary sequence from unicellular organisms to vertebrates. Deep-sea fish now, for example, have little use for color vision in their dark environment and tend to be color-blind, or sensitive only to the deep blue light that penetrates the abyss. Freshwater species whose environment is tinted by algae pigments in the water tend to have retinas containing predominantly cones sensitive to red and green light. It is sunlight that determines the overall photochemistry of visual pigments. The visual pigment rhodopsin, one of nature's most abundant pigments, absorbs the spectral wavelengths reflected by another, chlorophyll. Creatures whose lives are spent in the sun tend to have better color vision than those living in the shade—and those creatures tend to be brightly colored because the colors of organisms and color vision evolved together. It is a rule of thumb in nature that the more brightly colored the species, the more likely it is to possess color vision. Humans are the exception to this rule.

Human color vision is a complex process. Whenever photons of light stimulate a rhodopsin molecule, a change takes place in the electrical activity continually being transmitted to the optic nerve, to which the rods are indirectly connected. This change constitutes the electrical message conveyed to the brain. Rod signals reach their maximum size, and then their system is overloaded, when as few as 10 percent of the rhodopsin molecules (about 100 million per rod) are bleached.

There are three types of cones, containing three types of visual pigment called **iodopsin**, which resembles rhodopsin, although the exact chemical nature is unknown. They are bleached by light but regenerate much faster than rhodopsin molecules. Human cone pigments are sensitive to the three ranges of the spectrum we call red, green, and blue and are most sensitive to yellow light of 575 nanometers, green light of 535 nanometers, and blue light of 444 nanometers. Since the three types of cones each have broad absorption spectra, the eye is sensitive to a much wider wavelength range; the visible spectrum is between 400 and 700 nanometers. During the day, when the cones are active, the eye is most sensitive to yellow light of 550 nanometers because the retina has a predominance of "red" and "green" cones that, when equally stimulated, generate the sensation of yellow. There are comparatively few blue-sensitive cones, and almost none in the fovea, the fine-grained patch in the center of the retina. Rods are most sensitive to blue-green light of 505 nanometers. At twilight, when the eye responds to the fall in the level of illumination by gradually transferring from cone to rod vision, a change in spectral sensitivity takes place. As evening falls, the orange and red flowers in a garden begin to darken first, while blue and white flowers appear brighter by comparison.

Light falling on the eye is refracted by the cornea, the transparent outer layer, and enters the eye chamber through the pupil, the circular opening in the colored iris. The iris dilates in bright light and contracts in the dark, altering the size of the pupil and controlling the amount of light admitted. The pupil is black because most of the light entering the eye is absorbed. The lens is transparent to visible light but absorbs ultraviolet radiation. (Cataract removal often leads to ultraviolet light sensitivity.) Light that falls on the human retina must penetrate two complex but transparent layers of nerve cells before it reaches the photoreceptors. Only about 20 percent of the light falling on the retina is absorbed by the photoreceptors.

The photoreceptors translate the light they absorb into patterns of electrical signals that are transmitted across synapses (junctions between nerve cells) to the connecting layer of bipolar cells. These collate information from clusters of receptors and transmit it, in turn, vertically to the next layer—the ganglion cells. Horizontal cells and amacrine neurons distributed among the bipolar cells transmit the information laterally. Outside the fovea, individual bipolar cells collect signals from groups of rods and cones, and many of them converge on a single ganglion cell. But in the fovea one cone connects with one ganglion cell via one bipolar, to convey finer grained information. Fibers from ganglion cells all over the inside of the eye converge on the head of the optic nerve, which marks their exit to the brain.

Photons falling onto the retina are channeled along the photoreceptors to be captured by the visual pigments. The brighter the light, the more rhodopsin molecules are bleached, the more channels are closed, and the greater the reduction in the "dark signal" that the rods continually transmit. This arrangement may seem illogical, but the human eye is most often called upon to distinguish dark objects against light backgrounds, and it means that, in the light, less energy is consumed in generating electricity. It may also be an economical arrangement because the receptors consume less energy when the channels are closed during the day than when they are open in darkness—at night, for example, when the eye is at rest.

Only when the light and color signals from the eye reach the brain do we see color. The rod and cone cells, having absorbed light, convert it into electrical activity, which they transmit to the bipolar and ganglion cells. In transmission, these impulses are coded into temporal patterns that are then transmitted to the visual cortex at the back of the brain. In the retina, rods and cones respond to light stimuli by generating continuous electrical signals. These vary in size, up to one-twentieth of a volt, with the strength of the stimulus and last as long as it is applied. Retinal bipolar cells also use such signals to convey information about the retinal image to the ganglion cells. These slow, graded responses can transmit both positive and negative messages that excite or inhibit response, essentially indicating "go" or "stop." In this way, the continuous signaling of receptors and bipolars is converted into the discontinuous impulse traffic of the optic nerve. Variations in the frequency of "messages" to the ganglion cell fibers of the optic nerve constitute a code for the patterns of light, color, and shade that fall on the eye.

Neurophysiologists are now attempting to discover how the signals from the different receptors with different photopigments form this code. How the eye tells the brain that it is seeing red or yellow or brown can be discovered by intercepting optic nerve fiber messages on their journey from the retina to the visual cortex of the brain by means of a microelectrode. **Almost a third of the cerebral matter of the brain is involved in processing visual information**.

Defective Color Vision

It is essential that designers understand and be sensitive to color vision problems when working with clients since some form of defective color vision affects enough of the population to be worthy of consideration.

Only since the nineteenth century has it been understood that there are many types of defective color vision. Defective color vision is usually gender-linked. Defects are inherited by men and carried by women, although women can inherit them. A father with defective color vision and a mother with normal color vision produce normal sons and carrier daughters, and if a carrier woman marries a normal man half of their sons will have defective color vision. The term *color-blind* is misleading since almost everyone can see some form of color. People commonly described as color-blind can see colors, but they confuse hues that most people can distinguish clearly. For example, the majority confuse red and orange with yellow and green. They can distinguish colors most easily in the blue-green region of the spectrum. Colors probably do not all look the same to people with normal color vision.

A genealogical record of a family with defective color vision drawn up by an interested physician in 1777 went unremarked until John Dalton, the father of atomic theory, lucidly described his own defect in 1794, creating a stir of interest. Dalton was unable to distinguish between red and gray. He was a Quaker and is said to have attended a prayer meeting one day inappropriately dressed in bright red stockings. A colleague had exchanged them for his usual sober gray ones. Dalton suffered from a defect termed *protanopia*. Protanopes confuse red and orange with yellow and green. Deuteranopes confuse green and yellow with orange and red and cannot distinguish gray from purple. A third group, tritanopes, confuse green with blue and gray with violet or yellow. This is the rarest of the color-defective conditions.

Our understanding of the phenomenon of color vision and its defects stems from the **theory of trichromacy**, the idea that three colored lights, when mixed together in varying proportions, can produce sensations of other colors. During the seventeenth century, a French physicist first observed that white light would result not only from a mixture of all spectral wavelengths but also from a mixture of different colored lights. These ideas were published in 1780 by the French revolutionary, Jean Paul Marat, who was also a doctor of medicine. Around the same time, an obscure British physiologist first connected trichromacy and color vision, but our efforts to understand how the eye sees color are based on the theories of the British physicist and physician Thomas Young, who postulated that in the retina are a finite number of particles of three types: red, yellow, and blue. He believed all other colors were the result of these sensations being blended. These "particles" are now known to be the color receptors in the retina, the three types of cone cells. Each is primarily sensitive to either yellow, green, or blue light, although each has a wider spectrum of color sensitivity.

It is thought that people with defective color vision lack or have few cones receptive to specific parts of the spectral range or that they may lack certain visual pigments. Testing for color-defective vision may involve three or more tests. Most people know of color confusion tests such as the Ishihara test, whose purpose is to screen color-defective people from those with normal color vision. The test relies on patterns of variously colored dots in which a figure or a letter has to be recognized against a background. There are also many color-matching tests in which subjects are asked to arrange small colored samples of a known color specification into a color sequence to match a given hue with the standard proportions of red, green, and blue lights. For our purposes it is sufficient to know that complex and sophisticated testing for color-defective vision is available and that the issue is much too complex to do it yourself.

Some color vision defects are not inherited. Diseases of the liver and the eye may cause color vision anomalies, as can age. Reduced color discrimination may be a symptom of a brain tumor, multiple sclerosis, pernicious anemia, or diabetes. Industrial toxins and excess alcohol or nicotine consumption can also cause loss of color vision. In these cases the color vision may be restored if the disease is cured, but there is no cure for an inherited defect.

The color confusion that results from defective color vision can have very serious effects. Vision is our dominant sense. It informs us about our environment and has become essential for our survival. Jobs in the military, air traffic control, and transportation involve highly complex color coding. When lives are at stake, applicants must obviously be subjected to screening tests if color discrimination is part of the job. In the electrical, photographic, printing, dyeing, textile and paint, and design industries, good color vision is essential. Cotton buyers who have to grade raw materials, gem graders and setters who have to sort and match colored stones, and agricultural workers who have to judge the ripening of crops by their changing color all depend on effective color vision to do their jobs. Many people who have color vision problems do not become aware of them until adulthood because they have adapted so well to their environments.

We once knew an older man who had worked for an elevator manufacturing company for more than thirty years. His job was to assess the wiring by checking the color-coded wires to make sure they had been installed properly. Obviously, an error in judgment could have caused serious injury if a crowded elevator fell because of faulty wiring. In the decades he worked for the company, there had never been a problem with his work. The company was bought out by new owners, who decided to run color vision testing on all employees in color-sensitive jobs. You guessed it—the man we knew was found to have seriously defective color vision and was forced to take early retirement from his job in spite of the fact that his track record was perfect. We can only marvel at the adaptability that allowed him to find a way to distinguish between colors with such severely defective color vision.

Learning involves color, which is used in teaching mathematics, geography, and the sciences and is playing an increasingly important role in modern teaching methods, especially in computer use. Unless color vision problems are detected early, they may have a negative impact on the learning process, so, ideally, children should be tested for color vision early in their lives, prior to starting school. Children can be taught to adapt very well, particularly if their problem is discovered early.

Pigment Color

All matter absorbs and reflects light to some extent, but pigments are the most efficient agents of **selective absorption**. Selective absorption is the property by which colored objects are capable of absorbing photons of certain wavelengths from incident light and reflecting the rest. The carrot owes its orange color to pigments called carotenoids that absorb short-wave light and reflect the long wavelengths. Carotenoids also give salmon, lobsters, tomatoes, and autumn leaves their characteristic reddish color. Anthocyanin pigments color beets, rhubarb, hydrangeas, and red wine. Hemoglobin, the pigment that carries oxygen in the bloodstream, gives blood its red hue. Chlorophyll causes most plants to appear green because the chlorophyll absorbs all but the "green" photons, which it reflects. Dyes and paints make use of the pigment principle. Dyes and some inks actually form a compound with the molecules of the object they are being used to color. For example, henna, a natural vegetable dye favored by the ancient Egyptians, forms a compound with the protein keratin when used as a hair colorant. It actually bonds with the molecules in hair, forming a protective shield as well as providing a coloring agent. Paints and inks consist of a suspension of pigment particles in oil or water, which dries to leave a layer of pigment that will reflect only its own color and prevent light from reaching and being reflected from the surface beneath.

For thousands of years, dyes and paints were obtained from natural pigment sources only. Discoveries during the last century, however, resulted in the synthesis of pigments, and now an almost limitless range of colors is available for commercial use.

Working with Color

Fear stops many people from venturing into a circle of color wider than the one they have unconsciously established in their lives. Motivated by this fear, we surround ourselves with an accepted palette of neutrals, earth tones, or pastels, enlivened by small amounts of the one or two bright colors with which we feel comfortable. Most often these color schemes are arrived at by default. People often drift into a bland color scheme that is accepted by friends and family, and by its blandness it is accepted as good taste. The best way to overcome fear and to expand awareness is to directly work with color. Experimenting with color is great fun, and there is absolutely no substitute for the empirical learning that takes place when you actually mix and match colors yourself.

Learning color mixing is basic to any artist or designer, and it is helpful for anyone who is painting a car, applying cosmetics, or coloring the icing on a cake. The range of colors available for purchase is limited because no paint store could stock all the colors there are. Artists and designers should become so familiar with color that they can "eye match" a paint sample to a subject's eyes or a textile sample. For example, by working with color, interior designers develop a color memory that enables them to select fabrics and furniture based on a client's existing furnishings. They still need to check samples at the client's home because of changing light conditions, but after working with color for many years, a well-trained designer can select colors with remarkable accuracy.

With paint, only watercolors can be lightened by adding water; other kinds of paint are lightened by following the rules that apply to the mixing of all paints, including children's poster paints, polyurethane high gloss, artists' gouache, exterior paint, interior latex, and the oil paints of the masters. Colors are not immutable, but to change them requires a little knowledge. It is relatively simple to lighten or darken a hue, but there are complex rules for mixing colors just because there are so many, and the possible permutations are infinite. When two colors are mixed together, each is degraded to some extent. To work with color effectively, you will have to observe it closely and know how to use appropriate terminology to discuss it, which brings us to the topic of the vocabulary of color and color mixing.

The Vocabulary of Color

The basic colors or hues of the spectrum are **red, orange, yellow, green, blue, and violet**. The intensity of a color or a hue is known as its *saturation*. All colors have three dimensions: *hue, saturation*, and *value*. A *shade* is the result of mixing a pure color with black or gray. A *tint* results from mixing a pure color with white. Therefore, shades are darker than the pure color; tints are lighter than the pure color.

The human eye can discern the difference between several million colors of varying hue, saturation, and value (lightness or darkness). In spite of this, the basic color vocabulary in even the most sophisticated language is pitifully small—fewer than a dozen words. All other color terms are a matter of qualifying the basic descriptive color, such as red, light red, and dark red, or giving the color the name of an object, such as orange, lemon, or lime. When we discuss colors, we are usually referring to *hues*.

For centuries people wondered what caused the vivid bands of color in rainbows or in the sparkle of a diamond. Sir Isaac Newton stumbled on the answer quite by accident while working on another experiment. Newton discovered that if he passed light through a prism, the light on the prism's first surface was separated into its constituent wavelengths. The prism's second surface refracts the emerging rays, dispersing them more widely as they pass into the air, but they are not colored. The spectrum becomes visible only when it is directed onto a surface. Reflected from that surface, the component wavelengths of light produce the sensations of spectral color in the eye.

Newton found that if he isolated any color from the spectrum and passed it through differently colored solutions or reflected it from colored surfaces, he could not change its hue. The spectral colors he termed *primaries* and demonstrated that if they are all mixed together they will create white light. However, Newton did not carry his experiments quite far enough. Later it was discovered that white light can be produced by adding together only two or three primaries. When red, green, and blue light are projected at equal intensities on a white surface, white light appears where the three overlap. Where two of the colors overlap, the *secondaries* (yellow, magenta, and cyan) appear. This is called *additive mixing*.

So, we now know that **red, green, and blue (the additive primaries)** mix together to form white light. By mixing the additive primaries red, green, and blue in varying proportions, a wide range of colors can be produced. The additive primaries red, green, and blue are so named because they cannot be produced from each other.

Color can also be produced by *subtractive mixing*, in which the resultant color is produced by the simultaneous or successive subtraction of various colors from light passing through the combination. **Yellow, magenta, and cyan** are the **subtractive primaries**.

Since pigment colors are imperfect, it is not possible to produce the purity of mixing that is obtainable with light. For mixing pigments, paints in the six spectral hues make a good basis for experimental color mixing. If the six paints are mixed together, the resulting color will vary from deep brown to black, depending on the type of paint and the proportions used.

Pigment hues that appear opposite each other on a color wheel are traditionally called *complementary colors*, although opposite colors are truly complementary only in light. **The mixing of complementaries results in a neutral.** A true neutral is gray with no hue bias, but those with a hint of color bias can be used very effectively as a foil for stronger colors. For example, a neutral with a greenish tinge will intensify red used near it.

Color Glossary

Achromatic colors: Black, white, and the grays; colors devoid of hue.

Additive color mixing: Color derived from the adding together of colored light beams.

Additive primaries: Red, green, blue.

Chroma: The degree of saturation of a surface color.

Color: Synonymous with hue.

Complementary colors: Pigments opposite on the color wheel.

Dispersion: The separation of light into colors by refraction.

Fluorescence: The emission of light following the absorption of light of shorter wavelengths.

Fovea: A small depression in the retina that lacks rods but is rich in red- and green-sensitive cones.

Gray: An achromatic neutral intermediate in lightness between black and white.

Hue: Synonymous with color. The attribute of a color by which it is distinguished from another color.

Intensity: The measurable brightness of a light source. A synonym for saturation.

Metamerism: The capacity of colors to change under different lighting conditions.

Nanometer: One thousand-millionth of a meter.

Neutralization: The process of mixing a hue with gray, black, or white or the hue's complement.

Photon: A quantum of light energy.

Pigment: An insoluble coloring material that coats the color of the underlying surface rather than combining with it.

Primary color: One of a set of colors that can be combined in a color-mixing process to provide a wide range of colors. No two together will produce the third primary.

Refraction: The bending of light rays as they pass from one medium to another.

Retina: The light-sensitive inner surface of the eye on which the lens projects images.

Saturation: The vividness or intensity of a hue.

Shade: A color obtained by mixing a pure color with black.

Spectral colors: Colors that appear in the spectrum of sunlight ranging from red through orange, yellow, green, and blue to violet.

Spectrum: The color image formed when light is passed through a prism.

Subtractive color mixing: The production of color by the simultaneous or successive subtraction of various colors from the light passing through the combination.

Tint: A color obtained by mixing a pure color with white.

Value: A synonym for lightness.

Wavelength: The distance over which a periodic wave phenomenon repeats itself.

White light: A mixture of all visible wavelengths in the same proportion as they are found in sunlight.

Color Mixing

Color mixing has been likened to composing music. To mix and match colors, you have to analyze them visually, like picking out the notes in a musical chord. Like learning to play an instrument, this skill comes only from constant practice. The assignments in the workbook section have been designed to help develop basic color-mixing skills. Media differ, and techniques differ accordingly, but the principles of color mixing apply to all media. Only water-based colors can be lightened by adding water.

To experiment, begin by mixing the six colors of the spectrum with one another. Add a touch of white to each hue and to each mixture, then a touch of black. Try varying the proportions. A touch is just that—lightly touch the color with the brush and mix it in. Always compare and contrast your results. Colors are affected by the type of paint, as well as by the pigments used to create that paint. Pigment colors are not pure. They will almost always be slightly bluish, reddish, or yellowish. Only with practice and experience will you learn to "read" color as easily as reading the words on this page. (NOTE: When mixing paints, you may notice that colors are not consistent between brands. This is due to the different fillers that each manufacturer uses to give the paint stability. For example, one paint brand may result in much purer colors than another brand that produces murky undertones.)

Just as light exists as both a particle and a wave, color also has a duality. It behaves a little differently when it manifests itself as light color than it does as pigment color. While the color that reaches our eyes is always in the form of colored light, that light may have been colored at its source or it may have been reflected from a colored surface. Sometimes color theorists use the terms *additive* or *subtractive* when they refer to color mixing. Because we think the terms *additive* and *subtractive* color are confusing, we prefer to use the terms **pigment color** and **light color**, which are more direct.

Most of us have more direct experience with mixing pigment color than with mixing light color. In grade school, we may have learned to mix together red and blue paint to create purple or stirred blue and yellow paint to create green. We tend to think of color as a solid surface, as it looks when pigments or dyes are involved. When we envision color, we rarely think of it in terms of colored light. Whenever we select clothing, paint a room, or eat a piece of fruit, we are dealing with pigment color. What we see when we look at a colored surface is the light being reflected from that object. For example, a lemon is reflecting yellow light back at us. The colors **red, yellow, and blue** cannot be produced by any mixture of other colors, so they are called **primary colors of pigment**. By mixing together these pigment colors in various combinations, all the other colors are created.

Light Color Mixing

Most of us have little to do with light mixing on a daily basis, so we are less familiar with it. The most common use of colored light is in theatrical lighting, and this is a good example for explaining light color mixing. If you look up at a bank of stage lights, you will see three colors: red, blue, and green. From these three colors a lighting designer can mix light to create any other color. So, **red, blue, and green** are the **primary colors of light**. These same primaries are at work in your television set, your computer monitor, and anywhere else that light is mixed to create color. More will be said about the effects of colored light later in the chapter.

The Color Wheel

Exploring color contrasts is the basis of designing with color since colors are rarely used in isolation. Most people find combining colors is the most difficult part of working with color, perhaps because there are so many possibilities. Before a designer or artist can communicate with color, a system of color identification must be clearly understood. When we see a rainbow arching across the sky or observe the spectrum after a beam of light has passed through a prism, the resulting sequence of hues is red, orange, yellow, green, blue, violet. The red end of the spectrum can be joined to the violet to form a complete circle. This color continuum includes all the intermediate hues produced as each hue overlaps the adjacent hue and for practical purposes forms the basis of a standard twelve-hue color wheel (Figure 2-5). The twelve basic hues can be divided into what are termed primaries, secondaries, and tertiaries. (Remember that whenever we talk about color on the color wheel we are referring to pigment color.)

These divisions on a twelve-hue color wheel are broken down into:

Three primary colors: Blue, red, and yellow.

Three secondary colors: A combination of any two primaries such as violet, a combination of red and blue; orange, a combination of red and yellow; and green, a combination of yellow and blue.

Six tertiary colors: A combination of a secondary color with any additional quantity of one of its constituent primaries. (Commonly accepted tertiaries are blue-violet, red-violet, red-orange, yellow-orange, yellow-green, and blue-green.)

To communicate accurately with color, knowledge of the **three main qualities of color** is essential: (1) The relative position location on the color wheel of the particular hue being selected indicates the **hue family**, which is the first of the three qualities of color; (2) the second quality of

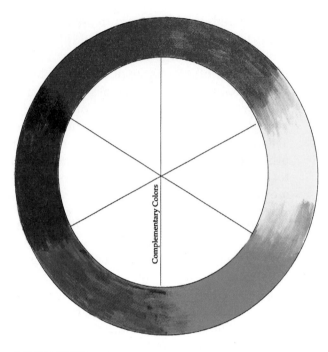

Complementary Colors

figure 2-5

COLOR WHEEL
This color wheel demonstrates the primary, secondary, and tertiary colors. Colors opposite each other on the color wheel are complementary colors, i.e., red/green, red-orange/blue-green. Any three colors adjacent to each other on the color wheel are analogous, i.e., red-orange, orange, yellow-orange. Split complements are one color and the color on each side of its complement on the color wheel. A triadic color scheme employs three colors equally spaced from each other on the wheel, i.e., red, blue, and yellow.

color, the lightness or darkness, is referred to as **value**; (3) the third quality is the degree of purity, intensity, or **saturation**, sometimes referred to as **chroma**.

Complementary Colors

Every color has an opposite on the color wheel. These opposites are termed *complementary colors*. When complementary colors are mixed together, a neutral gray results. Together, the two complementary hues have strange properties: Two lights of complementary colors—say, blue and yellow—if mixed together, produce white light. Similarly, yellow and blue pigments placed side by side reflect the three additive primaries of light. The yellow pigment reflects yellow and red wavelengths of light; the blue pigment reflects mostly blue wavelengths. In terms of combined reflected light, these two colors reflect the full complement of spectral hues. The same applies to the other pairs of complementary colors: red and green, orange and blue, and yellow and purple.

Contrasting hues, one of the simplest forms of color exploration, can produce a multitude of effects. When colors are juxtaposed, they play tricks with the eye because as soon as they are combined or laid one beside the other, they seem to change. To illustrate this, try the following experiment: Cut a hole in the center of a square of yellowish-green poster paper. Repeat this with a square of medium blue paper. Place each one on top of a square of deep turquoise so that the turquoise shows through each hole. Against the green, the turquoise will look blue; against the blue, it will look green. This phenomenon was called **simultaneous contrast** by the French chemist Michel Eugene Chevreul, director of the Gobelins tapestry works during the nineteenth century. His findings were used in the weaving of tapestries to give depth and clarity to the woven textiles.

During the eighteenth century, when textile printing was in its infancy, a color would often appear to change in transition from small-scale design to printed fabric. A green pattern in a blue field might turn yellowish; black against red might appear green. Chevreul, investigating these effects, realized that they were due to the influence of one color on another. **Simultaneous contrast** occurs whenever two or more colors or neutrals are juxtaposed. For example, gray placed next to yellow takes on a purplish hue, but when gray is placed next to blue, the blue looks yellowish. Such phenomena have fascinated artists for centuries. Many made careful studies of color combinations. The knowledge they gained is applied by craftspeople who use color. Weavers, for example, design checks with gray and blue yarn woven in such a way that a yellow stripe is visible, although no yellow yarn is used. The phenomenon of simultaneous contrast was later shown to be the result of after-image effects. The green pattern looked yellow because it was tinged with orange, the after-image of blue; the black was tinged with the after-image of red, which is green. Chevreul wrote, "The eye undoubtedly takes pleasure in seeing colors, independent of design and every other quality in the object which exhibits them." The principles of color harmony he established are the basis of modern aesthetic traditions governing the use of color.

He stated that colors of the same hue but different saturation harmonize when juxtaposed. Similarly, light and dark—or grayed—tones of the same hue should harmonize as long as the tones do not dull each other when put together. Complementary colors are harmonious, and there is harmony in a series of contrasting colors all having a dominant hue. Harmonious colors are always related in some way according to traditional teaching, but tastes change and with them the rules of harmony. What may seem harmonious in one decade may seem ghastly in the next.

The Bauhaus artist Johannes Itten explored the different ways of contrasting colors. He observed how colors divide naturally into blue-based or red-based colors (what are generally but incorrectly termed *warm* or *cool* colors) and how the two combined affect each other. Each generation of designers has come up with a signature variation on juxtaposing colors, which often can define a style or period. For example, those of us who lived through the 1970s will forever identify that period with avocado-, gold-, and copper-colored refrigerators and kitchen ranges. The 1950s may be remembered for their daring combinations of orange with pink or lime green and coral spiked with black.

Understanding the effect that one color placed next to another can have helps to create a desired atmosphere, or it can prevent the atmosphere subtly induced by one color from being destroyed by its proximity to another. Balance, harmony, and the creation of intentional special effects with color come only with practice and a full understanding of the nature of color and how the human eye sees color.

Color Schemes

Following are the basic color schemes. They will be dealt with in greater detail in subsequent chapters, but for the moment it is sufficient to understand them in general terms.

Achromatic

Achromatic schemes occur when only neutrals are used. They occur with surprising frequency in contemporary interior design, where white, beige, gray, and black form the basis for the "color" plan.

Monochromatic

In a monochromatic color scheme (*mono* meaning "one"), only shades and tints of one color family are used in the color plan. This is the simplest yet most artificial of all color plan possibilities, since monochromatic schemes do not occur in nature. If skillfully applied, monochromatic schemes can be very effective, depending on how well the chromatic and tonal values are handled. Any of the color families offers an extensive scale of tonal and chromatic variations, from light tints to highly neutralized tones. For example, a monochromatic scheme based on orange would include a wide range of tans and browns bearing little resemblance to the bright, highly saturated pure orange.

Analogous

Analogous color plans are based on a limited number (no more than two or three) adjacent hues on the color wheel. For example, you may select a blue- and green-based scheme with intermediate steps between, or a color plan based on reds and yellows.

Complementary

Complementary color schemes are based on direct opposites on the color wheel and may encompass primary, secondary, or tertiary options, for example, red and green, orange and blue, yellow and violet, and yellow-green and red-violet.

Color Harmony

Color combinations, like musical chords, can seem discordant. During the nineteenth century, Ogden Rood, an American physicist and color theorist, proposed that colors fall into a natural order, just as musical notes seem to fall naturally into ordered scales. Rood proposed that yellow is the lightest tone, orange is darker, red follows, and the scale descends through green, bluish green, and blue to violet, the darkest tone. Purples vary in tone between red and violet. If a color is lightened or darkened so as to be out of its natural order of tone and then used in combination with unmodified colors, Rood believed the resulting scheme would be discordant. This idea still persists and is the basis for some of the outmoded thinking regarding "clashing" colors. Although color combinations that would have been unacceptable half a century ago, such as blue and green or orange and magenta, are readily accepted today, some people find them unpleasant and discordant. Yet, so-called discords can be extremely pleasant, even exciting. Nature knows best when it comes to color, and nature has no discordant hues. Flowers have pink petals with yellow centers. The earth is brown with blue sky, yet under Rood's theory the earth is "unnaturally" darker than the blue. For centuries the Japanese have used the color combinations of nature in their design. Suffice it to say that there is no such thing as a bad color scheme. Taste is a matter of personal preference.

Understanding what makes one combination of colors pleasing and another combination of colors unattractive can be difficult to comprehend. Since color, like beauty, is very much in the eye of the beholder, there are no fixed principles of color harmony. There are, however, general guidelines that can help the novice until a level of expertise is reached. Briefly described here are five principles of color harmony. They will not cover all satisfying color combinations, and, in fact, some of the principles may seem to contradict each other. They are only guidelines. You will be the ultimate determining factor in whether a color combination is pleasing.

Principle of Familiarity

The principle of familiarity is based on the concept that familiarity is pleasing and readily accepted. As a result, color schemes based on nature will seem pleasing to most people. In addition, light and dark variations of the same color will harmonize.

Principle of Novelty

The principle of novelty argues that although people like harmonious or balanced color schemes, harmony quickly becomes boring. As a result, a new or unexpected combination will draw attention to itself and make the entire composition more pleasing and harmonious.

Principle of Resemblance

The principle of resemblance basically states that colors harmonize more when the differences between them are less. It justifies selecting light and dark colors of the same hue, or colors from an analogous color scheme. It argues against using multiple colors of different hue and lightness. However, the same range of lightness can also be pleasing—for example, a composition entirely of pastel colors.

Principle of Order

The principle of order suggests that colors should be based on an orderly plan. This might be an analogous color scheme, a contrasting color scheme, or a triadic color scheme. This principle also advocates using equal differences. For example, if you are using two shades of green, then the third shade of green you add should be exactly between the first two.

Avoidance of Ambiguity

Avoidance of ambiguity suggests that you should not use colors that seem incongruous with the rest of your color scheme. For example, gray in the middle of a vivid composition tends to draw attention to the gray and ruin the flow of the composition. An off-hue color in the scheme also creates disharmony as a viewer will not know whether the change in hue is intentional.

No matter what color schemes are chosen or what principles a color plan is based on, the goal should always be harmony. If done with expertise and skill, even seemingly outrageous color combinations can create a harmonious and balanced composition. The goal of any color composition should be to evoke a sense of wellness and to improve the human condition by its presence.

Lighting Basics

What follows is essentially a crash course in Lighting 101 because it is impossible to work effectively with color without understanding how it relates to light. To understand and manipulate lighting, the designer must learn to sympathize with its technology and create with the effects it produces. A prime function of light is disclosure. Light reveals shape. It can make an object appear flat, or it can increase its dimensional form. It can cause a subject to fade into the background, or it can emphasize the separation of planes. Illumination can add to or subtract from the value of articles, and interior designers must realize that costly furnishings can look cheap unless such properties as sheen and color are properly revealed with light.

Although the study of the effects of lighting on humans is in its infancy, we know that lighting has both conscious and subliminal effects on our physical and mental conditions. *Glare* makes us irritable, but *sparkle* leads to heightened appetite and enlivens conversation. The difference between glare and sparkle is the degree of brightness. Traditionally, color has been strongly related to human responses, but it is virtually impossible to separate the effects of color and light.

Lighting is an extremely flexible design element. With the flick of a switch, light can be made to alter pattern, color, and intensity. Lighting directs attention within a space because the eye automatically seeks out the brightest object in its field. By varying contrast and pattern, light can also direct movement within or through an environment. Increasingly, lighting is being used as a direct source of decoration by the use of silhouette projections, which form interesting surface patterns, and transparency projections, which can produce either impressions of detailed realism or wild flights of fancy.

There are six main concepts to be considered when you are beginning to design a lighting plan.

Visibility

The designer's first responsibility is to provide illumination that will let the occupants of a given environment see and be seen with appropriate speed, accuracy, and comfort.

Atmosphere

The mood or feeling created in an illuminated space is one of great interest to the designer, and yet this is the hardest concept to define or specify. The designer must consider whether the lighting is to be casual or formal, emotionally cool or warm, exciting or pacifying, cheerful or somber, and dramatic or evenly lit.

Composition

Overall shadowless lighting does not usually best define a space. The careful variation of a lighting system's direction, contrast, color, intensity, shape, pattern, and movement may best develop the visual environment.

Object Appearance

Objects respond differently to light. Diffuse or matte objects are more responsive to the direction of light, its intensity, and the brightness relationships developed with the subject and between the subject and its surroundings that are mirrorlike surfaces. White surfaces react rapidly to minor changes in intensity, while black merely absorbs additional light. Each object must be considered separately, as well as in coordination with the whole as it is revealed by the lighting system. The lighting designer must adapt lighting concepts within the limitations of structure, acoustics, air conditioning, budget, and environmental criteria.

Mechanical Development

Mechanical development is the review and selection of light sources from the wide array available. It may include natural daylight via windows or skylights and incandescent, fluorescent, halogen, or other types of artificial lighting sources.

Review and Correction

Before final design decisions are made, the proposed lighting plan should be checked against established criteria. The study of recommended practices of model installations can often save the designer from costly errors in judgment.

Light Sources

Three general categories of light sources are available to lighting designers: (1) natural daylight, (2) incandescent electric light, and (3) electric discharge lighting.

Natural Daylight

Natural daylight is a major factor to consider in any lighting plan, although it is often totally ignored. Natural daylight is not stable. It changes throughout the day in position, intensity, diffusion, color, and timing. Diffusion of the sun's rays is a variable caused by rain, haze, cloud cover, or atmospheric pollution. In any design utilizing natural daylight, three conditions should be considered: (1) light directly from the sun combined with reflected light from a clear sky, (2) light from a clear sky only, and (3) light from an overcast sky.

The color of daylight changes according to the composition of the atmosphere, the interreflection of objects in the environment, and the time of day. Typically, daylight changes from deep red, through a range of oranges and yellows, to blue-white, and then the cycle continues in reverse.

Daylight is also affected by various indirect variables, including local terrain, landscaping and waterscaping, location of windows, daylight control systems (shades, draperies, etc.), the color of the decor, and artificial light.

Incandescent Electric Light

The proper term for any artificial light source is **lamp**, not "light bulb." Technically, the bulb is only the glass used to enclose the other components. The sun and the incandescent lamp both create light by the heating of materials until they glow. For this reason, incandescent lighting is the closest to the sun.

Types of Incandescent Lighting. **General service lamps** (regular *light bulbs*) are the most commonly used, and they are the workhorses of the lighting industry. They come in a wide range of intensities and sizes. They scatter light in all directions and should be used in fixtures that will properly shield and direct their energy output in a useful manner.

Tungsten-halogen (also known as quartz or iodine lamps) are another class of incandescent lamp, boasting small size and a comparatively long life.

Reflectorized lamps are fully enclosed lighting instruments in their own right. They feature a light source, reflector, and lens within a single glass enclosure that can be screwed into any socket. They are more commonly known as *spotlights* or *floodlights*.

Decorative lamp classes are designed to be seen "as is" to provide special effects and are noted for bulb shapes that are flame-shaped, conical, tubular or globular.

Colors and Finishes of Incandescent Lamps. Incandescent lamps come in a variety of finishes and color coatings. The clear glass bulb is useful when a compact and bright point of light is required, to be further controlled by reflectors or lenses. However, any point source also creates strong shadows, and so lamp manufacturers produce two other standard bulb finishes to help spread the size of the source. Acid etching or sand blasting is the most efficient diffuser, but when a softer light is desired, the interior of the bulb may be coated with silica powder.

Five types of coatings are common: (1) painted surfaces; (2) sprayed lacquers, which can give a fragile but transparent color medium; (3) special plastic exterior coatings, which have a higher resistance to abrasion and weather; (4) ceramic enamels, which produce translucent or diffuse colors and may be used in higher-output lamps; and (5) dichroic filters, which are available for high-intensity sources producing very transparent and sparkling colors.

Specifying Incandescent Lamps. When specifying incandescent lamps, the user must always specify the wattage desired, the shape of the bulb, its size, the base or connector size (medium screw bases are common, but many of the newer European fixtures require intermediate base lamps, which can be difficult to locate for the average consumer), the finish or color, and the life expectancy expressed as average hours of life.

Electric Discharge Lighting

Electric discharge lamps are available in two types: (1) low-intensity discharge lamps, usually called fluorescent, and (2) high-intensity discharge (HID) lamps, which include the family of mercury vapor, multivapor, high-pressure sodium types. HID sources have traditionally been used in industrial, office, or streetlight applications, although they are now finding applications in all forms of interior spaces, including residential.

Both types have one thing in common: They must be used with a device called a ballast, which regulates the amount of electrical energy used. These lamps must not be installed in any household socket without a ballast. Also, both types produce light in a similar way. When the lamp is turned on, a flow of electricity is directed through metal terminals at either end of the enclosing chamber. After these terminals are heated, the electric current leaps between the terminals, creating an arc. In the fluorescent lamp, the arc produces invisible ultraviolet energy, which excites the fluorescent phosphors that coat the inside of the long tubular chamber. HID lamps have very short capsule-type chambers, and the arcs within them give off directly visible light. The capsule chamber of the HID source is usually enclosed within a larger glass enclosure, and the inside may be coated with phosphors to modify light output and color quality.

Incandescent versus Electric Discharge Lighting. In comparison with incandescent lamps, electric discharge sources have several advantages. Their life expectancy is longer, and they are efficient because they use very little energy to produce great amounts of light with relative little heat. However, they must always be used with the auxiliary ballasts, their color reproduction is poor, and there is considerable conjecture about the possible ill effects of fluorescent and HID lighting on the human body.

Luminaires for Interior Lighting

Luminaire is the technical term for what we usually refer to as a lighting fixture. A luminaire is a total lighting instrument: lamps, reflectors, lenses, housing, wires, and electrical connectors. Although there are wide variances in the designs of luminaires available (Figures 2-6.1 to 2-6.5) most fall into one of the following categories.

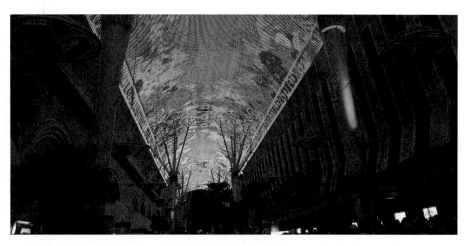

figure 2-6.1

Interior applications showing different uses of recessed and track lighting, both for general illumination and to accent art objects and architectural elements. *2-6.1, 2-6.2, and 2-6.4, © Dorling Kindersley. 2-6.5, © Dorling Kindersley, photo by Erik Svensson/Jeppe Wikstrom. 2-6.3, reprinted with permission of Lightolier, a Genlyte Company*

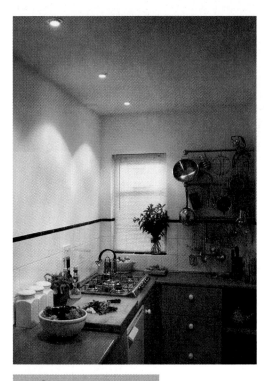

figure 2-6.2

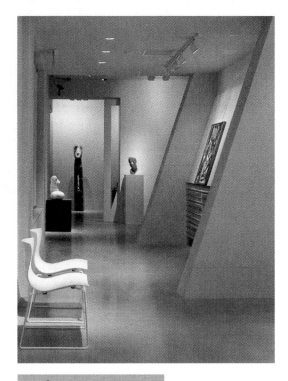

figure 2-6.3

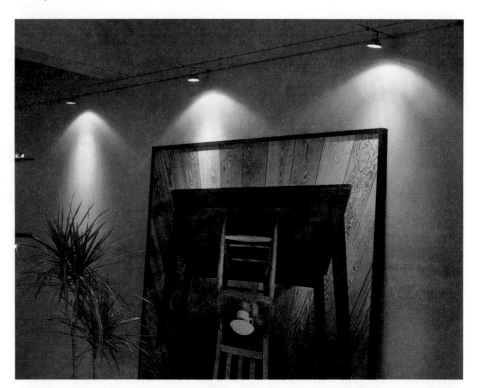

figure 2-6.4

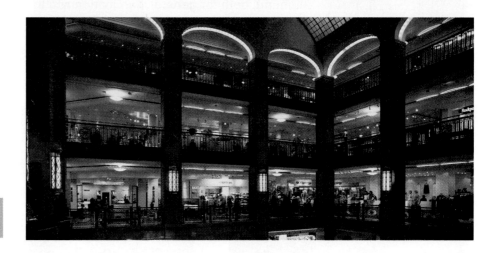

figure 2-6.5

Recessed Fixtures

This type of fixture uses a general service lamp in a polished metal reflector and is also referred to as an open reflector downlight. The reflector redirects the otherwise wasted upper portion of the light down through the ceiling aperture. The reflector also distributes light in useful ways and may be used to minimize the bright glare of the lamp in normal viewing angles. It is easy to maintain since it is simple to reach into the aperture to change lamps and wipe the reflector clean. However, because it is an open fixture, it does gather dust and dirt easily, and it has limited degrees to which light can be controlled.

Lens and Reflector Downlights

This type is not as efficient as the open-reflector counterpart, but the lens can add directional control to the light rays. The lens also covers the ceiling aperture, which retards the collection of dirt on the reflec-

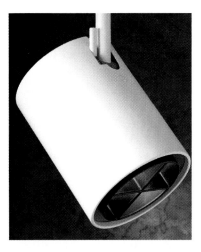

figure 2-7

Prospec Cylinders feature a classic design that is easily integrated into various architectural environments. Patented Tur-Lock aiming mechanisms and integral media cartridges are standard. Cylinders provide the best glare control and lamp shielding for the most dramatic accent lighting. *Reprinted with permission of Lightolier, a Genlyte Company*

tor's surface. One disadvantage of this type is that the lens tends to collect light on its surface and can cause an annoying brightness to the viewer.

Can Downlights

These fixtures are essentially cans mounted in a hole in the ceiling or on a track without reflectors or lenses (Figures 2-7 and 2-8). This type relies on reflectorized lamps to provide the requisite light control. There is one great advantage to this type: Each time the lamp is changed, a clean reflector and lens are automatically provided. This model is usually economically priced, but its low cost can be offset by the fact that the required reflectorized lamps cost much more than general service lamps.

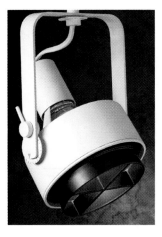

figure 2-8

This line voltage unit features a clean, minimal look that's ideal for museums, lobbies, and other institutional environments. Extremely versatile, it can be adjusted horizontally and vertically and then locked into place. Integral media cartridges are standard. *Reprinted with permission of Lightolier, a Genlyte Company*

Accent Lights

These are fixtures in which the axis of the light beam is adjustable (Figure 2-9). When they are supplied without reflectors or lenses, they rely on reflectorized lamps to direct beams of light on paintings, sculptures, and other highlighted objects.

Wall Washers

These are designed to evenly coat a wall with light (Figure 2-10). They are usually located in precise lines parallel to the illuminated surface. These luminaries enable the designer to treat the full vertical surface of a room independently from the horizontal working area.

Portable Fixtures

These include table and floor lamps, simple uplights that look like coffee cans with reflectorized lamps inside them. The uplight can be placed on a floor or other low surface to illuminate the ceiling. They are particularly effective when directed up through trees and plants, thereby casting interesting shadows on the ceiling.

Decorative Fixtures

These are more to be seen than to see by (Figure 2-11). They include the chandelier and sconce, as well as luminal art objects that derive their artistic quality from the interplay of light. This type of fixture often has design value but requires careful consideration for use as a functional light source.

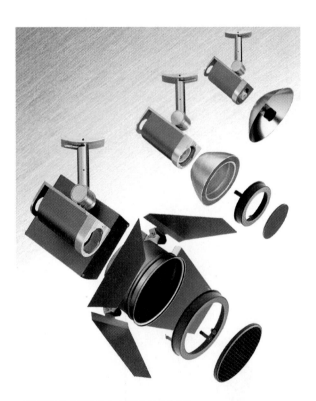

figure 2-9

LIGHTING EFFECTS ACCESSORIES
Lytespan track lighting offers a full range of high-performance accessories for tinting, coloring, and shaping the light beam. All accessories are designed to attach easily. Accessory holders hold one or two accessories: Simply choose the correct size needed for the attached shade. *Reprinted with permission of Lightolier, a Genlyte Company*

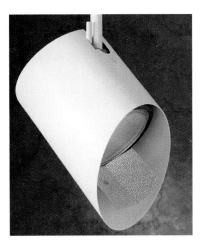

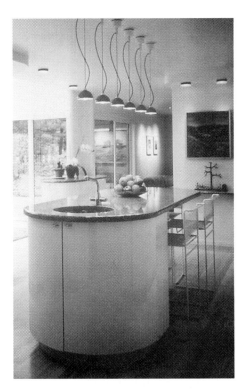

figure 2-10

WALL WASHER
ProSpec wall washer features an asymmetrical spread lens and an anodized aluminum kick reflector to distribute light evenly from ceiling to floor. Like ProSpec cylinders, it uses Lightolier's patented single-lever, Tru-Lock aiming mechanism. *Reprinted with permission of Lightolier, a Genlyte Company*

figure 2-11

MINIATURE PENDANTS AND SUSPENDED ACCENT LIGHTING (LOW VOLTAGE)
LyteJacks are a unique miniature, low-voltage halogen lighting system designed to create dramatic visual impact for accent and display lighting. Scale and proportion allow placement almost anywhere, and the lighting effects produced can highlight surfaces and objects without overpowering them. *Reprinted with permission of Lightolier, a Genlyte Company*

**Special Effects
Color/Light**

During the past couple of decades, theatrical lighting has been adapted for use in nontheatrical settings. Colored lighting may perform the same tasks at home or in retail applications as it does in a theatrical production (Figure 2-12). It can imperceptibly create a serene or lively mood, enhance decor, and make our complexions glow with the bloom of youth. The average person's experience with colored lighting is usually in an extreme setting: psychedelic light shows of the 1960s, the sometimes exaggerated lighting of home decorations at Christmas, the laser light effects at rock concerts, or the use of "black light" (ultraviolet) to make posters fluoresce. This type of lighting is used to grab your attention, but more subtle uses of colored light can also be very effective. Contemporary lighting systems enable anyone to have the same options a theatrical designer has. You can use colored lamps, dichronic filters that actively produce colored light rather than filtering white light. A

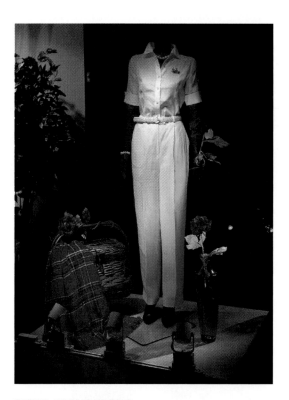

figure 2-12

RETAIL APPLICATIONS
From window displays that must accommodate changing outdoor light levels to floor displays that alter constantly, retail lighting poses many challenges. ATOM offers new ways to deal with these challenges by providing powerful features such as programmable time delays, fading effects, and scene cycling. Most important, lighting ATOM helps create a more visually exciting retail experience. A key feature for retail spaces is ATOM's track master module, which allows simultaneous communication with all ATOM modules in a space. Combined with Lightolier's Compose PLC Firewall, this permits a whole room or floor to be controlled in one easy step after initial programming. ATOM's powerful features make it easier than ever to create track lighting with all the drama and excitement required in today's demanding retail environment. *Reprinted with permission of Lightolier, a Genlyte Company*

variety of spot and flood lights, internal reflectors, and framing projectors are available to reshape the light beam for special effects.

The range of red, blue, green, amber, pink, and smoke-colored lamps is augmented with candle-tip and wild-flicker options. Rheostat dimmer switches can control it all. Most theatrical lighting is achieved by mixing the red, green, and blue light primaries in the proportions needed to achieve the required color, or by making use of filters. Today more than three hundred colors of filters are available to the public, and these can be used to great effect in homes and businesses. A very pale blue filter will give added luster to a collection of silver or an indoor pool. Pale pink or candlelight effects downlighting the dinner table can flatter any complexion. Subtle use of colored lighting can save on energy costs. Pinkish light makes us believe a room is a little warmer; bluish light can make a hot evening seem a little cooler. If you choose to use colored lighting, you will need to know its effects.

Colored light will distort all the colors in a room except its own. The effect can be so radical that the objects on which the light falls may become unrecognizable. Some of the effects you can expect from using colored light follow.

Red light destroys color. It converts pale and warm colors into a uniform red hue and makes dark colors look black. Even red is distorted under red light. Yellow-reds turn into blue-reds; dark reds turn into brown.

Pink light is more flattering and gives a sensation of warming up color, except greens and blues, which it causes to turn grayish.

Yellow light makes most colors appear more orange, while orange looks yellower. Light blues turn grayish violet. Dark blues look brown. Greens become grayish, and blue-greens look greener. A yellowish peach light can be flattering to skin tones, as it picks up the tones that flatter cosmetics.

Orange and dark amber lights redden yellows, intensify reds and oranges, and make greens, blues, and violets look grayish brown.

Green light grays all colors except green, which it intensifies. Pale green light is very tricky to use. It can enhance foliage but make complexions look ghastly.

Blue light can turn red into maroon and turn yellow into green. Dark blue light will gray everything except greens, blues, and violets, which it intensifies. Pale blue light looks cold and gives a ghostly glow to skin tones.

Violet light makes yellows look orange and makes oranges look redder.

The Effects of Light on Color

As just discussed, the color of light can make a dramatic alteration in how color is perceived (Figure 2-13). All light, whether natural or artificial in the form of incandescent, fluorescent, or sodium vapor, creates differences in the way color is viewed. The spectral characteristics of light falling on a surface, as well as the reaction of the surface itself to the light, must be considered. Virtually all objects and art forms will be seen under both natural and artificial light sources at some time; therefore, it is important to consider the effects of both on the colors selected. Most often colors are seen in a combination of light sources, such as natural daylight with incandescent, natural daylight with fluorescent, or a combination of incandescent and fluorescent sources (Figure 2-14).

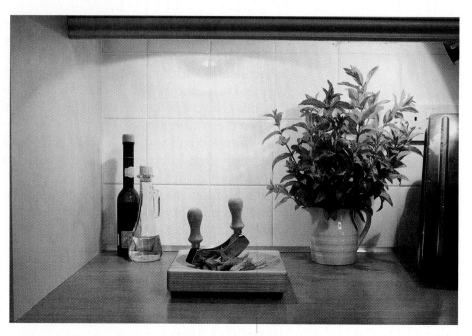

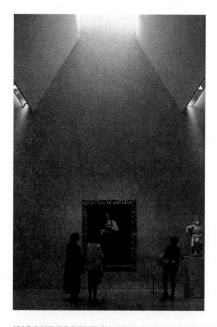

figure 2-13

CONCEALED LIGHTING
This concealed miniature track lighting system lets you bring light to places it's never been before. It is easily installed under shelves, beneath cabinets, or over a desk or work area. A choice of four compact lighting elements lets you provide general, accent, or task lighting. *© Dorling Kindersley*

figure 2-14

INCANDESCENT (LINE VOLTAGE) TRACK HEADS
Incandescent line voltage track fixtures offer superior glare control, adjustability, and accessorization particularly suitable for gallery use. *© Dorling Kindersley*

Natural Light

In interior environments, fenestration (placement of windows) is the primary consideration of natural lighting. Does the light fall from a skylight above? Is there a wall of windows on one side of the room? Is the low-level natural illumination from small or poorly placed windows? Whether you are an interior designer or an artist considering the placement of artworks, the source of illumination can make or break the image.

The designer must consider not only the size and placement of windows but also what is outside the windows. Are there large buildings outside that cast shadows? Are there many trees or green leaves, which will affect colors in the room? A room facing a white wall and a room facing a red wall will present very different color problems to the designer. We once lived in a small apartment where the kitchen window faced the white wall of the building next door. Our kitchen was also painted white, and in spite of having no view, it received adequate daylight and seemed bright and cheery. Then the building next door was painted a peasoup green, and our kitchen immediately took on a sickly hue that was quite disturbing. Food looked unappetizing, and even skin tones seemed sallow and unhealthy. We solved the problem by using a light-filtering shade, but it illustrated for us how **adjacent colors can affect an interior environment**.

The designer must consider how much or how little natural light there is to work with and decide whether to modify the situation. For example, rather than painting a small, dark room white to try to lighten it, it may be better to paint it in deep, saturated tones and juxtapose lighter furniture, so that the walls seem to float away. It is essential to consider the room's architectural definition when working with light and color. We do not usually promote formula design or design rules, but one rule is worthy of note: Good design does not fight the environment but blends with it.

Daylight can't be trusted. The natural light we see and dismiss as white is a constantly changing colored illuminant affecting the colored appearance of everything it illuminates. Because the human eye compensates and adjusts continually and rapidly, we scarcely perceive the variations, although we may experience an emotional response. The red and yellow light of a bright, sunny day is exhilarating, but we may feel downcast under the gray light of a cloudy sky.

The color composition of natural light changes from dawn to dusk, from winter to summer, from north to south, and from east to west. If you observe a white room from morning through evening, you will see a wide variety of colors. Morning light is faintly chill, varying from a pale yellow to a flat grayish white on a cloudy day. By midday the room will be flooded with "white" light and look more like its intended color than at any other time of the day. The late afternoon sun casts a rich, golden color that increases toward evening, when sunset produces warm reds, deep magentas, and longer shadows. These distinctions are of paramount importance to photographers, architects, and interior designers, whose work is always interfacing with natural light.

The orientation of different rooms in a house, or the way the house is placed on the lot, dictates the time and manner in which light enters. North daylight with its minimum of red, orange, and yellow wavelengths is cold-looking but valuable for reliable color matching. But even the north daylight so revered by artists does not afford a constant spectrum, even though the changes are minimal and gradual. North light is the ideal light in which to work with color.

Natural light changes dramatically with different latitudes. The degree of cloud cover common in northern Europe has conditioned the population to muted colors. Inhabitants of the Mediterranean region are accustomed to strong, mellow light. Pastels and deep, rich hues color the facades of houses in the diffused blue northern light, while bright, yellow-based hues reflect the California sun. Near the equator it is pointless to use strong colors on the outside of buildings because of the bleaching effect of the sun. Light's endless mutability makes it impossible to keep the indoor environment a constant color. The point is to use and appreciate the infinite spectrum offered every day.

Artificial Light

What we think of as a plain white electric light is, in fact, colored. Its hue is apparent in the windows of houses seen at night. The purpose of artificial lighting is not only to illuminate but also to add drama and impact to our lives. Warm white fluorescent tubes can increase the redness in meats and are often used in butchers' displays to enhance the product. Professionals use the terms *color appearance* (the apparent color of a light source) and *color rendering* (the effect of the light on the color of objects being illuminated). The most efficient form of illumination is low-pressure sodium-discharge lamps, but they render color so poorly that they must be relegated to the street, where safety is a higher priority than aesthetics. Sodium lamps are so effective because they radiate only those wavelengths to which the eye is most sensitive—the green and yellow—and provide the greatest visibility for the least expenditure of energy. They seriously distort colors, however, which can be illustrated by an event which took place in London, England. In 1936, mercury vapor lamps were introduced on a street in central London noted for its prostitutes. Within days, the prostitutes found other locations to ply their trade because the lamps were so unflattering to their makeup and skin tones.

In defining white light, we naturally associate it with normal daylight. But as we have learned, daylight changes constantly, varying with the latitude, season, and time of day. However, using color temperatures, we know that at approximately 5,000 K (K stands for Kelvin, a measurement of temperature) an ideal sample glows with a light that has spectral qualities approximating direct sunshine at midday on a June day in the temperate latitudes. The American National Standards Institute (ANSI) established 5,000 K as the graphic arts industry's viewing standard for the color temperature of lighting. This standard specifies not only the color temperature but also specific viewing conditions for the object being evaluated. Virtually all printing companies and film separation businesses use viewing booths equipped with 5,000 K lamps. Viewing booths are used for comparing a color original to a color proof or printed piece.

The color of light sources is a complicated relationship based on a number of different factors including correlated color temperature (CCT), color rendering index (CRI), and spectral distribution.

Correlated Color Temperature (CCT)

The first factor in choosing a color of lamp is to determine what Kelvin temperature is desired. For example, if a retail store wants accent lighting to blend in with warm halogen incandescent lamps, they may choose a lamp with a CCT of 2,700 Kelvin. This temperature is not simply an arbitrary number; it has a correlation to actual thermal temperature. Anyone who has seen a piece of metal being heated will notice that as the temperature of the metal increases, the color of the metal changes. This is a rough explanation of how the CCT of HID (high-intensity discharge) and fluorescent light sources is measured. **CCT is defined as the absolute temperature expressed in degrees Kelvin of a theoretical black body whose chromaticity most nearly resembles that of its light source.** From this standpoint, the CCT rating is an indication of how "warm" or "cool" the light source is.

Spectral Energy Distribution

When we look at a light source, we perceive seeing a single color, but in actuality we are seeing literally thousands of colors and variations of colors. The combination of different wavelengths of light makes up the color we see. The different combinations and the relative intensity of various wavelengths of light can be used to determine a light source's color rendering index or CRI.

Color Rendering Index (CRI)

In general, the CRI is an indication of a lamp's ability to show individual colors relative to a standard. This value is derived from a comparison of the lamp's spectral distribution compared with a standard (typically a black body) at the same color temperature. Incandescent lamps are the only light source that follow a true black body curve. Other sources are rated with a CCT. The CCT, however, does not provide information on the quality of color. For this, a color rendering index (CRI) is also necessary. **In general, the higher the CRI rating of a lamp, the better different colors will show.** However, this guideline can be misleading with certain lamp types. A high CRI sometimes makes different colors easier to distinguish, but standard colors may appear different than they actually are.

Incandescence is light produced by a heated material, examples of which are the sun, oil lamps, candles, gaslight, and the tungsten-filament lamp. The hotter the given material is heated, the greater the light it gives, first glowing red, then yellow, then nearly white. When the tungsten filament bulb became a mass production item, manufacturers could supply a subdued light with an almost infinite life or a bright white but short-lived light. They compromised on light slightly yellower than daylight but whiter than either oil lamps or candles, which would burn an average of 1,000 hours. Its color rendering is on the warm side of natural, enriching the reds, pinks, tans, yellows, and neutrals in the room, while dulling the greens and blues.

Fluorescent lighting is characterized by its flat, cold, bright illumination, which casts few shadows and no highlights. It is uniform, undramatic, and inexpensive to run. (See Chapter 4 for a discussion of how fluorescent light affects health.) It evolved from the original vapor tube devices, which produced light through the electrical excitation of gas atoms. The gas used determined color: neon made red, and mercury made blue. By coating the inner surface of vapor tubes with phosphors, fluorescent lighting was created. The color could be controlled by the phosphors selected.

Lighting manufacturers offer guidance on the color-rendering capabilities of their fluorescent lights. The trade names can be misleading. The first fluorescent tube marketed was called Daylight, but in reality it had a bluish cast and did not come close to duplicating daylight. Newer fluorescent tubes with names such as White, Warm White, or De Luxe Warm White more closely resemble the light from a tungsten lamp, but they still render color differently from natural sunlight and incandescent light.

Both shoppers and retailers have learned the importance of color rendering, often the hard way. A color consultant once developed a range of colors for a leading blanket manufacturer, but when the line was launched it created something of a mystery. In some stores the line sold remarkably well; in other stores the blankets barely moved at all. Lighting was the variable. The primarily rose and gold shades of blankets were popular in stores with incandescent lighting, while the fluorescent lighting in the other stores made the colors seem muddy. Similar errors occur among inexperienced buyers. **It is essential to view the item being considered under the same sort of light in which it will be used**. There are some tips for matching colors. If you want to buy fabric to match a carpet, take a sample at least six inches square and try out the match under *all* the different lights you have in the room. Dyes reflect differently under different types of lighting, a process called metamerism, and a yellow sample that matches the carpet exactly under tungsten light may look greenish under a fluorescent source.

The industry has inevitable stereotypes in artificial lighting. For example, cool and efficient fluorescents are supposed to equate with the workplace and contemporary design, while warm and cheerful incandescents equate with relaxation and tradition. In reality, there is a different light to suit every situation, mood, and response. For selecting lighting, current energy-conservation codes must be considered in conjunction with color rendering capability, as well as health and vision concerns (Figure 2-15).

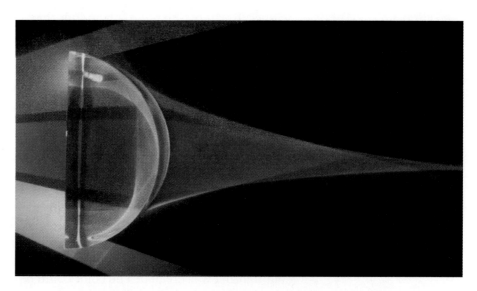

figure 2-15

Here, a large cylindrical lens mixes colors from colored light sources by refraction. *Reprinted with permission of Exploratorium, www.exploratorium.edu*

Light Measurement and Control

Measurement

There are four basic ways to measure light. The **lumen** refers to the quantity of light that is given off in all directions by the lamp itself. Lumen data are supplied to designers by all lamp manufacturers. Lumens are often compared with watts to give an indication of the lamp's efficiency. For example, if one type of 100-watt lamp produces 1,750 lumens and another produces 1,490 lumens, it is clear that the former gives off more light per unit of electric power.

Candlepower describes the amount of light given off in a particular direction and is measured in **candelas**. This measurement applies to the light issuing from a lighting fixture or a light-directing lamp such as reflector (spotlight or floodlight) types. It is important to remember that neither lumens nor candlepower has any relation to the distance that light must travel to strike its target.

The light falling on a target (**incident light**) is measured in **footcandles**. However, the viewer does not see by footcandles but rather by the light reflected from objects. A simple and inexpensive footcandle meter directly measures incident light.

Light that is reflected from an object is measured in **footlamberts**, and it is therefore footlamberts that reveal the environment. Because there are no foolproof formulas and tables that can help designers deal directly with footlamberts, reflected light is usually considered in terms of brightness relationships.

Brightness Relationships

The human eye responds to tremendous variations in brightness levels. It is capable of perceiving minimum differences of approximately 2:1 as well as maximum variations exceeding 100:1. Extreme contrasts can cause temporary eyestrain. When the eyes are forced to adapt beyond comfortable limits, the seeing process slows down and the viewer becomes fatigued or irritable. Contrast of some magnitude, however, is essential if seeing is to progress effectively both psychologically and physiologically. The designer must learn to work within a desirable range limit.

When contrasts in an environment are so great that they cause losses in visual performance or simply annoyance or discomfort, **glare** exists. **Direct glare** is usually caused by poorly shielded light sources, and correct baffling often improves the condition. **Reflected glare** results from disturbing reflections off mirrorlike surfaces, such as when you are trying to read in bright light from a book with shiny pages. When reflected glare is irritating, it is termed **discomfort glare**, but when seeing becomes difficult, it is called **disability glare** or **veiling glare**. The best remedy for reflected glare is to direct the potentially harmful reflections away from the eye or make the surface diffuse.

Lighting in the Office or Home

Office Placement Requirements

The basic lighting plan should be a design that will include proper spacing of luminaries to provide a pattern of lighting to fit any arrangement of furniture and equipment. Spacing between fixtures and the wall is usual at 2 feet, 6 inches. This spacing permits rearrangement of furniture with maximum utilization of illumination. For example, the conventional office desk is 5 feet long by 2 feet, 6 inches wide. In an application where desks are placed against the wall with the person performing the work facing the wall, the fixtures spaced 2 feet, 6 inches from the wall would be centered over the leading edge of the desk. Consideration should also be given for specifying that the end of fixtures be spaced as close as possible to walls. To assure satisfactory uniform illumination and minimizing of shadows, the ends of the fixtures should come within 6 inches to 1 foot from the wall.

Private Offices

Private offices in contemporary structures are often small, usually 8 by 15 feet or 12 by 15 feet. Either direct or indirect lighting can be applied satisfactorily since much of the lighting equipment of the ceiling itself is generally not within the visual field. The smaller the room, the more likely it is to find inefficient utilization of indirect lighting. The arrangement and orientation of furniture in the private office are fixed and permit the placement of direct lighting equipment to minimize both direct and reflected glare. A lighting system may literally be designed for and around the office desk and furniture. Not only is it necessary to provide satisfactory illumination for the occupant at the point of work but also sufficient brightness on walls, floors, and other areas is necessary to avoid high brightness ratios with the work. The use of dark paneled walls, desks, and floor coverings is not conducive to comfortable seeing, and higher reflectance materials are available with equal character, aesthetics, and decorative value.

Residential Placement Requirements

In most homes the average seated eye level is 38 to 42 inches above the floor. The lower edge of floor or table lamp shades should be at eye level when the lamp is beside the user. This is the correct placement for most table lamps and for floor lamps serving furniture placed against a wall. For user comfort, when the floor lamp height to lower edge of the shade is above eye level (42 to 49 inches), placement should be close to the right or left rear corner of the chair. This placement is possible only when chairs or sofas are at least 10 to 12 inches from the wall.

Working Toward a Balanced Lighting Environment

Gaining a balanced brightness environment can be a major problem in any office, but there are some established guidelines that can be used:

- Control window glare.
- Lighten desk tops. For good balance, tops ought to reflect about one-third of the light falling on them.
- Lighten walls and ceiling. Reflectance specifications are 80 to 90 percent for ceilings and 40 to 60 percent for walls.
- For furniture and machine reflectances, desk sides, files, and office machines should have a reflectance value in the 25 to 45 percent range.
- Floor finishes are equally important. Select materials in the reflectance range of 20 to 40 percent.
- Woodwork and trim such as door and window frames should be light if they are not to attract undue attention. They have a suggested range of reflectances from 25 to 45 percent.

Computer and Video Color

For some time, experimentation has been ongoing with colored light mixing. Until recently, these experiments had to be done by projecting and superimposing colored lights on a wall or screen. Now computer graphics have opened up a whole new area for color exploration. The CRT (cathode ray tube) used in televisions and computer video monitors has three electron guns that corresponds to the three primary colors of light: red, blue, and green. When these beams strike the light-sensitive phosphors on the surface of the screen in varying combinations and intensities, they can create a vast variety of colors.

There are many fundamental problems with displaying accurate color representations on a CRT tube. The real world is made up of reflected light, while the CRT creates images via transmitted light. When you add the variables inherent in the range of human color perception, which is unlike film or the electronic response of a video camera, accurate color matching can become a real challenge.

Color prints created from negatives require color balance or the addition of filters during the printing process to balance the enlarger's light color (sometimes called color temperature, which is represented in Kelvins) and remove the film's mask color (that orangish color you see at the edge of color negatives). Slides work in a similar way. If an outdoor slide was taken with full sunlight, then using a projector bulb with a similar color temperature closely reproduces the correct image coloration when the slide is projected. When working with video capture and reproduction via CRT, things are quite a bit different. It is difficult to correlate electronic parameters and relate them to the precise color temperature from an original. In this process, the color image is digitized to an electronic signal, assigned a set of color values, and then saved. When it is redisplayed, the process is reversed but also subject to the electronics of the display device. Viewing the same image on a number of different monitors is likely to result in a number of different interpretations due to different gamma values.

Most video systems use a *white balance* to aid in overcoming color problems created by adverse lighting conditions. The color balance assumes that under normal conditions, if a white object can be made to look white, then the remaining colors will be accurate too. If the original lighting is not close to the proper color temperature (typically daylight), the white balance may reproduce white at the expense of other hues. For example, suppose there is a white crystal in an image and we color it red. If we use the crystal to do a white color balance, the camera's electronics will make the crystal white by overcompensating for red. To compensate for the red, the image must be corrected with additional green and cyan (blue-green), thus other items in the picture may take on a green-cyan shade, while the crystal becomes white with gray shadows. White balance works well only when there is a truly white item in the image.

So how can we ensure that the images on the screen look like the original? We can't and we don't. If your monitor has a weak blue gun, then all images displayed on your CRT will show a yellow tint. We can only balance and make the image look very close to the original if the original is held near the screen and the screen image is corrected until the two look alike. It is possible to add an object with known color reference to every shot, but this is very impractical.

Computer-created color graphics are represented in **fractals**. A fractal (Figure 2-16) is a rough or fragmented geometric shape that can be subdivided in parts, each of which is a reduced-size copy of the whole. Fractals are generally self-similar and independent of scale. There are many mathematical structures that are fractals, for example, the Sierpinski triangle, Koch snowflake, Peano curve, Mandelbrot set (Figure 2.17), and Lorenz

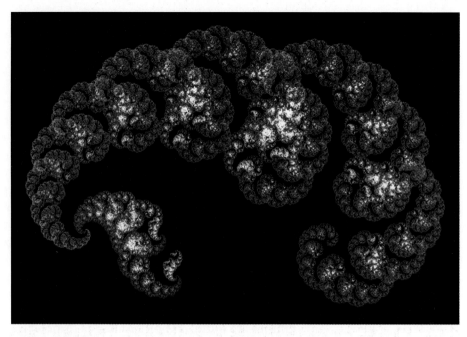

figure 2-16

FRACTAL IMAGE
A fractal is a geometric object that has two important characteristics: It is recursive; that is, the process of its creation gets repeated indefinitely. It is self-similar; that is, copies of the entire fractal may be found, in reduced form, within the fractal. *Used with permission of Edward S. May*

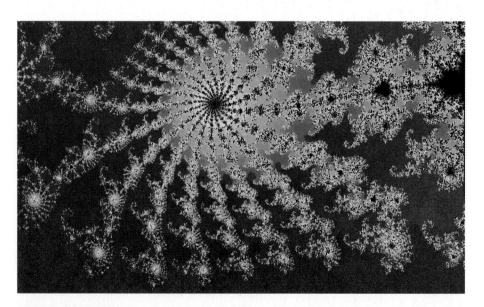

figure 2-17

MANDELBROT SET
The best known fractal object is probably the Mandelbrot set, named for Benoit Mandelbrot, who first investigated its fractal properties in the late 1970s. This is one computer-generated Mandelbrot image. *Used with permission of Edward S. May*

attractor. Fractals also describe many real-world objects, such as clouds, mountains, turbulence, and coastlines, that do not correspond to simple geometric shapes (Figure 2-18). Mandelbrot is reputed to have coined the word *fractal* from the Latin adjective *fractus* ("to break").

A digitized computer image is represented as an array of **pixels**, each of which contains numerical components that define a color. Three components are necessary and sufficient for this purpose, although in printing it is common to use a fourth component, which is usually black. In theory, the three numerical values for image coding could be provided by a color specification system, but because of its complexity, image coding uses different systems than color specification. (For more detailed information, see Chapter 11.)

An interesting feature of computer color is **gamma**, which is one of the most difficult computer terms to define. Even experienced computer technicians have a hard time understanding exactly what gamma is. Gamma, like color, is a complex interactive process. Gamma is a measurement, a mathematical formula reflecting a relationship between input and output. As simply as we can put it, gamma is a mathematical formula that describes the relationship between the voltage input and the brightness of the image on the monitor screen. Gamma has also been described as the measurement of contrast that affects the midtones of an image. Generally, gamma measurements range from 1.0 to 3.0. Different systems have different gamma measurements. An effective gamma rating delivers true colors and a good range of light, middle, and dark tones. Some computers come equipped with gamma correction built into their operating systems. Others require gamma correction to

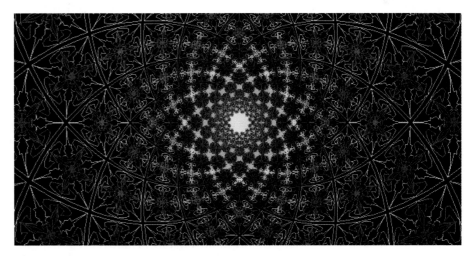

figure 2-18

The Fibonacci spiral on which the concept of the golden mean is based. At each concentric layer of a Fibonacci spiral, the ratio of a single component piece to one from the next inner layer is a constant, which varies according to how many radially symmetric parts of the spiral there are. This makes the expanding sequence of layers a kind of Fibonacci sequence: Each one is a certain linear combination of previous ones. These spirals occur frequently in nature, for example, in a nautilus shell or a sunflower. It seems that each growing layer of the organism must reproduce itself in a certain expanded version one layer out, thus guaranteeing a Fibonacci pattern. *Used with permission of Edward S. May*

achieve effective viewing conditions for images. The way things are at present, PCs and Unix require correction. Macs and Silicon Graphics workstations do not require correction. (The Macintosh comes equipped with a graphic card that automatically corrects the gamma.)

Colors viewed at uncorrected gamma appear different from those viewed at a corrected gamma. Gamma affects tonal differences and the range of grays assigned to a given color. Most important of all, gamma affects color. For example, let's suppose we have a color that is formed from a combination of 50 percent red and 25 percent green. When this color is viewed on a computer system with uncorrected gamma, it will be 18 percent red and 3 percent green. There is less green, and the color has shifted toward red. It is also darker. Differences in gamma create a nonlinear mutation of colors. By nonlinear, we mean that some colors may shift toward yellow, but others may lose their green hues and look bluer. Each color is individually altered.

At present the idea of a color standard is gradually evolving. The International Color Consortium is evaluating the differences in computer color with an eye to developing a standard that will benefit web pages of the future.

Lasers

The principles that underlie lasers are as complicated as the nature of light itself. A laser amplifies light waves, rather in the way that it is possible to amplify sound, but the problem with light is that it is naturally chaotic. Sunlight, electric light, or candlelight scatters a mixture of wavelengths in all directions in a way that is described as incoherent. Laser light is coherent, a single pulse of such intensity that it will emerge from a prism exactly as it went in. The first laser was created in California in 1960, when scientists produced a blinding pulse of light that could drill a hole through a diamond. The heat and brightness of lasers have boundless potential, from microsurgery to communications. Light has a far higher frequency than radio waves, and a laser beam can be used to carry millions of television or other signals through fiber optic cables that enable the beam to turn corners. Laser lights have become popular at rock concerts and events, but they are a valuable tool whose potential has only just begun to be tapped.

In this chapter we have discussed the evolution of color vision and the great impact that defective color vision can have. We have further explored the premise that only when the light and color signals from the eye reach the brain do we see color. This is a very important point to remember. We have presented explanations of pigment and light color, additive and subtractive color mixing, color schemes, color harmony, and the basis for working with color in both natural and artificial lighting conditions. This information readies us to move on to the next chapter, which exposes the deep-seated color prejudices that often prevent us from using color to its best advantage.

A Glossary of Terms Commonly Used in the Lighting Industry

Alternating current (AC): Current that changes its direction of flow through a conductor, going first one way, then the other. The usual rate used is sixty alternations (sixty times each way) per second.

Ampere (AMP): The unit for measuring rate of flow of electrical current.

Arc tube: A quartz tube in which a current traverses a gas between two electrodes.

Argon: An inert (will not unite with any other elements to form chemical compounds) gas used in incandescent and fluorescent lamps. In incandescent lamps, it helps to retard evaporation of tungsten filament.

Ballast: A part of every fluorescent lamp fixture. It is a circuit that controls the rate of flow of electrical current through a fluorescent lamp. It is also used for mercury vapor, sodium vapor, and other HID sources.

Beam candlepower: A measurement of beam intensity from reflector lamps as opposed to overall lumens of nonreflector lamps.

Blackbody: A theoretical body used by the lighting industry as a standard for establishing the "color" and spectral qualities of lamps. A perfect blackbody, when its temperature has risen to 3,500 K would give out light of a certain color; at 4,500 K it would give a whiter color, and at 5,500 K a still whiter color.

Bulb darkening: The darkening of an incandescent lamp caused by small particles of tungsten that evaporate from the filament and deposit on the bulb as the filament burns.

Candlepower (CP): Candlepower is a measurement of light intensity. It is used as a measurement of beam intensity at various angles from reflector lamps or fixtures.

Cathode: A cathode is an electrode that emits or gives off electrons. It is the type of electrode in a fluorescent lamp. The fluorescent lamp cathode emits or discharges electrons to the cathode (acting also as anode) at the opposite end of the lamp.

Color rendering index (CRI): A rating method by which fluorescent or any other light source is evaluated according to its ability to impart color to colored objects, with natural outdoor light having the RI of 100. Cool White has an RI of 62, and Vita-Lite has an RI of 91.

Color spectrum: all the radiant energy wavelengths that make human sight possible. The visible wavelengths include all colors and are measured in nanometers.

Direct current (DC): Electric current without alternations that flows in one direction only. Duro-Test has direct-current fluorescents available in 20-watt Daylite. DC does not affect incandescents adversely. High-voltage Fluormerics (230 v or higher) can be used on DC. They should be utilized with polarity switches.

Emission coating: An oxide coating deposited on a cathode that emits electrons when heated.

Filament: The threadlike tungsten wire that incandesces or lights up when an electric current runs through it; the light source in an incandescent lamp.

Fluorescence: Light resulting from the action of ultraviolet or other forms of energy on phosphors. Fluorescence occurs only while energy is being absorbed by the fluorescing material.

Footcandle: The unit of illumination. One footcandle is one lumen per square foot.

HID: Any class of high-intensity-discharge lamps, such as mercury vapor, metal halide, high-pressure sodium, xenon, and Optimarc.

High bay: High ceiling, usually above twenty feet and in an industrial plant. Because of height, it may be hard to reach for lamp changers without special ladders or scaffolding.

High output (HO): A fluorescent lamp designed for use with an 800-milliampere ballast. It usually operates at low temperatures near zero and still produces high light output.

High voltage: Voltage of 208 or higher.

Incandescence: Light emission by a heated filament or coil.

Infrared: Radiant energy with wavelengths that are longer than the wavelengths of the visible spectrum. Applications include photography, drying or baking materials in industry, medical heat therapy, and heating food.

Instant start: Refers to fluorescent lamps that start instantly, without preheating of cathodes and without the need of starters. "Instant start" lamps have coiled hot cathodes in contrast to "cold cathode" lamps. Both, however, start cold and instantly. A higher voltage ballast is required for instant start lamps than for preheat. Instant starts differ from rapid start lamps and cannot be used in rapid start fixtures.

Kelvin temperature: Term used to indicate the comparative color appearance of a light source compared with a theoretical blackbody. Yellowish incandescent lamps are 3,000 K. Fluorescents range from 3,000 K to 7,500 K.

Kilowatt: One thousand watts.

Kilowatt hour: One thousand watts of electric energy consumed in one hour, for example, one 1,000-watt lamp or ten 100-watt lamps burning for one hour.

Krypton: A very heavy, inert (will not unite with any other elements to form chemical compounds) gas that permits the filament in an incandescent lamp to glow hotter and brighter while still providing long life.

Louver: A frame fitted with slats or cross pieces that is fitted into an opening of a light fixture. For lighting fixtures, the cross pieces in louvers act to reduce glare from exposed lamps. They may also improve the appearance of fixtures, although they sometimes reduce light output somewhat.

Lumen (LM): The amount of light that is spread over a square foot of surface by one candle when all parts of the surface are exactly one foot from the one candle light source.

Lumen maintenance curve: This curve shows the loss of light output against the life of the lamp.

Luminaire: A lighting fixture complete with lamps installed.

North light: Scattered (not direct sunlight) light from the north sky at noon; about 7,500 K.

Preheat: A fluorescent system that requires starters. With this system, several seconds of heating time are necessary between the time the circuit is turned on and the time the lamp produces light.

Rapid start: A fluorescent system that does not require starters and usually requires one to two seconds to start. Current flows continuously through the electrodes, keeping them hot and electron emissive.

Spectral distribution charts: The term *spectral distribution* refers to the various wavelengths (colors) of light emitted by a lamp and to the intensity or power of the various wavelengths.

Starter: A starting switch needed for preheat fluorescent fixtures to "start" or light a lamp. It preheats the lamp cathodes and also provides a powerful electrical kick to jump the current through the lamp from cathode to cathode.

Ultra-high output (UHO): A fluorescent lamp that operates with a 1,500-milliampere ballast. It is used whenever higher footcandle levels are needed, using fewer lamps. It is also called VHO (very high output) or SHO (super high output). Power-Groove T-17 bulbs use the 1,500-milliampere ballasts.

Ultraviolet: Radiant energy of wavelengths shorter than the wavelengths of light. *Ultra* means beyond, so ultraviolet rays are beyond the violet end of the spectrum—that is, beyond the range of sight.

Visible spectrum: The complete range of energy wavelengths that activate human eyesight.

Watt: The unit of electrical power as used by an electrical device during its operation. The more lumens per watt, the higher a bulb's efficiency.

REFERENCES

Bouma, P., *The Physical Aspects of Colour*, Macmillan, 1971.

Boynton, R. M., *Human Color Vision*, Holt, Rinehart, and Winston, 1979.

Maas, J., Jayson, J. K., Kleiber, D. A., "Effects of Spectral Differences in Illumination on Fatigue," *Journal of Applied Psychology*, 59, 1974, 524–526.

Mehrabian, A., Russell, J., *An Approach to Environmental Psychology*, MIT Press, 1974.

Nassau, K. *The Physics and Chemistry of Color*, John Wiley, 1983.

Wurtman, R. J., "Biological Implications of Artificial Illumination," presentation at the National Technical Conference, Illuminating Engineering Society, Phoenix, September 8–12, 1960.

Wurtman, R. J., "The Effects of Light on the Human Body," *Scientific American*, July 1975.

Chapter three

Color myths and biases

**Color Fact,
Color Fiction**

Each and every one of us carries the baggage of color bias that we have been taught from the cradle. We cannot hope to approach color with a fresh perspective unless we can understand and free ourselves of the color biases with which we are encumbered. Most of what we are told is color fact is really color bias disguised as fact. As discussed in Chapter 1, color conditioning begins at birth and has more to do with language than with color. Color symbolism has been with us for centuries, from body painting to heraldry. Like it or not, we have come to accept certain color myths as fact, based on our cultural heritage and family values. Because of our close association with the cyclic changes of seasons, we have generally come to instinctively accept the earth colors—reddish browns, russets, and ochres—as associated with warmth and cheer. For most of us they represent a deep-seated sense of home, symbolizing elemental root qualities. But as with all things related to color, nothing is simple. While some find the earth colors comforting, others find browns and beiges boring and lifeless. The way certain colors become preferred or disliked may be traced to happy or unhappy childhood associations, or to reactions in favor of or against the traditional symbolic meanings attached to them.

Everything in life is colored, and a large amount of that color is subject to an individual's control. We select our own clothing, our own furnishings, the color of our car and appliances, cosmetics, flowers, and plants. Even our food choices are sometimes based on color rather than flavor. Our first perceptions of color may have been associated with the human body; the colors of blood and bodily emissions were the first to be given names. Almost the only thing universally agreed upon is that red, orange, and yellow are equated with fire while blue, green, and violet are associated with cool oceans, deep forests, and shadows. Beyond these two basic divisions there is little agreement about the physiological or psychological effects of color.

Color Symbolism

Early in the development of Western civilization, color in the form of heraldic symbolism was used to communicate with a population that had not yet developed reading skills. While reading and writing were not necessarily part of an upper-class education, a knowledge of heraldry was. By the mid-thirteenth century the rules of heraldry had become so well established that it had developed its own terminology, called *blazon*. This marvelously archaic and elaborate language based on Norman French is used to describe the ramifications of heraldry even in the present day.

In blazon, colors are called tinctures, comprising two metals, five main hues, and two main furs. The metals are Or and Argent (gold and silver); the hues are azure (blue), gules (red), sable (black), vert (green), and purpure (purple); *tenne* (orange) and murrey or sanguine (reddish purple) also make an appearance on rare occasions. The furs are ermine (actually illustrated as a pattern of spots that, depending on their relationship to the background, may be called ermine, *erminois, ermines,* or *pean*) and Vair, a blue and white pattern originally inspired by the belly fur of a squirrel.

During the considerable amount of warfare at the time, it was essential to distinguish the enemy from one's own troops. However, with the amount of armor worn, this was very difficult. Heraldry came into being as a way to immediately distinguish friend from foe on the battlefield. As the role of heraldry subtly developed from a means of identification into a declaration of family alliances, rank, and land, a man was entitled to join the coat of arms of his wife's family with his own on his shield, because he would have acquired new lands. Within a few generations the coats of arms of some great families had become a brilliant and chaotic jumble of colorful symbols that were kept in check and understood by the heralds.

Within heraldry, colors were often assigned symbolic meanings: red for blood or courage, white for honesty and purity, blue for loyalty. Subsequently, these colors with their associated meanings formed the basis for the American, British, and French flags as well as flags from other countries. To this day in the United States we make a strong association between patriotism and the colors red, white, and blue.

During the time of Henry VIII, green in England had come to stand for unfaithfulness, a concept derived from grass stains on a virgin's clothing. This is the subtle meaning of the ballad "Greensleeves," which has been attributed to him. Colors still provide us with a kind of shorthand in everyday speech. Red Army, yellow streak, purple prose, the blues, green thumb, and green with envy are just a few. Blue humor denoting an off-color remark is green humor in Spain, pink humor in Japan, and yellow humor in Hong Kong. In the United States, you are blue when you're depressed, but in Germany you are blue when drunk; if you're blue in Finland, you're just short of cash. The first step in freeing ourselves of color prejudice is to assess our own preferences in relation to our sociological and cultural backgrounds. By discussing each color or neutral in turn, with its associated biases, we can gain a better understanding of just how ingrained color prejudice is.

The Neutrals

Black

In our Western society, the neutrals black, white, and gray have very strong associations with language. Black (Figure 3-1) is inherently ominous in that it represents the unknown, maximum darkness, the negation of color. Most of our associations with black are negative: blacklist,

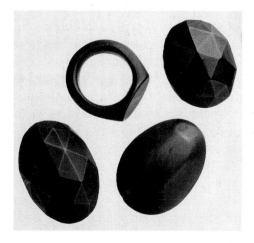

figure 3-1

© Dorling Kindersley

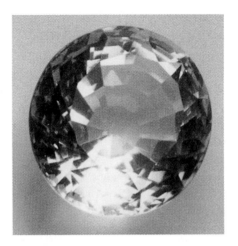

© Dorling Kindersley

figure 3-2

blackmail, blackball, black market, Black Mass, black looks, black sheep. Black is often the garb of the revolutionary, from beatniks to punks.

White

White is the opposite of black (Figure 3-2). White represents maximum lightness. In theory, a white surface reflects all light, but even the whitest materials like newly fallen snow will absorb 3 to 5 percent light. White's image is usually positive. White magic and white lies are benign; a white flag promises truce. One of the worst associations with white is a white elephant, which refers to a burdensome or cumbersome object, but even that is pretty tame compared to black's associations. We usually associate white with coolness, moonlight, the medical profession, and cleanliness. Until the 1960s kitchen appliances were invariably white, which contributed to our sense of hygiene associated with it. Whites vary from country to country. In the United States, we prefer whites with a blue or green cast, while people in Mediterranean countries such as Italy prefer white with a pinkish cast. Because white is the best-selling paint, manufacturers offer a wide range of whites with blue, red, yellow, and green undertones.

Gray

Gray (Figure 3-3), somewhere between white and black, is associated with technology, machines, aircraft, battleships, concrete, cement, and the urban environment. Gray can seem chilling and impersonal, but it also suggests the wisdom of age (gray hair) and the security of shadows.

One of our strongest language associations is evidenced by the phrase "Put it in black and white," referring to the printed word, which we often trust more than our own senses.

Red

Our associations with red (Figure 3-4) derive primarily from blood and fire. In Chinese the word for blood-red is older than the word for red, and in some other languages the same word means both red and blood. Because of these early associations, red is charged with passionate emotion. Red has strong associations with love and courage, lust, murder, rage, and joy. The bond between red and life has made it a significant

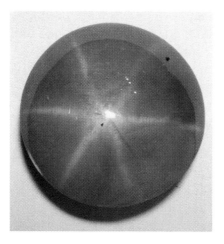

figure 3-3

color in every culture on earth. In ancient alchemy red denoted final attainment of the philosophers' stone, which was reputed to transmute lead into gold. Red is also very colorful within the context of language. For example, vermilion is synonymous with the archaic name for mercuric sulfide or cinnabar. This was sometimes called dragon's blood, and was the name of one of the earliest red dyes.

Ancient Egyptians began the tradition of marking important events or good dreams in red ink. The Christian church later continued the use of red to distinguish the order of service in prayer books and to show feasts on the ecclesiastical calendar. The latter practice contributed to the expression "red-letter day," meaning a fortunate event.

In myth and legend there are many strange associations with red, most of them expressing passion. It was once thought that the fat of a dead red-haired person (presumed to be of fiery temper) would make an excellent poison, and it was in great demand as a primary ingredient to rid

figure 3-4

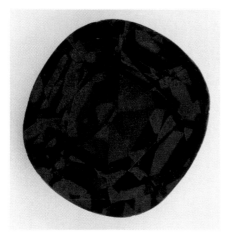

oneself of enemies. Being caught "red-handed" stems from the concept of the criminal being found still stained with the victim's blood. Lust is so integrated with red that adulteresses were branded "scarlet women" in Puritan times, and in later decades prostitutes were relegated to the "red-light" district.

Red is one of the few colors to change dramatically in association when mixed with white, for when it becomes pink it also becomes gentle and feminine in our minds. In medieval times pink was also called "nun's belly" or "nymph's thigh." It is difficult to find any bad associations with pink or rose. Being "in the pink" means everything is fine, as when everything's rosy. Red is associated with strength; white is associated with refinement. Pink, a combination of red and white, is associated with sweetness and gentility.

Red, symbolizing joy and happiness, is a primary color in old Persian and Turkish carpets that have been as valued as fine paintings for centuries. Up to a hundred years ago, red dyes were obtained from natural sources such as madder, and a variety of mordants (chemicals used to fix the dye to the yarn) produced different shades and variations. Today each shade of red is the result of a variation in chemicals. Color can now be measured and controlled precisely and the dyeing formulas stored and controlled by computer, giving a more reliable but often less interesting surface than the old natural dyes.

Orange

Orange (Figure 3-5) appears to be either loved or hated. It is a mixture of red and yellow and usually considered a warm color because of its association with fire. From a psychological viewpoint orange is similar to yellow, being considered cheerful and extroverted by most people. We usually associate orange with autumn from the changing of the leaves, and again link it with autumn because of the foods and spices we associate with the holiday season that have orange-brown tones—cinnamon, nutmeg, pumpkins, cloves, allspice, and so on.

When orange darkens into the browner tones, it is associated with comfort and security. Picture a steaming mug of hot chocolate spiced

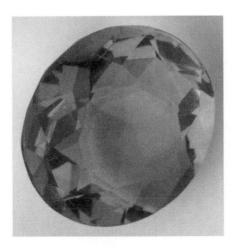

figure 3-5

© Dorling Kindersley, Natural History Museum, London

with cinnamon and perhaps a dash of orange zest: It just reeks of the cozy warmth of a fireside and the loving hands of someone caring for you, doesn't it? When orange becomes linked with metallics, we refer to it as copper and it then becomes exotic. In France there was an old custom of adorning bridges with orange blossoms, symbolizing the hope of fruitfulness because few trees are more prolific than the orange. The association of orange blossoms with weddings still lingers today.

The sunsets in the vivid oranges and salmons we take for granted today are a relatively new development. In a survey of people older than eighty, orange was remembered to be less predominant in sunsets than it is today. This has been explained by the amount of pollution now prevalent. A century or two ago when the air was clearer, there were fewer particles in the atmosphere to scatter the blue and violet wavelengths of light emitted by the setting sun, so sunsets were less vivid. With today's levels of industrial smoke and smog, the atmosphere is so polluted that by early evening most of the blue light has been scattered and only the long red, yellow, and orange wavelengths remain.

Fluorescent orange is one of the most conspicuous colors and is often used where safety through visibility is crucial. Life rafts are often orange, and the fluorescent version of the color termed Day-Glo orange is definitely attention-getting.

Yellow

Yellow (Figure 3-6) is usually considered a cheery, sunny color, yet it is also one of the least favorite colors chosen by people. Yellow has the highest reflectivity of all colors and is the first to be noticed, making it often the choice for fire trucks. Yellow is such a readily seen color that yellow cars are involved in fewer accidents than cars of any other color.

The first flowers to bloom in spring are often yellow: daffodils, crocus, primroses, forsythia. For obvious reasons, yellow is associated with lemons and citrus fruits and foods such as butter and cheese. The Chinese have always regarded yellow as a special color. During the tenth century they adopted it as the imperial color, and its use was reserved for only the emperor and those he selected by imperial order.

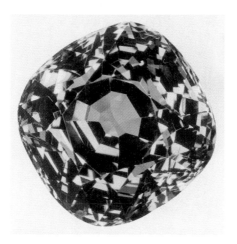

figure 3-6

© Dorling Kindersley

Yellow also has some negative connotations. Buddhist monks dyed their robes in saffron yellow as a constant reminder of mortality, for yellow is symbolic of death in that culture. In medieval art, Judas Iscariot was usually portrayed wearing yellow robes, linking the color with betrayal. Some countries passed laws demanding that Jews wear yellow because they betrayed Christ. The Nazis made Jews wear yellow armbands, continuing this trend. In sixteenth-century Spain yellow came to be known as a color of heresy and treason. The punishment for wearing yellow was burning alive. By 1833 priests were forbidden to wear it. Calling someone "yellow" suggests cowardice. Yellow press refers to unscrupulous or overly sensational newspapers, while a yellow-back novel was a vulgar or racy paperback book sold in Victorian Britain. Yellowing is often linked with age and decrepitude as well as with jaundice. From medieval times on, yellow has signified sickness. It is the color of the quarantine flag for ships at sea.

So yellow is something of a multiple-personality color, both happy and filled with misery and sickness. It is no wonder that many people either are ambivalent about yellow or find it disturbing, at least in its brighter forms. However, a recent study conducted by the Pantone Color Institute in conjunction with Roper Starch Worldwide Marketing found that yellow had improved in popularity, at least among the more affluent of the 2,000 consumers in the survey.

In nature, yellow means warning. Poisonous creatures are often colored yellow. The combination of yellow and black warns of special caution (consider bees and wasps). In fact, the combination of yellow and black was selected for the nuclear radiation warning symbol because of its natural associations with caution and danger.

Green

Green (Figure 3-7) also has ambivalent connotations. While most people associate it with growth, spring, and foliage, it is also associated with mold and decay, nausea, poison, and jealousy.

The ancient Egyptians were well aware of green's dual nature because it was the color representing Osiris, the god of both vegetation and death. Perhaps following the advice of Pliny, who said, "Emerald delights the

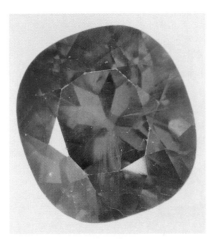

figure 3-7

© Dorling Kindersley

eye without fatiguing it," Nero was said to have peered through an emerald while watching the lions devour Christians. Belief that green is beneficial to the eyes lingers from ancient times, when the Egyptians used green malachite as a protective eyeliner.

Nature has lavished the Earth with green in foliage, but few green minerals that can be used as pigments are available. Because no bright green dyes could be obtained from nature, we had to wait until chemistry was able to produce them. Even though most leaves are green, there are many variations of chlorophyll that color plants different shades of green. Also, because of the presence of yellow carotenoid pigments, some green leaves have a yellowish hue.

Green is negatively associated with queasiness, seasickness, and poisoning. Extraterrestrials are often portrayed as green, from Mr. Spock of *Star Trek* to *The Incredible Hulk*. When asked to create something creepy, most children select green or purple. Green is associated with supernatural phenomena and eerie effects.

"Poison green" is a common color term based on a nineteenth-century arsenic-based pigment used in wallpaper. It was responsible for numerous deaths and brings to mind an occasion when we were invited to dinner at a prominent designer's Victorian home. The dining room walls were a stunning shade of emerald green, variegated and wonderfully mossy-looking. When we asked who had created the faux finish, the owner laughed and said they had simply stripped off the nineteenth-century wallpaper and left the arsenic-coated walls. It did create spirited conversation, particularly since the walls were in the dining room.

Green is equated with both security and jealousy as well as with the "green thumb" of a good gardener. It is the emblem of Irish patriots and the favorite color for camouflage. Green was symbolically worn at weddings in Europe, where it symbolized fertility.

Blue

The sky and the sea surround us with blue. Blue (Figure 3-8) symbolizes infinity, serenity. It also symbolizes depression, sadness, and isolation. Blue ribbons are awarded as first-place prizes. This tradition began in

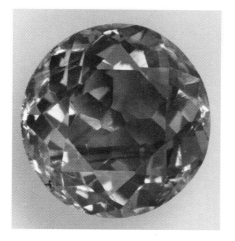

figure 3-8

© *Dorling Kindersley*

1348, when King Edward III of England recovered a garter shed by a lady during the course of a ball. He chose that moment to coin the phrase *honi soit qui mal y pense* ("shame to the person who thinks evil of it"), as he fixed the blue garter around his own knee and created the highest order of knighthood in England, the Knights of the Garter. "Blue chip" means high quality, particularly when applied to stocks. "Blue blood" indicates an aristocratic person. The term "bluestocking" means a pedantic female and dates back to 1400, when a Venetian society distinguished members by the color of their hose. This tradition was carried into eighteenth-century England.

Blue is the favorite color of Americans, particularly men. In a 1960s film, Sean Connery appeared in a blue shirt as British spy James Bond, 007. Suddenly men everywhere were wearing blue shirts. Blue denim has become practically a uniform and relies on indigo for its color. Blue sapphire and blue topaz are the two best-selling colored gemstones, probably based on their color. "Flow blue" is a particularly prized form of antique porcelain, and the blue transferware of old English Staffordshire pottery owes much of its great popularity to the deep cobalt on white color scheme. But blue is also linked with despondency, as in "the blues" popularized by Washington Irving in 1807 as an abbreviation of an older term, "blue devils." In music, the blues draws its inspiration from misery and woe, in the hopes that by vocalizing it the misery will disappear. Blue is also associated with transcendence, tranquility, and the ability to achieve balance.

Violet

There is often confusion between the terms *violet* and *purple*. Violet is a spectral hue, while purple (Figure 3-9) is a mixed color. Purple is the most significant color in the history of the dye process. For centuries, only royalty were permitted to wear purple. For that matter, it is doubtful that anyone but royalty could afford it because purple was so expensive to produce. The famous Phoenician-Tyrian purple color most prized in the ancient world was derived from the mollusk *Purpura*. Roman

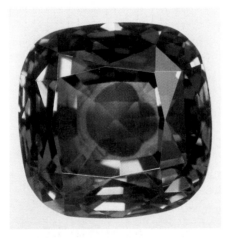

figure 3-9

© Dorling Kindersley

emperors used purple to represent their personification of the god Jupiter.

Synthetic purple dye was accidentally discovered in the nineteenth century by a young laboratory assistant named William Perkin. Purples and mauves became an immediate fashion sensation and were readily adopted by Queen Victoria and the British court in their extended period of mourning over Prince Albert's death. Mauves have come in and out of fashion ever since.

Purple is synonymous with sensuality and decadence, perhaps because of the purple stains of wine-soaked lips. In Christian ecclesiastical symbolism, purple is used to express mystery, penance, and sorrow, as identified with the periods of Lent and Holy Week.

Purple is seldom used in advertising and packaging, but its royal associations link it to luxury so that in advertising it usually represents a luxury item.

Purple is fairly rare in nature and is most frequently found in the flowers that have given names to their hues—violet, lavender, and lilac—and in the gemstone amethyst. Violets were used as medicine in medieval times, particularly to induce sleep. Oil of violets is still used as a perfume and flavoring. Candied violets are sometimes used as a garnish on elaborate pastries or desserts. Violet is the shortest wavelength of the spectrum and has the highest energy level. As it moves into ultraviolet, it becomes invisible to humans.

In psychology, violet is associated with internalization and sublimation; in the Lüscher Color Test a preference for violet indicates immaturity. Lavender is often considered effeminate and in some cultures has been linked with homosexuality. "Shrinking violet" denotes a shy person.

Color and Children

In Chapter 1 we introduced the topic of color conditioning, which begins the day we are born and follows us to the grave—unless we become aware of it and make a conscious choice not to be controlled by it. "Pink is for girls; blue is for boys." That old saying is such a part of our Western culture that we just accept it without thought. In Chapter 1 we reported that spending excessive amounts of time in a pink room can have a negative effect, yet how many female babies spend their formative periods in pink nurseries? If you go into most shops specializing in infant products, you will see pink, blue, cream, and pale yellow repeated again and again. Somewhere along the way we decided that when children get a little older, perhaps three or four years old, they suddenly prefer bright, primary colors. But is this true, or is this just something we impose on children, who are then forced to live with the colors we select for them?

In an attempt to answer this question, we delved into hundreds of color studies but found very few well-controlled studies aimed at children. Those well-controlled studies that we did investigate further had very mixed results, showing that some young children did like bright, primary colors, but that others seemed to prefer a much wider range of colors. One of the main problems we ran into while surveying these color studies was that the children being tested were offered only primary colors from which to choose, which obviously narrowed their range of selection. We ran our own study on a group of kindergarten children, allowing them to have a voice in selecting the colors that their classroom was to be painted. We provided the fifty children with lots of different colors of construction paper, including bright primary and secondary colors along with a wide range of pastels and neutralized gray tones, and asked them to choose their favorite colors. With almost no exceptions, the children selected a very sophisticated color palette with an excellent color balance. School administrators liked the colors the children selected, and their classroom was painted in those colors. The project was very successful, and the children expressed pride in having been able to participate in the decoration of their classroom. This project illustrated to us once again how often we are forced into selecting certain colors from early childhood, rather than being given the opportunity to develop our own color sense.

We have found that perhaps the greatest difficulty and disappointment we encounter in working in the design field is the chromophobic client who has the almost palpable fear of color that many people are saddled with. So often we have gone into blandly beige interiors and suggested that just a hint of color could create a whole new sense of the space, only to watch the client squirm uncomfortably at the mention of the word *color*. Yet during the conversation or while looking at photographs of interiors together, those same clients will remark how much they like blue or red or whatever their color preference really is. They have been conditioned to believe that safe beige is the only way to go to be "tasteful." As designers, we feel an obligation to free people from their self-imposed color prisons and help them express their true color sense. The least threatening way to do this is to first add just a touch of color in a portable form, perhaps by adding a silk pillow or two in the client's favorite color. Then, once client, family, and friends have accepted this small amount of color, a wider palette can be introduced gradually. Like it or not, part of any designer's job is to educate. By helping the client to understand the intricacies of design, the designer can produce a much better product, while helping to free the client from societally imposed dictates.

Color Trends

Color fashion trends are almost a form of dictatorship. Each season colors appear and we are expected to follow those fashion trends, no matter that the colors of the moment may make our skins look jaundiced or the color of a vampire's victim. If you happen to want to buy reds or oranges during a season when greens and blues are in fashion, you will have a very difficult time, often being forced to wait until your color preference appears once again or having to buy outside the area of your color choice. Economics makes this a necessity because manufacturers of home furnishings, appliances, automobiles, and clothing must find a way to relate their seasonal colors to other products being manufactured if they are to survive in the marketplace. Organizations such as the Color Marketing Group and the Color Association of the United States provide a forum for color consultants and designers to select and coordinate colors from one to three years ahead of a selling season.

Western technology has thrust new fabrics, building materials, cosmetics, dyes, and art materials into virtually every nation of the world.

Natural dyes have been exchanged for brilliant prints and vibrant colors, yet still each nation holds to perennial favorites regardless of fashion or availability. Germans and Austrians favor forest green. Highland Scots have a preference for subtly shaded tweeds. Muslims favor green as a sacred color derived from the legendary hue of the Prophet's cloak. China's Forbidden City is called purple, but is in fact predominantly red and yellow. It was thought that the camouflage of using yellow roof tiles to blend in with the yellow earth of the landscape would keep evil spirits from finding the city.

Climate has played a role in defining color biases. For example, the humid, foggy atmosphere prevalent in parts of Japan dictates soft, clear colors. We in the West have a distorted view of true Japanese color preference because of the harshly hued kimonos made for export. In fact, the Japanese have a very refined sense of color, and the bright purples, greens, and pinks of the export kimono are considered vulgar. The Japanese prefer the gentle colors of nature—sky, water, and wood.

Another criterion that has influenced color bias is complexion color. A rule of thumb seems to be: The darker the skin, the brighter the color. Pale complexions provide their own complexities, as cosmetics manufacturers have discovered. For example, the pigments of British cosmetics were considered too harsh for American consumers who, like Australians, prefer softer colors. In the United States, people on the East Coast favor cosmetics with a blue bias, while people in the West and Southwest prefer yellow-based cosmetics.

We pick up color signals from our families, from school, from television, from print media, and from our friends. Yet on the whole, these signals repeat the same color biases based on the same color myths that previous generations learned. Unless you take art classes, the educational process entirely ignores color. Even if you are trained to use color in the artistic sense, large gaps are left in the instruction with relation to the effects of color. The average student is not taught how color affects choices in purchasing, how color affects health and well-being, or how color can be used to influence people. Artists are taught how to use color in various painting techniques and are taught how to manipulate light and shadow in a two-dimensional medium, but that is a far cry from really understanding how to get the most benefit from the color that surrounds us every day of our lives.

In medieval times colors had great power and formed strong associations that have continued in European society. Color was linked to astral bodies: yellow for the sun, white for the moon, red for Mars, green for Mercury, blue for Jupiter. From heraldry we derived black for penitence, red for courage, blue for piety, green for hope, and purple for nobility or rank.

With such strong color associations ingrained in us from birth, we all have developed color biases. While it is beneficial for anyone to understand color and use it to advantage, it is essential for designers. A designer should strive not to let his or her personal color prejudice influence attitudes toward color when working with a client. If, for example, a designer is working with a client whose favorite color is yellow-green and the designer happens to detest that color, the designer should be able to put prejudice aside and prepare an appealing color scheme that both suits the client and meets the aesthetic requirements of the designer. Unfortunately some designers try to talk a client out of using a favorite color if the designer doesn't personally like it. This is selling a client short and should simply not happen. It is the designer's job to be proficient enough to make any color selection work by knowledgeable manipulation of color and light. Whether you work with color as a professional or you simply want to get the most from using color, freeing yourself from color bias is essential.

REFERENCES

Bruno, V. J., *Form and Color in Greek Painting*, Norton, 1977.

Buhler, A., "The Significance of Colour among Primitive Peoples," *Palette* 9, 1969.

Chevreul, M. E., *The Principles of Harmony and Contrast of Colors and Their Applications to the Arts*, Garland Publications, 1980.

Porter, T., "Investigations into Color Preferences," *Designer*, September 1973.

Chapter four

Color and health

Without light, life as we know it would not exist. Plants harvest solar energy by photosynthesis and then provide energy to other organisms through the food chain. Humans and animals depend on light through vision and other photoresponses. The biological effects of artificial light are the basis of a variety of medial treatments and diagnostic techniques. Light can also have deleterious effects. For example, ozone in the atmosphere protects living things from damage by ultraviolet radiation. Increases in the amount of ultraviolet light reaching the Earth's surface as a result of changes in the ozone layer may cause higher rates of skin cancer and skin aging, as well as undesirable effects on agriculture, oceanic plankton, and the aquatic food chain. Recognition of the importance of light in biology has led to the development of the science of photobiology: the study of the myriad effects of light on life.

This section describes a few of the many ways that animals and plants are affected by light. Some of these effects are beneficial (and, indeed, make life possible), and others are highly detrimental. Yet, in truth, we know relatively little about the influence of light on biological systems, including human beings. The goals of the science of photobiology can be roughly divided into several categories:

- The development of ways to control the beneficial effects of light on our environment
- The development of ways to protect organisms, including humans, from the detrimental effects of light
- The development of photochemical tools for use in studies of life processes and photochemical products to improve the quality of life
- The development of photochemical therapies in medicine

In recognition of the growing awareness of the influence of light (both beneficial and harmful) on living organisms and the need for scientific information about these effects, the American Society for Photobiology was founded in 1972. The society, with an international membership, holds annual scientific meetings, publishes the international journal *Photochemistry and Photobiology*, and in general serves as a resource for information about photobiology. Members of the American Society for Photobiology study a variety of scientific subjects concerned with the interaction of light and living things. The following sections introduce some active areas of photobiological research and outline their importance.

Photomedicine

To avoid the sun would be to exist without one of the great pleasures of life. But as with most enjoyable things, indiscriminate exposure and lack of understanding of the possible unpleasant consequences can bring problems and even serious aftereffects. More than twenty-five diseases are caused or aggravated by sunlight. The field of photomedicine includes the study of such diseases and their treatments.

Harmful Effects of Light

Sunlight is implicated in several skin diseases, including premature aging of the skin and skin cancer. Skin sensitivity to sunlight is controlled by the individual's genetic ability to produce melanin, the pigment that helps protect the skin from light-induced injury. Genetic variations in the capacity to form melanin, proximity to the equator, and personal habits of sun exposure determine the individual's susceptibility to skin aging (actinic elastosis) and cancer of the skin (basal cell carcinomas, squamous cell carcinomas, and probably malignant melanomas). Deficiencies in cellular capacity to repair sun-induced damage of DNA, as in the inherited disorder called xeroderma pigmentosum, are responsible for the early onset of sun sensitivity and freckling, which can lead to sunlight-induced skin cancer. Certain drugs or chemicals also augment skin reactivity to solar radiation and lead to transient phototoxic effects or chronic photoallergic reactions. In the synthesis of hemoglobin, the substance that gives the red color to human blood and carries oxygen, genetic deficiencies of certain enzymes lead to metabolic overproduction of hemoglobin precursors called porphyrins. These porphyrins absorb light and cause severe, disabling photosensitivity.

Beneficial Effects of Light

Photomedicine is also concerned with the beneficial effects of light. For example, phototherapy is useful for treating jaundice in premature babies, and light-based therapies can be effective in treating psoriasis. The use of light-based techniques to treat tumors and to inactivate the human immunodeficiency virus (HIV) that causes AIDS and other viruses present in blood is being explored. Phototherapies for several other diseases exist or are under development.

Photoprotection

Both tropical and systemic sunscreen agents prevent the acute and chronic effects of sunlight. They enable people to work outdoors and enjoy outdoor activities with reduced risk of sun-induced injury. The damage that absorbed light creates in the skin, such as the changes recognized as aging of the skin, is preventable with new types of water- and sweat-resistant sunscreens.

Photoimmunology

Light exposure can affect the immune system. For example, irradiation of mice with ultraviolet light not only produces skin tumors at the site of exposure but also alters the entire immune system, allowing transplantation of the tumors to areas not exposed to light. Studies of these effects may ultimately help explain the molecular basis for skin cancer in humans. This and other effects of light on the immune system are currently under active investigation in many photobiology laboratories.

Environmental Photobiology

Environmental photobiology is a new, multidisciplinary research area. It is concerned with the effect of artificial light on the human environment, the effects of sunlight on ecosystems, and human influences on the quality of sunlight reaching the Earth's surface.

By the release of chlorofluorocarbons, society has the capacity to change the spectral quality of sunlight by destroying the ozone layer in our stratosphere, which filters out much of the damaging short-wavelength ultraviolet radiation. What would be the ecological consequences of such a change? Could there be a harmful effect on agriculture? Would skin cancer risk increase? These are the kinds of questions studied by environmental photobiologists.

The role of artificial light in the human environment has only begun to receive serious attention. Mammalian cells grown in the laboratory are mutated by fluorescent room light. Light absorbed through the eye is known to affect the functioning of the pineal gland. Visible light, especially red light, penetrates deeply into tissues. Are there beneficial effects of light on humans other than those mediated by vision? The possibility of extraocular photoreception in humans is an exciting challenge for the future. (See Chapter 12 for more on this topic.)

Photosensitization

The phenomenon of photosensitization occurs not only in humans, as described in the section on photomedicine, but also in other organisms. For example, some plants contain potent photosensitizing chemicals. When cattle, sheep, or other animals eat these plants, they become light sensitive and may even die if they remain in the sunlight. Grazing animals with liver dysfunctions also become light sensitive because of the accumulation of chlorophyll metabolites that are photosensitizers. Even foodstuffs can suffer from photodamage. Some snack foods such as potato chips and corn chips develop an off flavor when exposed to light, apparently from the photooxidation of unsaturated oils that remain in the chips after cooking.

Ultraviolet Radiation Effects

Photobiologists working with ultraviolet radiation are concerned with identifying the photochemical changes that are produced in living tissue by the absorption of ultraviolet light and determining the biochemical and physiological responses of cells to this damage. the most important discovery in this research area in recent years is that all cells have a remarkable capacity to repair damage that is produced in their deoxyribonucleic acid (DNA) by ultraviolet radiation. It is now known that cells can also repair their DNA when it has been damaged by other types of radiation, such as x-rays, and by chemical carcinogens. Furthermore, normal cellular metabolism produces agents that damage DNA, and DNA repair systems play an important role in protecting the genetic material form the harmful effects of this damage.

Light-induced damage of DNA may lead to aging. Many of the earlier theories of aging have been unified into the genetic alteration theory. The basic premise of this theory is that the proper functioning of a cell or organism depends on the proper functioning of its DNA. If DNA damage is not repaired properly, the organism will undergo aging. Cells from patients with hereditary diseases that predispose them to early aging have been found to be deficient in DNA repair.

Photochemistry

Photochemical changes are responsible for biological responses to light and can have important effects on the environment of all organisms, including humans. Photochemistry is the study of the basic chemistry and physics of such transformations. Understanding and control of any photobiological process require knowledge of the underlying photochemistry. Photochemists investigate photochemical reactions using the tools of modern chemical analysis, including spectroscopic methods of many kinds. Once the detailed mechanism of a photochemical reaction is known, it is usually possible to learn how to modify the photochemistry and thus improve the efficiency of beneficial reactions or inhibit detrimental processes.

Photochemistry is becoming increasingly important as a tool in biological research. For example, the understanding of many complex photobiological processes can be enhanced through the preparation and study of synthetic photochemical models. Photochemistry can also be used to study the spatial relationships of molecules in complex biological structures. In this approach, light is used to induce chemical bonds between adjacent molecules. Subsequent identification of these attachments indicates the spatial relationship of the molecules in the native biological structure.

Many important industrial and manufacturing processes are based on photochemistry. Photocopying, photography, and photolithography are just a few examples. Also, natural and synthetic chemicals (e.g., medications, industrial chemicals, herbicides, and pesticides) can sometimes be altered by sunlight to produce compounds toxic to humans and other organisms or harmful to the environment. For example, the action of sunlight on automobile exhaust contributes to smog. It is therefore important to study the photochemistry of all common chemicals that may be exposed to sunlight.

Spectroscopy

The first law of photochemistry states that only light that is absorbed can produce chemical change. Spectroscopists study the absorption and emission of light by molecules. Spectroscopy can provide information about the chemical structure of a molecule and the energy states it can assume. It can also be used to determine the amounts of specific chemicals present in mixtures of materials. These analytical techniques are so sensitive that they are often the methods of choice for industrial quality control, medical analyses, monitoring of environmental pollutants and contaminants, and analysis of ores. Three are many spectroscopic techniques available to photochemists, including those based on lasers of various kinds. Photoacoustic spectroscopy is a recent innovation that allows the determination of the spectra of solid materials as well as liquid solutions.

Phototechnology

Continued progress in the science of photobiology depends on the timely development of new light sources to solve specific problems and of equipment to measure their intensity and spectral quality. For example, a commonly used phototherapy for psoriasis was fully developed only after suitable ultraviolet light sources were invented. Some of the more sophisticated developments in phototechnology have been the laser and laser-based equipment, such as biological cell sorters, cytofluorographs, and photoacoustic spectrometers.

Photosensory Biology

Chronobiology

The ability to distinguish time of day without reference to external light or darkness is found in both plants and animals. Light has important effects on this time sense, or circadian clock, as it is sometimes called. Light keeps the timing cycle synchronous with day and night, adjusts it to long or short days, and even stops or starts it under certain conditions. Animals respond to changes in day length with accompanying changes in reproduction, migration, and wintering behavior.

In humans, mental acuity varies with the time of day, as do body temperatures, hormone levels, and many other physiological functions.

Even sensitivity to drugs varies according to a circadian rhythm: A dose that is toxic at one time of day may be tolerated at another time of day. Most travelers have experienced jet lag, which is the result of the circadian clock getting out of adjustment. Understanding and control of circadian rhythms promise to lead to significant improvement in our quality of life.

As temperatures drop and daylight dwindles, it is natural to fall victim to the winter blues, but seasonal affective disorder (SAD) is a depression linked specifically to the lack of light brought on by shorter days. SAD can cause a need for more sleep, feelings of fatigue, significant weight gain, withdrawal, and lack of sex drive. While SAD's symptoms are those of clinical depression, its symptoms abate with spring. Other body rhythms are influenced by seasonal changes, but the light-dark cycle has the greatest effect. Until recently, a prime treatment for SAD was sitting in front of a therapeutic light in a medical office for up to six hours a day several times a week. Now, reasonably priced portable units can be set up on a desk or tabletop with full-spectrum lights positioned overhead that allow a person to read, work, or watch television while being treated. The typical patient responds within three to four days.

Lack of light also disrupts the pineal gland's secretion of the hormone melatonin. Normally, its production increases throughout the night, beginning around nine P.M. In SAD patients, that onset is delayed. However, it remains unclear whether this is a symptom of the disorder or its cause. (See Chapter 12 for more detailed information on these conditions.)

On the subject of light deprivation, photobiological researchers Richard Wurtman and Judith Wurtman are quoted as saying:

In recent years there has been growing interest in SAD and in two behavioral disorders, carbohydrate-craving obesity (CCO) and premenstrual syndrome (PMS), that share some of its symptoms. The symptoms include depression, lethargy and an inability to concentrate, combined with episodic bouts of overeating and excessive weight gain; they tend to be cyclic, recurring at characteristic times of the day (usually late afternoon or evening in CCO, month (just prior to menstruation in PMS) or year (generally fall and winter in SAD).

It now appears that these disorders are affected by biochemical disturbances in two distinct biological systems. One system involves the hormone melatonin, which affects mood and subjective energy levels; the other involves the neurotransmitter serotonin, which regulates a person's appetite for carbohydrate-rich foods. Both systems are influenced by photoperiodism, the earth's daily dark-light cycle. Indeed, photoperiodism appears to be the basis for the cyclic patterns of all three disorders.

It should be noted that even people who do not suffer from SAD, CCO, or PMS are still strongly affected by the light-dark cycle. Indeed, seasonal changes in behavior affect normal people as well as these sufferers. Among two hundred randomly selected subjects, 50 percent said they were less energetic in the fall and winter. Forty-seven percent said they gained weight during those months, 31 percent said they slept more, and 31 percent said they were not as interested in social activities. The study concluded that a significant percentage of the population suffers from a mild form of SAD. Further, it is suspected that contemporary lifestyles increase vulnerability to seasonal depression by diminishing the amount of time we expose ourselves to natural light. A study of healthy elderly subjects in San Diego, which has a sunny climate, found that men were in sunlight for only seventy-five minutes each twenty-four hours and women for only twenty minutes. Wurtman says, "We need not all live in California, but perhaps most of us need to be exposed to more light as our ancestors were. Perhaps much as office workers join health clubs to compensate for the lack of exercise, people with indoor jobs need to arrange for adequate exposure to light."

Photomorphogenesis

Nature has produced a number of light-absorbing molecules that enable organisms to respond to changes in the natural light environment. Light signals can regulate changes in structure and form, such as seed germination, leaf expansion, stem elongation, flower initiation, and pigment synthesis. These photomorphogenic responses confer an enormous survival advantage on organisms. For example, timing must be very precise for seed to be produced before the first killing frosts and yet allow the photosynthetic process to accumulate enough stored food to support seedling growth in the spring.

Currently, commercial greenhouse growers regulate the production of floral crops such as Easter lilies and poinsettias by artificially regulating the length of night and day. With more knowledge about light control of the photomorphogenic triggering responses, other commercial applications should be forthcoming. These may improve crop resistance to external stresses.

Photomovement

Photomovement is any light-mediated behavior that results in movement of an organism. A common example is the bending of plants toward a light source. Some flowers, such as the sunflower, move to face the sun throughout the day. Organisms that can move about can respond to light by moving either toward or away from the source. This ability can be ecologically important, as when it enables photosynthetic organisms to move into a favorably lighted environment. Such responses depend upon the organism's ability to determine the intensity and direction of light. Some organisms use the sun as a directional compass for migration (European starling) or food gathering (honeybee).

Since light is an easily manipulated stimulus. the study of photomovement is particularly attractive when compared with investigations of other stimulus-response systems. Photomovement studies will increase our understanding of the molecular basis of behavior. Much exciting research on how different organisms perceive the direction and intensity of light remains to be done.

Photoreception

The perception of light by receptors other than true eyes is well documented for both invertebrates and vertebrates. A classical example is the house sparrow. It uses the cyclic annual change in day length to synchronize its reproductive cycle with the appropriate season. The receptor for this light signal is not in the eye but in the brain. It receives light that passes through the feathers, skin, and skull at the top of the head.

In mammals, most responses to light seem to be mediated by the eyes. A well-documented exception is that photoreception outside the eye affects the level of the neurotransmitter pineal serotonin in newborn (but not adult) rats. If such extraretinal photoreception also occurs in newborn humans, then it is appropriate to be concerned about the occasionally extreme lighting conditions in hospital nurseries. It if occurs in adult mammals, then current artificial lighting schemes might require adjustment.

Current research indicates that light can penetrate and affect the human body by means other than through the eyes. The New York Association for the Blind has studied the neodymium light source for possible benefit to low-vision and blind patients. A neodymium lamp emits spectral energy in a different pattern than an ordinary incandescent lamp, emitting 30 percent less ultraviolet and 20 to 28 percent less infrared. The most important difference clinically in evaluating light for low-vision patients is a sharp drop in the emission of yellow light in the 570 to 610-nm range. The visual impression in viewing colored targets is a vivid "true" color similar to the view in full sunlight. This, for example, is significant for a diabetic who must see a color match strip for glucose and urine tests. In high-contrast acuity charts, contrast sensitivity chart tests, and reading material, there is an increased contrast between black and white. White appears whiter and black blacker because of the decreased yellow emission of the lamp. Favorable responses were elicited form patients with retinitis pigmentosa, optic atrophy, glaucoma with visual field defects, and diabetes with proliferative retinopathy.

We have previously established that color is electromagnetic radiation of a certain narrow band of frequencies that is registered by the eye and interpreted by the brain. Through the visual process, light/color influences chemical reactions in the body. We are also sensitive to electromagnetic radiation outside the range of visible light, as evidenced by sunburn, which stems form ultraviolet light that is invisible to us. On the most basic level, the body absorbs electromagnetic energy as pure heat. It is alarming to consider that the cells of the human body can cook in a radiation-filled environment just as food cooks in a microwave oven. This is why precautions are taken to block the dispersion of these waves in televisions, microwave ovens, and computers, even though some leakage may occur.

One question under study by photobiologists is whether additional biochemical reactions are happening simultaneously with color vision, reactions that may have extremely powerful effects on human physiology and behavior. The eye need not be involved in such color reactions. Color, like microwave or radio frequency radiation, may also be sensed by a totally separate process, such as directly through the skin. A remarkable study was done on a group of schoolchildren whose school room environment was changed from orange and white to gray and royal blue. The children in the class responded with blood pressure decreases by an average of 17 percent—yet all of the children were blind.

Color/Light and Human Health

Traditionally, architects, interior designers, and lighting engineers have tended to assume that the major role of light in interiors is to provide adequate illumination for working or reading or to add an ornamental accent to a room. However, recent studies show that our artificially lighted environments may actually be causing us damage. For example, lighting can have a great impact on how fast we fatigue.

In 1974 three researchers, James Maas, J. K. Jayson, and D. A. Kleiber, investigated the effects of lighting conditions on fatigue. Male and female undergraduate students took part in a study in which a university classroom was converted into a study room equipped with two independent fluorescent light sources installed in the existing ceiling fixtures. The first light source, Vita-Lite, was a full-spectrum light closely duplicating the spectral quality of natural sunlight. The second light source was a standard cool-white fluorescent light commonly used in institutional settings such as offices and schools. Tests for fatigue were administered to the subjects during the first and last fifteen minutes of each of the four-hour sessions during which the study was run.

In attempting to measure fatigue, the experiment considered two separate phenomena, subjective fatigue (feelings of weariness, ennui, and tiredness, obtainable only through self-report of the subjects) and objective fatigue (fatigue that can be monitored by objective measures of performance on various tasks).

The findings of the study indicated that the subjects became much more fatigued after exposure to cool-white fluorescent light than under full-spectrum Vita-Lite, which approximated natural daylight conditions. The study also found that the full-spectrum light resulted in clearer vision than the cool-white fluorescent.

This 1974 study indicated that people working under the cool-white fluorescent light so commonly found in offices and schools grew fatigued, were irritable, and had more eyestrain and headaches than people working under the full-spectrum light conditions. Vita-Lite, Chromalux, and other full-spectrum light sources are readily available, yet, to date, most institutions continue to fatigue workers and students alike with cool-white fluorescent lighting. Even worse, many architects, designers, and specifiers still promote it.

If fatigue were the worst offense of fluorescent lighting, it might be tolerable, but the list of negative effects of such distorted-spectrum lighting grows daily. Throughout history, humans have spent the vast majority of their time outdoors in natural sunlight. Only recently, within the last century, have we surrounded ourselves with artificial light, microwaves, radiation, and extended exposure to electromagnetic fields through computers, hair dryers, television, video games, and so on. The Industrial Revolution drastically changed the way we live. It brought us marvels of technology, but it also brought us lifestyles totally alien to our biological natures. Our technological society has created barriers that screen the sun's ultraviolet rays behind window glass, automobile windshields, and sunglasses, bombarding us instead with fluorescent light, sodium-vapor light, television screens, video games, and computer monitors.

The average person today wakes up to artificial light, goes about preparing for the day in a room where the window glass distorts much of the natural spectrum, goes directly to a car or public transportation that further screens out the natural environment, spends the large part of the day in an office, factory, shop, or school where the often windowless environment replaces sunlight with artificial light, and then spends evenings staring at the technologically generated radiation of a TV screen or video game. It is an alarming fact that the vast majority of the population spends its time in a totally unnatural environment with distorted color/light conditions that are radically different from the sunlight for which we were biologically designed to live compatibly.

Radiation Effects from Fluorescent Lights

For more than two decades, we have known that fluorescent lighting has harmful effects, yet we continue to put energy efficiency ahead of health as building codes demand the use of fluorescent lighting in schools, offices, and other public spaces. We must reassess this situation and put human health and safety ahead of cost concerns and profit margins. Standard fluorescent tubes emit three types of potentially harmful radiation: x-ray, radio frequency waves, and extreme low frequency (ELF). These types of radiation may completely shut off the activity of the immune system. ELF is a form of magnetic radiation that is also emitted from power lines, electric motors, computer monitors, televisions, and a variety of household appliances. Research studies have implicated ELF readings above 2.0 milligauss with a variety of diseases, such as leukemia and other malignancies. ELF dissipates quickly as one moves away from the source, and readings below 1.0 milligauss are recommended. If you are working under fluorescent lights for long periods, light sources need to be moved at least a foot away—and preferably three to four feet away—from the body. The Environmental Protection Agency (EPA) has categorized ELF fields as carcinogens in the same class as the toxic pesticide dioxin, formaldehyde, and PCBs with relation to causing cancer. A ten-watt fluorescent lamp produces a magnetic field that is more than twenty times greater than a sixty-watt incandescent bulb. Ceiling fluorescent fixtures with several twenty-watt tubes can produce a field of greater than 1.0 milligauss near the heads of people below.

ELF is often emitted in toxic proportions in older fluorescent boxes that utilize electric ballast (power transformer) as opposed to the new electronic ballast. Ballast is a form of resistance used to stabilize the current in the circuitry of fluorescent lamps. If human health is to be considered secondary to profit margins and energy efficiency, then at least the newer fluorescent lights should be used. Sinusoidal electronic dimming ballasts increase the frequency of the spark in fluorescent lamps from 60 to 20,000 cycles per second. This makes the frequency of the spark faster than the human eye can see, which eliminates the annoying flickering and hum of old types of electric ballasts. These newer ballasts also significantly reduce ELF, while producing brighter light with less energy. X-rays can be effectively stopped by lead tape shielding around the cathode portion of fluorescent tubes to decrease harmful emissions. John Ott first observed that geraniums placed near the ends of fluorescent tubes adjacent to the cathode portion often withered and died. Ott-Lite full-spectrum fluorescent products are shielded.

The Healing Aspects of Light

The ancient Greeks recorded the sun's healing power. Downes and Blunt in 1877 discovered the sun's ability to destroy bacteria. In 1903 Niels Finsen won the Nobel Prize for successfully treating tuberculosis with the ultraviolet portion of light. The importance of color/light on the human body has been researched for some time, but, as we have seen, only within the last decade or so has it developed into the full-fledged scientific specialty of photobiology.

Photobiological research is now beginning to uncover the effects of color/light on the human body. Full-spectrum light (sunlight) has been found to increase the body's resistance to infections by boosting the immune system, to increase the oxygen-carrying capacity of the blood, to increase adrenaline in tissues and thereby increasing tolerance to stress, to increase production of sex hormones, to improve the cardiovascular system, and to help stabilize the blood sugar levels of diabetics. In an article published in *Scientific American*, photobiological researcher Richard J. Wurtman stated, **"Visible light is apparently able to penetrate all mammalian tissues to a considerable depth."** It has even been detected within the brain of a living sheep. Think about that for a moment. **It means that each of the various effects of light on mammalian tissues has either a direct or an indirect effect—but it has an effect—even though we may not be aware of it.**

One of the first widely accepted medical treatments with color/light began during the 1950s with the introduction of a radical new treatment of jaundice in newborn babies. The condition, called neonatal jaundice, stems from a buildup of incompatibilities between the mother's and the baby's blood, which results in a waste serum called bilirubin. The infant's immature liver is often incapable of filtering the wastes fast enough to prevent the ensuing brain damage and death. Until the 1950s, blood transfusion was the only available treatment. Then, a sharp-eyed British nurse noticed that when jaundiced babies in the hospital nursery were wheeled near windows and left in the sunlight, their jaundiced yellow skin color began to fade. Further research indicated that the sunlight had an effect on the babies that enabled them to excrete the toxic wastes that had been building up in them.

At first, it was thought that the light broke down the bilirubin or stimulated the production of sluggish liver enzymes to speed up filtration of the toxins, but it has since been discovered that the sunlight penetrating the babies' skin produces a photon of visible blue light. When the blue light comes in contact with a molecule of bilirubin, it changes its physical structure in a way that makes the toxins water-soluble and easily excreted.

Some molecules in our bodies act as **photosensitizers**. They are able to be catalysts in the oxidation of other compounds. Research has shown that photosensitizers in human tissues can include constituents of foods and drugs such as the antibiotic tetracycline, which can greatly increase response to light in some people. Sunbathing while taking tetracycline can greatly increase the chance of sunburn in sensitive individuals, as can other chemicals and cosmetics. The indirect responses of a tissue to light result not from the absorption of light within the tissue but from the actions of chemical signals liberated by neurons or the actions of hormones as the blood circulates. In an experiment where young rats were kept continuously under light, their hormones were affected to such an extent that their reproductive organs developed at a highly accelerated rate.

The color of light is also under study to see what effects it may have on us. Green light is the most potent in changing the phase of the temperature cycle, and ultraviolet and red wavelengths are the least potent. In another study, similar findings showed that green light was the most effective in inhibiting certain glandular actions. Recent research on the effects of the color/light phenomenon have resulted in remarkable findings. A few examples can help to make the point.

- Experiments on cattle have led to a new hypothesis on human obesity. Cattle kept for extended periods under artificial light were 10 to 15 percent beefier than cattle left outdoors. From the ranchers' point of view, this leads to higher profits by producing fatter cattle without the cost of extra feed. From the viewpoint of human beings, it may lead to an obese populations or a lot of extra money spent on diet aids.
- Mohr and colleagues at the German Red Cross Blood Transfusion Service studied virus inactivation of blood products by phenothiazine dyes in combination with light. This study was successful in photodynamic virus inactivation of blood and blood products, such as therapeutic plasma. The researchers noted that the procedure was further improved when the fluorescent tubes routinely used for illumination were replaced by more intense light sources, such as light-emitting diodes or low-pressure sodium lamps. It was noted that using this method the improved virus kill was accompanied by reduced damage to plasma proteins.
- Ben-Hur, Oetjen, and Horowitz researched the effects of a photosensitizer in combination with red light at the 600 to 800-nanometer range, which was found to kill 99 percent of HIV-infected cells.
- Photochemical decontamination of red blood cells with a photosensitizer and red light to enhance the viral safety of blood transfusion is being studied by Zmudzka and coworkers.
- Moor and associates found that photodynamic sterilization of red blood cell concentrates was possible, although the mechanism of photoinactivation of viruses is not completely understood.
- In another study, Hudson and colleagues compared natural pigments for their light-mediated antiviral efficacies testing two target viruses, herpes simplex virus type 1 and Sindbis virus. The study showed that while various antiviral effects occurred in combination with light, none of the active compounds showed significant activity in the dark.
- Tong and Lighthart studied the effects of solar radiation on bacterial levels in the outdoor atmosphere and found that pigmented bacteria could increase as a result of increased solar radiation in the atmosphere under areas of stratospheric ozone depletion.
- Mims reported from the Sun Photometer Atmospheric Network in Texas that there is an increased incidence of respiratory, cardiopulmonary, and other diseases associated with severe air pollution, but the responsible biological mechanisms are unknown. The bactericidal effects of solar ultraviolet-B are well known, and significantly reduced UVB resulting from severe air pollution in regions where UVB levels are ordinarily high might allow the growth of harmful organisms.
- In an exciting study, Michelsen and coworkers are researching the effects of using suitable photosensitizers for the photodynamic therapy of cancer.
- In another study, Chin and associates explored the virucidal treatment of blood protein products with UVC radiation.

- The National Eye Institute is conducting a study to determine if there is a link between fluorescent lighting used in neonatal intensive care units and loss of vision due to retinopathy of premature infants. Each year, approximately six hundred premature babies go blind or suffer some loss of vision from this condition.
- Mark Rea and Richard Stevens of Pacific Northwest Laboratories and George Brainard of Jefferson Medical College are collaborating on a study to understand the role of light in breast cancer, based on the hypothesis that artificial lighting is linked to breast cancer through melatonin suppression.

A new area of research is the study of drugs that are activated by light. Because these drugs are inert when they are not exposed to the correct wavelength radiation, they enable the medical practitioner to target only those tissues exposed to both the drug and the appropriate wavelength of light. A rethinking of ancient techniques has produced a drug known as 8-MOP that has been effectively used in combination with light to treat a form of cancer called cutaneous T-cell lymphoma (CTCL). The ancient Egyptians recognized that *Ammi majus*, a weed that grows on the banks of the Nile, had medicinal properties when used in conjunction with light. Early Egyptian physicians noted that, soon after eating the plant, people became much more easily sunburned. It is now known that the active ingredients in the plant are psoralens, the class of compounds to which 8-MOP belongs; it is the prototype for a new generation of drugs activated by light.

The body of evidence grows daily that color/light energy is so much more than just a passive component of the environment. Color/light energy is vitally connected to all living things. We cannot survive without it, yet we are only just beginning to understand its profound significance and to discover the negative effects of its improper use.

By living in improper color/light conditions, we may be causing incomplete metabolic or biological processes to occur in our bodies. Richard J. Wurtman, a photobiological researcher at the Massachusetts Institute of Technology, commented on the importance of properly balanced light sources:

We are just now becoming cognizant of possible biological implications of tampering with our lighting environment. Recent evidence shows that rats raised under cool-white fluorescent light (the kind found in most schools and offices) have retarded gonad growth whereas exposure to high-pressure sodium vapor bulbs (also found in many schools) have resulted in abnormal brain growth and adrenal hypertrophy. Further, in recent reports of illness in children attending school lit by the same sodium vapor lamps, the FDA began requiring that lighting companies assess the biologic consequences of prolonged exposure to novel light sources before they are released for indoor use.

The Department of Biology at Chicago's Loyola University reports a study in which the most significant abnormal conditions resulted from animals raised under pink fluorescent light, which represents a concentration of wavelength energy in the narrow part of the red end of the visible spectrum. The abnormal responses included excessive calcium deposits in heart tissues, smaller litters, lower survival rates of litters, significantly increased tumor development (which has since been confirmed by six major medical centers), a strong tendency toward irritability, aggression, and cannibalism.

Wurtman and Neer of Massachusetts General Hospital reported in the *New England Journal of Medicine*:

> *Most Americans spend much of their time indoors exposed to artificial light, light sources whose spectra differ appreciably from sunlight. Daylight fluorescent tubes provide very little long-wave ultraviolet light and emit yellow and red radiations in a ratio quite different from that present in sunlight. It does not seem wildly imaginative to speculate that prolonged exposure to this unplanned phototherapy might have physiological consequences. Perhaps it is not too early to suggest that appropriate federal bodies give thought to the ultimate necessity of regulating the spectral composition of commercially available light sources.*

Perhaps one of the most alarming light experiments was run during the late 1950s at the Ben May Cancer Research Laboratory of the University of Chicago under the direction of Katherine Sydnor. For six years she administered carcinogenic (cancer-causing) chemicals to rats while keeping them under different lighting conditions. Some were kept in total darkness, and others in varying periods of artificial light. Sydnor noticed that the fur of the rats kept in total darkness was soft and smooth in texture but thick and fully developed. The same breed of rats exposed to artificial light were completely bald on the top of their heads, with baldness continuing down the ridge of their backs. Tumor development in the rats kept under artificial light was significantly greater than in those kept in total darkness.

In a further study undertaken by the Environmental Health and Light Research Institute from 1970 to 1973, full-spectrum fluorescent light closely duplicating sunlight was compared to cool-white, warm-white, pink, and black fluorescent light on the development of melanoma, a particularly virulent form of cancer. Mice were injected with cancer cells and divided into the various lighting groups. When the mice were autopsied, those kept under cool-white fluorescent light showed more tumors of greater size than those kept under full-spectrum light that nearly duplicates sunlight. It should be noted that cool-white fluorescent light is the type most commonly found in schools and offices.

Sunlight is the ideal form of light both for color rendering and for maximum human health. With artificial lighting, the goal should be to duplicate sunlight as closely as possible because sunlight represents all the colors visible to humans and more—sunlight contains the much maligned and much misunderstood ultraviolet rays.

Lasers as Healers

Thomas Dougherty of Rosswell Park Memorial Institute in Buffalo, New York, started working with the idea of utilizing light with certain light-sensitive chemicals in the treatment of cancer. In 1972, he noticed that if he took a certain photosensitive chemical, which he called photofrin, and injected it into the bloodstream of an individual with cancer, even though the chemical went throughout the body and collected in all the physical tissues, within three days it began to leave the tissue that was healthy. It seemed to collect within the tissue that had malignant cells in it. Dougherty found that he could then shine a violet or ultraviolet light on the patient's body, and, if there was a malignant growth somewhere near the skin's surface, that part of the body would fluoresce in response to the light as if lighting up to announce its presence. Dougherty then found that if he took red light and focused it on the spot, within ten minutes the tumor started to self-destruct. Initially he worked with visible noncoherent light but is now using laser (coherent) light. In the last twenty years his research has been done on eighteen to twenty different kinds of cancer. It is called photodynamic therapy and now is done in about seventy to eighty centers in the United States and Canada. The success rate is reported to be quite good, and the primary reported side effect is sensitivity to light for four to six weeks, but further research may prevent that.

While there are more than seven hundred frequencies in full-spectrum sunlight, much research is now being done on only one frequency, or monochromatic light, for activating specific cell functions in damaged cell tissue and accelerating the body's normal healing process. For the past thirty years, scientists in the United States, eastern Europe, and Asia have researched the clinical use of lasers. Laser is an acronym for *light amplification by stimulated emission of radiation*. Lasers used in surgical applications are called *hot lasers* and are used to cut, cauterize, and destroy tissue. More recently, *cold lasers* or *soft lasers* of lower power have been used in a process called laser photobiostimulation. Research has studied their ability to stimulate a variety of cellular functions in a nonthermal and nondestructive manner. Cold lasers are available in many clinics, research facilities, hospitals, and medical offices around the world. Researchers have used cold lasers to isolate the most potent individual frequencies or monochromatic lights in their explorations of the effects of different wavelengths on human tissue samples. There are currently only two available methods for producing monochromatic single-wavelength light beams. The first is with a laser, the second with a light-emitting diode or LED. Lasers produce coherent light, whereas light-emitting diodes emit noncoherent light. Human cell tissue has been observed to respond more powerfully to a single wavelength than to exposure to more than one wavelength at a time.

According to David Olszewski, president of the Light Energy Company, which markets phototherapy products, much of the monochromatic light research has focused on isolating the most potent frequencies for wound healing and the relief of acute or chronic pain. Research demonstrates that **cell tissue responds best to certain frequencies that appear to be within the red and infrared spectrum, such as 630 nanometers (nm), 660 nm, 880 nm, 940 nm, and 950 nm**. The water and hemoglobin within the body's tissue restrict the full absorption of light frequencies outside the range of 600 to 980 nm. From the preliminary research, it appears that one frequency of light may be a primary resonant frequency for the body, while the others may be harmonics. It has been demonstrated that a **single wavelength within the middle of the red spectrum (e.g., 660 nm) is the most resonant frequency to human tissue because it stimulates the production of cell tissue and rapidly promotes the regeneration of skin and blood tissue in the areas exposed to it**. For example, on a half-dollar-size wound, the application of a 660-nm LED or cold laser for several minutes every two hours can, within one or two days, stimulate the generation of new skin without scabbing or the formation of scar tissue.

It is thought that photons are absorbed by the skin and underlying tissue, triggering biological changes within the body in a process known as *photobiostimulation*. Although the exact mechanism of action is still undergoing study, what is known is that **monochromatic light increases oxygen and blood flow, aids wound healing, stimulates nerve functioning, and facilitates muscular relaxation.** Proponents contend that monochromatic light in the blue, red, and infrared regions enhances and speeds up certain cellular metabolic processes, such as changing the electrophysiological properties of the cell membrane and activating enzymes that, in turn, activate key chemical reactions.

The Relationship of Light Therapy to Acupuncture Points

Until fairly recently, acupuncture was looked at with extreme skepticism by the Western medical community. It was often though of as quackery. Now, its healing benefits have been embraced by Western medicine, and acupuncture is often prescribed or performed by contemporary medical doctors and health practitioners. While light therapy is still looked upon with mild suspicion by the medical profession at large, there are those who are beginning to recognize its benefits, particularly when it is used in conjunction with the acupuncture points.

The acupuncture system contains twelve meridians on each side of the body and two master meridians along the center line. Each meridian contains from 25 to 150 acupuncture points (acupoints) and terminates at the end of a finger or toe. The meridians are named for the specific vital organs they traverse, such as lung or stomach. Energy (called *chi*) flows through the meridians in a predictable manner. Health problems in the body are reflected as abnormal conditions in the meridians. Acupuncture treatment is directed toward restoring the energy flow and balance, thereby improving the health problem.

Acupuncture points can be activated by light (photoactivated). In acupuncture, lasers and LEDs are being used instead of needles to stimulate the flow of life energy in the meridian system. The advantages of light are that the laser and LED are painless, can achieve quick results, and are safe from transmitting infection to either the patient or the acupuncturist. Since the LED has a wide dispersion, there is a larger margin for error for hitting the acupoint than with a laser or needles. LEDs allow a range of about three-quarters of an inch because of the scatter of the light beam. It is much more comfortable for the patient to use LEDs, particularly for sensitive acupuncture points around the face, such as the sinus and ear points.

In countries outside the United States, laser therapy has become an accepted extension of physiotherapy techniques that use the other arts of the electromagnetic spectrum, such as microwaves, shortwaves, infrared, and ultraviolet, to help stimulate the healing process. Much research is still needed to know how best to apply laser therapy to specific conditions, such as length of exposure time and frequency of treatments; however, low-power lasers are winning acceptance for use in a number of bone, nerve, and soft tissue conditions.

Problem areas can be reached by applying the light beam directly to the skin, where it penetrates as much as one inch into the soft tissue. If more extensive or deeper application into the body is required, the light can be applied to the acupuncture points. Using a combination of both direct application and acupuncture point techniques, most problems can be reached and treated by light. Since 660-nm red light lasers penetrate only 8 to 30 mm (deep enough to affect muscle tissue), it is most useful for superficial conditions such as scars, wounds, ulcers and a variety of skin conditions, such as acne, psoriasis, eczema, and rashes. Local treatment with infrared lasers in the 830-nm and 950-nm range penetrate somewhat deeper into the 30- to 40-mm range and are used to treat conditions of the joints, tendons, muscles, and fascia, such as osteoarthritis and rheumatoid arthritis. They may be effective with conditions involving both acute and chronic pain, swelling, and stiffness. Studies show that most effective results occur with tissues that have ample blood supply, such as muscles and soft tissue. Tissues with less blood supply, such as ligaments and tendons, respond more slowly to light treatment.

The laser acupuncture studies and research papers are growing rapidly, with new results being reported almost daily. In fact, a huge number of research and clinical studies are looking at the uses of low-power lasers on health problems, using both direct application to damaged tissue and indirect application through acupuncture points. The whole field of soft lasers in medicine and physiotherapy is new. Much is not known, but preliminary indications are that soft lasers are an effective, relatively safe, and useful therapeutic tool. The use of LEDs as an even safer, longer lasting, and less expensive alternative to low-power lasers is growing. The FDA has increased its regulations governing the use of low-energy lasers and is issuing consent forms for acupuncturist research and practice. Laser acupuncture treatment protocols vary, because it is based on the power of the laser (5 to 50 milliwatts) and the time applied. No units above 50 milliwatts should be used in treatment, and pain results when the power reaches 200 to 300 milliwatts. There has also been considerable discussion concerning the use of *continuous* light beams for acupoint sedation and *pulsed* (intermittent on-off) beams for stimulation of acupuncture points. This same concept applies to direct application of light to tissue, where continuous beams are used for pain relief and pulsed light to cause rapid regeneration of cells. Several studies seem to correlate the use of pulse rates between 200 to 300 pulses per second with a 50 percent on and 50 percent off cycle. Pulse rates from as low as 1 per second up to 20,000 per second have been employed. At this point, from preliminary studies it appears that it is the monochromatic single wavelength that is crucial to evoking a cellular response, not whether the light is laser or LED. LEDs are increasingly replacing cold lasers because they demonstrate comparable effectiveness without the laser's side effects.

There is concern with the use of even low-power lasers in terms of the potential harm and negative side effects. The FDA classifies low-power lasers as class III, nonsignificant-risk medical devices for investigational purposes only. Studies at the University of Washington cautioned that cold lasers can detrimentally affect or damage a particular acupoint if used for a prolonged period and can lead to reduced effectiveness. Laser treatment is based on the power of the laser and the duration of time that it is applied. Either one of these components can be overdone. Since photostimulation has a triggering effect, LED light allows the photoacceptor mechanism and the cellular functions to be in greater control than with the ore powerful laser light. With lasers you need to know the exact location of the acupuncture point. LEDs give a larger light dispersion beam and allow a greater margin of error in locating and activating the acupuncture point. LED biostimulation has been applied in the field of dermatology, neurology, physiotherapy, and dentistry, as well as cosmetic applications. The LEDs used in phototherapy are primarily manufactured in Southeast Asia and are similar to the indicator lights frequently seen in electronic equipment, such as those on your stereo or smoke detector, although the therapeutic LED is 200 times brighter. Advantages of using LEDs over lasers include the lower cost, longer life (approximately 50 years at 2,000 hours per year use), increased safety, and ease of professional and home use. Because LEDs are diffused light, they can be used anywhere on the body without side effects such as damage to the eye. LED phototherapy units can be used on a much wider range of problems than the soft laser.

A growing body of research in countries outside the United States supports the use of light therapy in treating medical conditions. In Stelian and colleagues' study in the *Journal of the American Geriatric Society*, pulsed monochromatic red light helped relieve pain and disability from knee osteoarthritis, suggesting that it can be a useful addition to medication. The monochromatic light was applied on both sides of one knee for fifteen minutes, twice a day. After ten days, the group getting red light scored 50 percent lower on pain tests and 40 percent lower on tests demonstrating a reduction in disability than the control group, which received a placebo light treatment.

Research led by Russian Olympic team psychologist, Gregory Raiport, describes the use of laser acupuncture to treat organic problems, as well as depression, anxiety, and addictions. The cosmetic industry has used both low-powered lasers and LEDs on acupuncture points on the face to help give a "facelift," as point stimulation helps tone slack muscles, ease lines, and improve blemishes. This method of light stimulation encourages the production of collagen and elastin and gives the skin tissue greater elasticity and a healthier and younger appearance.

Dr. Pankratov of the Institute for Clinical and Experimental Medicine in Moscow has verified that the acupuncture meridian system conducts light, particularly in the white and red spectral range, when the light source is held against or within 1 to 2 millimeters of the acupoint. This means that the body's meridian system acts as a biological fiber optics network for the distribution of light. The meridian ending points lead to an avenue for applying light deeper into the body than the normal red and infrared penetration depth of 4 to 80 millimeters, literally providing a conduit into specific organs and tissues.

With the light-conductive properties of the acupuncture system now being studied more fully, it appears that the increased effectiveness of acupuncture treatments when used in conjunction with monochromatic light may be due to the effect of two modalities at work simultaneously: The stimulation of energy (*chi*) and the triggering effect of light on the photoacceptors in the problem area together result in accelerated tissue regeneration from the molecular level.

Most recently, studies have shown that stimulation of the acupuncture meridians is effective in cases of environmental illness, such as poisoning from pesticides, air and water pollutants, and radiation sickness; substance abuse (alcohol and chemical dependencies); and process addictions to gambling, sex, work, and eating disorders. In addition, acupuncture point stimulation has been an adjunct treatment for severe mental disorders such as anxiety, depression, obsessions, compulsions, and schizophrenia. Acupuncture has been shown to support and improve immune functioning in patients with compromised immune systems, such as those with AIDS.

Ultraviolet: Friend or Enemy?

Humans are not able to see ultraviolet light, but it is still there affecting us anyway. Ultraviolet light is directly related to human health. It can contribute to skin cancer if exposure is excessive, but the benefits far outweigh the negative effects. This is not to advise anyone to bake in sunlight. What is suggested is moderate daily exposure, no more than ten to fifteen minutes a day in the sunshine. This minimal exposure can especially benefit those who spend most of their lives locked away in offices under artificial lighting conditions. A few minutes of walking in natural sunlight during the lunch break can work wonders.

For over a hundred years, it has been known that the sun's ultraviolet rays have an antibacterial effect. The bacteria causing anthrax, plague, strep, cholera, staph, and dysentery all show ultraviolet sensitivity. With these discoveries, the era of sunbathing therapy evolved, culminating in 1903, when Niels Finsen won the Nobel Prize for his work in curing tuberculosis through sunbathing. Sunbathing as a form of therapy continued well into the 1930s but was abruptly discontinued with the invention of the wonder drugs, beginning with penicillin in 1938. The progress of modern technology soon all but obliterated what were thought of as the antiquated methods of sun therapy. Yet an alarming problem has surfaced in recent years. More and more bacteria are now becoming resistant to the wonder drugs, while the antibacterial effects of sunlight have not been reduced.

In spite of the enormous amount of ongoing drug research, photobiologists continue to research ultraviolet wavelengths of sunlight in fighting diseases. Independently published reports show ultraviolet light used to cure peritonitis, viral pneumonia, mumps, fungal infections, and bronchial asthma. In 1976, L. D. Heding reported in *Cancer Research* that ultraviolet light could inactivate and destroy cancer-producing viruses. Further studies in humans have shown that exposure to limited amounts of ultraviolet light or natural sunlight (but not enough to redden the skin) increases the number of white blood cells, which play a leading role in the body's immune system and defense against bacteria. A single sunlight treatment increased the white blood cells of laboratory animals for up to three weeks following treatment. It cannot be stressed too strongly that exposure to sunlight must be in small doses that do not cause sunburn. If you expose yourself long enough to get a sunburn, then the negative effects can outweigh the positive.

Color and Light in Health Care Facilities

The color/light selected for health care facilities may have a marked effect on patients (Figure 4-1). A case in point is Methodist Hospital in Indianapolis, Indiana. The hospital decided to use the power of color to promote the health and welfare of patients and staff during a phase of new construction. A color consultant who specializes in health care design was called in. The color consultant suggested avoiding colors from the lavender-purple family in treatment areas because they disturb

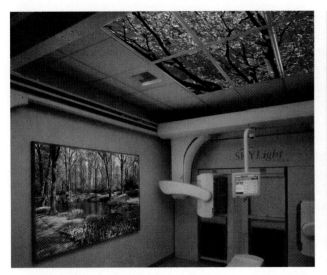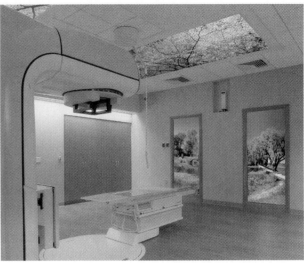

figure 4-1

If you have ever spent time staring at the ceiling of a medical facility you will really appreciate this use of colored photographic images. Using colored imagery in this way helps to calm the patient and provides a focus away from the often dehumanizing medical equipment. **Nature imagery**, shown in recent studies to *reduce patient anxiety*, is displayed in backlit color photographic *Ceiling Mural* and *WallMural Transparencies*, surrounding patients and medical equipment in a new healing interior architecture for the high-stress treatment environment known as **Visual Therapy**. Surveys consistently show that when nature imagery is introduced to a patient's field of view before and during treatment, patients walk away with *a positive perception of their treatment experience*, and, interestingly, were *acutely aware* and *deeply thankful* of *"someone's effort on their behalf to make things visually better."* Bright and uplifting healing environments contribute to increased staff satisfaction as well as reduced employee turnover. *Wall and ceiling imagery by Joey Fischer, Art Research Institute, © 2002 www.visualtherapy.com http://www.visualtherapy.com/. Used with permission.*

the focus of the eye and have an afterimage of sickly yellow-green. White was found to be emotionally sterile, with little therapeutic application. Yellowish green was not used because its reflection on human flesh gives the complexion a sickly pallor. The consultant advised against stripes, which are a constant source of tension, especially if they are crooked or off-balance on the wall of a patient room.

The consultant also suggested that uniform color in any patient environment is wrong. Color variety adds a stimulus that is necessary in health care. The design team developed three sets of complementary colors for the hospital complex: Green and rose, representing the green and red color wheel combination, and blue and peach, as values of the blue-orange combination, were used in the patient areas such as surgery, intensive care units, and individual rooms. Because the sidewalls and headwall (where the head of the bed is) in rooms reflect color off walls, the sidewalls and headwall are always neutral, leaving the footwall as the accent. A plum and yellow combination, derived form the purple-yellow complementary pair, was used in more specialized areas of the hospital, such as clinical or public spaces, but generally not in patient areas. By confining colors to specific floors and areas, the design team was able to eliminate the possibility of the housekeeping staff putting the wrong chairs in the wrong rooms. These colors evolved from grayed tones to the correct values of lightness and darkness. Complementary colors give an alternative soothing-stimulating effect, and the combination provides a balance that is effective for the long term. A warm neutral—grayed beige—was used as a background throughout the hospital. Pure gray is not a good color for health care environments. It is cold and tends to go black, fostering depressive emotions. This neutral was specified for larger surface materials such as marble tile floors, ceramics, and laminates and opened up a variety of color directions for future replacements of materials that are more susceptible to wear, such as paint, fabrics, and carpet.

REFERENCES

Apperly, F. L., Cary, M. K., "The Deterrent Effect of Light upon the Incidence of Spontaneous Breast Cancer in Strain 'A' Mice," *British Journal of Experimental Pathology* 23 133.

Belkin, M., Schwartz, M. "New Biological Phenomena Associated with Laser Radiation," *Health Physics* 56 1989, (5) 687–690.

Ben-Hur, E., Oetjen, J., Horowitz, B. *Silicon Phthalocyanine Pc4 and Red Light Causes Apoptosis in HIV-Infected Cells*, VITEX, 1997.

Bergold, O. "The Effect of Light and Color on Human Physiology," 1 1989, 33–39.

Bouma, P., *The Physical Aspects of Colour*, Macmillan, 1971.

Chin, S., Jin, R., Wang, L., Hamman, J., Marx, G., Mou, X., Andersson, I., Lars-Olof, L., Horowitz, B., *Virucidal Treatment of Blood Protein Products with UVC Radiation*, VITEX, 1997.

Felber, T. D., reported at the American Medical Association Conference, June 1979, Atlantic City, New Jersey.

Fing, C., Cleland, J., Knowles, C., Jackson, J., "Effects of Healing: Neon Laser Experimental Auriculotherapy on Pain Threshold," *Physical Therapy* 1990, 24–30.

Hudson, J., Imperial, V., Haugland, R., Diwu, Z., *Antiviral Activities of Photoactive Perylenequinones*, Department of Pathology and Laboratory Medicine, University of British Columbia, 1997.

Karu, T. "Photobiology of Low-Power Laser Effects," *Health Physics* 56 1989, 691–702.

Lewy, A., Sack, D., Singer, C., White, D., "The Phase Shift Hypotheses for Bright Light's Therapeutic Mechanism of Action: Theoretical Considerations and Experimental Evidence," *Psychopharmacology Bulletin* 23 1987, 349–353.

Maas, J., Jayson, J. K., Kleiber, D. A., "Effects of Spectral Differences in Illumination on Fatigue," *Journal of Applied Psychology* 59 1974, 524–526.

Mandel, P., *The Practical Compendium of Colorpuncture*, Energetik-Verlag, 1986.

Mandel, P., *The Pharmacy of Light*, Mandel-Institut fur Esogetische Medizin, 1955.

Meltzer, H. Y., "Beyond Serotonin," *Journal of Clinical Psychiatry* 52 1991, 58–62.

Michelsen, Kliesch, Schnurpfeil, Sobbi, and Wohrle, *Unsymmetrically Substituted Benzonaphthoporphyrazines: A New Class Of Cationic Photosensitizers for the Photodynamic Therapy of Cancer*, Institute für Organische und Makromolekulare Chemie-Universitat Bremen, 1997.

Mims, F., *Significant Reduction of UVB Caused by Smoke from Biomass Burning in Brazil*, Sun Photometer Atmospheric Network (SPAN), 1997.

Mohr, H., Bachmann, B., Klein-Struckmeier, A., Lambrecht, B., *Virus Inactivation of Blood Products by Phenothiazine Dyes and Light*, German Red Cross Blood Transfusion Service, Institute Springe, 1997.

Moor, A., Wagenaars–van Gompel, A., Brand, A., Dubbelman, T., VanSteveninck, J., "Primary Targets for Photoinactivation of Vesicular Stomatitis Virus by AIPcS4 or Pc4 and Red Light," *Medical Biochemistry* 1997.

Nassau, K., *The Physics and Chemistry of Color*, John Wiley and Sons, 1983.

Ott, J., *Light, Radiation and You*, Devin-Adair Company, 1982.

Prevent Blindness in Premature Babies, P.O. Box 44792, Dept. P, Madison WI 53744-4792; www.rdcbraille.com.

Rivlin, R., Gravelle, K., *Deciphering the Senses*, Simon and Schuster, 1984.

Shapiro, R. S., Stockard, H. E, "Electroencephalographic Evidence Demonstrates Altered Brainwave Patterns by Acupoint Stimulation," *American Journal of Acupuncture* 17 1989, (1).

Stelian, J., Gil, I., Habot, B., Rosenthal, M., Abramovici, I., Kutok, N., Khahil, A., "Improvement of Pain and Disability in Elderly Patients with Degenerative Osteoarthritis of the Knee Treated with Narrow-Band Light Therapy," *Journal of the American Geriatric Society* 40 1991, 23–26.

Tong, Y., Lighthart, B., *Solar Radiation Is Shown to Select for Pigmented Bacteria in the Ambient Outdoor Atmosphere* Institute of Microbiology and Epidemiology, Beijing, 1997.

Wurtman, R. J., *Biological Implications of Artificial Illumination,* presentation at National Technical Conference, Illuminating Engineering Society, Phoenix, September 8–12, 1960.

Wurtman, R. J., "The Effects of Light and Visual Stimuli on Endocrine Function," *Neuroendocrinology* 12 1967.

Wurtman, R. J., "The Effects of Light on the Human Body," *Scientific American*, July 1975.

Wurtman, R. J., "The Pineal and Endocrine Function," *Hospital Practice* 1968, 32–37.

Wurtman, R. J., Weisel, J., "Environmental Lighting and Neuroendocrine Function: Relationship between Spectrum of Light Source and Gonadal Growth," *Endocrinology* 85 1969, (6) 1218–1221.

Wurtman, R. J., Baum, M., Potts, Jr. J., "The Medical and Biological Effects of Light," *Academy of Sciences* 453 1979.

Wurtman, R., Wurtman, J., "Carbohydrates and Depression," *Scientific American*, January, 1989, 68–75.

Zmudzka, B., Strickland, A., Beer, J., Ben-Hur, E., "Photosensitized Decontamination of Blood with the Silicon Phthalocyanine Pc4: No Activation of the Human Immunodeficiency Virus Promoter," Food and Drug Administration, Center for Devices and Radiological Health. 1997

Chapter five

Color and psychology

In both consumer and design-related publications, we often encounter statements of absolute certainty about the psychological aspects of color. However, it is very difficult to make such statements with any accuracy, for two reasons: (1) Psychological measurements are often highly subjective and open to individual interpretation, and (2) the interactions taking place with regard to color/light are so intricate and intertwined that it is difficult to separate them even in a laboratory. Because of this complexity, the outcomes of psychological color/light studies are often contradictory. Some of the original laboratory studies have come under sharp criticism for their often small and nonrepresentative sample sizes, failure to define stimulus variables, confusion of stimulus and experimental design variables, and extrapolation beyond the evidence provided by the data. Subsequent authors who rely on these early studies have often merely cited their findings and drawn conclusions that are actually unwarranted and unsubstantiated.

The work most often cited in terms of how color affects behavior is that of Kurt Goldstein (1942), but there are serious problems with the controls in this study. He postulated a behavioral theory of color based on the observations and experimentation of patients with organic diseases of the central nervous system. These patients manifested impaired motor function such as unstable gait or trembling and distortions in estimates of time, size, and weight. His experiments were conducted on only three to five patients. The color stimuli used were pieces of colored paper, colored rooms, colored lights, or colored clothing that were not controlled for variables such as saturation, value, or texture. Further, neither numerical results nor statistical analyses of his observations were ever presented. What he observed was that in the presence of green, abnormal behavior became less deviant, while in the presence of red these behaviors became exaggerated. For instance, patients who overestimated or underestimated short time spans demonstrated more accurate estimations in the presence of green and more distorted estimations in the presence of red. From his work with brain-damaged individuals, Goldstein formulated a theory that he believed applied to all individuals. He viewed red as having an "expansive" effect on the senses and being capable of inducing a state of excitation in both emotional and motor behavior. He found green to be "contractive" in nature and to promote tranquility. Goldstein's theory was based on the notion that there existed a one-to-one mapping between color states and emotional states, which seems to be a gross oversimplification of the complex processes linking color and behavior. His theory has not been confirmed by the work of subsequent researchers, yet it has become firmly entrenched within both our culture and the popular press that red excites while green (or blue) is calming. Unfortunately, the majority of the early color studies on which our concept of psychological responses to color are based were equally poorly controlled, with questionable outcomes.

Even though it is very difficult to accurately measure psychological responses to color, some trustworthy research has been done that clearly indicates the significant relationships involved in psychological responses to color, including research in such areas as color preference, the association between color and perceived temperature, the effects of color on the perception of an object's weight, color and spaciousness, color's effect on the flavor and acceptability of foods, and color and the arousal response. Although absolute results are difficult to ascertain, the search for answers in the area of color psychology is an intriguing one.

Arousal Properties of Color

Most people believe that red is exciting while blue is calming, but is this true? Many studies have been run in an attempt to answer this question. Some have studied the physiological responses, such as heart rate, blood pressure, or galvanic skin response; others have concentrated on more subjective psychological responses. Humphrey (1976) postulates that red may carry unique signal properties. He notes that red is the most common color signal in nature, arising from the fact that red contrasts well with both green foliage and blue sky. Also, because it is the color of blood, it is easily accessible by animals for the purpose of changing their coloration. Problems arise from the ambiguity of its signal: It can signal either approach through sexual display or edible food, or it can signal avoidance through aggressive behavior or warning of a poisonous substance. According to Humphrey the response to red is a reflexive one, serving the purpose of preparing one to take some form of action that is defined by the context.

Red may carry with it signal properties that function as an arousal mechanism for an organism; however, it is unlikely even in nature that such arousal lasts beyond a short duration, especially if presented within a context. Therefore, claims that certain wall colors will arouse an individual or make a person more alert and therefore more productive are not supported by studies run so far. Goodfellow and Smith (1973) found no support for the general notion that red impairs fine motor coordination while blue facilitates it. Hammes and Wiggins (1962) found that red and blue color illumination had no effect on high-anxious or low-anxious subjects in a perceptual motor steadiness task. Smets (1969) asked subjects to estimate the amount of time spent under red and blue light conditions, with mixed results. Caldwell and Jones (1985) found no significant difference in rates of counting under red, blue, or white illumination.

Two common physiological measures of arousal are changes in electrical activity in the brain (EEG) and changes in skin conductance or resistance, called galvanic skin response (GSR). Gerard (1958) ran a comprehensive and well-controlled study using red, blue, and white light and found statistical significance between the red and blue conditions for all physiological measures except heart rate. Blood pressure was lower in the blue illumination than in the red and yielded a lower respiration rate and increased alpha wave frequency. Gerard does caution the reader regarding the generalizability of these findings, because his study was conducted only on male college students, who may not represent the population at large.

The findings from other studies have not been so clear-cut. When Erwin and colleagues (1961) presented lights of four different colors—red, blue, green, and yellow—for five minutes the results were mixed, but the authors did not mention how or if the brightness variable was controlled. The list of studies trying to determine if red is more arousing than blue is an extensive one and contains a variety of mixed results. In an attempt to clarify this condition, we undertook to examine the red and blue question ourselves in preparing research data for a doctoral degree. While our study investigated the physiological effects of color, we have included it in this chapter because of its investigation of the arousal properties of color.

Our study investigated the effect of interior pigment color (blue, red, or yellow) on task performance and arousal (determined by a combination of GSR and pulse scores) to determine the optimum color use for the interiors of educational facilities and residential and commercial environments (Figure 5-1). It was anticipated that a better understanding of the effects of color on human beings could prove an effective means toward improving the ability to perform tasks with greater accuracy and lessen stress in interior environments. Pigment color was selected for this study because of its practical applications in interiors. A distinguishing feature of this study was the precise control of the colors used. Red, yellow, and blue were selected and precisely controlled for saturation and brightness by using the combined technologies of spectrographical analysis and computer technology. We used a sample of forty-two randomly selected male and female subjects following color-blind pretesting and a pilot study.

In our study, subjects were alternately placed in specially constructed environments colored with the controlled pigment colors red, yellow, and blue in controlled daylight conditions to eliminate the variable of illumination fatigue. In these constructed environments the subjects performed mathematics, reading, and motor activity tasks while being monitored for galvanic skin response and pulse rate. Based on previous studies we expected to find that red would cause more arousal or excitement than blue and that there would be a difference in performance across the three colors. Unlike previous studies, this study precisely controlled the color and lighting conditions. It was found that pigment colors of equal saturation and brightness resulted in comparable arousal and task performance scores; the results did not support the belief that red is more arousing than blue.

It appears that poorly controlled color studies are most likely to find a difference in the effects of red and blue on arousal, while those studies

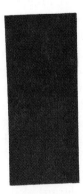 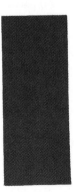 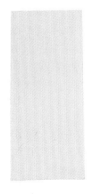

figure 5-1

FEHRMAN COLOR STUDY
Our research used controlled pigment colors of red, blue, and yellow to study their effects on task performance and arousal on human subjects. Our findings did not support the belief that red is more arousing than blue. We found that pigment colors of equal saturation and brightness resulted in comparable arousal and task performance scores and that red does not cause more excitement than blue.

that utilize good controls do not find a significant difference in physiological measures. There may still be a difference in the red and blue response, but it seems likely that this is more aligned with learned response. If we have learned to believe red is exciting, we will find it exciting.

Color Preference

Color preference is one of the most intensively researched areas within the color field. Almost a hundred years of investigations have explored the relationship between feelings, emotions, and color. Part of the problem in researching this area is determining exactly what is being studied in color preference. Early research studies supported the views of a strong associative relationship between particular preferences with given colors. Many of these associations were of an emotional quality that led researchers to question whether certain colors were able to elicit certain emotional responses consistently. They wondered if there might be an inherent physical relationship between color and people that resulted in consistent emotional reactions, or if the linkage between specific colors and emotions was a purely cognitive one. Researchers wanted to discover whether the color-emotion link was biological or learned.

Several of the early studies measured color preference in terms of one evaluative dimension, such as pleasantness or unpleasantness. A high pleasantness rating for a given color then became synonymous with a high preference rating. In the late 1950s a research specialty developed that investigated the hypothetical relationship between colors and various mood tones or emotions. From this research came the popular concepts of "secure colors," "happy colors," "active colors," and so on that have become so favored by popular authors, interior designers, and fashion consultants without a full understanding that these responses are only one tiny and questionable part of the color/light response.

It is no secret that early research in color preference lacked adequate controls. The three psychological dimensions of color—hue (the color itself), value (the lightness or darkness of the color), and saturation (the intensity of the color)—were rarely controlled in experiments and were not considered in statistical outcomes. This led to severely skewed or even invalid results. Another problem with these early studies is that they did not control for the order in which colors were presented, nor was illumination adequately considered.

Early color preference studies focused almost entirely on the color itself, without regard to the other important variables. Researchers presented their findings in terms of most and least preferred colors. Red, blue, and green were usually reported to be most preferred, while yellow and orange were judged to be least preferred. Little if any consideration was given to the ability of color value or saturation to affect judgment. For example, a person may find a pale blue sky attractive but might not like a dark navy or murky indigo blue; someone else might find a deep burgundy red appealing but might not like pink. Yet all of these variations come under the two colors, red and blue.

In studies that did provide adequate controls, it was found that the colors blue, green, and red were preferred in light tints over darker shades and that saturated colors were preferred over unsaturated colors (Figure 5-2). (Remember that saturated colors are those that contain more pigment

Preferred Colors in Order of Preference

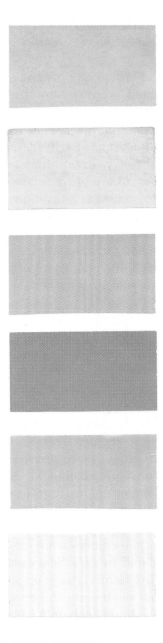

figure 5-2

CONTROLLED COLOR STUDIES
In studies with adequate controls, light tints of blue, green, and red were preferred over darker shades, but saturated colors were preferred over unsaturated colors. Saturated colors contain more of the color pigment and less of gray or neutral tones. The size of the color sample also played a strong role in preference, as people often liked small samples of yellow and orange but found large samples of the colors unpleasant.

or intensity, i.e., the amount of redness in red.) Another factor that was discovered in later studies was that the size of the color sample used in the experiment had a bearing on the outcome. For example, people often liked small samples of yellow and orange but found large amounts of the colors unpleasant. In a study of over 21,000 people, it was found that colors were preferred in the following order: blue, red, green, violet, orange, yellow.

Another study found that blue-greens were most preferred while least preferred were yellows and yellow-greens. This held true across all levels of saturation or brightness. As brightness increased, perceived pleasantness also increased. People responded more favorably to the brighter colors. However, direct application of this study cannot be made to real-life situations without further research because color combinations, color as applied to objects, and the interaction of color, light, and texture must all be considered in a real situation. Color remains complex. From the studies so far presented on color preference, the emerging trend appears to be consistent that blue is a preferred color while yellow is not. Researchers wanted to know why.

One of the areas they explored was that of background. Was it possible that the background against which the colors were displayed made a difference in color preference? It was not until the work of Helson and Lansford in 1970 that color combination effects were systematically studied. Previous studies had been run with the colors displayed on neutral backgrounds of gray or black. The Helson-Lansford study was the first to try something different and is probably the single best controlled experiment on determining preference of color combinations. The researchers presented 125 color chips against 25 colored backgrounds under 5 different lighting sources to 10 subjects for a total of 15,250 ratings. Although the small number of people taking part in this study has been criticized, the total number of ratings is significant. Subjects were shown 12 color chips on a background and made absolute judgments on a 9-point scale.

The Helson-Lansford study showed that color preference ratings were the product of an interaction between light source, background color, and object color. Background color was the single most important component of preference judgments due to contrast effect. Men were reported to prefer blue, violet, and green. Women preferred colors in the red, orange, and yellow range. It was also found that value contrast was the most important factor for pleasant color harmony—the greater the lightness contrast, the more the color combination was preferred (Figure 5-3).

The Helson-Lansford study is important to color research because it was the first to show that color preference could be influenced by variables other than those of the color itself. It showed that the interaction of the light source with the color was of prime significance in color preference.

Another study showed that even the size and shape of light sources and their placement within a room have an effect on color preferences. It showed contrast to play an important role in color preference relations and indicated that the perceived pleasantness of a color is changeable and not an invariant quality within the color itself.

These color studies may give the impression that color preference has been regarded as a static state, invariable across time and circumstance, but evidence is beginning to indicate an alternative view. When office

Colors Preferred by Men

Colors Preferred by Women

figure 5-3

COLOR PREFERENCES ACCORDING TO GENDER
The Helson-Lansford study was the first to show that color preference could be influenced by variables other than those of the color itself and that the interaction of the light source with the color is of prime significance. In this study, men and women showed different color preferences.

workers were asked to select the color they preferred every fifteen minutes over the course of five to forty hours, color choices varied with time. Individuals did not prefer one color every time. This has tremendous implications for trying to decipher color preference and make color selections for public spaces.

So far, only one dimension of color preference has been considered, that of pleasantness or unpleasantness, but means have been devised to measure other aspects of color preference. In one study, color was judged on a rating scale with people rating a number of colors against these scales. In this study yellow was rated most favorable. Activity seemed to be related to the color dimension: Red and yellow were seen as active colors while green, violet, and blue were viewed as passive. Potency was directly dependent on a color's saturation.

The results of these studies suggest that an acceptable color is defined by the object with which it is associated, and this relation is probably the product of cultural norms and expectations or subjective color bias.

Interesting psychological color studies have been undertaken by a Swiss research group using the Swedish Natural Color System (NCS), which is based on an individual's perception of color. According to the NCS there exist six pure color perceptions: yellow, red, green, blue, black, and white. (In the United States, we consider black and white to be neutrals, not colors.) According to the NCS system, the perception of any color is based on the degree of its perceptual similarity to these six elementary reference colors that are assumed to be a component of one's own visual system.

Within the NCS system, three parameters define a given color: degree of whiteness, degree of blackness, and purity of color (chromaticity or saturation). The results of this study showed no difference exhibited between colors with equal chromaticity or saturation on the excitement factor. This finding upholds the findings of our study and contradicts the long-held stereotype that "warm" colors (red, orange, yellow) are exciting while "cool" colors (green, blue, violet) are calming. Both the NCS and our studies show no increased excitement factor in the red areas and no calming factors in the blue areas. It is possible to have a dull red or an exciting blue, based on the purity of the color. **With regard to excitement or arousal, the intensity of the color appears to be of greater significance than the color itself.**

To summarize, many factors influence color preference, including:

- Learned color bias
- Variations in the saturation or value of the color under study
- The interaction between light source, background color, and the color of the object being viewed
- The contrast between colors in combination
- The size and placement of light sources

Cultural factors and the effect of texture also play a role in color preference. Colors do not inherently contain exciting or calming effects. The commonly believed stereotype that red is arousing while blue is calming has been disproved. The arousal value of a color lies in its purity, not in the color itself. Finally, the preference for one color over another is not a static state but changes over time. Color perception is a highly complex process. Attempts to simplify it generally lead to inaccuracies and the perpetuation of myths.

Color and Emotions

The research in color preference led to a spin-off area of research, that of color and emotional response or moods. Researchers asked whether a reliable mood-color association exists and whether color could influence one's emotional state. Well-controlled research studies have shown that a definite color-mood association exists, although the color-mood association differed widely among people participating in the study. In fact, the studies showed all colors to be associated with all moods in varying degrees of strength. Although certain colors are more strongly associated with a given mood or emotion, there was no evidence to suggest a one-to-one relationship between a given color and a given emotion. What seemed to make the difference was how strongly a person associated a particular color with a particular mood or emotion.

Colors have been stereotyped by the public when it comes to emotions. In spite of physical evidence to the contrary, most people continue to equate red tones with excitement and activity and blue tones with passivity and tranquility in color-mood association research. **This is a learned behavior.** From the time we are very young, we learn to associate red with fire engines, stop lights, and danger signals that cause us to form an alert or danger association with red. Further, the red, orange, and yellow tones in fire further cause association between those colors and heat and kinetic energy. We have seen how cultural biases that are a part of our language further support the red-equals-excitement myth. These subconscious messages clearly affect the response to red. Blue tones, being associated with cool streams, the sky, and the ocean, continue to be equated with calm and tranquility. This, too, is a learned response with which we are subtly surrounded from early childhood. **In understanding color, it is important to differentiate between these culturally learned color associations and true biological responses.**

Research on the emotional aspects of color has for the most part resulted in a gross oversimplification of a very involved process. Unfortunately, this oversimplification has been promoted heavily in the popular press. The design community, too, has jumped on the bandwagon, often making sweeping statements about color that are totally unsupported by anything but myth or personal belief. For example, one book refers to blue as "communicating cool, comfort, protective, calming, although may be slightly depressing if other colors are dark; associated with bad taste." There is, of course, no basis for these statements except as the personal opinion of the author, but too often these personal opinions become accepted as fact.

Colors do not contain any inherent emotional triggers. Rather, it is more likely that our changing moods and emotions caused by our own physiological and psychological makeup at the moment interact with color to create preferences and associations that we then link to the color-emotion response itself.

The Effects of Color on Flavor

A particularly interesting area of color research is that of studying color in relation to the flavor of various foods (Figure 5-4). It has been shown that color can outweigh the impression made by flavor. People show a

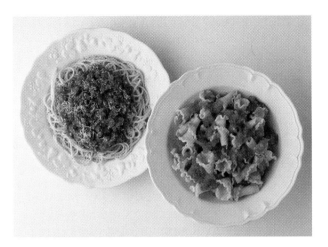

figure 5-4

People reject foods that are identified with a specific color if the color differs from what is expected. For example, if this pasta were dyed blue, it would be unpalatable to most people. © *Dorling Kindersley*

low preference for yellow and yellow-green foods on the whole and have ascribed greater sweetness and greater flavor to orange, red, white, and pink foods. Wines have been judged sweetest when white or pink but less sweet when yellow, brownish, or purple.

While foods are rarely chosen solely on the basis of color, foods that are identified with a specific color are rejected if the color differs from what is expected; for example, bananas dyed blue, red mashed potatoes, and green oatmeal are unacceptable to most people. Our almost immediate suspicion and rejection of foods in the blue-green range is well founded in our inherent suspicion of molds; any association of mold or mildew makes us instinctively reject foods in this color group. This response is so strong that in tests many people could not bring themselves to sample prepared food colored blue or purple, and many of those who tried felt sick afterward. Nature does not create blue food, with the possible exception of blueberries, which are really more of a dark purple. Consequently, we do not have an automatic appetite response to this color range. We appear to have deep-seated instincts to avoid blue and purple foods because many blackish-purple and blue fruits and berries are poisonous. A million years ago when our earliest ancestors were foraging for food, blue, purple, and black became ingrained as color warning signs of potentially lethal food.

An interesting exception to the dislike for blue foods came about recently when the makers of M&M candy added a surprising new color to its candy bag—blue. The company reported that the blue selection was made as the result of a vote by M&M fans. It would be interesting to know how much of the blue candy is actually consumed or if it is the last color left in the bag. Of all the colors in the spectrum, blue is an appetite suppressant. Weight-loss plans suggest putting food on a blue plate or putting a blue light in the refrigerator to suppress your appetite. The most dramatic result can be achieved by using a blue lamp in your dining area.

The color of medicines also has an effect. Scientists at the University of Amsterdam looking at studies of common drugs found that people expect white pills to be weak and black ones strong. Such beliefs can be powerful: Medical students who were told they would receive stimulants or sedatives were then given blue or pink placebos. The students taking blue pills reported feeling drowsy; those who got pink pills felt perked up.

Studies run on common foods such as orange juice, raspberry jelly, and strawberry sherbet show that these foods are preferred when colored with food coloring to intensify their natural colors. Orange juice colored even oranger was preferred over natural orange juice and thought to be sweeter. The same held true for raspberry and strawberry products. The redder they looked, the more they were preferred, even though the flavor was identical to the natural, undyed product. This has obvious implications in the processed food industry.

Red has such strong associations with flavor that in some countries tomatoes and other red vegetables are grown commercially in brightly colored varieties that have almost no flavor at all, yet the association with redness and ripeness (and paleness with disease) is why pale tomatoes do not sell as well as the flavorless red type.

Golden brown is so thoroughly associated with appetizing bakery products that the baking and roasting of bread, cereals, and nuts is precisely controlled so that they emerge neither too dark nor too light for consumer taste. Bakery goods are often packaged in some type of golden brown wrapping to suggest their inner goodness.

Children's responses to color in food are not as conditioned as those of adults. Most children will consume food and drink of any color, but foods dyed in unfamiliar colors such as blue, purple, or yellow-green sometimes make adults feel nauseous. Give children or adults a drink that is orange-colored yet flavored with lime, and both will think they are drinking orange juice.

White in foods has associations with refinement and delicacy. Refined white flour, sugar, and rice have long been favored as status symbols in preference to the coarse-textured and brown-colored unrefined foods that were associated with the peasant class. That trend is now beginning to reverse because of the renewed interest in healthful diets. We now know that the peasants got the best of the deal. Still, more white flour, sugar, bread, and rice are sold than their brown counterparts. Studies run by airlines have shown that women generally prefer white meat and fish, so they usually take on more chicken and fish for women passengers than for men. (This may have more to do with dieting habits than with color choice.)

Dark-colored foods are often preferred by men and have become associated with strong flavor and spiciness. Coffee beans are generally roasted to a deep brown and packaged in brown or red to suggest richness and strength. Similarly, beers are color coded: Light beers are pale yellow to deep gold, while strong beers are deep brown to black. Most food items aimed at the male market are tinted or packaged in brown because of male-oriented preferences in this area. Dark brown sauces and chutneys, relishes, or smoked meats are also presented in some form of brown wrapping.

Food color conditioning begins at birth and can be overcome or altered only by education to the potential dangers of some artificial food coloring or by training on proper nutrition. Even so, food color conditioning is one of the most entrenched and most difficult of all habits to break.

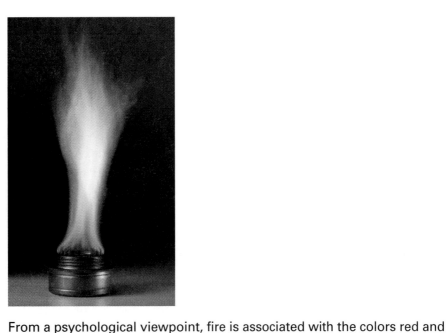

figure 5-5

From a psychological viewpoint, fire is associated with the colors red and yellow, which we then extrapolate to mean warmth, so that red and yellow are thought of by most people as "warm" colors. *© Dorling Kindersley*

Color and Temperature Perception

We previously touched on the idea that visual metaphors in language make stereotypical use of color and temperature through images that are prevalent in our culture, such as fires being red or yellow (Figure 5-5) and those colors thereby being associated with warmth, or blue-green, the color of the sea (Figure 5-6), being associated with cold. An obvious association exists between color and temperature in human experience. The scientific search for color-temperature relationships has centered primarily on three types of questions:

1. Do certain colors reliably and unvaryingly communicate particular temperature expectations?

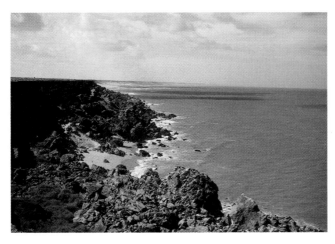

figure 5-6

The ocean is associated with blues, greens, and coolness, which causes people to think of blues and greens as "cool" colors. *© Dorling Kindersley*

2. Will the application of surface or lighting colors serve to change the perceived temperature of objects or spaces?

3. Can the use of interior colors affect the thermal comfort of a room's inhabitants?

One of the most interesting color-temperature studies showed a strong relationship between existing temperature and color selection. When the indoor temperature was cold, people preferred red; when the temperature rose, people preferred blue. Again, blue and red appear to be cognitively connected to temperature states.

Increased concern for energy conservation has renewed interest in whether interior colors can aid thermal comfort. Would it be possible, for example, to reduce a room's overall temperature if the walls were painted in a color such as red, which is associated with warmth? Could air conditioning be somewhat conserved in a room painted in tones of blue or blue-green, which are associated with coolness? Studies indicate that this is a real possibility. Subjects have consistently reported feeling warmer in rooms colored in red or orange tones and cooler in rooms colored within the blue or green range.

In a well-controlled study the researchers used an experimental climatic chamber modified with wood paneling, acoustical ceiling tiles, and red carpeting, along with residential-style pictures, chairs, and lamps. They found that subjects felt significantly warmer in the modified chamber during two-hour exposure periods. It should be noted, however, that these responses were strictly psychological. Physiological measures taken during the study showed no physiological changes in skin temperature.

Later work by the same research team tested people in an open-plan office environment. They found that for periods of up to one hour, orange work stations were judged more comfortable than blue ones. They also found that in a cooler than neutral environment, people were more comfortable when the walls were dark than when they were light.

A large part of the color-temperature relationship depends on the overall design considered as a whole. It is possible within the context of an overall design to use color as part of an environment's holistic effect on thermal comfort. Since the perception of temperature changes in relation to color is strictly a psychological phenomenon and is not accompanied by physically detectable warming of the person, any design conditions that can contribute to an overall sense of comfort will increase the feeling of warmth.

Color and Weight Perception

Dozens of studies have tried to make a permanent connection between color and the perceived weight of objects. As with many other color studies, early research in this area used poor controls, so the outcomes are questionable. In the early 1960s a study was done in which cubes were covered with various colors of paper that were controlled for saturation and brightness. It was found that the apparent weight of the blue, red, and purple colors differed significantly from the yellow, green, and gray colors taken as a group, but that within groups they did not differ from each other.

A much larger field study in Germany found that the brighter the color, the lighter in weight it was judged. Another study found red the heaviest, then blue, green, orange, and yellow in descending order. It was concluded from this research that colors themselves can convey weight and that indirect cognitive associations are likely to be the same. Contrarily, though, another study found yellow to be significantly heavier than blue, indicating once again that the variables and controls in a study, or the lack of them, can produce widely different results.

Across a variety of research studies it appears that the brightness and saturation of colors may be employed to communicate perceptual impressions of weight. Although there have been no definitive studies in real environments to test these effects, much interior design seems to confirm these basic concepts. Often perceived heavier colors are placed above perceived lighter colors to decrease the perceived height-to-width ratio of an enclosed room in order to enhance furniture appearance and spatial impressions. Spatial orientation also apparently influences sensations of lightness. Deliberate manipulations of spatial position in lighting direction affected impressions of lightness and perceived weight in one research study.

In trying to draw conclusions from the vast amount of conflicting data relating to this topic, it appears that while there is unequivocal proof that a real psychological relationship exists between color and weight perception, the major effect may be attributable to the saturation and brightness of the color, rather than the color itself.

Color and Space Perception

One of the most common uses of color in interior environments is in the alteration of perceived spaces. For decades, design students have been taught that "warm colors advance and cool colors recede." But do they? In fact, such a rule is now outdated and far too oversimplified to be of any use to today's designer, given the complex interactive processes related to color and color perception.

Many haphazard studies were run early on to determine color's relation to space perception, but as early as 1918 a researcher noted that the perceived distance of colors was dependent in part on how far apart the pupils of the observer's eyes were. This was one of the first clues that distance effects of colors were not as simple or as direct as we have been led to believe. Unfortunately, this very important point went virtually unnoticed for years.

Another piece of faulty research took place in 1930, when subjects were asked to view either red neon or blue argon lights through slits that compensated for the relative size of the retinal image as the lights were moved. When the lights were placed an equal distance apart, researchers found that the blue light was judged nearer. This was particularly puzzling given that the standard explanation for advancing and receding colors, chromatic aberration in the lens of the eye, was contrary to these results. Even with much evidence to the contrary, this explanation has persisted to this day as gospel among some color practitioners.

More recent studies have shown that when the apparent distances of different colors are held constant, the brighter colors in the study (white, yellow, green) were seen as farther than they appeared to be, while darker colors in the study (blue, black) were seen at their actual position. **In other words, at constant distances bright colors appear nearer than dark ones.**

This evidence was borne out by an Italian study run at the University of Bologna that showed that colors offering the most contrast appear to stand out or advance more than colors that blend better with the background. **The operative factor in advancing and receding colors appears to be the contrast between colors and their backgrounds rather than the colors themselves.**

Brightness is the operative cue for apparent color distance. Brighter seems nearer. Objects showing high contrast with their background will be judged as standing out from the background and therefore nearer. The results of a 1956 study by Mount and colleagues are worth quoting: "No color variable has an inherent or unique position in space, and thus color can influence judgments of distance only in a specific context involving primary and other secondary hues of relative position." This indicates a far greater complexity to advancing and receding colors than is generally thought.

An intricate study conducted in 1960 gives even further evidence that this is so. Researchers had subjects compare standard and variable circular figures in all combinations of achromatic (colorless) and chromatic (colored) figures and backgrounds. They found that the apparent size of the figure increased as its brightness increased and the brightness of the background decreased, regardless of the color of figure and ground. They also note that the effects of color on apparent size resemble its effects on apparent weight in that brightness is the dominant force. The controller for apparent distance is strong contrast, induced primarily by brightness but also by saturation between a judged element and some established reference frame that can be a background or a homogeneous room.

Taking all these research studies into account, what can we then conclude about color effects on distance and spaciousness?

- **First, perception of spaciousness is not attributed to specific colors but rather to the brightness or darkness of a color.**
- **Second, spatial impressions are highly influenced by contrast effects, particularly brightness differences between objects and backgrounds.**

There appears to be something additionally compelling about bright red, probably due to its strong signal properties, but the spatial differences between red and blue surface colors are due to their relative brightness levels.

Spaciousness is enhanced by increasing lightness of the walls and by decreasing the contrast between elements that intrude into a space and the background (Figure 5-7). For example, painting out obtrusive fixtures such as pipes and ducts will increase the sensation of spaciousness. Color plays a vital role in the perceived spaciousness of interiors but not as simple a role as is commonly believed. Color's role in the perception of spaciousness rests more on color's ability to be a carrier of contrasts that help to define interior perspectives, rather than on any inherent powers of a specific color.

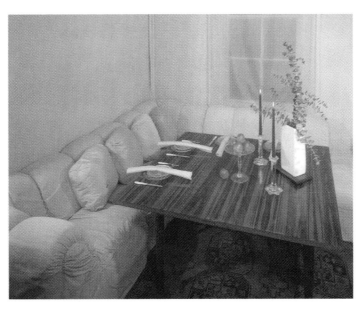

figure 5-7

Spaciousness is enhanced in this small dining area by making the seating banquette blend with the walls, which fools the eye into enlarging the space. Scrim fabric over the window allows filtered light and screens an unattractive view without adding bulk. *Interior design by Fehrman & Fehrman.*

Psychological Color Testing

Although color has long been associated with personal characteristics, it was not until the publication of the Rorschach Inkblot Method in 1921 in Switzerland that a systematic exploration of the relationship between color preferences and responses and personality traits was begun. Until recently, most of this research was conducted in Europe. For example, the Color Pyramid Test (CPT), a semistructured, color-oriented test, was devised in 1950 by Max Pfister, a Swiss psychologist, and introduced into the United States by K. W. Schaie in 1963. Max Lüscher published a popular book, *The Lüscher Color Test*, in 1965, and although many psychologists feel that this type of book written by a recognized authority should not have been published for popular consumption, it sparked a renewed public interest in color and personality.

The Lüscher test relates various personality characteristics to a person's ranking of several series of colors. Any self-testing material in the area of personality can be dangerous to the layperson and may give the false impression that he or she can determine individual personality structure, weaknesses, and strengths in a few easy minutes. Making any serious decisions on this type of perfunctory analysis would be foolish.

The Rorschach Inkblot Method is often employed in clinical psychology. Even though it is widely accepted, it is one of the most criticized instruments. One of the major criticisms leveled against it is the lack of basal work with "normal" subjects as a criterion against which pathological groups could be compared, thereby slanting obtained scores. Another criticism deals primarily with Rorschach's hypothesis that color responses are measures of the emotional state. He stated that neurotics are subject to "color shock," as exhibited by a delayed reaction time when presented with a color blot. He also noted that red evoked the shock response in neurotics more often than did other colors.

Research has sometimes contradicted Rorschach's hypotheses, but no method has come along to date that has proven better. The popularity and usage of the Rorschach test increase annually, and the weight of evidence favors the color-emotion theory. In this theory, responsiveness to orange, yellow, pink, or red characterizes emotional impulsivity, and responsiveness to blue or green characterizes emotional control. Color responses have also been related to a desire for or feeling against social participation and to ego control, spontaneity versus passivity, and depression. The latter category is the one area of near unanimous agreement: The diminished interest of the depressed individual in the environment is reflected in a lack of color interest.

The Color Pyramid Test

The Color Pyramid Test (CPT), another personality measurement device, is nonverbal, projective, and minimally structured. The subject is given a five-step pyramid of fifteen fields, each one inch square, and a group of colored paper squares. The subject is then asked to fill in the fields to make first a "pretty" pyramid, then an "ugly" pyramid. The scoring procedures are based on the standardization of the instrument in Germany and later modifications in the United States.

The CPT was designed particularly to yield information on those aspects of personality that are relevant to affect expression and impulse control. It is believed that a global view of the person may emerge by inferring behavior characteristics that would be expected on the basis of the observed emotional structure. Every color is believed to have stimulus content and stimulus quality. The CPT is based on the theory that the high-wavelength colors (red, orange, yellow) possess strong excitation potential and high arousal qualities and induce elated mood states. The low-wavelength colors (green, blue, purple) are believed to have limited excitation potential and relatively low arousal value and are associated with sedate mood states. The neutrals, brown and gray, represent low excitation potential or a depressed effect, while white and black may be seen as the extremes in this scheme: White represents extreme arousal and impulse release, and black represents extreme inhibitory and repressive impulse control.

Interpretations of the CPT are given in terms of high or low color choices. For example, "high red" is associated with impulsivity, and "low red" is characteristic of reduced emotional tone and responsiveness to stimuli. It must be remembered that the CPT is based only on a specific theory, one that may or may not be accurate. **The results of many color studies show no reason to believe that red is any more arousing than green. In fact, the saturation of a color is more important to arousal properties than the color itself.** However, the CPT assesses color personality as follows: Orange is considered an index of extroversion or introversion, with high orange characterizing a highly sociable person. Persons with high yellow scores are considered skilled in the establishment of interpersonal relations, but they are more objective, cool, and poised than the emotional high oranges. High black reflects depression, withdrawal, and regression. High purple is characteristic of the emotionally disturbed, anxious individual. High white characterizes schizophrenic blandness and lack of inhibition control. High browns are negative and need-deprived. High blues are introspective and rational in approach, whereas low blues are irrational and poorly organized. High green indicates sensitivity and an active inner emotional life, whereas low greens lack sensitivity and spontaneity and are bland. Colors in combination also have distinct implications and are scored as *color syndromes*. It should be noted that scoring the CPT is a very complex matter. The information given here is merely skimming the surface and should not be considered at all a defining account. In other words, if you happen to be wearing black today, don't assume you are plunged into the depths of depression. You may be, but you may also just be dressing according to fashion's whim.

It is interesting to note that this type of color personality testing does not seem to be affected by the usual cultural norms. A study done in Taiwan compared the differences between schizophrenics and normal people in a color-usage task. Schizophrenics used fewer colors, were less conventionally oriented, and used more deep green and black than did the normal group. These results are generally in keeping with results obtained in the United States and suggest that cultural differences are not of great importance in color personality tests.

Other psychological studies have investigated personality scores when correlated with the frequency of color dreams and vividness of color in dreams. The results indicated that there are two kinds of color in dreams: reality color and symbolic color. Reality color is a reflection of the conscious world; symbolic color is representative of inner processes. Individuals who respond objectively and in detail to their environment have dreams that are often a duplication of their daytime environment. Individuals who react to experience with emotion and in a highly personalized way tend to dream in symbolic color. For these people, color in dreams represents emotions as part of their makeup or the failure to discharge or clarify an emotional situation or experience.

Barbara Brown of the Department of Psychiatry at the UCLA Medical Center conducted some interesting studies with color visualization. She had been fascinated by the variations among people who have the ability to internally visualize in color. Some people are capable of thinking and dreaming in full color, while others report visual images that are limited to gray tones, like a black-and-white film. She attempted to distinguish one from another by their response to color. Her experiments showed that people capable of color visualization respond differently than nonvisualizers to flickering colored lights. When a visualizer is exposed to rapid flashes of red, brainwave recordings showed a kind of startle response that was out of phase with the frequency of the flashes. Nonvisualizers showed a relaxation response to the color red, indicating an electronic confirmation of their lack of internal color visualization.

A psychoanalyst who has worked with blind patients reports that the congenitally blind, along with most of those blinded before the age of five, do not have visual dreams. They imagine such nonvisual elements as speech, smell, and other sensory elements instead of visual imagery. However, those who are blinded after the age of seven tend to retain visual memory and visual dream imagery.

The Rorschach, Lüscher Color Test, and Color Pyramid Test mentioned here are three of the best-known instruments for measuring personality through color choice. Many other color personality tests are available to the psychologist. Because of the large number of tests available, and because of the widely diverse interpretations that can be made from each of the tests, the results are often interpreted differently by different practitioners. Only trained personnel should be entrusted to decipher the implied connection between color and personality. It is too important and too complicated to be simplified into a parlor game.

The Retinex Theory

Finally we come to a perplexing phenomenon known as the retinex theory, developed by Edwin Land, inventor of the Polaroid Land camera. Land's research in color photography led to a new view of how we see color. The retinex theory perhaps more properly belongs in a discussion about the brain's role in the perception of color, but because the brain-mind combination results in the way we see and interpret color, we have chosen to present it here, within a discussion of the psychology of color.

Land demonstrated color constancy with displays of patchworks of different colored rectangles that are called Mondrians because they resemble the paintings of the Dutch abstract artist. In one demonstration, Land measured the wavelengths coming from an orange Mondrian patch in normal white light. Then by adjusting the intensity of three projectors equipped with different color filters, he changed the wavelength composition of the light striking the Mondrian until the light reflected from a green patch exactly matched the light previously reflected from the orange patch. The trichromatic theory developed by Maxwell (on which our red, blue, and green primary system is based) predicts that this green patch should now appear orange. In fact, to the normal observer it remains quite green. This same procedure can be carried out for blue, yellow, and red patches. In each case our visual system seems to ignore the wavelength composition of the incident light in order to capture the "true" color of the patch—the one we expect to see. But how?

The key to Land's retinex theory is that we do not determine color in isolation. For example, let's take three berries—one green, one pink, and one red—all hanging against a green leaf. As the rosy rays of dawn illuminate the berries, everything in the scene will reflect the red light. Yet, the red berry will continue to reflect more red light than the pink berry, which, in turn, continues to reflect more red light than the green berry and the green leaf. The ratio of the intensity of the red light coming from each berry to the red light intensity of the surroundings remains nearly constant. The increase in red light coming from a pink berry at dawn is thereby canceled by the increase in red light coming from the leaf. The retinex theory says that is how we manage to see the berry as pink—by computing center-to-surround intensity ratios for each of the three wavelength bands of red, blue, and green.

Through the process of living we expect to see certain things, and those are the things we see. Oranges are supposed to be orange, limes are supposed to be green, and lemons are supposed to be yellow. In fact the Chinese use the word *Ch'ing* in Mandarin to describe the inherent color of an object. The word can mean green, blue, black, or red, depending on what is being described, because it denotes the natural color of an object, the color that we *expect* to see. Such subtleties are absent from European languages and yet the expectations remain. **Part of our visual process is that of learned response. We expect a lemon to be yellow, and so we are likely to see it remain yellow, even if lighting conditions change.** If a lemon is bathed in red light, it should appear much redder, but the brain compares the lemon to its surroundings. As long as the ratio of the lemon to its surroundings remains constant, we will continue to see a lemon as bright yellow even in the reddest sunset light. **Through elaborate calculation our visual system is able to ignore changing conditions of light and to retain our learned expectations of color, even under adverse conditions.**

Color psychology is a complicated and subjective topic. In view of this complexity, the outcomes of psychological color/light studies are often contradictory. However, research has clearly indicated the significant relationships between color and psychological states, including color preference, color and perceived temperature, color and perceived weight, color and space perception, color and the flavor of foods, and the arousal properties of color.

In summary, color preference has been widely studied. Early research was often poorly controlled and led to inadequately investigated conclusions that were adopted by the popular press and that formed the basis for much of our current misconceptions about color. Recently conducted well-controlled research has shown that color preference ratings are the product of an interaction between light source, background color, and object color. Color preference is not a static state. Individuals do not prefer one color every time, but choice can vary dramatically within short periods of time.

As with the physiological results of our color study that investigated the arousal response of red and blue, a Swedish research group also found that neither red nor blue had any inherent arousing or calming effects from a psychological viewpoint. With regard to excitement or arousal, the intensity (saturation) of the color is of greater significance than the color itself.

Research on the emotional aspects of color has resulted in a gross oversimplification of a very involved process. Colors do not contain any inherent emotional triggers. Rather, it is more likely that our changing emotional states interact with color to create preferences and associations that we then link to the color-emotion response itself.

With regard to color and flavor, it has been shown that color can outweigh the impression made by flavor. Our expectations influence flavor. If an orange drink is flavored with lime, people think the flavor is orange. Food color conditioning is one of the most entrenched and most difficult of all habits to break.

While studies have shown a relationship between color and temperature, a large part of the color-temperature relationship depends on the overall design as a whole. While there is unequivocal proof that a real relationship exists between color and weight perception, the major effect is attributable to saturation and brightness of the color rather than the color itself.

In space perception, the operative factor in advancing and receding colors appears to be the contrast between colors and their backgrounds rather than the colors themselves. Brighter seems nearer. Color's role in relation to spaciousness rests on color's ability to be a carrier of contrasts that help to define interior perspectives rather than on any inherent powers of a specific color.

Various tests have been devised to assess the relationship between color and personality, the three best-known of these being the Rorschach Inkblot Method, the Lüscher Color Test, and the Color Pyramid Test (CPT). Color testing should always be left to trained personnel and never simplified into a parlor game.

Finally, Land's retinex theory has led to a new view of how we see color. The key to the retinex theory is that we do not determine color in isolation. We compute center-to-surround intensity ratios for each of the wavelength bands of red, blue, and green, and we are strongly influenced by what we expect to see.

REFERENCES

Alexander, K. R., Shandky, M. S., "Influences of Hue, Value and Chroma on the Perceived Heaviness of Colors," *Perception and Psychophysics* 19 1976, 72–74.

Beck, J., "Apparent Spatial Position and the Perception of Lightness," *Journal of Experimental Psychology* 69 1965, 170–179.

Blank, H. R., "Dreams of the Blind," *Psychoanalytic Quarterly* 27 1958, 158–174.

Caldwell, J. A., Jones, G. E., "Effects of Exposure to Red and Blue Light on Physiological Indices and Time Estimation," *Perception* 14 1985, 19–29.

Erwin et al. "Some Further Observations on the Photically Elicited Arousal Response," *Electroencephalography Clinical Neurophysiology* 13 1961, 391–394.

Eysenck, H. J., "A Critical and Experimental Study of Color Preferences," *American Journal of Psychology* 54 1941, 385–391.

Farne, M., Campione, F., "Colour As an Indicator for Distance," *Giornale Italiano di Psicologia* 3, 415–420.

Fehrman, K. R., "The Effects of Interior Pigment Color on School Task Performance Mediated by Arousal," doctoral dissertation, University of San Francisco, 1986.

Gerard, R. M., "Differential Effects of Colored Lights on Psychophysiological Functions," doctoral dissertation, UCLA, 1958.

Gerard, R. M., "Color and Emotional Arousal," *American Psychologist*, 1959.

Goldstein, K., "Some Experimental Observations concerning the Influence of Color on the Function of the Organism," *Occupational Therapy* 21 1942, 47–151.

Goodfellow, R. A., Smith, P. C., "Effects of Environmental Color on Two Psychomotor Tasks," *Perceptual and Motor Skills* 37 1973, 296–298.

Guilford, J. P., Smith, P. C., "A System of Color Preferences," *American Journal of Psychology* 62 1959, 487–502.

Hammes, J. A., Wiggins, S. L., "Perceptual Motor Steadiness, Manifest Anxiety, and Color Illumination," *Perceptual and Motor Skills* 14 1962, 59–61.

Helson, H., Lansford, T., "The Role of Spectral Energy of Source and Background Pleasantness of Object Colors," *Applied Optics* 9 1970, 1513–1562.

Humphrey, N. K., "The Color Currency of Nature," in *Color for Architecture*, Van Nostrand Reinhold, 1976, 95–98.

Judd, D. B., "A Flattery Index for Artificial Illuminants," *Illuminating Engineering* 42 1967, 593–598.

Kay, C. Y., "Differences in the Usage of Colors between Schizophrenics and Normals," *Acta Psychologica Taiwanica* 6 1964, 71–79.

Kearney, G. E., "Hue Preferences as a Function of Ambient Temperatures," *Australian Journal of Psychology* 18 1966, 271–275.

Luckiesh, M., "On 'Retiring' and 'Advancing' Colors," *American Journal of Psychology* 29 1918, 182–186.

Lüscher, M., *The Lüscher Colors Test*, Random House, 1969.

Montgomery, G., "Color Perception: Seeing with the Brain," *Discover*, December 1988, 52–59.

Mount, G. E., Case, H. W., Sanderson, J. W., Brenner, R., "Distance Judgment of Colored Objects," *Journal of General Psychology* 55 1956, 207–214.

Osgood, C. E., Suci, G. J., Tannenbau, P. H., *The Measurement of Meaning*, University of Illinois Press, 1957.

Payne, M. C., "Apparent Weight as a Function of Hue," *American Journal of Psychology* 74 1961, 104–105.

Pinkerton, E., Humphrey, N. K., "The Apparent Heaviness of Colors," *Nature* 250 1974, 164–165.

Restak, R., *The Brain—The Last Frontier*, Warner Books, 1979.

Rohles, F. H., Laviana, J. E., "Indoor Climate: New Approaches to Measuring How You Feel," Proceedings of CLIMA 2000, World Congress on Heating, Ventilating and Air Conditioning, Copenhagen, 1985 1–6.

Sivik, L., "Color Meaning and Perceptual Color Dimensions: A Study of Color Samples," *Goteborg Psychological Reports* 4 1974.

Sivik, L., "Studies of Color Meaning," *Man-Environment Systems* 5 1975, 155–160.

Smets, G., "Time Expression of Red and Blue," *Perceptual and Motor Skills* 29 1969, 511–514.

Smets, G., "A Tool for Measuring Relative Effects of Hue, Brightness and Saturation in Color Pleasantness," *Perceptual and Motor Skills* 1982, 1159–1164.

Suinn, R. M., "Jungian Personality Typology and Color Dreaming," *Psychiatric Quarterly* 40 1966, 659–665.

Walters, J., Apter, M. J., Sveback, S., "Color Preference, Arousal and Theory of Psychological Reversals," *Motivation and Emotion* 6 1982, 193–215.

Wright, B., "The Influence of Hue, Lightness and Saturation on Apparent Warmth and Weight," *American Journal of Psychology* 75 1962, 232–241.

Chapter six

Color and interior environments

Within an interior environment, color can define space, indicate function, suggest temperature, influence moods, and project personality. Color may well be the most important element in an interior space. There are many factors to consider in choosing color effectively; room size, shape, function, lighting, cost, and personal preference are all factors that must be considered, in addition to the human health factor.

The emotional effects of color can make a living space feel exciting or subdued. A person's working environment can and should be taken into account in choosing color for the home. People working in dull jobs may need some excitement at home, and vice versa.

Everything in a room makes a color statement, but the governing items are paint or wallpaper, draperies, carpets, and upholstery. Accent colors come from area rugs, lampshades, bed and table linens, and other accessory items. In all interior color decisions, the proposed color must be examined in the environment in which it is to be used so that the true effects of lighting can be determined during both daylight and artificial light. To match fabric to carpeting, for example, take a sample at least six inches square and try it out under all the lighting conditions you live with to avoid the problem of metamerism, the capacity of colors to change under different lighting conditions.

What we think of as plain white electric light is actually subtly colored. The purpose of artificial lighting is not just to illuminate; aesthetic and health considerations are also important. The most energy-efficient form of artificial illumination is the low-pressure sodium discharge lamp, but these lamps render color so poorly that they are usually chosen only as street lamps, where safety has a higher priority than appearance.

Incandescent light radiates a broad spectrum closest to sunlight. Incandescence is light produced by a heated material, and sun, oil lamps, candles, gaslight, and tungsten-filament lamps are examples. The hotter the material is heated, the greater light it gives—first red, then yellow, and then nearly white. Contemporary incandescent lamps render color on the warm side of natural, which enriches the reds, pinks, tans, yellows, and neutrals in a room while dulling greens and blues.

Fluorescent lighting is characterized by its flat, cold, bright illumination, which casts few shadows and no highlights. In it uniform, undramatic, and economical, but it may have health hazards ranging from headaches to chromosome damage. Various fluorescent tubes are available that can alter interior colors: Daylight is a bluish hue that tends to dull reds and turn blue colors purple; White, Warm White, and DeLuxe Warm White fluorescents attempt truer color reproduction, but they, too, fail. More research needs to be done in this area before we collectively accept fluorescent lighting as a viable alternative to incandescence.

Colored lighting done with skill and restraint can be used very effectively in the home. A pale blue filter can give luster to a collection of silver; an amber lamp can increase the color of a yellow flower arrangement; a pale pink lamp enhances skin color and is most flattering. Colored light distorts colored pigments and this must be remembered when using colored lights. The psychological impact of color in the home is so great that the subtle use of warm or cool tones can save heating and cooling costs. Since amber and pink are associated with warmth and comfort, they can make a cool evening seem warmer, while blue light can make a hot room seem cooler.

For beginners experimenting in the field of interior design, the old theatrical rule of thumb still holds true: project on a color light of the same color for a decorative or atmospheric effect. This is a good place to begin, but only with training, study, and experimentation can the student of color and light succeed in this complex and sensitive field.

The Relationship of Color/Light in Interiors

Lighting conditions always have an effect on color, especially in interior spaces where colors will be viewed under both natural and artificial light sources. An earlier chapter discussed the phenomenon of metamerism, where the relationship of dyes and light plays a large role in how color is observed. The directional orientation of a room also has a part in how color is seen. For example, northern exposures tend to make colors appear more toward the blue end of the spectrum, which is perceived to have a "cool" cast, and a southern exposure reveals more of the yellowish, red, or perceived "warm" tones. To achieve a harmonious balance in the environment, take directional orientation into consideration when selecting colors for a room. Spaces with northern exposures tend to appear more inviting if color selection runs to the red or yellow end of the spectrum because these colors counteract the blues and create a natural balance. Spaces with southern exposures can appear more pleasing if blues and greens are used. If you have a northern exposure and you want to paint your walls green, then select a green with a warm yellowish undertone rather than one that is bluish. The same balance can be achieved in a southern exposure where you want to use reds. To avoid an overly "hot" feeling in a red-toned room with a southern exposure, select reds with a bluish undertone to maintain a harmonious balance with the natural light (Figure 6-1).

This all changes, of course, during evening, when artificial light is introduced. Then you must consider not only the impact of natural light on the colors you have selected but also how they will look under a variety of artificial lighting conditions, such as fluorescent, incandescent, halogen, and candlelight. It can be very tricky to find colors that look equally well under all lighting conditions, so a blend of similarities and contrasts is often the best way to go. That way, no matter which lighting source you use, you will get a flower garden effect, where many tints and shades of a color appear to blend and harmonize seamlessly. It takes practice and experience to make this work so that colors do not look spotty or patchy (Figure 6-2).

Recently we accepted a project to redecorate a medical office. New carpeting was needed in the lobby and reception areas and through a rear hallway that led into several office spaces, separate from the examining rooms. The lobby area had halogen lighting, the reception area had incandescent lighting, the rear hallway had overhead fluorescent fixtures, and each office had a different combination of natural and artificial light. Carpet that looked great under the incandescent light looked hideous under the fluorescent light. Another carpet that looked wonderful in the reception area was far too harsh in the natural light of the offices. Yet, we and the client wanted to use a single carpet for continuity. After many attempts to find a color that would work in all areas, we decided on the "flower garden" trick. We selected a subtle multicolor

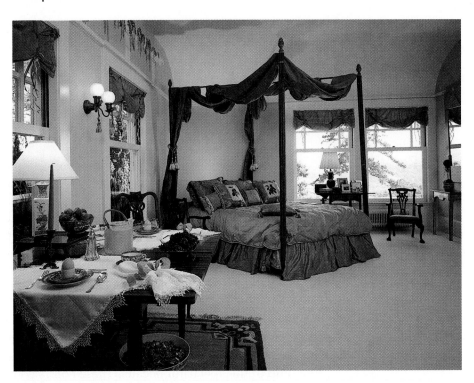

figure 6-1

Recent well-controlled color studies indicate that the more intense a color, the more likely it is to cause arousal regardless of the hue. Based on this, the pale celadon, amethyst, and taupe color scheme of this master bedroom is intended to induce rest and relaxation. *Interior design by Fehrman & Fehrman. Reproduced by permission of E. Andrew McKinney, photographer.*

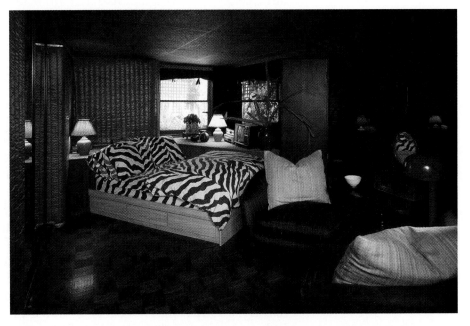

figure 6-2

This bedroom contains every color of the spectrum plus the neutrals. They are incorporated seamlessly without appearing patchy or spotty. This provides a balanced environment for the users. *Interior design by Fehrman & Fehrman. E. Andrew McKinney, photographer.*

pattern for a central ground and bordered it with a heather-effect carpet made up of many tiny specks of different colors, which the eye read as a solid color harmonizing with the central field. Many colors in small amounts fooled the eye into blending the colors under all of the different lighting conditions, and the carpet looked great in each space. Pointillist painters such as Seurat used small dots of color effectively, and individual pixels combine to create color in computer and television monitors.

Whenever we use color in an interior, we always strive to maintain a balance of color in each room by including a sampling of all colors. If this is done expertly, the room will seem very inviting and relaxing, and the user will feel a sense of well-being. When people come into our home, they usually let out an involuntary breath. They may not even notice that they do this, but it is something we have noted over time. Visitors immediately relax, probably without knowing why. It is because the colors are in balance. As an example, we will share with you how we achieved this effect.

Our double-parlor living room has a very sunny southern exposure, but we wanted to use a soft terra cotta color for the walls. We knew that using a reddish tone on the walls would be unbalanced in this exposure, so we first painted the walls a soft bluish mauve and then did a series of three transparent color washes over it: a pale apricot, a medium-toned terra cotta, and finally a light glaze of mineral red. The effect is very subtle, and the layers of color also help to conceal the years of aging since our home was built prior to 1860. Although we used the same pale bluish mauve for the ceilings in both of the double-parlor rooms that make up the living room, the front room, which is closer to the southern light, always appears a soft gray, while the second room, which is farther away from the front bay windows, appears more like the color in the can—a bluish mauve. At night, the colors change again with the addition of candlelight and chandeliers, and the ceilings appear to be the color of a dove's wings. This subtle color change repeats the constant light changes that occur in nature.

We selected dual-colored shot silk for the draperies. The threads going one direction are a soft teal, and the threads in the other direction are a coppery color, so as the light hits the fabric, it reads both teal and copper simultaneously. This fabric enabled us to bring in some of the cooler blue and green tones while bridging the colors of the terra cotta–toned walls. Turkish carpets in patterns of teal, a coppery orange, and cream set the stage for accessories in a range of greens, golds, and beige tones. Every color of the spectrum is used somewhere in the room but with subtlety, and the whole effect is one of harmony, a space that seems perfectly natural and relaxing.

Our kitchen area has a northern exposure with lots of green reflections from the trees in the garden outside. Because of this strong green reflection, we decided on a green granite for the countertops. While our initial preference had been for an alternate color of granite, the strong green reflection made other colors unappealing. We selected a green granite with a yellowish undertone to counteract the bluish northern light. To balance this light, we painted the walls a "white" that is really the palest possible shade of apricot. The eye reads it as white, but the undertones of yellow-orange give the room a warm feeling rather than the harshness that would have come from stark white. We then added the golden tones of aged pine in cabinetry and furniture to further balance the color with very pleasing results.

Color in Interior Environments

In an attempt to analyze the various effects of color related to interior environments, hundreds of color studies have been run on an international level. Many of these studies address the psychological properties of color, while some are more concerned with the effect that color has on spatial dimensions. Although these studies sought to define the effects of color in interior environments, most were run in laboratories with small color chips. Perhaps the most important thing to be learned from all the studies run on color in interior environments is this: **Extrapolations cannot be reliably made from color taken out of context in laboratory experiments because of the way humans process color information.** In a real situation, there is always a background, always a contrast effect, and always an interactive process between light, eye, and brain. Selecting color on chips in isolation simply does not give the same data as in a real three-dimensional environment with all its inherent complexities. When research is done in settings that closely simulate a real interior environment, results are usually different from the outcomes of studies run in isolation.

Several countries have systematically performed color assessments of real or simulated interiors during the past twenty years. Considered as a whole, the following results from Japan, England, and the United States begin to provide a really coherent body of evidence about color.

Japanese Interior Color Studies

Masao Inui of Japan undertook several surveys of the actual types of colors used in different environments. His idea was to make a careful and thorough survey of colors in common use and, by analyzing these patterns, to reveal underlying principles of color psychology at work among people. Inui used the Munsell color system for his studies and reported results in the Munsell vocabulary. (See Chapter 11 for an explanation of this system.) He found that in most Japanese interiors the "warm" colors were used more frequently than the "cool" colors. Yellow-red hues centered around the color of natural wood (Munsell 10YR) strongly dominated. Munsell values are distributed in a blunt, cone-shaped pattern, peaking at value 8, while chroma reaches maximum frequency at 2. So, the "warm" colors of high value and low chroma most often used in Japanese interiors contradicts predictions extrapolated from color preference literature.

Inui also found that color preference was often heavily influenced by the room type and the surface to which it was applied. For example, theater foyers used much brighter colors than would be found in the average living room. Hospital consultation rooms and operating rooms employed more green-yellow and green with very high value and low chroma. Ceilings were mostly colorless, but floors were very colorful. Since the color impression of a room is primarily experienced as an integrated experience by an observer, Inui found that the less bright the color (heading toward neutrality), the more pleasant the interior was thought to be. However, movie theater lobbies were an exception. They were considered to be more pleasant as they became more colorful, indicating that **color preference in real settings is partially determined by the social**

function of the interior space. People often accept interior colors in one setting yet find the same colors objectionable in another setting. Appropriateness is the key to acceptance.

Inui also had subjects rate more than thirty scale models of interiors made with colored paper. Observers were asked to picture themselves in the ten types of rooms represented in the study and to state a preference for each room. Only one color composition was found to suit any type of room. This corresponded to the colors of natural wood with foliage. Other combinations were considered appropriate for certain types of rooms only, and some were found unsuitable for any application.

Kunishima and Yanse (1985) also investigated the pleasantness of different wall colors in residential living rooms. Their results confirm much of Inui's earlier work. The most successful wall colors for living rooms were those perceived as "warm" in hue, high in brightness, and low in saturation.

British Interior Color Studies

A pair of English color investigators produced some very interesting studies into what makes different colors seem appropriate for different kinds of interiors. Slatter and Whitfield (1977) based their study on the hypothesis that the judged appropriateness of certain colors varied with the function of an interior. They labeled a perspective drawing of an unfurnished room as either a bedroom or a living room and asked subjects to select appropriate wall colors. When the drawing was perceived as a bedroom, slightly more saturated yellow, yellow-red, and red were selected than when the drawing was regarded as a living room. Living rooms were most often selected as neutrals.

Following this study, Slatter and Whitfield (1978) extended considerations of color appropriateness to the style of a room as well as its function. Subjects were asked to rate appropriateness of nine wall colors of a domestic interior furnished in either modern, Georgian, or Art Nouveau styles. They found that the neutral white was perceived as highly characteristic of modern, dark red was considered most suitable for Georgian, and a light green was most often related to Art Nouveau.

United States Interior Color Studies

The color studies run in the United States are much less concentrated and systematic than the European and Japanese work. During the past thirty years, there has been a scattering of work that only recently has begun to focus on specific questions, primarily about enhancing productivity in high-technology workplaces.

Srivastava and Peel (1968) were interested in color's influence on human movement through interior space. They compared visitors' movement patterns as they viewed art museum exhibits when the walls were painted light beige or dark brown. By using a hodometer (which unobtrusively measures footsteps), they found that visitors to the dark room took more footsteps, covered twice as much area, and spent less time in the room than visitors to the light room.

In a color-productivity study, Bill, Margulis, and Konar (1984, 1985) had office workers state preferences for described colors, pick color chips of the most preferred colors for workstation features, and rate the colors. Based on one-time data for 1,000 workers, they found that office personnel preferred colors for walls and dividers that were low in saturation. Preferred selections were light blue, light aqua green, and off-white. Work surfaces in light wood were preferred, with chair seats in a highly saturated color. These findings reaffirm the apparent desire for a workplace that is predominantly light for surroundings, but with visual interest introduced by strong color and value contrasts in small-scale elements.

A Westinghouse study (1986) showed more productivity in a light-walled room than in a dark-walled room. A wide variety of poorly controlled studies attempted to determine color preference in workplaces and residences, color as related to productivity, and color appropriateness in public spaces, with generally unreliable results. However, the well-controlled studies described in the preceding paragraphs demonstrate a satisfying coherence. They strongly suggest that it is not productive to apply color theory to real settings based on the results of laboratory experiments done in isolation. Color as applied to real three-dimensional interior spaces involves the experience of color in context, color in a perceptually rich setting. Much environmental color meaning and acceptability seem to rely on cognitive appraisals between what is viewed and a preconceived stereotype that is dependent on individual education, experience, and sociocultural norms, all of which define taste.

Color and Spaciousness

One of color's most compelling uses in design is to alter the perceived size of interior spaces. One of the first things learned in most design programs is "warm colors advance; cool colors recede." It has even been written that blue appears to recede and can therefore affect the height of ceilings or the perceived distance of walls. But is this true? Experiments in color perception during the twentieth century have given much more insight into color's effects on perceived spaciousness than this oversimplified rule would suggest. As early as 1918, Luckiesh investigated the "retiring" and "advancing" effects of color. Pillsbury and Schaefer (1937) tested subjects with red and blue neon and argon lights viewed through slits that compensated for the relative size of the retinal image as the lights were moved. When the lights were placed at equal distances, the researchers found, to their surprise, that the blue light was judged to be nearer, in direct contradiction to the accepted standard "cool colors recede."

Experiments conducted by Taylor and Sumner (1945) and Johns and Sumner (1948) found that when the apparent distances of different colors are held constant, **the brighter colors appear nearer than dark colors**. Their introduction of brightness into the color-distance questions reveals an alternative explanation for the peculiarities of the previous research. If brightness controls apparent distance rather than "warm" or "cool" colors, then blue light (which appears brighter than red at low luminance levels) would appear nearer as it did in the Pillsbury and Schaefer study. Viewing colors through squinted eyes is a favorite trick of the trade for color designers to gauge brightness differences independent of hues. In this context, one loses hue sensations while brightness contrasts remain.

After reviewing these and many other well-controlled studies, **we conclude that brightness is the operative factor in the perception of**

advancing and receding rather than "warm" or "cool" colors, with bright colors appearing nearer than dark colors regardless of hue. An object's distance is also judged somewhat in relationship to its similarity or to contrast with its background. Objects showing high contrast with their background will be judged in apparent position before their background. The controller for apparent distance seems to be strong contrast induced primarily by brightness but also by saturation between a judged element and some established reference frame such as background. **Spaciousness is enhanced by increasing lightness of the enclosing surfaces and by decreasing the contrast between elements that intrude into a space and background.** Therefore, the old trick of "painting out" obtrusive fixtures or unwanted visual elements is well founded. Color plays a role in creating a sensation of spaciousness, but it is far from a simple task. Color's role in the perception of spaciousness relies more on its ability to be a carrier of achromatic contrasts that help to define interior perspectives than on any intrinsic powers of hue.

So, how can we apply this information directly to interiors? Color creates perspective. The length, width, height, depth, and area of interior space can be masked or accentuated with color. Advancing colors make distant walls seem nearer and box large rooms in, thereby reducing their perceived size. Painting a ceiling in a bright color (regardless of hue) will make the ceiling seem lower. Light-reflecting colors emphasize space. Uniformity of color also plays an important role in defining interior space. Uniformity of color can increase the perception of spaciousness or make a space seem boxed in. The caveat here is that uniformity of color used throughout an entire house to create a sense of spaciousness can have the reverse effect. For example, when all rooms in a house are painted the same color, the degree of uniformity causes us to perceive that the interior space taken as a whole is actually smaller because we lose the ability to differentiate the rooms. The operative factor here is balance. To gain the most from using color effectively, a harmonious balance is the goal. Remember, there are no nice, neat formulas to rely on. For dealing with color in interior spaces, there is no substitute for experience.

The Aesthetics of Color in Interiors

Color plays a vital role in any interior environment. It can dramatically change the way objects look, both individually and in relation to each other. A good interior designer should be sensitive to the physiological and psychological effects that color has on the inhabitants of an interior space (Figure 6-3). Using color in an interior is a subtle and detailed process because the completed interior color is an amalgam of a multitude of color areas that are affected by artificial and/or natural light, as well as the observer's interpretations. Interior color themes are drawn from the variety of materials incorporated into the interior: natural materials (wood, granite, marble, slate); textiles (drapery, upholstery, tapestries); wall and floor coverings; paintings, sculpture, and other artworks and collectibles; and plants and floral arrangements. All these elements contribute to the overall color image of the interior space. To make the most of color, its aesthetics must be considered. To achieve this, the color palette must be compatible with the purpose of the room, its physical size, form, and source or sources of light.

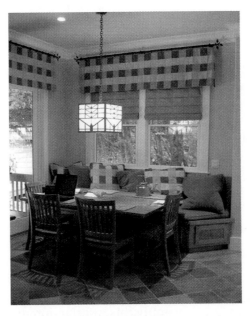

figure 6-3

This breakfast area is decorated in a geometric pattern, yet the overall feeling is one of calm and serenity because of a sophisticated and well-thought-out color scheme. *Interior design by Island Architect (www.islandarchitect.net), formerly PDI. Reprinted with permission.*

Over the years attempts have been made to reduce the principles of color harmony or color aesthetics to a formula, but this effort usually fails because the result is static and boring—much like comparing a paint-by-number picture with the real work of a trained artist whose soul shines through in the finished product. In the world of color, nothing teaches like experience. Only by using color can we really develop our own sense of it and, in the process, perhaps arrive at something unique and truly inventive. A really experienced designer does not use prescribed color charts or fixed formulas. Each interior space is as unique as the client for whom it is being designed, and each deserves a fresh eye and a sense of newness not possible with formula thinking.

Color charts can be very helpful for the beginning student of color and for a textile or product designer's initial color combination testing. The interior designer, however, has a unique problem to face. The colors used in a room are on surfaces that are viewed at various angles. They also vary in texture and receive different degrees of light, depending on their placement in the space. For example, the color of the small piece of fabric provided in the typical fabric sample can look very different when it is spread over the surface of a very large sofa or used to cover walls. The tonalities in a pattern, its location in the room, and the light sources are all factors that affect whether the color plan works (Figure 6-4).

Color Harmony in Interiors

Interior designers work with three dimensions—space, volume, and texture—as well as lighting. An interior designer must also consider that the interior space is a background for the humans who will inhabit it. In residential projects, the personal preferences and feelings of the client must be considered. In commercial projects, the designer must consider the

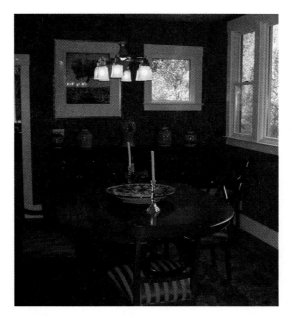

figure 6-4

Red is a good color to select for a dining room because it causes salivation, which may aid in the digestion of food. We have noticed in our design practice that even people who are very hesitant to use red in large quantities readily accept red in dining rooms. *Interior design by Island Architect (www.islandarchitect.net), formerly PDI. Reprinted with permission.*

vast range of people who will use the interior, whether it is a hospital, restaurant, hotel, or other public space. To this end, any color selected must be considered within the context of both **chromatic and tonal values**. The degree of vitality and chromatic relationships are of critical importance in bringing certain colors together (Figure 6-5).

The experienced interior designer considers several questions while developing a color plan. Is there a client preference? Do the uses and purposes of the space suggest neutral or color solutions? Does the level of illumination demand light, medium, or dark tonalities? With these basic questions answered, the designer can then proceed to widening the color composition by considering the contrast and variety of color areas, the interplay of chromatic and tonal values, and the use of pattern. When initiating a color plan, the interior designer usually divides a space into main areas (floor, walls, ceiling), secondary areas (window treatments and large upholstered pieces), and minor areas (small chairs, paintings, pillows, small objets d'art, and other accessories).

Establishing Interior Color Themes

An interior color theme is established by the treatment of the main and secondary areas. Accent areas are important to create a general effect, although greater unity is achieved when the same color accents are repeated in various parts of the room. For example, the red accent color of a pillow could be repeated in a lamp base, a flower vase, or small lacquered boxes used as table accessories. There are probably as many ways to make a color theme "work" as there are designers. There really are no hard-and-fast rules. In fact, the most successful rooms do not rely on rules but on the years of training and experience it takes to develop an

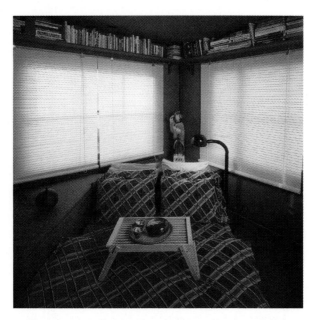

figure 6-5

Red, green, and violet are not easy to use together in an interior, but here they bring a vitality to the space. The walls are upholstered in a soft gray-green denim with red ribbon trim, which tie the colors together. *Interior design by Fehrman & Fehrman. E. Andrew McKinney, photographer.*

eye for color. There are, however, helpful tips an interior designer can consider.

Complementary Color Scheme

In interiors, a complementary color scheme generally employs two complementary hues, one for the main area and one for the secondary area. (Remember, complementary colors are opposite on the color wheel, i.e., red-green, blue-yellow, and orange-violet.) Exact complements are less effective than complements that are tinged with the same underlying hue. For example, a yellow-based red harmonizes better with a yellow-based green because the underlying yellow relates the two hues. The same pleasing effect could be derived from using a blue-based red with a blue-based green. Here the blue is the underlying link between the two.

Analogous Color Scheme

This type of scheme is usually limited to two or three adjacent colors on the color wheel, such as green-blue with intermediate steps in between, or yellow-orange or orange-red might be used.

Monochromatic Color Scheme

This one-hue plan is based around a single color. In monochromatic schemes that work most effectively, a variety of tonal and chromatic values are employed in the same plan.

Monotone Color Scheme

Monotone schemes are composed of one color, one tone, and one level of saturation throughout. While this scheme can be done with any color, the most popular choices are the neutrals gray and beige. Monotone schemes are often dreadfully boring, and their common use in institutional settings or commercial interiors must be questioned since they provide virtually no stimulation or interest. However, galleries often use monotone schemes to set off their works of art, and this approach can be quite effective if handled properly.

Achromatic Scheme

Achromatic schemes are quite popular today, perhaps because they offer little challenge. Achromatic schemes use the neutrals black, white, gray, and brown. They rely on a varying range of beiges and browns or of grays from near-white to charcoal black (Figure 6-6).

Chromatic Distribution

Making decisions about how much color to distribute and to what areas can be tricky for the color novice. In traditional rooms, the most neutralized values are generally used in the dominant areas, with brighter colors saved for smaller areas or accessories. However, the opposite approach has been used with great success. Because colors are never seen in isolation, the designer must consider how color placement will affect the overall color image. For example, two complementary colors placed in juxtaposition will heighten the intensity of both. Depending on the tonal values and saturation, a bright green sofa with bright red pillows might be unnerving, as the colors will appear to flash. However, adjusting the tonal values to a forest green sofa with burgundy pillows could create a quite pleasing impact. In interiors where heightened stimulation is desired, juxtaposed complementary colors may be the perfect

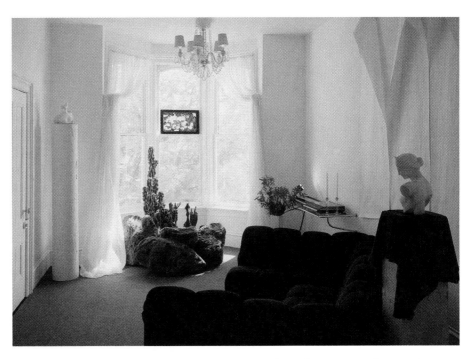

figure 6-6

This interior was an interesting challenge. The client wanted a modern minimalist look in a Victorian home without altering the architecture. This was achieved with a primarily achromatic scheme of black, white, and gray in combination with large, wall-mounted paper sculptures and a dramatic rock and cactus garden. *Interior design by Fehrman & Fehrman. E. Andrew McKinney, photographer.*

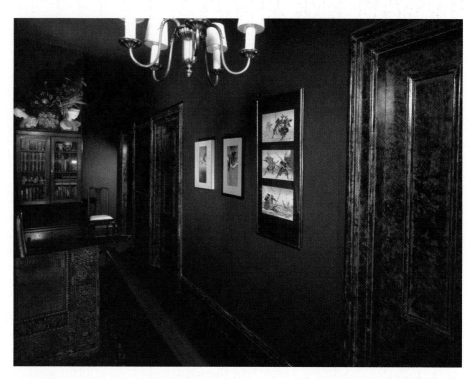

figure 6-7

On the surface, there appears to be no connection between this hallway and primal humans, but the colors selected here reflect our earliest conditioning to color. The dark value of the floor makes us feel secure by grounding us, while the medium value of the green walls subconsciously reminds us of trees and plants. *Interior design by Fehrman & Fehrman. E. Andrew McKinney, photographer.*

choice. It really all depends on the level of training and experience the designer brings to the project.

Tonal Distribution

Since humans began walking upright, most of us have become conditioned to a dark value beneath our feet (earth), medium value around us (trees and plants), and a lighter value above (the sky). Darker materials are imbued with a psychological sense of weight, and gravity has conditioned us to feel safest on a weighty, sturdy base (Figure 6-7). Because of these millennia of conditioning, most of us continue to feel most comfortable if these values are continued into our interior environments. The tonal value of a color is highly influenced by adjacent values and may appear lighter or darker by contrast. Furniture placement can be greatly affected by tonal distribution and vice versa. If a light-value sofa is placed against a dark-value wall and floor, the sofa will appear to float in space. This effect is not usually desirable and can be unsettling to people. We are affected by our interior spaces at a subliminal level. The average person may not always be able to identify what makes a space comfortable or uncomfortable, but subtleties such as this contribute to the overall comfort or discomfort. To correct the problem of the floating sofa, we simply need to adjust the surrounding values more closely to that of the sofa so that all surfaces—wall, floor, and sofa—appear in proper proportion. A dark floor, medium sofa, and lighter walls provide the greatest level of comfort for the largest number of people (Figure 6-8).

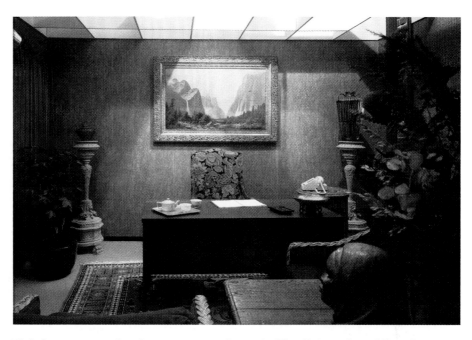

figure 6-8

This is an example of a room out of synch. The light-colored flooring makes the desk and area rug appear to float strangely in space. The gridded ceiling with fluorescent lighting appears oppressive and casts glare on the painting. *Authors' collection*

Interactive Color Schemes

If you choose a color and its complement, the shadows that are cast from either color are the complements (Figure 6-9). Using a complementary color scheme such as two tertiaries, yellow-green and red-violet, the shadows cast by the red-violet are yellow-green, and vice versa. Therefore, the eye reads only pure color with no interference from other colors casting other shadows. Interactive color works best for tertiary colors, which are a combination of primary and secondary colors, because the colors are already blended and harmonically balanced. If you are doing a drawing or rendering for interiors, you should use the complement as the base for the shading of the object you are drawing. For example, if the object is yellow-green, use red-violet for the under-base of the shading. To achieve the best color for the shading, mix the complements together and use the resulting neutral gray as the shading.

Color/Energy Relationships in Interiors

Colors selected for interiors can have an impact on energy costs. According to the Environmental Protection Agency (EPA), artificial lighting accounts for 25 percent of electrical energy use nationwide. Since light walls reflect more efficiently than dark walls, much more lighting is required for dark-walled rooms. Previously we discussed how our psychological state can affect our perceptions of color. The color of a room can affect your perception of temperature. For example, studies have shown that colors associated with warmth and fire, such as reds and oranges, can cause people to estimate the temperature in a room to be six to ten degrees warmer. The opposite holds true for colors perceived as cool, such as blues and greens. Major paint manufacturers can provide the light reflectance value (LRV) of colored paint chips. White

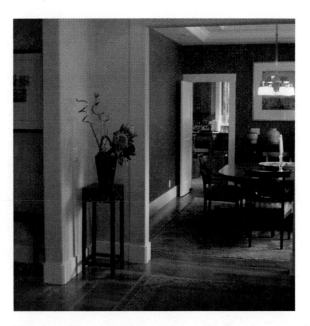

figure 6-9

This interior uses tints of the complementary colors yellow-green and red-violet in a blended, harmonically balanced, interactive color scheme. *Interior design by Island Architects (www.islandarchitect.net), formerly PDI. Reprinted with permission.*

reflects 80 percent of light; black 5 percent. The higher the LRV number of the paint color, the less artificial lighting will be required.

Historical Interior Colors

We cannot have a complete understanding of how to use color in interiors without at least a basic knowledge of the historical uses of color. This brings to mind a client of a few years ago who had some lovely antiques, ranging from original eighteenth century to late Victorian. One piece in particular stood out from the rest, a Victorian rosewood sofa by Belter that had been re-covered in bright yellow shiny vinyl! While this material may have its place as a rain slicker, it was totally inappropriate for use on an antique. The discordant note it struck overpowered the rest of the room. With a little knowledge of historical uses of color (and, of course, textiles), this unfortunate incident could have been avoided. Although experienced professionals may produce a pleasing effect when they choose to break from tradition from time to time and use colors or textures more appropriate to a different period, inappropriate colors chosen from ignorance can be quite horrifying.

An in-depth study of the history of interior decoration is beyond the scope of this book, but a basic understanding of the color preferences of previous eras is important to the study of color in interiors.

Color in the Colonial Style

The term "Colonial," as applied to interior style produced in America, covers the period from about 1650 to the late 1700s. Strong regional differences stylistically influenced furniture and interiors from different parts of the country. French Huguenots and a few prosperous British settled in the Carolinas, while affluent Dutch and Quakers and poorer Germans, Swiss, and Swedes made New York and Pennsylvania their destination. Each national group brought its own style to the melting pot, including the British styles of William and Mary and, later, Queen Anne. Even as American craftsmen created furniture based on the designs of Chippendale, they were introducing their own inspirations and innovations. For example, in England mahogany was the preferred wood, but in New England cherry became an alternative, and oak, birch, maple, and walnut were used in rural areas, each providing subtle differences in color.

In terms of color, the predominant hues were those that we refer to today as "natural" or "earth tones" since most were derived from natural earth pigments (Figure 6-10). Walls, however, were often treated with bright paint that was often uneven in its application because of the

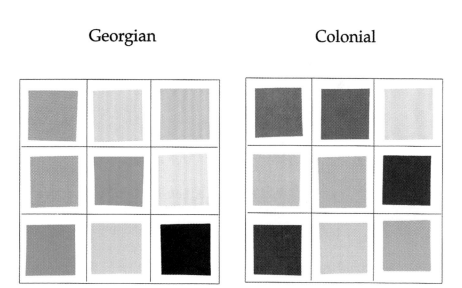

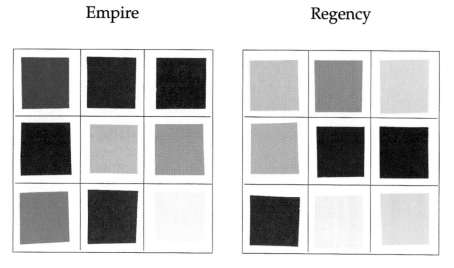

figure 6-10

Historical color palettes showing colors favored in the Georgian, Colonial, Empire, and Regency periods. *© Copyrighted 1998 by Kenneth and Cherie Fehrman*

imperfect consistency of pigments. Rich ochres and reds, a range of subtle grays, and browns, deep peacock blue, and lemon yellow define this period.

Color in the Georgian Style

The eighteenth century is noted for the style commonly known in England as Georgian. The Georgian era covers the period from about 1714 to 1780. The early Georgian era was dominated by Palladianism, based on Andrea Palladio's sixteenth-century Italian villas. The mid-Georgian period flirted with Gothic, chinoiserie (following the opening up of trade with the Far East), and a touch of Louis XV style. The famous furniture designer Thomas Chippendale incorporated all of these styles in his work. The late Georgian period was much influenced by the archaeological excavations of Pompeii and Herculaneum and was characterized by lighter, finer decoration and furniture. One of the great British architects known for his interiors was Robert Adam (1728–1792). Adam made detailed studies of classical remains and used his knowledge to create a deliberately eclectic style. Magnificent examples of his work can be seen in England at Syon House, Kedleston Hall, and Osterley Park. Adam and Chippendale worked together on a number of projects, both believing that furniture and interiors should be considered as an integrated whole. Although Adam has become known for soft colors such as pastel rose, greens, blues, and yellows (Wedgwood's jasperware typifies the colors used by Adam), he was very comfortable working with strong, unusual color combinations. On a visit to London's Victoria and Albert Museum a few years ago, we encountered a surprising example of work by Adam. The exhibit was a room reassembled from one of England's stately homes. Rather than the pastels most associated with Adam, the walls were a bright scarlet embedded with minute flecks of gold, giving the impression of a candy-apple metal-flake hot rod paint, which he had combined with a grayed turquoise for an unusual yet pleasing effect.

During the Georgian period, the walls of houses were often paneled. In wealthy homes, the paneling might have been exotic mahogany, but it was often painted "softwood," such as pine, treated to a faux finish to simulate more exotic woods or simply left in one of the popular "drab" pigments such as gray, off-white, olive, or brown. Later in the period, paneling was painted pea green, sky blue, or a soft pinkish color known as "blossom." Color was often used to emphasize the division of the wall into sections. Although there are exceptions, when the room was paneled, the cornice was usually painted to match the wall. When the walls were painted or papered, the cornice was usually painted to match the ceiling. Typical colors of the Georgian period were soft gray, pale green, blue, pink, and white. Gilding was also very important. Georgian ceilings were generally finished with a coating of whitening or crushed chalk for a soft, matte look. As the eighteenth century drew to a close, rooms became more colorful, sometimes with unusual and unexpected combinations defining the different architectural elements, often set off against white moldings.

American styles of the eighteenth century were, of course, similar to those of England and Europe, with Britain being the most influential force, at least until 1776. Chippendale's work inspired a school of cabinetmaking in Philadelphia that developed into one of the most sophisticated furniture design movements of the century.

Color in the Empire Style

When Napoleon ruled France from 1799 to 1815, a style developed based on military symbols such as crossed swords, spears, arrows, and torches. Ingenious styles in campaign furniture made military life more comfortable. This furniture included folding desks, beds, chests, and very slim chests of drawers. After Napoleon's campaign in Egypt, Egyptian symbols were included on the typically heavy mahogany furniture. Sphinxes, winged griffins, slave figures, pharaonic heads, and palm fronds found companions in the swan's necks, acanthus leaves, laurel wreaths, caryatids, and lions that had been borrowed from classical Greek and Roman designs. The Empire style is associated with bright colors. Bright green, bright yellow, crimson, and bright, deep blue are typically Empire, often used in combination. Touches of black and white, deep red, and Prussian blue can also be found in this period. Prussian blue, formulated in 1720, was the first chemical colorant. By the end of the eighteenth century, brilliant lead-chromate yellows and reds had been developed.

Color in the Regency Style

Stylistically, the Regency period lasted from about 1790 to the 1830s. During this period, smaller houses were built, which led away from the elaborate and costly applied ornamentation of the Adam era to a more consistent use of motifs from the ancient Greek and Egyptian civilizations. The increasingly relaxed style of room layout encouraged less formal types of furniture, such as the recamier. Key motifs of the style include the Greek key patterns, swans, sphinxes, and winged griffins, used with much more restraint than in the Empire style. Since the Regency style is very adaptable to today's room sizes, it has remained quite popular. Colors of the Regency style are rich, lustrous, and lively—light, clear blue, aqua, pale yellow, and deep reds set off with white or cream.

Color in the Federal Style

The Federal style developed in the United States in the late eighteenth and early nineteenth centuries. It continues to be a popular style. Federal furniture is usually made of mahogany, rosewood, cherry, or bird's-eye maple and is highly prized for its sense of refinement and elegance. The intense blue popularly called Williamsburg blue and the deep, dusty Federal green are hallmarks of this style. Gray, mustard yellow, and deep lavender in muted tones are distinctively Federal colors, in combination with white or cream (Figure 6-11).

Color in the Biedermeier Style

The Biedermeier style has made a huge resurgence in the past decade or so. It was first popular between 1815 and 1850 in central Europe, Germany, Austria, and Sweden. At the time, it was commonplace furniture, with its popularity based on its inexpensiveness, simplicity, and practicality—it was perfect for the middle class for whom it was created. Much of the furniture is veneered in light, honey-colored fruitwoods such as cherry, walnut, and pear, although birch and ash were used in Scandinavia. Ebony inlay or ebonized ornamentation makes a striking contrast to the pale, glossy wood. As with most Scandinavian design,

Federal

Biedermeier

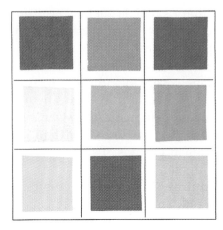 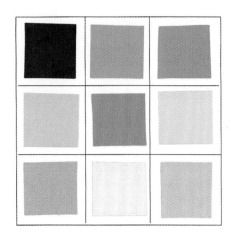

Edwardian

Arts and Crafts

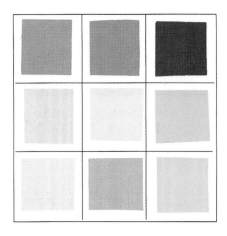 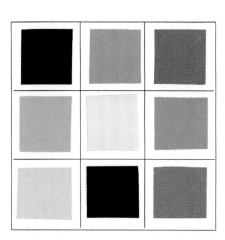

figure 6-11

Historical color palettes showing colors favored in the Federal, Biedermeier, Edwardian, and Arts and Crafts periods. © Copyrighted 1998 by Kenneth and Cherie Fehrman

light is of the essence. Light, clear colors such as pale green and yellow are associated with the latter part of this period, and bright, strong colors such as reds and blues were more often used when the style was first introduced.

Color in the Victorian Style

The Victorian era began in 1837 with the ascension of Queen Victoria to the British throne, and it ended with her death in 1901. There is no one Victorian style, but a series of substyles that merge and blend into one style that we have labeled Victorian. Some of the substyles include Gothic Revival, Rococo Revival, and Renaissance Revival. The Victorian age was one of great eclecticism. England ruled the world and brought back much of it to England in the form of cultural souvenirs, ranging from fabrics to carpeting, carvings, porcelains, and curiosities. Wallpaper was first mass-produced in Britain in 1841, and it became the primary treatment for walls for more than a century. In general, the Victorian era relied on somber colors such as deep crimson (particularly popular in dining rooms), dark green, maroon, browns, grays, and black (Figure 6-12). The excavation of Pompeii, buried under volcanic ash in 79 A.D., had an enormous impact on interior color. Pompeiian red and Pompeiian blue-green were often used in late-Victorian dining rooms and parlors. A craze developed for anything from ancient Greece; even

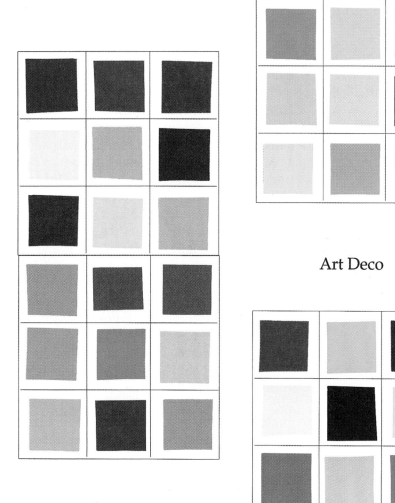

figure 6-12

Historical color palettes showing colors favored in the Victorian, Art Nouveau, and Art Deco periods. © Copyrighted 1998 by Kenneth and Cherie Fehrman

the colors of Greek pottery decoration heavily influenced the colors of the aesthetic movement that followed. The Victorian era was earmarked by opulent ornamentation, which eventually became so overpowering that it spawned a revolutionary movement protesting it—the Aesthetic Movement.

Color in the Aesthetic Style

In 1868, when Charles Eastlake published his book *Hints on Household Taste*, he frequently used the term "aesthetic" in reference to the lighter, less eclectic style he preferred, thus providing the banner under which his followers gathered. The two main styles embodying the Aesthetic Movement were Queen Anne and Japanese. A breakthrough came with E. W. Godwin (1833–1886), who designed many innovative interiors, including the house that Oscar Wilde leased in London's Tite Street, Chelsea. It was decorated in subtle shades of white and gray and is thought to be the precursor of Syrie Maugham's white-on-white style of the 1930s. Most of the colors of the Aesthetic Movement were not so subdued. Yellow satin upholstery set against walls washed in blue and green were often seen, and, while color was kept light, it was used liberally and decoratively. The Aesthetic Movement spanned 1875 to 1890 and showed a preference for purples, pinks, mauves, greens, and yellows.

Color in the Arts and Crafts Style

The Arts and Crafts Movement came about, at least in part, to offset inferior-quality mass-produced furniture that was being foisted off on the British working class. The movement began about 1870, when William Morris's concepts inspired the overthrow of Victorian gloom, and it continued in one form or another through the end of the century. Architects C. R. Ashbee and W. R. Lethaby were the founders and leaders of the Arts and Crafts Movement. Other powerful leaders in the movement were William Morris, and C. F. A. Voysey, among others. This movement loved anything homespun and handcrafted. Morris can be credited with creating a backlash against the chemical artificiality of Victorian colors (especially the aniline dye colors of mauve and magenta); he preferred colors derived from natural sources. Anything to offset the idea of mass-produced mediocrity was popular in this movement. Oak made a huge comeback as the primary choice for wooden furniture, and color took on a lighter but dull tone. Dull green became particularly popular.

In the United States, the Arts and Crafts style was taken up by members of the Roycroft Community under the direction of its founder, Elbert Hubbard (1856–1915), who published the magazine *Philistine*. Roycroft furniture also preferred oak, although ash and mahogany were occasionally used. The most sought-after American furniture maker of this style is Gustav Stickley (1858–1942), who made oak furniture noted for its strong rectilinear lines. Stickley and other leaders of the American Arts and Crafts Movement derived their color palette from what they imagined were the similar paint colors of seventeenth-century Colonial America. In keeping with the British end of the movement, color was light to medium in tone, featuring a lot of wood and natural or earth tones such as greens, tans, and browns, as well as deep blue, black, grayed green, ochre, deep purple, and dull gold. Even though the Arts and Crafts Movement was a revolt against the often gloomy interiors of the late Victorian era, it still seems dark by current standards.

Color in the Art Nouveau Style

French Art Nouveau, also called Le Style Moderne, began about 1892 and ended in the early 1900s. Art Nouveau was noted for its combination of Rococo and botanical forms. Sensuous curves and tendril-like patterns denote the period. The tendency toward lighter interiors that began in the Arts and Crafts Movement continued into the Art Nouveau style. Art Nouveau also adopted the idea that color can be used to create a mood in interiors. White suddenly became associated with progressiveness in decoration. Other popular colors were lilac, mauve, salmon, gray-green, indigo, and black, all applied so that the overall effect was one of light airiness.

Color in the Edwardian Style

The Edwardian era began in 1901, with Edward VII's accession to the British throne, and ended with his death in 1910. Perhaps its most defining feature is its continuance of the tendency toward lighter interiors. Homes of this time reflected the eclecticism of many styles, including all the substyles of Victoriana, a rebirth of the Queen Anne style, Turkish and Moorish furnishings from the Victorian smoking rooms, and fragments of the newer Arts and Crafts and Art Nouveau movements. White and pastel shades dominated the Edwardian color palette as people threw off the Victorian age and its dark, heavy color schemes. The Edwardian palette may be considered the first "modern" color palette, as we still use it regularly today. A preference for light, bright interiors dominated. Shiny white or cream paint was the preferred treatment for interior woodwork. Soft pink, blues, greens, grays, and occasionally pale mauve define this style.

Color in the Modernist Style

The so-called Modern Movement of the 1930s is most often associated with white, but, in fact, the modern era ushered in vibrant colors as well as making white extremely popular. Dutch architect Gerrit Rietveld (1888–1964) greatly admired the work of American architect Frank Lloyd Wright and became a leading member of a young group of artists, architects, and designers called De Stijl (the style). Rietveld used primary colors and abstract rectangular forms to create a modern design that had no links to the past. His severe "Red and Blue Chair" of 1918 heralded the era of color that was to follow in Art Deco and the 1950s and 1960s. Wright's design philosophy was similar to that of German architect Walter Gropius (1883–1969), founder of the Bauhaus School. In this environment, Gropius trained a new generation of teachers who were to change the appearance of interiors and furniture throughout Europe and to influence design worldwide. In *The New Architecture and the Bauhaus* (1935), Gropius anticipated "the desire for a universal style of design stemming from and expressive of an integral society and culture." The Bauhaus designs drew on abstract art and machine imagery for inspiration, producing brightly colored abstract patterns and severe chrome-and-leather furniture.

It is always interesting to be at a place in history that lets us look back to see how the past influences the present. The machine-dominated influences of the Modernist Movement were softened by interior designers such as Syrie Maugham, wife of the novelist Somerset Maugham, who became noted for her pickled and waxed white wood furniture and white-on-white interiors of the 1930s. She did not invent the all-white room, but she was the first to market the idea so successfully that it became her signature.

Although others had used white before, Syrie reinvented the term in a range of names taken from nature whose images evoked luxury and elegance. Her rooms were not just white—they were parchment, ivory, oyster, and pearl, conjuring up visions of exotic origins, ancient manuscripts, and precious jewels. When *Harper's Bazaar* devoted an article to her house, the music room was described as having white walls, white satin curtains, white satin slipcovers, white velvet lampshades, and a pair of white porcelain camellia trees four feet high. The dining room's pine paneling had been stripped and waxed, providing the background for rock crystal, white-painted chairs, and a dining table covered to the floor with an ivory filet lace tablecloth, on which was an arrangement of white porcelain, white flowers, and white-porcelain-handled flatware. The living room was noted for its long sofas upholstered in parchment satin, its modern sculptured carpet in varying pile heights in two tones of cream, its Louis XV chairs painted and upholstered in creamy pearl, and its famous mirrored, chrome-framed panel screen.

The screen provided a stunning effect, reflecting the room to infinity like a marvelous faceted jewel, but it was not without its problems. A frequent visitor commented that during hot weather the bonding medium softened, causing enough flying glass to decapitate the unwary. Syrie even went so far as to have her white canvas draperies dipped in white cement to repeat the sculptural effect of the carpet. The finishing touch was provided by the dozens of white lilies, camellias, gardenias, and chrysanthemums that filled the space. It was a totally impractical design, yet it earned her the title of the White Lady. The publicity generated by Syrie Maugham and her contemporaries went a long way toward imprinting the image of white on the era, when, in reality, others, most notably by the proponents of Art Deco, were using considerable amounts of color.

Color in the Art Deco Style

The Modernist Movement found its antithesis in Art Deco. The Art Deco style was named after the Exposition des Arts Decoratifs, which took place in Paris in 1925. It was influenced by the earlier arrival of Diaghilev's Ballet Russe in Paris in 1909. The Ballet Russe had an enormous effect on color, fashion, and interior decoration. Strong, exotic colors such as purple, jade green, and orange were immediately adopted by the avant-garde. These colors were often set off against black or gold. Other popular colors of the era included more muted tones such as the ubiquitous *eau-de-nil* green (pale grayish green), gray-blue, and primrose yellow set against white. Other popular Art Deco combinations were gray, black, and green, orange with brown, and cream with green.

Art Deco combined elements of Neoclassicism, Orientalism, and exotic elements introduced by the Ballet Russe. The discovery of Tutankhamen's tomb added Egyptian influences, and the developing Cubist and Fauvist painters of the period added their influences derived from African and primitive art. All of these influences combined to form the brilliant colors, exotic finishes, geometry, and pyramid shapes that define the Art Deco style. Interior color came from many things, certainly paint and wallpaper, but also the exotic lizard skin, tortoiseshell, lapis, ivory, and shagreen surfaces used by designers such as Jacques-Emile Ruhlmann (1879–1933). A renewed interest in lacquer added another layer of color as the works of Jean Dunand (1877–1942) and Eileen Gray (1878–1976) brought sensuous layers of color to screens and furniture. Wrought iron and bronze were crucial elements of Art Deco design. Toward the end of the 1920s, Jean-Michel Frank became known for his pale, natural silk, parchment, or undyed-leather walls, concealed lighting, contrasting textures, and simply shaped, luxurious furniture. Gold-plating and engraved glass, cream and gold tiles, elaborate metalwork and friezes, and contrasting woods all appeared in the Art Deco style. Whereas the Modernist Movement applauded the work of the machine, Art Deco thumbed its nose at mundane mass production, preferring instead luxurious materials worked by the hands of master craftspeople. Art Deco and opulence were soulmates.

Color in the Fifties Style

By the end of World War II, people felt like celebrating. In the United States, new subdivisions sprang up like weeds as people freed from war concentrated on raising families and beginning new lives. A massive need for housing and furniture, combined with technological experimentation based on wartime inventions, revolutionized the home furnishings industry. Charles and Ray Eames offered their wood-laminate technology. George Nelson provided his innovative storage wall and furniture designs. Florence Knoll, while known for her own designs, contributed her wisdom in letting talented designers and artists follow their own hearts in the designs they presented at the Knoll showrooms. Despairing of the poor quality of textiles available after the war, the Knoll Planning Unit engaged the help of master weavers and colorists to develop a new line of textiles that have become a signature of the fifties era. From 1949 to 1955, Eszter Haraszty was director of Knoll Textiles. Her transportation cloth and Knoll stripe were revolutionary. This Hungarian émigré was known as a brilliant colorist. She began using the then-startling combination of orange and pink (Figure 6-13). It shocked, it surprised, and it was just what was needed to define a new era. Suddenly, pink became de rigueur in fabrics, fashion, and cosmetics. Pink in the fifties became so wildly popular that it was spoofed in the Audrey Hepburn film *Funny Face*, in which the song "Think Pink" poked fun at the whole concept.

The 1950s are remembered for some unusual colors and combinations, such as turquoise paired with lime green, coral and lime green, pink with charcoal, pink with orange, and black accents. It was a decade of technological advances in fabrics and finishes. The dyeing industry met the challenge with furnishing fabrics in orange, pistachio, and turquoise, often used together. Color invaded the kitchen. (I can still remember the awe I felt as a child when I saw my first turquoise-colored refrigerator at a local department store.) Colored enamel kitchenware became popular. Dyes and pigments were used to color the new plastics. Moisture-proof paints, wallpapers, flooring, and surfacing materials appeared in bright pinks, orange, red, gold, and turquoise, but metal cookware remained because the heat-resistant colored metal coatings that made a color-coordinated kitchen possible did not appear until the sixties.

1950s   1970s

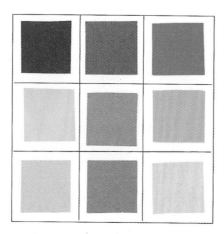
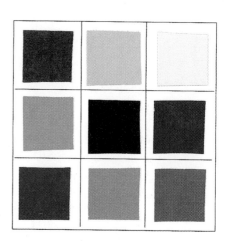

1960s   1980s

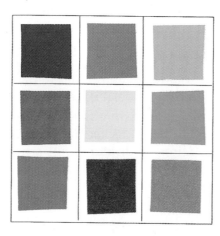
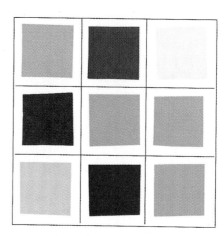

figure 6-13

Historical color palettes showing colors favored in the 1950s through the 1980s. © Copyrighted 1998 by Kenneth and Cherie Fehrman

**Color in the
Sixties Style**

The sixties continued the color revolution even further. The popular phrase of the day, "Let it all hang out," certainly applied to color. The development of new technologies in the dye industry allowed the introduction of color vibrancy that was embraced in the extreme. Suddenly color exploded in fashion and interiors. Whatever our parents had tried to teach us about good taste and appropriateness were trampled underfoot in our rush to experience color as it had never been experienced before. Ultraviolet of pulsing intensity, paired with vibrant acid green, pink, and orange, went to the Day-Glo edge. Screaming Yellow Zonkers described much more than the name of a snack food. It was the most appropriate description of the shockingly bright yellows that became available in the sixties. The trend toward op art that intentionally used color to create often disturbing optical effects was extended to interiors. Colors were intentionally paired so they would flash, such as a red sofa placed against a green wall. Huge geometrical or floral wallpapers employed a multitude of colors never before used together in interiors and topped it off with splashes of shiny chrome Mylar. Everything was flash and fantasy. Suddenly it was desirable and kicky to do the bizarre. Even some of the middle-aged completely relinquished their dignity in an attempt to be "with it." (It was undoubtedly during this time that our client had gone over the edge to cover that Victorian sofa with the screaming yellow vinyl.)

Success in discovering dyes able to color synthetic materials and fabrics allowed a new range of cheap and versatile furnishings to appear in an unprecedented range of colors. In 1960, Vernor Panton, a Swiss architect, designed the first plastic chair with no joints. From then on, synthetic molded furniture became the rage, in geometric shapes from solid molded foam cubes in bright colors to air-filled colorless transparent plastic chairs and sofas. These forms, together with an unprecedented use of color, epitomized the sixties look in interiors. The decade of the sixties was a time of experimentation on many levels, and color was no exception. As with any era or style, it is always easy to be the critic from the vantage point of hindsight, but the perceptive designer will take the best and leave the rest.

Color in the Seventies Style

The early seventies continued the experimentation with color and synthetics fibers that had begun in the sixties, but the mid- to late seventies saw the birth of high tech. This sophisticated new movement in architecture and interior design turned the artifacts of industry into an art form. The use of industrial materials and products in a domestic setting was the hallmark of high tech (a synthesis of high style and technology). High-tech industrial metals and synthetics often had no indigenous color. High-tech designers often contrasted the gleam of chrome or polished steel with the dull grays and browns of industrial carpeting or the embossed patterns of rubber industrial flooring. Color was sometimes applied to decking or exposed steel framing, and when color was used, it was often bright and primary.

Color at the End of the Century

With the advent of the eighties, high tech gradually evolved into the postmodern style that retained some of the hard edge of high tech but softened it somewhat by employing grayed-green or grayed-pink and a general softening of the industrial look in domestic interiors (Figure 6-14). As the eighties blended into the nineties, no single look defined the period. There was a return to opulence in the mid-eighties, which saw a rebirth of elaborate fabrics and drapery treatments and the reintroduction of passementerie to fringe and tassel furniture and window treatments. Color was used sparingly, with color combinations that were often borrowed from earlier eras that complemented the fabrics and trims being used. A tightening of the economy in the early nineties

1990s

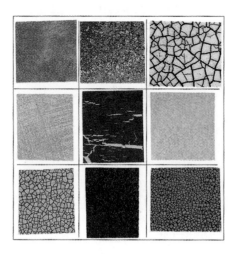

Beginning the New Millennium

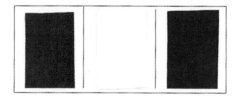

Color palettes showing colors favored in the 1990s and beginning the new millennium. The 1990s favored a wide range of faux finishes in paint techniques to suggest aged plaster, crackle glazing, marbleizing, and a variety of rag and sponge finishes, as well as a trend toward Mediterranean colors of soft golds, greens, and terra cotta. The tragic events of September 11, 2001, began the new millennium with an intense return to patriotism, symbolized by the colors red, white, and blue.
© Copyrighted 2002 by Kenneth and Cherie Fehrman

slowed the frivolous spending of the eighties and, perhaps, encouraged the trend toward faux finishing that seems to have hallmarked the period. Not for decades had faux finishing and trompe l'oeil ("fool the eye") techniques been in such demand. They introduced usually subtle colors to interiors in the form of painted marble or granite, soft washy mural landscapes, and re-created ancient, crumbling wall finishes in residential and commercial interiors. Although employing artisans to create these effects may be costly, do-it-yourself kits and instructional videos sprang up like toadstools, making at least some level of faux finishing available to the general public, with varying degrees of success.

Just as the excavations of Pompeii and Herculaneum revolutionized the use of interior color, we may now be experiencing a similar phenomenon. Current scientific investigation of Colonial era colors has begun to reveal a bolder palette than we ever imagined—one that may again radically alter the way we color our interiors. In the new millennium, we have experienced war, which has led us in the United States of America to a renewed appreciation of the patriotic red, white, and blue. We can only speculate as to our future, but we believe it will be one in which color/light plays an increasingly important role.

Personal Interior Color Plan

After reading all the foregoing information about color in interiors, you are now ready to develop your own personal color plan. Whether you are a color student, a design professional, or a homeowner eager to redecorate, the following list outlines the sequence of considerations to address.

Architecture

The architecture should always be the first item to consider in developing an interior color plan. For example, even the world's greatest interior designer could have trouble making a case for bright orange ceiling timbers in an Elizabethan interior. The architectural style should point the way to the general scope of the colors to use. If you do not want to use colors accurate to the period of the interior, as a general rule of thumb, it works better to access earlier periods than to "modernize" by using colors from later periods. For example, a Victorian home can work well decorated in the soft colors of the Georgian period, but trying to use the Mylar wallpapers and colors of the 1960s in a Victorian just looks bizarre. **Always take your cue from the architecture.** Keep in mind that ceilings in very dark colors look weightier and therefore lower. Bright colors that advance make distant walls seem nearer, therefore reducing their perceived size. The way color is applied can either unify or separate the background from the foreground area. For example, if a dark color is used only on the ceiling of an eight-foot-high room, the ceiling may appear lower. The same color used on the ceiling and walls can unify the space and confuse the eye enough to make the ceiling appear higher (Figure 6-15).

Use of Space

The next thing to consider is the way the space will be used. Is this a public space that needs to accommodate the preferences of numerous and varied people? This must be a prime consideration if you are doing a color plan for a hotel, a hospital, or a commercial space, but it is equally important to consider it for your own living room. This is not to suggest that "committee beige" should be a prime choice. However, when you select color for the public spaces in a residence, the use of the space should be considered (Figure 6-16). Will the space be used primarily for quiet contemplation or conversation? Will large, noisy parties be the norm? Is this a bedroom, living room, dining room, den, or even a studio space that must incorporate all of these activities? Having a clear picture of what the space will be used for helps immeasurably in developing an appropriate color plan.

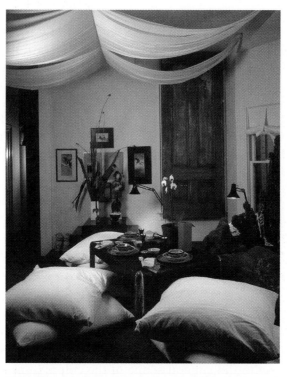

figure 6-15

This interior includes a blend of Western and Japanese elements. The low dining table, large floor pillows, rock garden, and Japanese woodblock prints bow to Japan. The very high ceiling in this room was visually lowered with the use of billowing silk to better relate the space to the low seating. *Interior design by Fehrman & Fehrman*

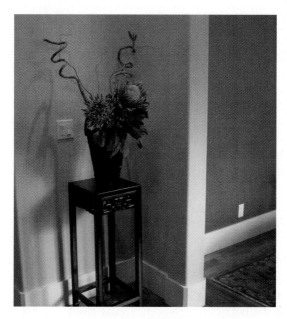

figure 6-16

This small corner of a hallway is made inviting by an antique Chinese stand with a flower arrangement that lends a nod to the Asian heritage of other furnishing used in this home. *Interior design by Island Architects (www.islandarchitect.net), formerly PDI. Reprinted with permission.*

Keeping in mind that there are no formulas, common spaces are usually more acceptable to the most people when neutralized color is used. Saving bright colors or unusual combinations for use in the private areas of the space can be easiest on guest and host alike. We are noted for making frequent and often dramatic changes in the colors in our own home. We have gone from a pale Georgian palette accented with off-white, to deep teal walls accented with verdigris woodwork, to the "crumbling Italian villa" look, to walls glazed with layers of sunset colors, but the look that received the most attention was black.

Many people who work a lot with color find they need some respite at home, so they use white or beige monochromatic schemes in their own environment. At one point, for the same reason we decided on black for our living room (Figure 6-17). It was a very sparse look. Walls were black, furniture was upholstered in beige silk, and the only decoration came from a grouping of lava rocks with large specimen cactus. The adjacent dining room was also black, with gray carpeting, a low Japanese lacquer dining table, and very large cream silk floor pillows. Windows were treated with copper-clad shutters. We found the whole look very low key and peaceful. Some of our friends agreed with us, but others had

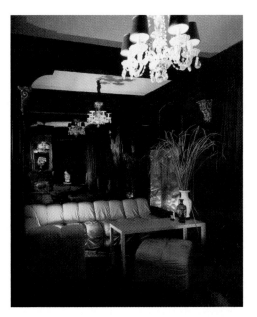

figure 6-17

In previous chapters, we have shown how color selection affects perception. This is a photo of our living room during the 1970s when it was painted black with a mirrored wall, copper shutters, and chocolate moire silk draperies. It had such an impact on people that a policeman who came collecting for charity asked if we were devil worshippers, and another man refused to come into the room because he thought it embodied evil. A woman friend seeing it for the first time clasped her hand over her mouth and stood staring wide-eyed, saying she would never have the nerve to do a black room. We were quite surprised by the responses. Since we had freed ourselves from such color conditioning, we just thought of it as an interesting room. *Interior design by Fehrman & Fehrman. E. Andrew McKinney, photographer.*

the most extreme reactions. One person refused to come into the black space because he believed black embodied evil. This person was an educated colleague with a doctorate, yet he believed it so strongly that we had to let him in by the back door and entertain him in the kitchen, which was then painted white. Another person literally walked around the room with her mouth open, completely speechless. Finally, a policeman came to the door collecting for a charitable cause. We invited him in to wait while we got the checkbook. As soon as he entered the black room, his eyes widened, he looked horrified, and he asked, "Are you guys into devil worship?" The black experience really showed us what an extreme effect the selection of color can have on how people relate to your interior space and, by association, to you.

Color Preference

Both the color novice and the design professional must always consider the color preference of the people who will inhabit the space. If "spice tones" are the popular trend of the moment and you hate spice tones, don't use them in your own space. This advice may seem obvious, but so often people follow color trends without giving any thought to whether they like the colors that are popular at the moment. With the wide range of colors available to everyone today, it is easy to have paints custom-mixed to your specifications and almost as easy to find fabrics and accessories in your selected color range. Even though there are color trends in interiors and home furnishings just as there are in the fashion industry, selecting colors you (or your client) truly like will extend the life of the interior immeasurably. Also, the psychological benefits of living with colors you really like are inestimable. (We sometimes wonder if the number of violent outbursts by postal workers might not stem from the dismal battleship gray interiors within which they work for hours on end.) It can be trickier and may require considerable communication and compromise to accommodate all the members of a household, but the results will be well worth it. If one family member has strong color preferences that the rest do not like, it is usually best to select a neutralized color that will please most for the living room, dining room, and kitchen areas and leave bedroom and private area color selection to the individual.

Period or Style of Furnishings

The period of furnishings to be used also affects color selection. Each period and style of furnishings has specific colors associated with it that should be considered in developing an interior color plan. An example of what not to do comes immediately to mind. Recently, we were in a medical waiting room with Bauhaus-inspired chairs that had been covered in a wine mohair plush much more suitable to Victorian furniture. It was extremely discordant, and we noticed that people avoided sitting in these chairs even though they looked comfortable. Even though the person decorating the office had missed the point, it seemed that most people realized on a subconscious level that there was something wrong about those poor chairs. It would be interesting to see if they continued to be shunned if they were recovered in a suitable material.

There is no substitute for knowledge about periods and styles of furnishings. Studying historical materials and visiting museum exhibits can develop a sense of appropriateness. When you thoroughly know and understand the concepts of color in relation to historical styles and periods, then you can begin to express yourself in your own personal style.

Interior Color for the Age Wave

In the twenty-first century, the reality is that the housing industry will be catering to a more mature population. A significant part of the nation will be at or near retirement age. Breakthroughs in medicine have extended life expectancy. Escalating costs, a shortage of retirement facilities, and a desire for independence will result in baby boomers remodeling their homes to accommodate elderly parents or themselves. These factors have spurred research in creating interior design for the age wave of a maturing population.

When we think of selecting color for an interior, we rarely consider its effect on the visual process, but it should be a primary consideration. Like it or not, as we mature into seniority, our eyes grow weaker. Older eyes have trouble with small print, glare, and low-contrast color schemes. With an aging population, visual impairment must be considered. Products labeled with poorly contrasting colors or stored in cases that produce glare may be passed over. In the home or office, similar color/light conditions can cause irritability, eyestrain, and headaches. As life expectancy has increased because of better health care and improved nutrition, the number and proportion of older Americans have grown dramatically. In 1960, 16.7 million Americans aged sixty-five and older accounted for 9 percent of the U.S. population. In 1990, the number had risen to 31 million with a 12 percent share. By 2025, there will be 62 million people this age, accounting for nearly 18 percent of the population, according to Census Bureau projections.

Virtually everyone suffers some loss of visual acuity by age sixty-five. Many factors contribute to visual impairment, including a number of normal aging processes. The first to strike many individuals is the loss of focusing ability at close range, otherwise known as farsightedness. This typically occurs at about age forty-five and is caused by weakening eye muscles. It occurs when the lens is no longer flexible enough to change shape properly when focusing on close objects. Reduced flexibility of the aging eye also makes adjusting to changes in light and darkness more difficult. Glare can be a particular problem, but it can be controlled by screening window treatments and the use of matte surfaces.

The lens of the eye yellows with age. This means that older people are less sensitive to colors at the blue end of the spectrum, making it difficult for them to see the difference between blues and greens. (To simulate this condition, you can hold a strip of yellow plastic up to your eyes and view through it.) Another normal physiological change that makes distinguishing between colors more difficult is the loss of cells in the retina. As retinal cells are lost, it is more difficult to see the contrast between two colors and to see in dim light.

Although increased lighting can visually expand a space, caution must be exercised in using overly dramatic lighting schemes that may impair the occupants' vision. Walls, floors, window treatments, and furniture should be selected to avoid excessive reflection. To counteract these limitations, avoid subtle color contrasts. Pink on red or red on pink is likely to be a difficult combination for the elderly eye to distinguish. The same goes for light brown and dark brown. As the aging eye loses much of its sensitivity to blue and green colors, every effort should be made to establish an attractive alternative palette to enhance declining depth perception. The strongest color contrast and the easiest to see is black on white. Signage is particularly effective in this combination of neutrals.

In summary, perhaps the most important thing to be gained from this section on color in interiors is the willingness to put aside what you think you know about color and be willing to experiment. The best color studies are those that were run in actual interior environments rather than laboratory studies using small paint chips or swatches of color. The studies run under real-life conditions had far different outcomes than those run in labs because in a real situation there is always a background, always a contrast effect, and always an interactive process between light, eye, and brain. Using human subjects to select color on chips in isolation simply does not give the same data as studies in a real three-dimensional environment with all its inherent complexities. The other thing that must be remembered about using color in interiors is that the color will change with differing lighting conditions. The importance of light's effect on color can never be underestimated.

Color preference in real settings is determined, at least partially, by the social function of the interior space. People are often willing to accept interior colors in one setting that they would consider unacceptable in another setting. Appropriateness is the key to acceptance.

Color can be used in interiors to alter the perception of space. Bright colors appear nearer than dark colors, regardless of hue. Spaciousness is enhanced by increasing the lightness of the enclosing surfaces and by decreasing the contrast between elements that intrude into a space and background.

Although attempts have been made to reduce the principles of color aesthetics to a formula, such efforts usually fail because of the complexity of color/light interaction. To work effectively with color in interior spaces, it helps to have a basic knowledge of color use in various periods and styles and to be willing to experiment within a framework of appropriateness.

REFERENCES

Aksgur, E., "Effects of Surface Colors of Walls under Different Light Sources on the 'Perceptual Magnitude of Space' in a Room," in F. W. Billmeyer, G. Wyszecki, eds., *AIC Color 77, Proceedings of the Third Congress of the International Colour Association*, Adam Hilger Ltd., 1977, 388–391.

Brill, M., Margulis, S. T., Konar, E., BOSTI, *Using Office Design to Increase Productivity*, Volume I, 1984.

Brill, M., Margulis, S. T., Konar, E., BOSTI, *Using Office Design to Increase Productivity*, Volume II, 1985.

Inui, M., "Colour in the Interior Environment," *Lighting Research and Technology* 1 1969, 86–94.

Inui, M., *Practical Analysis of Interior Color Environment*, Building Research Institute, 1966.

Inui, M., *Proposed Color Ranges for Interiors*, Building Research Institute, 1967.

Inui, M., Miyata, T., "Spaciousness in Interiors," *Lighting Research and Technology* 5 1973, 103–111.

Johns, E. H., and Sumner, F. C., "Relation of the Brightness Differences of Colors to Their Apparent Distances," *Journal of Psychology* 26 1948, 25–29.

Kunishima, M., Yanse, T., "Visual Effects of Wall Colours in Living Rooms," *Ergonomics* 28 1985, 869–882.

Luckiesh, M., "On 'Retiring' and 'Advancing' Color," *American Journal of Psychology* 29 1918, 182–186.

Pillsbury, W. B., and Schaefer, B. R., "A Note on Advancing-Retreating Colors," *American Journal of Psychology* 49 1937, 126–130.

Sivik, L., Hard, A., "Color-Man-Environment: A Swedish Building Research Project," *Man-Environment Systems* 9 1979, 213–216.

Slatter, P. E., Whitfield, T. W., "Room Function and Appropriateness Judgments of Color," *Perceptual and Motor Skills* 45 1978, 1068–1070.

Smets, G., "A Tool for Measuring Relative Effects of Hue, Brightness and Saturation in Color Pleasantness," *Perceptual and Motor Skills* 1982, 1159–1164.

Srivastava, R. J., and Peel, T. S., *Human Movement as a Function of Color Stimulation*, Topeka, 1968.

Taylor, I. L., Sumner, F. C., "Actual Brightness and Distance of Individual Color When Their Apparent Distance Is Held Constant," *Journal of Psychology* 19 1945, 79–85.

Chapter seven

Color in architecture and landscape design

Color in Architecture

Historical Exterior Decoration

We have come to accept the lack of color in our public buildings. Today we expect to see gray, beige, and black in corporate towers and even in newly constructed religious buildings. From a historical perspective, however, lack of color in public buildings is unusual. Historically, color was laid on lavishly in architecture, not from civic pride but because of the desire to glorify gods or kings or to celebrate the marvel of building itself (Figure 7-1).

The prototypes of all Western neoclassical architecture were the finely proportioned temples of ancient Greece. Far from being the bare, neutral stone structures we have come to accept, they were richly painted with deep jewel-toned pigments. For example, the marble of the Parthenon was colored in bright greens, blues, and reds to celebrate the divine events it housed. Statuary was deeply dyed, often with garish pigments. The marble figure of a woman found on the Athenian Acropolis was colored red, green, blue, and yellow. Quite often statues had red lips, glowing eyes made of precious stones, and even artificial eyelashes. One relief was painted with a blue background against which figures were painted in red clothes with a blue border, blue helmets with red ornamental stripes on the edges, and blue and red shields. Lions were depicted with red manes, harnesses, and yokes, and the tails and manes of the horses were red.

The colors of ancient Greece may have served the function of giant billboards, where color played a strong symbolic role (Figure 7-2). Blue was associated with truth and integrity. Red represented love and sacrifice. In fact, red has played a strong historical role in the emergence of architectural color. The eighteenth-century discovery of Pompeii and Herculaneum, almost perfectly preserved beneath the volcanic ash of Mt. Vesuvius, forever changed our views on Roman architecture. The brilliantly applied colors shocked a world that had grown to accept a more neutral palette.

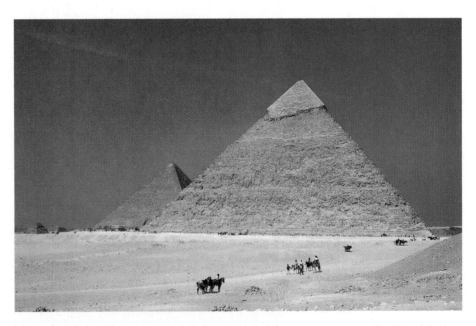

figure 7-1

We have come to accept ancient monuments stripped bare by the winds of time, but ancient monuments were once brightly colored with painted images and symbols. The pyramids were once faced with gleaming white limestone. © Dorling Kindersley

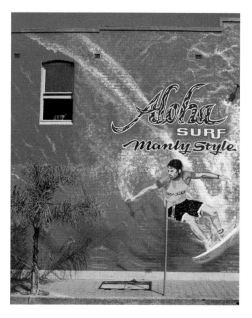

figure 7-2

Like this contemporary advertising sign painted on a building, the colors of ancient Greece may have served as giant billboards with a strong symbolic role. © *Dorling Kindersley*

Primitive peoples endowed red with magical properties (Figure 7-3). Corpses were daubed with red ochre to prepare them for life beyond the grave. Red is as common to all peoples as the color of blood and is believed to have been used extensively in the buildings of ancient cultures. Colored images were thought to offer protection from the physical forces of nature. Strong, saturated colors were used in red, blue, green, and yellow, as well as neutrals in black, white, gold, and silver metallics. The layered ziggurats

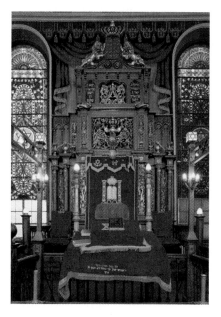

figure 7-3

Primitive peoples endowed red with magical properties, and red continues to be a symbolic color in many of the world's religions. © *Dorling Kindersley*

of Mesopotamia were colored according to hues assigned to the planets. A surviving ziggurat from ancient Ur (now in Iraq), among the oldest structures ever built, uses brilliant blue, red, black, and gold on its four concentric walls. The temples, shrines, and pyramids of the Inca, Maya, and Toltec cultures of Central and South America all used brilliant color surfacing.

In ancient Egypt, the temples were even larger and more awesome. Columns were carved to resemble palm trees and papyrus. The capitals were painted to represent flowers and leaves. Mythical scenes enacted on walls and pylons were full of fierce gods and detailed rituals. The colors of these skillfully painted buildings shone out against the brilliant blue sky, green foliage, and yellow desert. The interiors of the temples contained blue-painted ceilings symbolizing the heavens and green floors representing the meadows of the Nile valley.

The cathedrals of medieval Europe were also painted. As the focal point of social life at the time, they were deemed worthy of the finest decoration. The somber facades to which we have grown accustomed were once brightly painted. As the sunlight poured through the brightly illuminated stained-glass windows, it was rivaled by the vividly painted interiors and the pigmentation and gilding of the external facades. Traces of medieval colors can still be seen on some of the French cathedrals, such as the flecks of red, blue, and green at Angers and the red stain on Notre Dame. In *Colour Decoration of Architecture*, James Ward wrote:

> *The coloring occurred principally on the moldings, columns, sculptured ornaments and figure work. The outside coloring was much more vivid than the inside work. There were bright reds, crude greens, orange, yellow ochre, blacks and pure whites, but rarely blues, outside, the brilliancy of light allowing a harshness of coloring that would not be tolerable under the diffused light of the interior. The large gables of the transept also bear traces of old painting. There is also evidence that the greater portion of similar edifices of the thirteenth, fourteenth and fifteenth centuries were decorated in color.*

Only centuries of scrubbing and weathering have removed the paint that adorned the saints and angels in their niches. Some cathedrals, such as Wells in England, were plastered or whitewashed and painted with black or red lines to simulate the mortar between blocks of stone. In *Gothic Adventure*, Cecil Stewart refers to Wells Cathedral, stating:

> *Its one hundred and seventy-six full-length statues were brilliantly coloured. The niches were dark red and the figures and drapery were painted in yellow ochre, with eyes and hair picked out in black and the lips in red. In the central group of the Virgin and Child, the Virgin's robe was black with a green lining, while the Child's robe was crimson, the composition being set on a background of red and green diaper. There is evidence, from plugholes, that the statues were further enriched with gilded metal ornament. Above, the row of angels were painted rosy red.*

The Reformation and the Puritans scrubbed and whitewashed religious buildings in the name of piety to rid them of their pagan overtones, thereby destroying their original intent.

The secret of building to last is, of course, to select stone as the building material. The ancient Egyptians, whose bronze and copper tools were among the first to be equal to the hardness of stone, built the massive Step Pyramid of Zoser more than 4,500 years ago out of blocks of brownish limestone. The outer casing was carefully finished in a finer-grained near-white limestone, just as the Great Pyramid was. Using the local stone has the advantage of allowing the building to harmonize with the landscape, and both the pyramids and the medieval castles and cathedrals of Europe frequently appear to grow from the ancient outcrops of rock on which they are built.

We have come to think of Japanese architecture as based primarily on a subdued color palette drawn from wood and stone, but their buildings were also color enriched. The Toshogu Shinto Shrine at Nikko was lacquered, painted, and gilded lavishly both inside and out so that even after 350 years its brilliant reds and yellows and intense blues and greens are still visible. It is said that during the seventeenth century the shrine blazed with nearly six acres of gold leaf.

The builders of ancient Rome could draw their color from all the quarries of the known world but used mostly what was on their doorstep. The interior of St. Peter's exemplifies the amazing range of colored marbles that enabled the Romans to dispense with the Greek habit of painting buildings. They borrowed the pattern of architecture from the Greeks; they simply scaled it up and created more militaristic monuments out of patterned stone and bronze plating. It is said that Caesar Augustus found Rome in brick and left it in marble (Figure 7-4).

In areas where stone was scarce, people built from the most durable materials at hand. Five thousand years ago the religious shrines of Mesopotamia were made of mud bricks covered with copper sheets and decorated with shapes of archetypal coloring: red sandstone, black shale, and white mother-of-pearl. Later generations raised their glittering shrines high above the plains on huge, constructed mountains called ziggurats. Many have survived to this day, but their bright mosaic patterns formed from thousands of colored clay cones, their blue tiling, and gilded metal roofs have disappeared into dust.

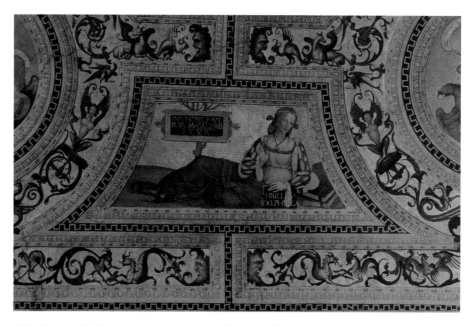

figure 7-4

This beautifully painted Roman ceiling typifies the luxurious ornamentation often found in buildings of ancient times. © *Dorling Kindersley*

The Muslims of Central Asia produced the most brilliant wall facings ever devised. Techniques of glazed faience were nearly as old as the cities themselves. Nebuchadnezzar used them in the bright blue bricks and golden heraldic beasts of the main entrance to Babylon that he rebuilt in the sixth century B.C. Nearly 2,000 years later, whole mosques were covered in complex mosaics of turquoise and sky-blue glazed tiles. The Islamic empire stretched east to the Atlantic and west to the China Sea, and its architecture is as diverse and colorful as the area it covered. Consider the red-tiled Alhambra palace of Spain with its fantastic stalactite plaster hangings; the mauve, blue, brown, and umber hues of Tamerlane's mausoleum at Samarkand; and the glistening whites and reds of Akbar's Mogul pleasure dome, south of Delhi.

In the rain forests of Central America, the Mayan masters of stucco adorned their magnificent pyramid-form temples with elaborate and brightly colored carvings and designs. The awe-inspiring city of Palenque in Mexico was discovered in conditions of almost pristine color by successive expeditions in the seventeenth and eighteenth centuries. Eager to expose its glories more fully, they unfortunately hacked and burned down the surrounding jungle of trees, thereby destroying the delicate microclimate that had protected the stucco coloring.

The Chinese selected the simplicity of wood for their early buildings. As one of the five key elements of Chinese philosophy, wood alone provided fit accommodation for the gods. But they did paint columns, lintels, and beams and added polychrome decoration to the eaves of roofs whose semicircular ceramic tiles were green, blue, purple, or, in the case of imperial residences, yellow. When a home was built, red firecrackers were exploded from the upper beam of the roof. A piece of red cloth was suspended to promote felicity. Green pine branches were placed on the scaffolding to deceive wandering evil spirits by making them believe they were passing over a forest.

In the palaces and temples of China, color symbolism can be found everywhere. In the Forbidden City, the hues symbolize the five elements, virtues, and vices (Figure 7-5). Red shows as the positive essence, the heavenly and masculine principle. Yellow is the negative essence, the earthly and feminine principle. The walls of the city are red, symbolizing the south, the sun, and happiness. The roofs are yellow, symbolizing the earth.

For generations we reproduced Greek designs in bland neoclassic beiges because we did not realize they had originally been colorfully painted. What a shock it must have been for the tasteful society patrons of the day to realize that their carefully selected neutral palette was based on error. From the mid-nineteenth century, bold use of color began to appear in Western architecture. Color was a vital element in a shift of attitudes that changed the face of architecture across the Western world in the form of Art Nouveau.

British, French, and Belgian Art Nouveau had a recognizable coherence, while the style's most unique practitioner, Spain's Antonio Gaudi, brought to the style an interpretation strictly his own. Gaudi was passionate about color. He deemed color essential to producing a sensation of life, and he used it freely in his building facades, which were embedded with bits of rubble and brick, shards of pottery and tiles, paint, and whitewash.

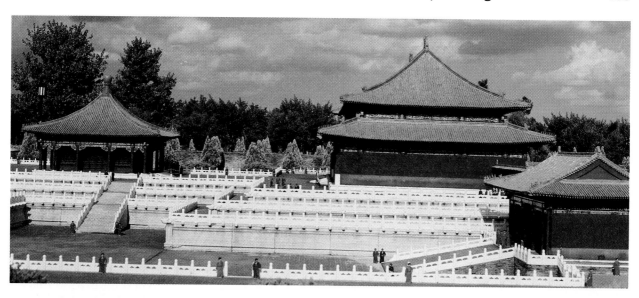

figure 7-5 China's Forbidden City utilized color symbolism extensively in its yellow and red exterior. The red walls symbolized the south, sun, and happiness. The roofs are yellow, symbolizing the earth. © *Dorling Kindersley*

The turn of the century brought a series of movements that unified painting, sculpture, and architecture for the first time. Constructivism used color to emphasize function. Moving parts such as doors were distinguished from fixed parts such as walls. Purism used color to define space. Piet Mondrian's abstract canvases painted in primary colors with black, white, and gray deeply influenced the architects of the Dutch De Stijl movement, such as J. J. P. Oud and Gerrit Reitvelt. In Germany, the Bauhaus School evolved a utilitarian aesthetic that saw architecture as indivisible from the socioeconomic conditions out of which it grew. This vision was to dominate European and American building for decades, and it still makes its impact known.

Perhaps the best-known designer to affect modern building facades with his work with reinforced concrete was French architect, painter, and writer Le Corbusier (Figure 7-6). Although Le Corbusier endorsed the utilitarian link between color and object, color and space, his palette extended beyond the primary colors of his contemporaries to include natural colors. However, the concrete with which he made such a design statement became clumsy cubes in less capable hands, and we are now having to live with its effect. Although the use of concrete made possible the amount of building necessary after the appalling destruction of two world wars, it is also the material most associated with the dehumanization of contemporary urban environments.

The inevitable backlash against raw concrete came when the Germans responded by dressing facades with tiles or bright colors directly derived from their rich tradition of folk art. Their instincts were soon echoed throughout Europe and America, where a reaction against drab, utilitarian buildings and the social emptiness of a soulless environment sparked a new and colorful expression in domestic architecture (Figure 7-7).

Color abounds in traditional domestic architecture the world over (Figure 7-8). In Brazil, houses are painted in pastels and primary colors.

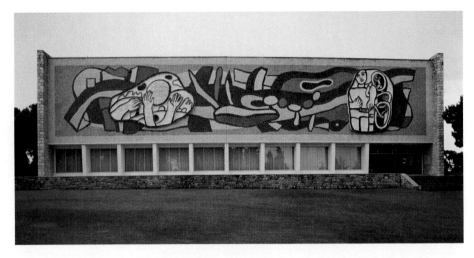

figure 7-6

Early-twentieth-century design brought about a series of movements that unified painting, sculpture, and architecture for the first time, as in this building that incorporates a Leger piece. © *Dorling Kindersley*

The chalets of Austria and Switzerland display facades adorned with floral motifs. San Francisco's Victorian "painted ladies" display very colorful exterior facades. The problem confronting anyone responsible for decorating the facade of a building is whether to blend safely and discreetly with the surroundings or to be conspicuous at the risk of being controversial. Something in the collective consciousness of the corporate mind seems to regard bright color as frightening or dangerous. In the right hands, strong color can be used on architectural facades and, by its presence, add to rather than detract from the community. When color is handled poorly, as is often the case with some of the gigantic exterior

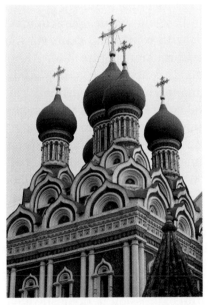

figure 7-7

This Russian building shows a wonderful use of color that is intrinsic to its elaborate architecture. © *Dorling Kindersley*

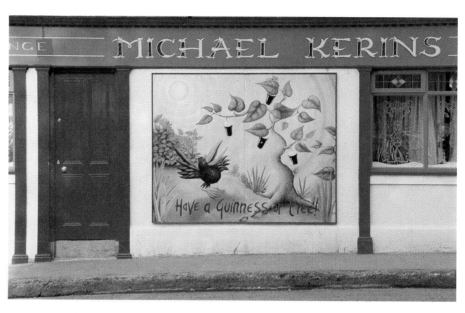

figure 7-8 Sunny climates often spawn colorful painted building exteriors. These colors might seem far too bright in the cooler, grayer light of colder climates. *© Dorling Kindersley*

murals on urban buildings, it is not only an eyesore but a daily irritant that may add to the difficulties of living in an urban environment.

Exterior color must be considered in context with neighboring structures and also with the indigenous climate. For example, bright colors can work very well in warm, sunny climates, but they may seem overpowering in cooler, grayer lighting conditions (Figure 7-9). A good example of this occurred in areas of London where many Jamaicans settled. They

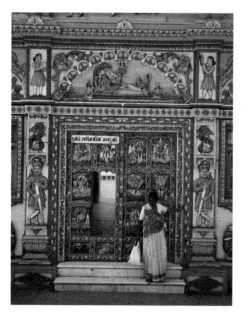

figure 7-9 This brightly colored temple in India is beautiful in the strong sunlight of that climate, but in a cold climate it might appear garish. *© Dorling Kindersley*

brought with them their free color sense and painted front doors and windows of traditional English brick houses in hot pinks, yellows, and mauves that looked totally out of place in the gray English light. The traditional English forest green, black, or white trim was much more in keeping with the rosy brick. While the Jamaican color sense works wonderfully in sunny climates, it is overpowering in England. Another example is a Spanish-style house that was painted bright banana-skin yellow with cobalt blue trim. Among the subdued pastels and creams of its neighbors, it really was very scary. A walk through the streets of your own city or town will undoubtedly turn up many similar examples of people who did not consider the neighboring environment in selecting architectural color.

Wall Painting

The materials of most historical wall paintings are similar, although the results of the work may be quite different (Figure 7-10). Even though four or five thousand years separate the Egyptian tomb paintings and Michelangelo's masterpieces in the Sistine Chapel, the same ground mineral pigments were used, from ochres and iron oxides for reds, yellows, and browns, to green malachite and blue azurite. The painting surface was also similar: a basic plaster made of sand and lime. It is the composition of the painting surface and its preparation that cause the very different color effects.

To begin with, much wall painting that is termed *fresco* is misnamed. True fresco belongs largely to the Italian Renaissance, when pigments mixed simply with water were applied directly to wet plaster (Figure 7-11). There was no medium in which the pigments were ground; the binding process took place when the plaster set with the pigments embedded in it. It was mainly because organic pigments such as madder

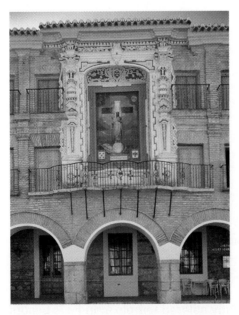

figure 7-10   Historical wall paintings such as this one often used ground mineral pigments to achieve their colors. © *Dorling Kindersley*

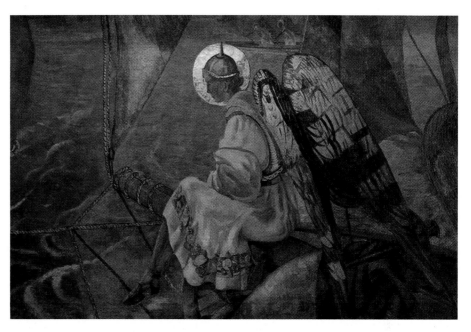

figure 7-11 This is a true Italian fresco in which pigments were applied directly to wet plaster. © *Dorling Kindersley*

and woad were destroyed by the alkaline lime that the fresco palette was restricted to a range close to that of the ancient world. The Egyptians seem to have painted on dry plaster with a tempera consisting of pigments bound in gum or egg white. The bright, flat colors appeared on Egyptian walls from temples to palaces, tombs, and houses. In the workers' village of Kahin built around 1900 B.C., a typical dwelling had a brown-painted surround with red, blue, and white striped walls topped with large tan areas containing brightly decorated panels.

The Minoans of Crete were geographically well placed to inherit the arts of the Egyptians and subsequently to funnel them to mainland Europe. Their early monochrome wall washes graduated to stencil designs in black and red on white plaster. They introduced natural forms. An early example at Knossos shows a boy gathering saffron in a meadow filled with crocuses. The remarkable thing about Cretan artists is that they seem to have employed true fresco and to have carried the technique to Mycenae around 1500 B.C.

Analysis of one Mycenaean fragment showing two women in a loggia casts further light on the technique they employed. The ground colors of blue, yellow, and red were painted *al fresco* while the plaster was still wet. The remainder of the color was superimposed in a tempera *al secco* on the dried surface.

The consummate skill required to produce a fresco is not often fully appreciated (Figure 7-12). The wet plaster was applied in only a sufficient quantity for one day's work at a time (so that it did not dry), so there was little possibility of alteration except by replastering. It was necessary to get it right the first time. Also, the working conditions were quite uncomfortable. Hours were spent on a cramped scaffold with often inadequate lighting and no way of judging how the colors would look when dry except by

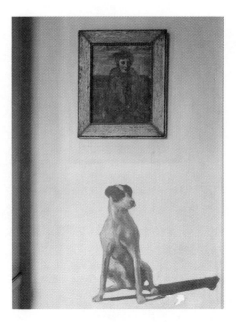

figure 7-12 This fresco is also a trompe l'oeil image, which means "fool the eye." In this case the fresco fools the eye into believing the family dog is sitting beneath the portrait of an ancestor, bringing with it a charming sense of humor. © *Dorling Kindersley*

experience. Yet wall paintings such as those in the Sistine Chapel are masterpieces that have never been equaled, nor are they likely to be.

Although it has not reached the heights of historical frescoes, wall painting has undergone a rebirth that began in the 1960s. While faded advertising signs dating back to Victorian times can still be seen on exterior building walls in Europe and some of America's older cities, it was not until the middle of the twentieth century that exterior murals made a major comeback (Figure 7-13). Some began as protests to social and political problems of the day; others sprang from the need to celebrate local heroes or history or were painted by ethnic minorities to express their pride. Some murals are obviously executed by talented, trained artists, but some reflect only the good intentions of their creators without any matching skill. Murals are often used in dilapidated areas to counteract the ravages of graffiti or to enhance the temporary scaffolding on new construction sites. Although the intentions of the sponsors and artists are good, the results are often mixed, with questionable color palettes and artistic abilities finding a large captive audience who must live with these murals in their communities. Even at their worst, however, public murals executed by unskilled artists do represent an attempt at creative, positive self-expression that should be encouraged.

A Graffiti Abatement Project

In an attempt to bridge the gap between murals and faux finishing techniques, we became involved in an experiment with a local high school that was having terrible problems with vandalism and graffiti. Its student body is over 95 percent minority members, and many are recent immigrants whose families have little economic means. The school's vice principal, a noted authority on gangs, identified approximately fifteen different gangs on campus. While the school's administrators grapple

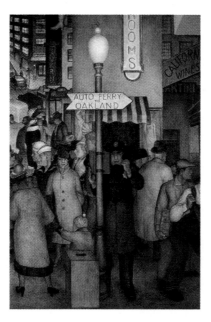

figure 7-13

Wall painting had a rebirth in the early twentieth century, as shown in this mural from San Francisco's Coit Tower painted in the 1930s.
© Dorling Kindersley

with insufficient funding, they find the resources to remove or paint over the graffiti that appears on campus almost daily. Too frequently, the gangs, tag artists, or graffiti artists view the administration's efforts as a challenge and hit the campus buildings yet again. Because of our own frustration with urban graffiti, we teamed up with educators and artists to create an innovative joint project with the high school to address this issue. In collaboration with the school's art teacher and another professor, we formed the Aesthetics Project as an experiment to combat graffiti. The project sought to teach faux finishing skills and mural techniques to high school students who had demonstrated artistic expression outside the bounds of establishment art. It was hoped that these learned skills would serve as an avenue toward later employment within the arts.

The physical objective of the Aesthetics Project was the design and execution of faux finish and trompe l'oeil painting on the exterior of the school building. A marbleized faux finish was applied to the entrance portico of the school's gymnasium, and a mural incorporating faux finishing was painted on the east facade of the main building. Paints, brushes, ladders, and other materials were donated by local businesses. The painting was completed in approximately ten weeks' time and was executed in water-based paints. Faux finishing, a highly marketable skill, is the craft of painting something to replicate another surface material. In this project, for instance, the gymnasium's classical entrance portico was painted to look like marble. The mural incorporated both faux finishing techniques and the art of trompe l'oeil painting (literally, "fool the eye") to create a colonnade of Roman arches supported by columns made to look like marble that extend the length of the main building's east facade. Each arch forms a frame for a distinct painting depicting a scene of the school community as interpreted by a student artist. Images include a view of break-dancers at a school dance, a class in progress, a basketball match, and other school-related activities.

Twenty-two high school students were selected by the fine and industrial arts departments as project participants. University students with advanced standing in design collaborated on the murals and shared their artistic skills, particularly faux finishing, with their high school counterparts. They also served as excellent role models for the younger students. The project's educational benefit from the interaction between high school and college students cannot be overstated. Not only did university students share their marketable faux finishing skills with students but also they served as mentors and ethnically diverse role models. They exposed the high school students to the academic and social responsibilities of a university community. In particular, the minority university students were models for their high school counterparts of successful university students pursuing professional careers in interior design. The university students also had much to gain through this collaboration because the project presented an opportunity for the advanced design students to work with inner-city high school students and to give back to the community. Perhaps the most noteworthy observation is that at the time of this writing, more than six years after completion of the project, the faux finishes and mural areas remain free of graffiti.

Wall art has become an intrinsic part of the urban experience. It is our belief that the graffiti that so often blights the exteriors of buildings in our cities may be a response to the lack of creative outlets afforded young people today because of budget cuts in education. It is unfortunate that the arts are often the first subject areas to be cut from educational budgets, because they produce the defining images of cultures so prized by archaeologists and anthropologists.

Environmental Color

If you are a frequent flyer, you may have noticed that cities have their own defining colors (Figure 7-14). London is a rosy city, colored by its brick structures. San Francisco is primarily an ivory city, with whites and off-whites predominating. Historically, the color of local building materials defined the primary color of a town. For example, Oxford in England is known for its ochre-toned sandstone buildings. In historical settings, the structure was usually related directly to the earth upon which it stood because it was made from the earth, trees, or stone of the immediate environment. When they were available, colored pigments were added in the form of paint for exposed woodwork or stucco facades. Today we have nearly unlimited color selection available to us, but in earlier times an association formed between brighter colors and wealth, stemming from the fact that blues, organic yellows, reds, and some greens could be as much as a hundred times costlier than the common earth pigments.

In order to protect color traditions, certain cities such as Venice have legislated color control. Its citizens are prevented from painting facades in anything but a prescribed range of the earth pigments ochre, umber, sienna, and red. In towns throughout America, advisory boards of historians and designers have researched the specific colors used historically. It would be unthinkable to change the color of certain buildings that we

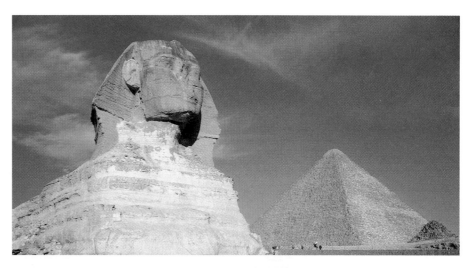

figure 7-14

Cities and monuments all have their own defining colors. Although ancient monuments might have once been brightly colored, we now associate Egypt, the Sphinx, and the pyramids with the natural color of sandstone and may find it hard to accept that they ever looked different. © *Dorling Kindersley*

have come to view in one way only—the White House, for example, is irrevocably white.

Turin is an example of a city that has embraced environmental color on a grand scale. In 1800 a council of builders was established to devise a color plan for the entire city. Their concept was to designate principal streets and squares with a uniform architecture and coordinated colors. The basic scheme allowed about eighty different colors that were used in a way that ensured a continuous but varied progression. The council was abolished in 1845, and during the ensuing decades the city has evolved monochromatically due to the pervading "Turin yellow" that has proliferated throughout the city. Because of its predominance, it tends to blur architectural detailing and spatial relations between buildings and the environment. In 1978 a program was set up to restore the original plan, and the program is progressing at a rate of about a thousand buildings a year. It has been suggested, however, that such restrictions might freeze cultural evolution into a single phase and may therefore not be desirable.

Among other things, San Francisco has become well known for its "painted ladies," the multicolored Victorian houses that were once painted drab gray (Figure 7-15). Again the expressive mood of the 1960s was the spur for this movement. During the decade when "flower power" was the catch phrase of the Haight-Ashbury district, artistic colorations began to appear on the gingerbread fretwork and, gradually, on the entire building fronts of the Victorian homes and flats that predominated in the area. The resultant sea of often discordant colors spawned the new industry of the exterior color consultant, who provided coordinated color palettes that were often based on historically reconstructed colors or were, for the most part, at least pleasing to view. The best of the exterior color consultants took many things into consideration when developing a color plan: architectural history, location and setting, exposure to weather, and relation to neighboring color schemes. One building

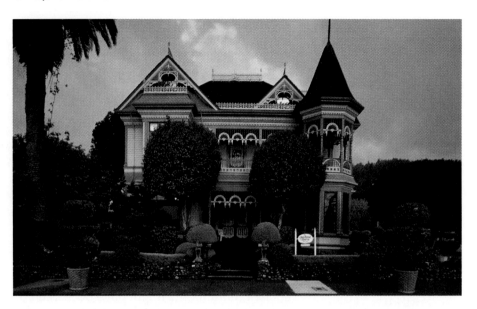

figure 7-15

This Victorian "painted lady" is brightly colored according to today's concept of Victoriana, which originated in the 1970s. The Victorians themselves favored colors that were much more somber, and this house might originally have been painted gray or brown. © *Dorling Kindersley*

in particular still stands out from its neighbors, a Victorian painted in forest green with a monumentally scaled and well-executed jungle cat sprawling across the facade.

The most successfully painted Victorians in San Francisco adhere to a formula that was developed in the mid-1970s. Four or five colors are used to pick out the gingerbread detailing and architectural features of the building. A background color of high lightness value covers the flat wall surfaces. A highly saturated color is used in small quantities to delineate columns, plinths, and corbels. Pairs of colors in strong hues are targeted for door panels, moldings, and so on. A dark color of low value is employed as shadowing and, finally, a color or neutral of high lightness value may be used to highlight any particularly fine examples of ornamentation. More recently, some of the finely ornamented areas have been picked out in gold or silver leaf, which, when done with restraint, is very attractive.

Perhaps the most important message of environmental color is harmony. When environmental color is harmonious within the context of the building, the neighboring buildings, and the environment at large, it is both beautiful and enlivening.

Architectural Color in Service Systems

Mid-twentieth-century industrial buildings were once a vast vista of gray prefabricated concrete. Gradually, this depressing scene gave way to more individual expression in color as architects realized the new role that color could play in identifying major structural elements. This coincided with the high-tech dismembering of form whose structures exposed their private areas of wiring, plumbing pipes, and so on. Vitreous enamel, tinted glass, colored brickwork, infused stucco, anodized metals, and concrete stains and paint are now regularly in use.

The seventies postmodernists began experimenting with color by using it as an important facet of their designs. West Coast architect

Joseph Esherick used strong colors to introduce a territorial legibility to the facades of low-income housing projects, while Charles Moore used seventeen shades of earth pigments in a design for a private residence. Chicago architect Stanley Tigerman's Illinois Regional Library for the Blind and Physically Handicapped crossed into new territory in its use of color. His concept of creating a brilliantly colored external and internal system for a library for the blind is not as odd as it might first seem. In fact, his explanations show that a great deal of thought went into his color choices. He noted that the legal definition of blindness does not necessarily imply total loss of vision. A partially sighted person can and often does perceive contrasts among colors. Tigerman's colors break with the expected levels of institutional austerity by incorporating red for exterior walls, bright yellow for the structural system, and blue for ducting. An exterior wall is left in exposed concrete, with openings and doors picked out in contrasting black.

Michael Graves's use of architectural color is noteworthy. Graves states that the classical origins of form have thematically derived from nature and humans. The floor represents ground, the ceiling sky, and columns represent trees. He finds the classical language of color derived only from nature and nature's materials, such as green "meadows" painted on the floors of Egyptian temples and blue "sky" applied to medieval vaulting. He goes on to explain that although color is two-dimensional, our understanding of it is in three-dimensional terms. "No matter how one might know color to be an application to a surface, we see color first as representational. To some degree, therefore, it possesses the quality of an object, an artifact."

The experimentation of twentieth-century designers and architects has freed architects, at least for the moment, to use color with the most creativity available for centuries. Perhaps in the twenty-first century color will finally come into its own, once again re-creating the brilliance of historical styles.

Architectural Color Selection

The selection of color for architectural applications requires knowledge and consideration of the same confines that affect all color selection: lighting and context. Color selections should always be made or examined under light sources that will be used in the final scheme. Unfortunately, architects too often select color under the fluorescent lighting conditions in their offices, although the colors will be used in the natural light of outdoor situations. In spite of our ability to adapt visually by the automatic adjustment of the eyes to prevailing levels and color of illumination, the discrepancies are often too great and the exterior colors seem distorted from the original concepts. Standardized color measurement systems such as Munsell or Pantone (see Chapter 11 for an explanation of these systems) can be helpful in architectural color selection, but it is important to use samples that are large enough to achieve accuracy. For example, one of the basic problems of color selection in architectural design is the nature of the work itself. The design process usually takes place at a very small scale on the drawing board. Color schemes that are created with small swatches of color and materials may not work when enlarged to full size. **The larger the area of color, the greater the visible saturation.** Colors that may appear to mix or blend well in small paint chips may appear discordant or too intense on a large wall. Background color may influence judgment of a color sample. If the color samples are placed on a white board, for example, the colors will appear one way. If a light gray sample board is used, the colors will appear less bright and closer to their true saturation. This color discrepancy is the reason why it is important to apply a large test area of the colors under consideration directly to a wall before committing to the final color scheme. Only then can the colors be seen in the true lighting conditions and in interaction with the other colors under consideration.

An effective way to determine color selection on architectural facades is to take line drawings of the building exterior and do test patterns of tonal quality by blocking in areas of light, dark, and intermediate grays. Once a pleasing tonal pattern is established, various color plans can be considered. Effectively colored architectural facades always consider the neighboring natural and built environment. A study of the soil colors and natural plant materials of the site can give a clue as to the best colors for the building. The brownish-black of loamy soil areas may suggest deeper tones of forest green, chocolatey browns, and charcoal with lighter accent colors. California's ochre-toned soil may suggest soft terra cotta, Naples yellow, yellowed ivory, and so on. Using the immediate environment to influence color selection is one of the simplest ways to arrive at environmental color harmony. One of the most effective ways to see what color will actually look like on the completed building is to construct scale models and paint them with the actual colors under consideration. Bringing the color into a three-dimensional medium will again change it from the flat two-dimensional medium of the sample board or scale drawing and will enable the designer and client to make adjustments before moving on to the actual application on the finished structure.

Le Corbusier made the following comments in a paper written for students, "If I Had to Teach Architects":

> *Here is a golden rule. Use colored pencils. With color you accentuate, you classify, you disentangle. With black you get stuck in the mud and you are lost. . . . Color will come to your rescue.*

The Sivik Study of Exterior Color

Perhaps the most comprehensive and meaningful study of colors as applied to architectural exteriors was conducted by L. Sivik (1974) in an investigation of the connotations of colors as applied to objects. He utilized black-and-white slides of buildings that could be combined with a color print overlay to make it appear that the building color had changed while all else remained constant. Sixty-seven color samples were prepared that could be attached to two different types of buildings, an apartment house and a single-family dwelling with garage. A stratified sample of passers-by on the street rated ten colors attached to each picture on thirteen different scales.

Sivik found that three factors he called "emotional evaluation," "social evaluation," and "spatial factor" described the judgments. Adjectives such as beautiful, friendly, and pleasant were considered to mean the same thing when used to describe exterior colors and were used to rate emotional evaluation. Social evaluation is more heterogeneous in meaning, while spatial factor deals entirely with concepts of spaciousness. It was found that the yellow- or red-colored buildings were regarded as more beautiful than the blue-colored ones, which was not expected from the results of color chip preferences alone, when blue is often preferred. People apparently like houses that are painted in various shades of yellow through beige or that appear as natural wood. People most disliked dark or violet-colored buildings, but much of the social meaning read into an exterior building color depends on the degree of saturation of the color, rather than the color itself. The darker the color, the more people felt enclosed by it.

In an actual survey of 136 residents of apartment buildings, Sivik found that the residents rated their gray buildings lower than others. People who lived in buildings colored in highly saturated blue approved of the exteriors, but this was highly contradictory to the results of the laboratory study and to a study in which the residents were asked to imagine what the blue color was like. From these studies it can be inferred that color viewed in real situations is evaluated differently from that of laboratory experiments. As previously stated, color is an extremely complex topic that is influenced by lighting conditions, personal bias, and the perceived appropriateness of the color to specific applications.

Architectural Color and Energy Conservation

When planning color for an exterior application, the climate should be considered because color can influence energy consumption. White reflects the radiant energy rays of the sun, and black absorbs them. The hotter the roof, the hotter the rooms below. Light-colored roofing or reflecting coatings reflect the radiant energy and keep the rooms below cooler. On a 90-degree clear, sunny day a white roof shows a temperature of 110 degrees Fahrenheit (F), an aluminum-coated roof 140 degrees F, and a black roof 190 degrees F. That makes quite a difference when it comes to heating and cooling bills. Under ideal conditions, the attic would be well ventilated, and heavy insulation would dissipate much of the temperature difference, but in fact most buildings do respond to the color selected for the roofing material. A study conducted in Florida revealed that homeowners could save up to 23 percent of their cooling costs by selecting a reflective roofing material. According to a study by the Lawrence Berkeley laboratory, increasing the reflectivity of roofs and surfaces in metropolitan areas nationwide could result in a $10 billion savings in energy and equipment costs.

Color in Landscape Design

Photosynthesis is one of the most important biological processes on earth. The process that consumes carbon dioxide and liberates oxygen has transformed the world into the hospitable environment we know today. Directly or indirectly, photosynthesis fills all of our food requirements and many of our needs for fiber and building materials. In order to sustain life on this planet, we need to encourage plant growth. In spite of the recent publicity regarding the disappearance of the rain forests and the detrimental environmental changes this portends, the importance of plants is often forgotten in urban areas, where the largest growing thing seems to be concrete. Ideally, architecture and landscape design should blend seamlessly into a harmonious and beautiful composition. The primary ingredient of harmony or discord is color. While plant shape and size should complement architecture, a garden's first impact comes from its color. The shape and scent of plants are secondary to the initial visual impact of color.

While in times past it might have been true that nature never makes mistakes with color and, therefore, the colors of all flowers work well together, this is often not the case today, because humans have intervened to create plant hybrids in colors that nature never intended. Today we must be more selective in our choice of plantings to complement the color of architecture and the nearby environment.

Historically, gardens have reflected the artistic and architectural styles of their day. For example, the formal knot gardens of the English Tudor style employed the colors of heraldry. Victorian gardeners preferred sensational color selection, mixing scarlet geraniums and blue lobelia, thereby ignoring the good advice of nineteenth-century gardening guru Gertrude Jekyll. Jekyll applied the laws of complementary colors, choosing each group of foliage and flowers to prepare the eye for the next color chosen (Figure 7-16). A typical Jekyll plan would include a gray foliage border, progressing to darker gray with blue, gray-blue, and white flowers, then gradually incorporating pale yellow and pink that gave way to stronger yellows and finally orange and red, so that the color reached a climax in the middle and then receded again toward the quieter colors at the edges.

Jekyll exploited successive contrast by planting monochromatic flower borders in which flowers of palest pink, for example, would merge gradually into blooms of progressively stronger shades of the same hue. Their brightness would be accentuated by contrast with the paler blooms. She noticed that although the orange African marigold has dull green leaves, after looking steadily at the flowers for 30 seconds the leaves appear bright blue. She made spectacular use of this afterimage

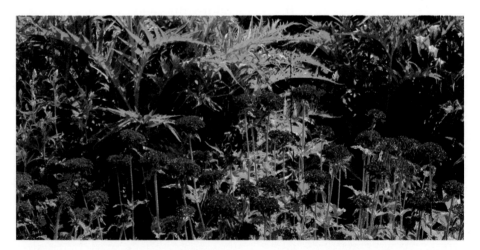

figure 7-16

Nineteenth-century gardening guru Gertrude Jekyll applied the laws of complementary colors to gardening, choosing each group of foliage and flowers to prepare the eye for the next color chosen and allowing the colors to "bounce" off one another, as in this picture. © *Dorling Kindersley*

effect in monochromatic borders edged with flowers of a complementary hue. She devised series of monochromatic schemes in which, for instance, a garden planted with grayish-blue flowers would lead into another planted with flowers in shades of yellow and orange, whose brilliance would be intensified because the eye had been prepared for it. Gertrude Jekyll was also known for monochromatic gardens in which she planted a variety of species in the same color range, producing a whole greater than the sum of its parts.

Seasonal Color

Certain colors naturally evoke specific seasons of the year. The first flowers of spring are so often yellow that most of us associate daffodils, crocus, and forsythia with the awakening of spring. Summer brings with it a feast of all colors, gradually waning into the tawny shades of marigolds, chrysanthemums, and crisp fallen leaves as autumn settles in. Then, in many climates, the complements of red and green predominate against the crisp backdrop of fallen snow as deep evergreens and bright winter berries herald the winter season (Figure 7-17). Urban dwellers can keep in touch with the seasons by creating interior landscapes of seasonal arrangements. A mound of miniature pumpkins, dried corn, and pomegranates immediately brings to mind the harvest season. For a holiday buffet, a tabletop can be transformed by nestling dishes of food among fragrant pine boughs tucked with pine cones and sprigs of holly berries. Giant clam shells can be transformed into vases holding exotic blush-tinted protea and pale mauve freesia in spring or summer. Creating small interior landscapes is a good way to practice using color, light, and texture before moving on to the more expensive and permanent outdoor landscape design.

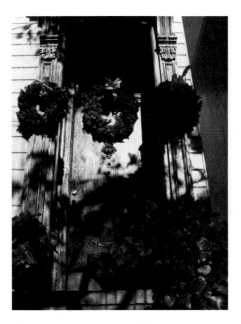

figure 7-17

Certain colors naturally evoke seasons of the year as in this Victorian house decorated for Christmas in red and green. *Author's collection* © *Copyrighted 1998 by Kenneth and Cherie Fehrman*

Architectural Color in Landscape Design

The same laws of complementary colors, harmony, and contrast that affect color use in other applications also apply to garden design. They apply not just to neighboring blooms, but to foliage, light and shade, position, season, and architectural elements such as walls, paths, hedges, ornaments, and furniture. Color creates atmosphere in landscape design, but color can be derived from more than the plants selected for the garden (Figure 7-18). The color and texture of neighboring architecture plays an important visual part in any landscape design. For example, the shiny white paint of a neighboring wall will reflect more light than the mossy surface of a stone wall. In a garden of subdued color, the eye is naturally drawn to the subtle contrasts between the textures and shapes of different leaves and the subtle variations of greens. Selection of paving materials, benches or garden furniture, fencing materials, ornaments, and the amount of light and shadow in the garden are also important elements to consider. Natural wood and stone team more naturally with the colors of trees and plants than synthetic materials do. The selection of paving materials, from the rosy tones of bricks to the pale beige of sandstone to natural or pigmented concrete, will alter the color effects of plantings. Garden ornaments can be made to seem to advance or recede by their placement in relation to color. For example, a verdigris bronze deer may peek shyly from a grove of similarly colored trees, but will dominate a bed of red flowers.

A particularly important aspect of color to understand in relation to landscape design is an optical phenomenon known as the **Purkinje shift**, named after the Czech physiologist who discovered it. This color-related phenomenon describes the gradually changing emphasis on different parts of the spectral range that will create distinctive atmospheres at different times of the day. For example, if a red and a blue object of equal

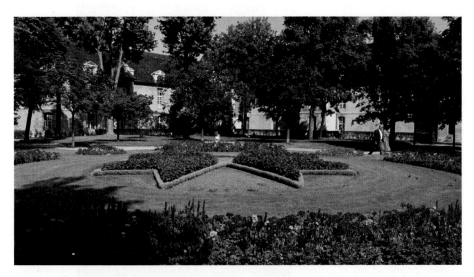

figure 7-18

Relationships between the architecture and the landscape should always be considered. The landscape design and architecture of this house could better relate to each other if the bank of trees did not block the view of the garden from the house. © *Dorling Kindersley*

saturation are placed side by side and viewed at the beginning and end of the day, the red will look brightest in daylight, while the blue will look brightest in twilight. This, of course, occurs because of the changing light conditions. A garden planned to exploit the changing light of day takes on a whole new dimension, for when red and orange flowers so brilliant in daylight begin to fade in the twilight, the barely visible blue flowers can dominate with a wonderful luminescence.

Mosquito Notes   There is one other aspect of color that relates to gardens, that of insects. While we must respect the bees and other insects that pollinate flowers and promote the continuation of plant life, there are those pesky creatures of the outdoors without whom we would all be happier—namely, mosquitoes. Mosquitoes are particularly affected by color. Studies have shown that the common European malaria-bearing mosquito alighted most frequently on dark blue, red, and brown and avoided yellow, orange, and white. This study suggests that hikers or nature lovers would do best to dress in yellow, orange, or white when outdoors and to avoid khaki or blue denim. A similar South African study found that pink and yellow mosquito netting was the most efficient in keeping mosquitoes away.

Color has an important impact on the artificial urban environment, in terms of both architecture and landscape design. While we have all become conditioned to the monochromatic schemes of most major urban centers, the browns, beiges, grays, and blacks to which we have grown accustomed are really an invention of the modern machine age. Historically, architecture was brightly colored. Because the effects of time wore off the layers of bright pigmentation, when we discovered ancient civilizations we believed their color schemes were monochromatic and based decades of exterior decoration on that erroneous belief. In planning architectural color, it is essential to consider it in relation to existing landscaping and neighboring structures as well as the predominant weather patterns and lighting of the indigenous area. Color in landscape design should always be executed in harmony with architecture and the neighboring environment.

REFERENCES

Baldwin, H., *Colour on Buildings: 1500–1800*, Oxford Polytechnic, Department of Architecture, 1978.

Birren, F., *Light, Color and Environment*, Van Nostrand Reinhold, 1969.

Chochron, I., *Color Natural*, Ediciones del Grupo Montana, 1970.

Faulkner, W., *Architecture and Color*, Wiley-Interscience, 1972.

Graves, M., personal correspondence with authors.

Kuppers, H., *Color: Origins, Systems, Uses*, Van Nostrand Reinhold, 1972.

Larsen, M., Pomada, E., *Painted Ladies: Those Resplendent Victorians*, E. P. Dutton, 1978.

Marx, E. *The Contrast of Colors*, Van Nostrand Reinhold, 1973.

Porter, T., Mikellides, B., *Colour for Architecture*, Studio Vista, 1976.

Prizeman, J., *Your House—The Outside View*, Hutchinson, 1975.

Sivik L., "Color Meaning and Perceptual Color Dimensions: A Study of Exterior Colors," *Goteborg Psychological Reports* 4 1974.

Chapter eight

Color in advertising and marketing

Color Impression

Marketing psychologists say that a lasting impression is made within ninety seconds. Color accounts for 60 percent of the acceptance or rejection of an object or person. Because color impressions are both quickly formed and hard to change, decisions about color are critical factors in the success or failure of an encounter or a sale. Color can influence thinking, change actions, and cause reactions. Because of our associations with traffic lights, red means stop and green means go. Traffic lights send a universal message, and so do the colors used for a product. Whether on your business card or your business suit, color adds a subliminal note that plays a critical role in the success or failure of your message.

In advertising, the term *weasel words* refers to the way language is used to drain the meaning from a product claim. The weasel is said to be able to attack a chicken coop, suck out the inside of eggs without breaking the shells, and sneak out undetected. The hollow eggs look fine until you examine them and find out they're empty. Common weasel words such as *helps, improved, up to, as much as,* and *the look of* are all used to confuse the consumer. In the same way, there are "weasel colors" that are even more insidious because they act on a subliminal, subconscious level. For example, the favorite food colors—red, yellow, orange, and brown—exert a measurable effect on the autonomic nervous system, stimulating appetite. This physical effect is exploited by producers who can pass off almost flavorless food by using food coloring and appropriate food packaging colors to make it appear more appetizing. You are influenced the moment you see color, and the influence of color is a clever tool of persuasion. Because color exerts its effects on a subconscious level, people do not realize that they transfer its effects onto the contents of a package or onto an advertising message. Because consumers are not aware of the decisive influence of color on them, they do not build up a defensive attitude the way they do with language. Consumers tend to mistrust advertising because they have come to realize it is a form of manipulation.

Colors can help sell and manipulate in subtle ways because consumers not only view them but also react to them in predictable ways that are controlled by the advertiser. Color plays a vital role in the transmission of messages in advertising. Colors are not merely decorative; they are loaded with meaning. It is, however, essential that sender and receiver assign the same meaning to the colors used if the message is to be successfully transmitted. If, for example, a happy, active feeling is desired, a good choice in our society might be yellow, but in many Asian cultures yellow symbolizes death and would obviously transmit quite a different message. Every social group has its common group of symbolic colors that correspond to the experience, opinion, and values the society has acquired.

Extensive research to predict the specific associative relationships between colors and taste and colors and smell is regularly used in advertising and marketing campaigns. Color influences us every day in a thousand different ways. Restaurants and food ads stimulate our salivary glands and make us want to eat by using orange, pale yellow, vermilion, pale green, and pale brown (Figure 8-1). Thirst corresponds to a tension

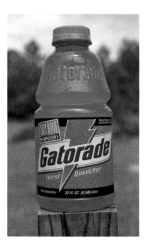

figure 8-1

Thirst corresponds to a tension between a feeling of dryness and a desire for a liquid. In color language, the greenish-blue and reddish tones of this bottle of Gatorade were designed to trigger thirst. © *Dorling Kindersley*

between a feeling of dryness and the desire for a liquid. Expressed in colors, this translates to a combination of yellowish-brown or reddish-yellow (dry) and greenish-blue or blue (liquid). In the proper combination, these colors can trigger thirst.

Advertising uses red to symbolize eroticism, lilac to portray a sentimental sensuality, and pink or soft pastels to express the care and tenderness of motherly love (Figure 8-2). Our need to feel important or prestigious is addressed by the use of violet, wine red, white, golden yel-

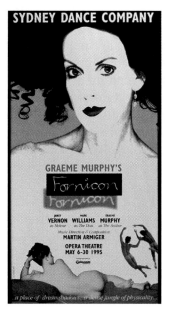

figure 8-2

Advertising uses red to symbolize eroticism and lilac to portray a sentimental sensuality, as in this poster. © *Dorling Kindersley*

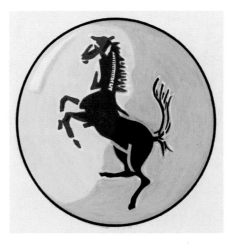

Golden yellow and black portray our need to feel important or prestigious—perfect for this Ferrari logo. © *Dorling Kindersley*

low, and black (Figure 8-3). Many of today's upscale advertisements make extensive use of these colors (Figure 8-4).

Today's consumers are exposed to thousands of advertising messages and special offers. Because of the large number of products in a self-service store, it is estimated that the average time a consumer looks at each individual product is between a twenty-fifth and a fiftieth of a second. This time corresponds to a spontaneous visual shock that stamps an impression on the retina with the speed of light, almost without a person being aware of it. We register only a small portion of the impressions that constantly bombard our senses. For a product to be noticed, it must please us, because we tend to ignore unpleasant colors no matter how bright they are. Experiments have shown that orange and red attract attention best of all (Figure 8-5). While yellow is a striking color, it is not popular and is often ignored. On the other hand, blue is not especially visible, but it is well liked and frequently noticed.

Colors can easily be used to manipulate consumers. Colors can influence the subjective appreciation of the quality of goods or the perception of an advertising message. In one experiment, 200 people were asked to judge a coffee that had been served out of four colors of containers: red, blue, brown, and yellow. Seventy-five percent found that the coffee from the brown container was too strong; 85 percent considered the coffee in the red container to be rich and full-bodied; the coffee in the blue container was judged to be mild; and the coffee in the yellow container was thought to be too weak. All the containers held exactly the same coffee. In another experiment, a panel of women tried out two face creams. One was pink, the other white. The formulas were identical, but the women were not informed of this. All the women said that the pink cream was milder and kinder to sensitive skins and more efficient than the white cream.

The consumer is endlessly and continually manipulated by color use in product marketing and advertising. The background color of an ad, the color of the clothes or cosmetics worn by the model, and the color of the coffeepot shown in the advertisement play a major role in how we respond to a product. In a market research survey, women were given

Colors That Influence Taste

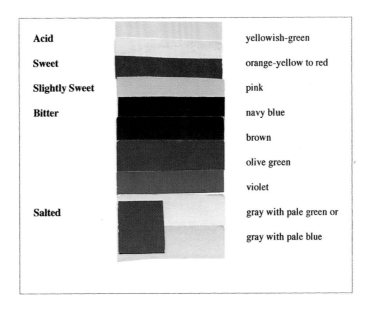

Acid	yellowish-green
Sweet	orange-yellow to red
Slightly Sweet	pink
Bitter	navy blue
	brown
	olive green
	violet
Salted	gray with pale green or
	gray with pale blue

Colors That Influence Smell

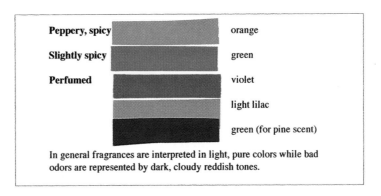

Peppery, spicy	orange
Slightly spicy	green
Perfumed	violet
	light lilac
	green (for pine scent)

In general fragrances are interpreted in light, pure colors while bad odors are represented by dark, cloudy reddish tones.

figure 8-4

Colors that influence taste and colors that influence smell.

three different packets of laundry detergent to try for a few weeks. The detergents in each package were identical, although the women were not informed of this, but the packages were different. One package was primarily yellow, the second primarily blue with no yellow, and the third a combination of blue and yellow. At the conclusion of the test, the women thought the detergent in the yellow packet was too strong. Some said it even damaged the material being washed. The product in the blue package was considered not strong enough to get the washing really clean. The third package of blue and yellow was considered "marvelous." This difference can be accounted for because the blue and yellow packaging triggered exactly the right response in the consumers. The yellow signified strength and an ability to get the job done; the blue indicated a gentle but antiseptic cleaning power; together, the yellow and

Most Easily Perceived Colors and Neutrals Based on Color Preference in Packaging

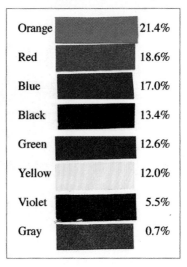

Orange	21.4%
Red	18.6%
Blue	17.0%
Black	13.4%
Green	12.6%
Yellow	12.0%
Violet	5.5%
Gray	0.7%

Most Visible Colors Recognized from a Distance

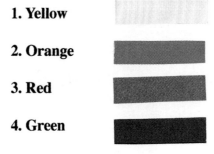

1. Yellow

2. Orange

3. Red

4. Green

figure 8-5

Colors and neutrals most easily perceived and colors most visible from a distance.

blue gave just the right impression to promote a "perfect" detergent—at least in the minds of the consumers.

Color is a kinetic element. Each color has a specific symbolic language or value. In marketing terms, this means that the possibility exists to enhance the identity and characteristics of a product or an object. Colors may be grouped into psychologically active or passive categories (Figure 8-6). The active colors, particularly red and yellow, provoke immediate psychological reactions and may even be irritating. The passive colors, especially blue and green, are more static. Active colors are used to upgrade aggressive qualities of a product, while passive colors are more associated with harmony, tranquility, and achievement. For example, a red package of detergent carries the psychological implication that this brand really gets in there and fights dirt. A blue package is also appropriate for detergent because it implies antiseptic cleansing, but this product would suggest that the cleaning effect is brought about through a chemical harmony whereby dirty linens are restored to their original brightness.

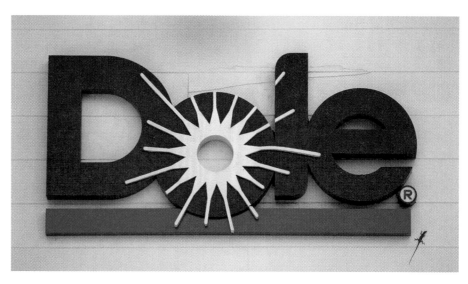

figure 8-6

This Dole sign is a good balance of active (red) and passive (blue) colors while utilizing yellow to symbolize pineapple. The result is a very effective, attention-grabbing sign. © *Dorling Kindersley*

When consumer psychologist Louis Cheskin conducted the original research for Cheer detergent in the 1950s, he tested three different colors of flecks in the product: red, blue, and yellow. Consumers reported that the yellow flecks did not get clothes clean enough, and they claimed that the red flecks actually were so strong they damaged the clothing. The blue flecks were singled out as the best for getting clothes clean. In reality, there was no difference in the product content, but the blue flecks helped make Cheer one of the longest-lived detergent brands on the market. Likewise, when Tide was created in the 1950s, it was Cheskin's idea to make the product white and the packaging a bold orange because it psychologically conveyed the message of powerful cleaning. The white powder suggests cleanliness, but the addition of the bright orange Tide package conveys power and strength (Figure 8-7).

It is a well-known marketing fact that people tend to buy psychological and social satisfaction rather than products. In recent times gaudy and bold packaging has given way to enticing packaging that plays on a consumer's dreams and fantasies. The Ralph Lauren Collection is a brilliant example of successfully marketing a dream—that of moneyed rusticity, the equivalent of designer jeans, a look of instant "old money." Lauren has cleverly marketed tradition to a society that increasingly reflects a desire for security and routine in a world characterized by constant change. Lauren's colors tend to burgundy, forest green, tans, and dark blues, all of which are associated with tradition, money, and security.

Advertisers rely heavily on cultural conditioning in using color. A color that is associated with a certain idea or emotion, if that association is repeated frequently, will become symbolic of the emotion or idea. In our culture, red is generally associated with danger, blue with coolness, green with growth, and yellow with sunny warmth. An awareness of these effects is necessary to avoid undesirable visual communication. In Palo Alto, California, an architect used a blue mosaic around the entrance to his building to provide a cool, refreshing atmosphere. But

The following colors evoke certain feelings within our society but it should be noted that different perceptions vary from culture to culture.

RED signifies strength, vivacity, virility and dynamism. Red is used in advertising to indicate primitive strength, warmth, efficient or the fortifying properties of a product.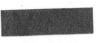

ORANGE expresses radiation and communication. It is the color of action. Receptive and warm, it characterizes a fire burning in the hearth and symbolizes generosity.

YELLOW is the most luminous of all colors. It is the first noticed, the loudest and brightest, although one of the least liked colors. Golden yellow is more tolerated, but greenish yellow is a sickly, unpleasant color to most people.

GREEN symbolizes growth and hope. It is considered a quiet color which has a sunny character when tending toward the yellow green or a more pensive mood when tending toward the blue.

BLUE evokes images of relaxation. It is the most favored color in our culture. Blue expresses an inner spiritual life and symbolizes infinity in its darker shades and a dreamlike quality in its lighter tints.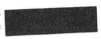

VIOLET is the mysterious color. It is equivalent to meditative and mystical thought. Violet is the color of dignity. In some subcultures within our culture violet symbolizes mourning.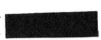

GRAY is a neutral, signifying nothing. It is symbolic of indecision and inertia and is associated with monotony and depression in its darker shades.

figure 8-7

THE HIDDEN MEANINGS IN COLORS

because the entrance to the building was always out of the sun, the combination of shadow, the blue mosaic, and a fountain provided an image that was uninvitingly cold. Another architect, this time in San Francisco, used a very bright red-orange rope barrier system in a restaurant to direct consumers into a buffet line. The architect did not consider, however, that people subconsciously interpreted red as a danger signal. When customers lingered behind the barrier and hesitated to enter the buffet line without considerable encouragement, the restaurant soon removed the red-orange ropes, and business increased.

Much of color's selling power can be traced back to the emotional memories associated with various hues. Color has the power to communicate emotion and the essence of the product inside (Figure 8-8). Without words, color can communicate sexiness, fragility, durability, youth, freshness, and leading-edge concepts. Some colors convey universal messages, while others may vary by ethnicity, region, or socioeconomic background.

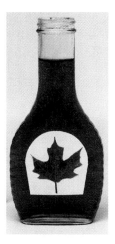

figure 8-8

Sometimes a product itself is its own best advertising, such as this bottle of maple syrup with a simple maple leaf label. Its reddish-brown color says syrup better than anything else could. *© Dorling Kindersley*

Color plays a larger role in the success of a product than the performance of the product itself (Figure 8-9). Butter has to be colored yellow. It will not sell if it is a natural creamy color. Bread does not sell well in green or blue wrappers, but the addition of yellow to the wrapper boosts sales. Candy of all one flavor in assorted colors sells better than candy of one color alone. A product can fail miserably in the marketplace if it is colored unappealingly, even though it may perform remarkably well. A classic commercial application of color was used by an advertising man who persuaded a food chain to rearrange its meat section. The meat had been arranged in white trays set on white cabinets, lighted by an ordinary light, and surrounded by a sawdust-covered floor. This enterprising individual surrounded the meat with various green decorative materials and lit the cabinets with a pink light source. The red of the meat, when

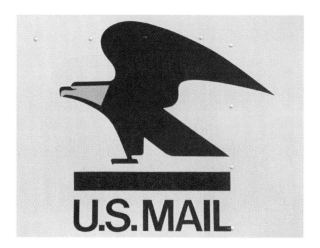

figure 8-9

A brilliantly simple, highly effective sign for the U.S. Postal Service that effortlessly relates reliability, strength, and patriotism. *© Dorling Kindersley*

emphasized by the complementary green surroundings, looked fresher and more appealing. Sales tripled. This use of color juxtaposition is now standard in supermarkets, where complementary colors are used to enhance each other.

Like it or not, we are products of our cultural conditioning, and a large part of that cultural conditioning relates to color. When you reach for an object, are you buying it for its performance or for the hidden color message promising to fulfill your fantasies? Knowing how to interpret those hidden color lures can save you money when you go shopping.

Psychographics

In the world of color, choices about hues, tones, and shades can make or break a product (Figures 8-10 and 8-11). Color is such an important brand recognition factor that in a landmark 1995 decision, the Supreme Court deemed color such a potent brand identifier that a particular shade alone can serve as a legally defensible trademark. Color can challenge the established order of things, drawing fresh attention to an existing product by making it stand out from the crowd, but to do this the product must appeal to the consumer. Some consumers never willingly accept new colors. When so much depends on color choices, the decision to use a particular shade can seem unbearably difficult. Will this year's new color invite or turn away buyers? To help answer that question, marketing surveys attempt to identify psychographic groups. For example, Cooper Marketing Group of Oak Park, Illinois, identified three consumer color preference psychographic groups: color forwards, color prudents, and color loyals. Color forward shoppers tend to be either young and ethnic or higher-income, better-educated women over age forty-five who define themselves by their fashion savvy. They are the most willing to try daring colors. Color prudents are the mainstream. They usually wait for a color to gain acceptance before they adopt it. By the time color prudents accept a new color, it has already passed from avant-garde to mass market. Color loyals resist color change and are usu-

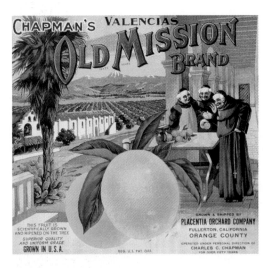

figure 8-10

In the world of color, choices about hues can make or break a product. This label for lemons is colored to attract attention while easily making brand association with the product. © *Dorling Kindersley*

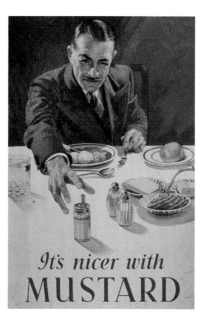

figure 8-11

The golden tones of this vintage ad for Coleman's Mustard subliminally reinforce the advertising message. © *Dorling Kindersley*

ally dragged, kicking and screaming, into new color directions. Most products are geared to color prudents, because they represent average color preferences.

It can be difficult to assess just how people fall into these categories. For example, color forward consumers are not necessarily identifiable by income. Early in the comeback phase for chartreuse, Cooper found the color in three outlets—a French fashion magazine, a Nordstrom's catalog, and a Wal-Mart ice cream dish—proving it no longer true that color comes from the top. The color forward customer wants new and is just as likely to shop at Kmart as at Bergdorf Goodman. Gender is not necessarily a good predictor, either. For example, men tend to be more color forward in the automotive category, which plays up the male tendency to idolize the automobile. Men have been overheard to say how good mud looks against the metallic green of a truck; they can more easily relate to color when it is linked with a product they idealize.

Youth is another huge color divider. Color is even more powerful a stimulant for children than for adults. A Moscowitz and Jacobs study found that for the majority of children, the color of a food product is more important than its taste. Since about 1991, children have loved neon colors, with green and yellow topping the list. When asked to select their favorite color for new products, they choose green. Boys are slightly more likely than girls to take their favorite colors from their favorite sports teams. Children are capable of noticing extremely subtle differences in color related to marketing. When tests were being conducted for a board-game manufacturer, a target audience of girls aged five to seven was selected. They overwhelmingly hated the packaging of a new game called "Perfect Wedding." The pictures on the box showed a brunette bride, an engagement ring, and a picture of a cake-top bridal couple. After studying the problem it was discovered that the cake-top groom's hair looked gray in the picture. Once the hair was changed to a youthful dark color, sales increased. Children have sharp visual acuity and often see things that no adult would notice.

Color marketing is not a simple process. One color or neutral can send different messages to different groups of people. For example, according to a Pantone study, black signifies mystery to 30 percent and power to 27 percent of the public. While 23 percent consider black masculine, 20 percent found it depressing and 18 percent considered it conservative. It is therefore essential to match a given color with the appropriate demographic group the product is trying to appeal to.

Color Preference

Every year a small group sets the palette for consumer goods. This is the Color Marketing Group, a 1,300-member group of design and industry professionals who reach a consensus on color based on socioeconomic and other trends. The result limits consumer choices but allows for better coordination of items across manufacturing. In addition to random selection, the Color Marketing Group also considers color preference surveys in determining its color selections. In a consumer color preference survey, 5,000 consumers were asked questions about cards of 100 numbered colors representing 17 color families. Asked to rate the colors that best convey power, 25 percent of the respondents from the 1997 survey chose scarlet red, 17 percent chose black, and 13 percent chose bright violet blue. More than 55 percent of the sample picked three out of a total of 100 colors. This is a very strong support for the universal meaning of some colors. If all colors were equal, each could be expected to be chosen by 1 percent of respondents. Of the consumers surveyed, 45 percent of participants chose three colors that most represent fragility. Pale pink represented fragility to 27 percent, white to 9 percent, and pale lavender to 9 percent. Preferences also varied by ethnicity. In choosing a color that represented power, whites were more likely to select red, while more African Americans chose black, and Hispanics favored bright blue. Similarly, pale pink was most linked with fragility for whites, while African Americans were more likely to select white. When selecting for romance, black and red were universal favorites. However, there were subtle differences by ethnicity and gender. African American women are more likely to choose gold and silver as romantically attractive; Hispanics are more likely to prefer bright red, orange, or fuschia; and white women favor cobalt blues and pinks.

Respondents to a Pantone Color Institute survey indicated what colors of clothing, home products, and cars they owned and what colors they might choose when they next purchased an item. The results: Blue, red, and black were favored for clothing, with red-violets and blue-greens next in popularity. Beige was the favorite for big-ticket home products such as carpets, upholstered furniture, and paint, with blue gaining in popularity. Economic insecurity may motivate people to choose safe neutrals such as beige for expensive items because they want them to stay in style for a long time. For cars, blue, gray, red, white, and black were the most popular, with blue-green gaining fast. Interestingly, the survey found no strong regional color preferences. This was attributed to the effects of mass media. Fashion magazines, catalogs, television, and megachains all present the same options.

Naming Color

Another issue to consider in color marketing is the name associated with the color. If color can make or break a product, the name can make or break the color. When paint manufacturer Benjamin Moore changed the name of its ivory shade to "antique silk," the color went from twentieth to sixth in sales volume in two years. When industry recycles color it invents new names to make the color seem new and fresh. Chartreuse may seem dated, but calling it limone gives it a fresh new edge. Other old colors with updated names include salmon mousse (soft orange), Creole spice (terra cotta to copper), ragin' Cajun (earthy red), antique bear (golden brown), iceberg blue (purplish blue), green bayou (blue-green), fortune teller (neutral metallic gray-silver), and macabre (plum-black). Such names evoke immediate emotional response and are essential to sales of everything from nail polish to cars. Doubtless you would rather tell a friend you just painted your living room Sahara sand rather than number 3457 or plain old beige.

Because of the strong emotional associations of words, consumer color preference surveys are conducted by identifying the colors with numbers rather than words. In 1994 and 1995, Pantone and Roper Starch Worldwide asked 2,000 consumers for their color preferences. The study found that blues were in vogue, greens were on the rise, and oranges were out. Young adults aged 18 to 29 favored bright and deep colors, while those aged 45 and older preferred pastels and candy colors. Blue was the number one color. It has always been America's favorite, with a soft, sky blue proving particularly popular among men.

Packaging

Mass communications theorist Marshall McLuhan revealed the secrets of media manipulation in his works *Understanding Media* (1964) and *The Medium Is the Message* (1967). The observations of the people he termed "the frogmen of the mind" were deployed to manipulate the consumer. Their findings were confident: "People have so much to choose from that they want help—they like the package that hypnotizes them into picking it ... it takes the average woman exactly 20 seconds to walk along a supermarket aisle without pausing, so a good package design should hypnotize her like a flashlight waved in front of her eyes. Colors such as red and yellow are helpful in creating such hypnotic effects." It has been said that when you work with colors, you work on the subsymbolic level (Figure 8-12). There is a hierarchy of communication. At the top are high-order symbols such as words. Next there are illustrations and overt symbols such as crowns, and crosses. Then there is the subsymbol world of color, which is so primitive that color reactions may be closer to physiology than perception.

Dr. Max Lüscher, while a professor of psychology at Basle University, worked on the effects of color on the human mind to test his belief that colors have emotional value and that a person's color preferences reveal basic personality traits (Figure 8-13). It is accepted as doctrine in the advertising industry that color is one of the most important means by which an impression can be created. It is no secret that colors from the long-wavelength end of the spectrum, primarily yellow and red, seem to leap out at the eye. Because red appears to advance, it can make a package look larger and more visible than a neighboring blue one. Red is intrusive and attention-getting. Most "sale" tags are in red, yellow, or a

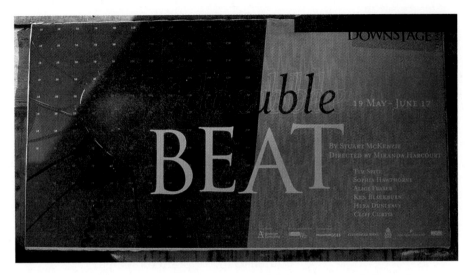

figure 8-12

This advertising sign portrays two powerful images to reinforce its message—a strong red color and the beating heart. © *Dorling Kindersley*

combination of the two. Orange is particularly common on baked goods packaging. Combinations of yellow, red, orange, and blue are often used for cleaning products because they create an energetic impression.

The advertising industry has spent a great deal of money running surveys on preferred colors broken down by age, gender, race, income bracket, and so on. It has been found that primary colors and bright colors appeal to lower-income consumers, who make few purchases and prefer each one to stand out as much as possible. Pastels and neutrals appeal to upscale, sophisticated consumers. Dark colors appeal to older people and to men. Greens, blues, and bluish reds appeal to women and

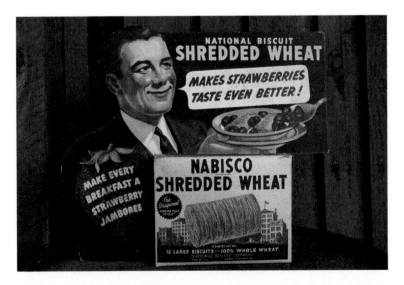

figure 8-13

Red is intrusive and attention-getting, something well known to the designer of this Nabisco Shredded Wheat advertisement. The blue-and-white packaging also sends a subliminal message of wholesomeness. © *Dorling Kindersley*

are used on cosmetics and skin care preparations. Violet and purple are reserved for especially luxurious products such as jewelry or expensive chocolates. Black, silver, gold, and sometimes white are also linked with luxury, as well as with technology.

Once the customers' attention has been attracted, the package must make them feel good about what they are buying. If the product is expensive, it must look worth the cost. Whenever goods are competitively priced, a more attractive package can make the crucial difference in clinching the sale. Cigarettes provide extravagant examples of the importance of color in packaging. Blindfold tests have proved that some smokers cannot tell one brand from another without the packaging.

People may think they never notice ads, but in fact the ads register at the periphery of consciousness. Tests reveal that the gaze of the consumer glancing along a supermarket shelf rests on each package for less than three-hundredths of a second. In that fraction of time, packaging experts must not only attract attention but also convey content and plant the desire to buy deep in the shoppers' subconscious. Products can have their sales careers made or broken literally in a split second. In advertising and packaging, colors call attention, impart information, and create lasting identity. The object is always the same—to sell the product.

Lüscher developed a test based on color that he claims can reveal personality traits by the analysis of individual preference for, dislike of, or indifference to certain colors. Lüscher proposes that colors have objective psychological significance and from this he has derived what he describes as the "psychological primaries"—greenish blue, red, yellow, and dark blue. Applying his theories to packaging, Lüscher devised a color range he considered psychologically effective. He suggested that package colors correspond to the real or imagined need that the product fulfills. Products offering security, for example, should be packaged in dark blue, while those whose promise is the enhancement of life should be in red packs. Lüscher proposed that a package in the colors of the psychological primaries creates a subliminal need for the complementaries, because the mind responds to color as a whole. For example, a package of a greenish blue color would cause a deep psychological craving for the color red. Greenish blue is a common color for men's aftershaves and may create an inner desire for yellowish red, a color to which Lüscher ascribes masculine characteristics.

A survey of the most successful brands on the market seems to bear out Lüscher's theories, yet few packaging designers claim any knowledge of them. Their choices seem to be intuitive and aided by long experience of trial and error. Lüscher describes many poor choices in packaging that have hurt product sales: pepper in a sky-blue pack instead of the brilliant yellowish red that suggests heat and strength; caffeine-free coffee in a red pack that indicates strength; a grayish-violet color that symbolizes decay for a canned meat label.

One of the world's first mass-produced food products was Heinz baked beans. It was packaged in a greenish-blue can, yet it sold very successfully. Greenish-blue, according to Lüscher, corresponds to a need for clarity and certainty. His theory is that this color is an expression of firmness and resistance to change. The person who places a greenish blue high on the color preference list values possessions as symbols of both security and self-esteem. One of the best-known symbols in the world is the red label of Coca Cola. While it might seem more appropriate to package a cool, refreshing drink in blue, the sparkling red of Coke labels practically screams youth, zest, energy, and life-giving properties, not to mention a caffeine jolt. Kodak is so renowned for its yellow and red logo that the color is sometimes referred to as Kodak yellow. It is one of the most successful packages in advertising history.

Color Symbolism in Signage

Color provides immediate information and has been used for centuries to help in product or location recognition. The red-and-white-striped poles outside barber shops or the glass bottles filled with colored liquids in apothecary shops were immediate advertisements as to what service was available. These early examples of signage were very effective and directed at a largely illiterate public for whom alphabetical signage would have had little or no meaning. Today we still rely on color coding for signage. Blue and white designates handicapped facilities, a green curb means limited parking, a white zone means passenger drop, yellow curbs indicate loading zones, and red zones mean no parking. In England black and white "zebra crossings" indicate pedestrian crosswalks.

Color is one of the most important aspects of visual communication. It can be used to catch the eye or communicate ideas and feelings. Contrasting hues lend power to visual communication. The strongest contrasts occur between complementary colors, or colors that are opposites on the color wheel. However, complementary colors do not always provide the best legibility. Red and green are complementary colors, but while a red message on a green background may attract attention, the flicker effect it causes makes it very difficult to keep in focus. Legibility and contrast are influenced more by value than by hue. Any combination of colors with similar values will provide low visibility. While the combination of red and green is very hard to read, a combination of yellow and purple provides a strong value contrast and therefore is very legible. **The most readable color combinations in descending order are black on yellow, black on white, yellow on black, and white on black** (Figure 8-14). (This is something to keep in mind for Web site text designs, many of which are unreadable.)

The value of color for visual communication was demonstrated by Patty and Vredenburg (1970) in a study of recall of electric signs. They found that colors were not only important in attracting attention but also were a significant factor in memory retention over time, although it was also discovered that too many colors confuse and negate memory-building effectiveness.

An important thing to remember about color in relation to humans is that our bodies constantly seek to restore equilibrium. If we are presented with a situation that causes a state of unbalance, we naturally try to restore balance as quickly as possible. This is particularly true when dealing with color, as stated by Johannes Itten, German painter and instructor at the Bauhaus:

> *Harmony implies balance, symmetry of forces. ....If we gaze for some time at a green square and then close our eyes, we see, as an after-image, a red square. ....This experiment may be repeated with any color, and the after-image always turns out to be of the complementary color. The eye posits the complementary color; it seeks to restore equilibrium of itself.*

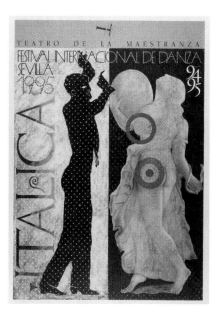

figure 8-14

Black and white create one of the most easily read combinations. The addition of the red circles brings an air of eroticism. © *Dorling Kindersley*

The physiological reason for the phenomenon of **afterimage** is that on the retina of the eye the cone receptors that register the yellow and blue wavelengths tire after prolonged exposure to green, and when faced with a neutral background they temporarily function less efficiently than the other receptors. The result is that the neutral background is perceived predominantly by those cones that register the wavelengths of red.

Color in Print Media and Web Site Design

The advent of true commercial color printing was brought about by the development of cost-effective photographic processes and the improvement of ink. In printing the problem has always been to find an ink that is transparent enough not to block off the color in which it has been laid but dense enough to reproduce a color accurately. Modern offset lithography, so called because the image is "offset" onto a rubber roller before being transferred to the paper, owes a debt of gratitude to the ink manufacturers. Because the roller has to be moistened before ink is applied, the difficulty had been to obtain a proper balance of ink on every impression. Modern, highly concentrated inks have not only solved the problem but also met the stringent demands of food manufacturers for print on packaging that is light-fast, scuff-resistant, odorless, nontoxic, and able to withstand boiling and freezing conditions. Today's inks can handle virtually any surface, from plastic to cardboard to metal, and they largely account for the explosion of color in packaging that took place in the 1960s.

The proliferation of color television in homes nationwide put great pressure on printers to keep up with the deluge of color that consumers had come to expect. Magazines, books, posters, and all the eye-catching handouts at the supermarket had to appear as colorful and be competitive with TV commercials as much as possible. But a costly impediment still stood in the way: the lengthy process of hand-correcting color on a negative before the printing plate was made. At the time there was no alternative. A blue shirt advertised in a catalog had to look the right color of blue in print. Because it was easier to color-correct a drawing than a photograph, more than 90 percent of book covers before the 1960s were hand-drawn. Electronic scanners changed everything. They provided the ability to scan in an original transparency, remove any unwanted color in specific areas, and produce a perfect four-color film ready for platemaking in a matter of minutes, without any of the telltale brush-marks that had often been visible in hand-corrected color.

Color Separation in Printing

We see masses of color in print every day and have come to take it for granted, but the process of producing it is quite complicated. An image that is to be printed in full color first has to be separated into three images, each containing one of the transparent ink colors: yellow, magenta, and cyan (Figure 8-15). These are translated onto three printing plates, with black as the fourth in a four-color printing process. The separations are made by photographing the image through three filters of red, green, and blue. With a blue filter, red and green light are absorbed and only blue is transmitted, producing a negative with a record of the yellow content of the image contained in the light areas. A positive will reverse these light areas into solid areas of yellow. The same process is repeated with red and green filters to produce magenta and cyan separations. A fourth, black separation is usually made from a yellow filter.

Once the original image has been separated into positives of yellow, magenta, cyan, and black, the positives are ready to be screened. Glass screens consist of a finely ruled grid pattern placed between the camera's lens and the film. Contact screens consist of a pattern of vignetted dots that is placed in direct contact with the unexposed film. The image is photographed through the screen, which essentially breaks down the image into thousands of tiny dots, small in the light areas and larger in the dark. These result in gradations or *halftones*, which is also the name of the process. These dots are then engraved on plates, one of each of the primary colors and usually one black plate. The plates are superimposed one on the other during the printing process to reproduce the original image in full color.

While we have come a long way with inks and paper, we still do not have the capability of reproducing color perfectly. Halftones give the impression of solid color but an enlargement reveals that a halftone is really composed of millions of tiny dots. These are mixed by the eye of the observer to form the expected color. A similar effect was achieved with the painting technique known as **pointillism** that was employed by such artists as Seurat.

Color in Web Site Design

The human eye is capable of seeing more than ten million colors. In contrast, at the present time only 256 colors are available in Web browsers and only 216 colors are common to all Web browsers. The images you see on the Web are getting their colors from the browser software. If the image contains colors that don't exist on the browser, the software tries to mix the color from the 256 available colors. It tries to patch tiny dots (pixels) of its colors together to make it look like the color it's trying to replicate. This is called **dithering**. Web site designers should use caution

Yellow Plate

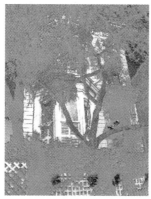

Magenta Plate

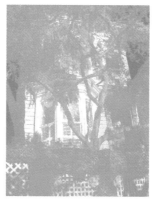

Cyan Plate

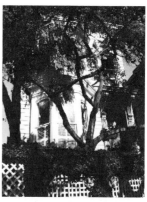

Black Plate

Yellow Plate

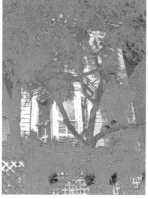

Yellow & Magenta Plates

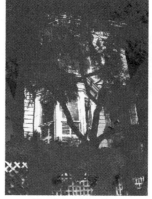

Yellow, Magenta & Cyan Plates

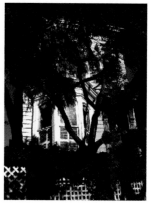

Yellow, Magenta, Cyan & Black Plates

figure 8-15

COLOR SEPARATION IN THE PRINTING PROCESS

An image that is to be printed in full color first has to be separated into three images, each containing one of the transparent ink colors yellow, magenta, and cyan. These are translated onto three printing plates, with black as a fourth, making up the four-color printing process. The separations are made by photographing the image through three filters of red, green, and blue. With a blue filter, red and green light are absorbed and only blue is transmitted, producing a negative with a record of the yellow content of the image contained in the light areas. A positive will reverse these light areas into solid areas of the yellow. The same process is repeated with red and green filters to produce magenta and cyan separations. A fourth, black separation is usually made from a yellow filter.

when selecting background colors and text colors. Some computer systems may read these backgrounds as so speckled that the text becomes unreadable. For example, if you had red, yellow, and blue paint and you needed green paint, you could select yellow and blue, mix the paints together, and come up with green. Web browser software can't mix colors together in the same way. The browser brain is digital, meaning that it is computing numbers to arrive at the colors. The software brain has to make a lot of little dots to create a color that exists outside of the 256-color range, resulting in tiny speckles of color instead of a solid color.

The images you see on the Web are either GIF or JPEG images. These acronyms refer to the computer language that is working within the graphic images. Some graphic images speak GIF and some speak JPEG.

The GIF or JPEG images can be viewed by all computer operating systems—PCs, Macintosh, and Unix. They also contain color information and this information is based on RGB, or how much R (red), G (green), and B (blue) is in the image.

As stated in Chapter 2, *gamma* is one of the most difficult computer terms to define. It is, essentially, a measurement tool for color. Gamma is also a mathematical formula that reflects a relationship between input and output and describes a critical relationship between electricity and what happens on your monitor. To be as succinct as possible, gamma is a mathematical formula that describes the relationship between the voltage input and the brightness of the image on your monitor screen. Gamma can also be described as a measurement of contrast that affects the midtones of an image. Usually, gamma measurements range from 1.0 to 3.0, with different systems having different gamma measurements. An effective gamma rating will deliver true colors and a good range of light, middle, and dark tones. Some computers such as the Macintosh come equipped with automatic gamma correction and provide optimally accurate color. Colors viewed at uncorrected gamma appear different from those viewed at corrected gamma by way of lightness and darkness differences, tonal differences, and color differences.

Let's consider an example of corrected versus uncorrected gamma. Suppose we want to view a color that is 50 percent red and 25 percent green. If this is viewed on a computer system with uncorrected gamma, it may show as 18 percent red and 3 percent green. There is less green and the color has shifted toward red. It will also look darker. Differences in gamma create an alteration of colors that may cause some colors to shift toward yellow, while others may lose their green tones and look bluer. Each color is individually altered.

You might ask why all computers can't render color the same way. The International Color Consortium is evaluating the differences in computer color, and it is hoped that in the future a simplified standard for computer color will be developed.

REFERENCES

Albers, J., *Interaction of Color*, Yale University Press, 1971.

Birren, F., *Color Psychology and Color Therapy*, Citadel Press, 1978.

Brochmann, O., *Good or Bad Design?* Studio Vista, 1970.

Color Engineering, Chromatic Publishing Co.

Color Research and Application, John Wiley & Sons.

Itten, J., *The Art of Color*, Reinhold, 1966.

Patty, C. R., Vredenburg, H. L., *Electric Signs: Contribution to the Communications Spectrum*, Rohm and Haas, 1970.

Color in fashion and textile design

Chapter nine

Color Symbolism in Apparel

The colors of fashion mirror the spirit of the time. Their changes reflect the changing influences at work on society, from the religious symbolism of the Middle Ages that dictated the popularity of red as a symbol of courage, to later centuries when the reigning monarch dictated what was fashionable and stylish. The color of clothing has complex meanings rooted deep in history. The psychology of color in dress is studied in great detail by costume designers, who use it in the interpretation of the characters they dress. A good costume designer knows that the color of the costume makes its presence felt more rapidly than the form of the garment. The Woody Allen film *Interiors* illustrates a great example of color in relation to character. The depressed and suicidal characters in the movie consistently wore drab neutrals, while the emotionally healthy character wore vibrant, lively colors. The contrast was startling. We believe *Interiors* depicts one of the most brilliantly symbolic uses of color in film. If color can have such an impact in theatrical design, what does your clothing say about you? To better understand the hidden meanings of color in apparel, we must first understand it in a historical context.

Alchemy and the Christian church were essential influences on color use in the Middle Ages. In fact, many alchemical symbols were adapted from church doctrine. In the drably colored world of the Middle Age populace, the church was the center of life and a dominant force. All the important occasions in life were linked to the church, from baptism to funeral. The richly colored stained glass of religious buildings was probably the most splendid color that common Europeans had the opportunity to see. Not only did they illustrate familiar biblical scenes, but their colors depicted older traditions, such as the green of spring and the golden colors of autumn harvest.

The colors of church vestments hold strong symbolic associations. White and gold are worn at Christmas and Easter, representing purity. Red is worn at Pentecost and the feasts of the martyrs. The red robes of cardinals symbolize blood and the reminder that blood may be shed to defend the church. Green vestments represent hope and vitality, reminding the faithful of God's bounty. Purple symbolizes Lent and penance and was the most sacred and royal color from earliest times, partly because it was a very difficult color to obtain. Purple, being a mixture of blue, symbolizing spirit, and red, symbolizing blood, represents both the divinity and humanity of Christ.

Outside the church, other forms of color symbolism prevailed. In medieval times people believed that the world was composed of four basic elements—earth, air, fire, and water—each of which had its distinctive hue. Black represented earth, white was for water, red symbolized fire, and yellow the air. In the human body of medieval times, black represented bile, white phlegm, yellow the spleen, and red blood. Medical practitioners of the day thought it essential to maintain a balance between these elements. The Chinese had a color system even older than that of Europeans. In China there were five elements instead of four: earth, water, wood, metal, and fire. They were represented by yellow, white, black, blue-green, and red, respectively. Each element and color corresponded to an animal, a part of the body, a season, a planet, and a cardinal point of the compass, with Earth in the center.

In Europe, color symbolism reached its apex in the Middle Ages and then soon lost much of its influence. In Elizabethan times and beyond, green was used for bridal gowns to symbolize fertility, based on the greening of spring. The symbolism became debased when green gradually came to stand for the loss of virginity represented by grass stains on a virgin's garment. Such subtle variations have all but vanished from the language, but colors still possess enormous powers of suggestion and continue to have great influence, especially in fashion.

Color Trends in Fashion

Many influences come to bear on the colors of fashion. During the sixteenth and seventeenth centuries, the dark tones in dress painted by artists such as Holbein and Caravaggio inspired contemporary fashion colors in dress, while the influence of the clear, delicate, pastel tones of eighteenth-century painters was evidenced in interior decoration as well as in costume. New interpretations of color attributed to Renoir, Monet, Pissarro, and Sisley had a great influence on the colors of clothes between 1860 and 1885. Even today, fashion is influenced by movements in art or by great art exhibitions, such as the Tutankhamen exhibit that influenced fashion and jewelry design of the 1920s, or the 1960s remake of the film *Cleopatra* that regenerated Egyptian hairstyles.

For decades the French court was the undisputed leader in European fashion. Then when Worth, the Empress's couturier, began designing for foreign aristocrats in 1855, Paris became the center of the world fashion trade. It remained so for decades, only to be challenged by the glamour of Hollywood and the allure of movie stars when Jean Harlow created a craze for platinum blond hair and James Dean gave new meaning to black leather jackets. Black has continued to be a constant among the revolutionary young, with the notable exception of the sixties' "flower children," who were captured by color, the brighter the better.

Once, technology dictated trends in fashion. Only royalty could wear purple because the cost of producing the dye was exorbitant. Now, the availability of textiles and dyes is virtually endless, and we depend on other trends to influence the colors of fashion. One of the most important influences comes from color consultants, who have a marked effect on the colors that are available to the consumer. Color associations such as the Color Marketing Group meet internationally to decide which colors to use for the seasons ahead. This allows coordination between clothing, makeup, accessories, and jewelry. Because the influential apparel fashion fields change faster than the home furnishings, automotive, or kitchen appliance industries, it is usually the textile manufacturers who make early crucial decisions as to color. Working about six months ahead of each launch season, they arrive at their color collections and seasonal color buzzwords such as "oyster" or "eggplant" or "jewel tones" to promote their ideas and appeal to the consumer.

At least twice each year in Paris, Milan, New York, and London, makers of cotton, silk, wool, and synthetics meet with design and color consultants from all over the world and with members of such organizations as the American Color Marketing Group or the British Colour Council, as well as with designers, manufacturers, and retailers. The mass-market fashion world is not a place for the loner. The investments required are so great that accessories and cosmetics produced by different manufacturers must coordinate to promote national and international sales trends.

Color consultants bring their ideas and interpretations with little color cards of custom-dyed yarn. The dyers will have worked from ideas as abstract as a photograph, a tear sheet from a magazine, an object, or a scrap of old fabric—essentially anything the color consultant could find to suggest the desired new colors. Remarkably, time after time the color cards brought from all over the world are already so attuned that only slight adjustments are necessary. How does this happen? The ideas for a new season's colors generally grow out of the existing popular palette. They assimilate the impact of everything from media events, such as a hit film, book, or major art exhibition, to living trends, such as an increased desire for health or physical activity, smaller apartments, or a return to the country, to economics, such as recession or inflationary trends. The initial ideas must then be made feasible by considering the cost. For example, red pigments are costlier than earth pigments, so red clothing may cost more to produce than beige clothing. Other factors considered when adopting a color might include limiting the number of variables in pattern or color to prevent problems with color matching, making sure the dyes are suitable to the fibers selected, and envisioning the way the color will look when massed on clothing racks in stores. Color is the first thing to capture a shopper's attention.

Twentieth-Century Color in Apparel

Turn of the Century

In the twenty-first century, some of us may look back fondly at the turn of the twentieth century, when the influence of London's Great Exhibition of 1851 created an icon of technology, with which we soon fell in love. The colors, the wonderful gadgets, and the promise of the future loomed high on the horizon and people faced the new twentieth century with hope and perhaps a little awe. The late Victorian era's somber colors of mourning gradually gave way to the delicate colors of Art Nouveau (Figure 9-1). Replacing the maroons, purples, and black of

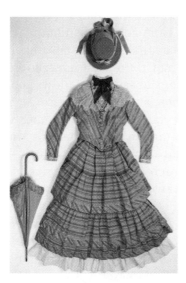

figure 9-1

Example of an average woman's dress from the mid-nineteenth century, indicating the typical somber color of the time. © *Dorling Kindersley*

the nineteenth century were the favorite new colors taken from the delicate tints of the sweet pea. Girls wore white, and mature women wore mauve, a newly developed color dye that became the rage. Women's shoes and stockings were always black in the city—cotton stockings for the poor, silk for the rich. Brown shoes were reserved for the country, with serviceable lisle stockings to match. The favorite accessory of the era was the feather boa dyed to match the outfit, and the favorite fur was pale gray chinchilla. Daytime wear was primarily white, pale gray, or beige. In the evening the pastel sweet pea tints were supplemented by brilliant sequins and white, elbow-length gloves. Men's clothes were somber. Suits were formal and dark. Black suits were worn with black top hats to do business in the city. Women were expected to be fragile, and men protective.

In June of 1909 the Ballets Russes arrived in Paris and changed everything. Instead of pastel tints, the Russian artists who designed the sets and costumes for the Diaghilev ballets used brilliant primary colors in wild combinations unknown to Europe. Canary yellows, bright blues, jades, and shades of fuchsia were favored in Léon Bakst's sets and costume designs. The exotic, erotic images he created with the widest range of colors ever seen on the European stage were an immediate sensation. Mustards, violets, yellows, and blues suddenly became popular in daytime dress. Within a year, cosmetics, fashion, and home decor were completely changed (Figure 9-2). Picasso, Matisse, Braque, and Utrillo designed set decorations and costumes for the Ballets Russes. Cartier began setting emeralds and sapphires together, and Fortuny designed pleated dresses dyed in glowing jewel tones. Fashion designer Paul Poiret seemed ahead of the trend when he designed the first of his revolutionary high-waisted gowns in 1905. By exchanging the corseted **S**-curve figure in favor of a natural outline, Poiret liberated the female form. His bold and unusual colors, including canary yellows, bright

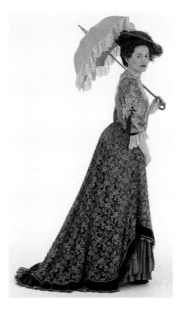

figure 9-2

Continuing into 1900, colors in fashion were still quite subdued, favoring primarily white, pale gray, or beige. © *Dorling Kindersley*

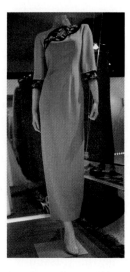

Even the average woman's daywear around 1910 began to show a preference for color, while trendsetters embraced colors influenced by Leon Bakst's Ballets Russes, which drew inspiration from oriental influences such as the sleek silhouette and bold colors as shown in this parrot green cheongsam. © *Dorling Kindersley*

blues, jade greens, and fuschias, predated the colorful trend set by the Ballets Russes (Figure 9-3). Poiret's designs were often trimmed or executed in black, and black kohl rimmed the eyes of his exotic models. To accompany his new look, Poiret introduced short hairstyles topped by a turban with a tall aigrette.

How strange it must have been for the soldiers returning home from World War I. When they left, their mothers, wives, and sisters were in long, tight hobble skirts with tightly corseted waists. Now they wore full skirts in which they could freely move and even show off their feet and ankles—body parts that had not been seen for decades in polite society (Figure 9-4). Painted faces also arrived about this time. Suddenly, cosmetics were not just for ladies of the evening. With the introduction of rouge in 1911 "to protect a lady's skin against the coarsening effects of sun, wind, and dust" from motoring, cosmetics gradually became socially acceptable for all women. In 1912 *Vogue* magazine legitimized the use of cosmetics in its pages, and the first American lipsticks in slide tubes appeared about 1915.

The Twenties

By the early 1920s, people were becoming tired of the bright, exotic colors introduced by the Ballets Russes. Women were also becoming emancipated and venturing into entirely new areas of sport, flying, and careers. Chanel was the driving force behind the subdued neutrals of the 1920s (Figure 9-5). It has been said that she chose beige for her salon to use up an abundance of army surplus material that she acquired cheaply, but, whatever her motivation, she stood the fashion world on its ear by borrowing from the understated elegance of gentlemen's tailored clothes to create her slim skirts and collarless tweed jackets woven in subtle shades of beige. She introduced flesh-toned stockings and pale beige shoes with toes and heels of black to emphasize the length of the leg. She

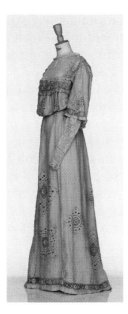

figure 9-4

This linen dress dating from 1911 shows a looser, less constrictive silhouette, allowing for more freedom of movement than in the Victorian era. © *Dorling Kindersley*

designed simple pullover sweaters in pale tints worn with magnificently opulent costume jewelry in emerald greens and ruby reds.

Nights on the town in the twenties were gleaming occasions set off by pale, lustrous satins, crepes, silks, velvets, and taffetas trimmed with gilt lace, rhinestones, and beads. Bracelets and rings encircled with diamonds were the height of fashion, and owning a string of pearls became

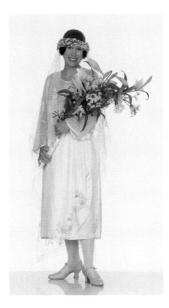

figure 9-5

This 1920s bridal gown features the dropped-waist silhouette typical of the period. © *Dorling Kindersley*

a must for every fashion-conscious woman. Also in vogue was black-and-white jewelry made from unusual materials, such as rock crystal or black onyx set with diamonds and mounted in white gold, silver, or platinum.

Film star Jean Harlow influenced fashion with her platinum blond hair, red lips, and sultry image. By 1924 it was estimated that 50 million American women were using 3,000 miles of lipstick a year. Soon after, red nail polish became popular. By 1929 men wanted equal time, and a group of men in London formed the Men's Dress Reform Party to try to establish more colorful and comfortable fashions for men. They suggested replacing trousers with tunics or with one-piece zippered suits. While this seemed too far-fetched to gain much popularity, the group did succeed in establishing shorts for tennis or the beach as appropriate apparel for men.

The Thirties

Actor and dancer Ginger Rogers epitomized the 1930s in her films with Fred Astaire. The pale colors of the twenties continued in favor for a while, but color slowly began returning to fashion by 1934 (Figure 9-6). Pale evening dresses in crepe, matelassé (a pure silk with a crinkled surface), or ciré (lacquered satin) were worn with long, dark gloves. Hats and gloves of brightly patterned material were added to plain suits and dresses, and floral patterns returned. Certain color schemes of the thirties are distinctive to the period and have rarely been seen since. Cocoa brown with hyacinth blue, prune with turquoise, and mustard yellow with gray are characteristic of the period (Figure 9-7).

The year 1930 ushered in an event as influential as the Ballets Russes had been to the turn of the century. The Museum of Modern Art in New York exhibited works by Van Gogh to such an explosion of interest that the doors had to be closed. Suddenly, sunflower prints were everywhere,

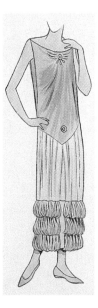

figure 9-6

A 1930s shift continues the long lines of the 1920s. Movie star glamour was the rage, although the Great Depression made that unavailable to most of the population except in movie daydreams. © *Dorling Kindersley*

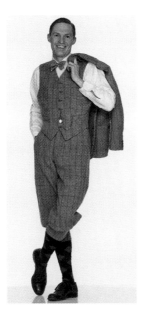

figure 9-7

This example of men's country attire in the 1920s and 1930s shows the colorful argyll socks that were so popular at the time for casual wear.
© Dorling Kindersley

and fabrics appeared in bright yellows, greens, blues, and browns taken from Van Gogh's color palette. Another influential designer of the period was Schiaparelli, who transformed ideas culled from London's Surrealist Exhibition of 1936. With the help of Salvador Dalí, she designed a hat shaped like a shoe and launched a vivid new color, "shocking pink," which was intended to fulfill its name.

World War II

By 1940, most of the world was at war. The February issue of *Vogue* magazine dedicated a few paragraphs to color in fashion. "Dusty lime … cherry red, tulip pink and orchid mauve; shrill peacock blue; much yellow; much gray … this is the spring palette divided between smoky pastels and clear bright colors. As war goes on it may be more difficult to get the strong dark shades of navy, brown, gray and black because they use up such a quantity of dye; but if we're reduced to pastels—so much the gayer." Strong colors became morale-boosters: gray and red, yellow and brown or black, navy or black with red (Figure 9-8). Soon the square-shouldered military silhouette was translated into khaki or olive and became the standard for most women. Because of a shortage of dyes, colors became subdued. Bright reds became muted plums, while the lime greens yellowed, and faded blacks, grays, and browns predominated.

Wartime Paris made up for drab colors and uniformity by inventing extraordinary hats with flowers and ribbons and adding color in accessories whenever possible. The United States had been cut off from Paris during the war and turned to South America and Polynesia for inspiration, choosing bright scarlets, yellows, and magentas favored by Mexicans. By 1947, with the war at an end, Christian Dior had created his revolutionary New Look in soft, gentle colors with yards of skirt made possible by the availability of postwar goods.

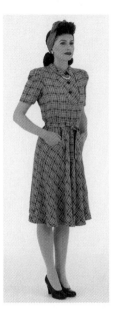

World War II brought big shoulders and short skirts. © *Dorling Kindersley*

The Fabulous Fifties

The 1950s reveled in color: green, turquoise, pale yellow, amethyst, lilac, pink, and soft red. Most evening dresses were strapless affairs that defied gravity, held in place by cleverly boned bodices. Dior became noted for his elaborate jewelry designs to match: emeralds or peridots with green, turquoises or sapphires with blues, topaz with yellows, and tourmalines with pink. He also introduced Italian stiletto-heeled shoes in matching colors (Figure 9-9).

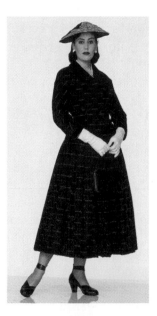

Dior's "New Look" featured small waists and full skirts, often with the oriental influence of a "coolie" hat. © *Dorling Kindersley*

In fashion, the matching ensemble was of primary importance in the early to mid-fifties. A billowing wrap or semifitted coat in taffeta or satin opened to reveal a slim dress of the same fabric and color, but often rich with an allover design. Colors were brilliant: green, turquoise, pale yellow, amethyst, lilac, pink, and geranium. Until the fifties, turquoise dyes were of inferior quality and stability. In 1951 the Bayer Company in Germany perfected Alcian (kingfisher) blue, the first fast turquoise dye for cotton. The color immediately became a fashion sensation.

During the fifties, Italian design based in Florence began to rival the designs from Paris. Pucci and Simonetta designed in magnificent fabrics and showed their collections in Renaissance palazzos. Hot pink was the color of the decade. The hot pink silk fashions launched by Jacques Fath in 1951 were so popular that the next year an even brighter "very hot pink" surfaced. This color was promoted by *Vogue*, not without controversy, but became a runaway hit in fashions for the home as well as on the runway. In fact, the fifties were so engrossed in pink that the 1956 musical film *Funny Face*, starring Audrey Hepburn and Fred Astaire, included a song, "Think Pink," that spoofed the decade. By 1955 even men's shirts had turned pink, promoted even by the conservative Brooks Brothers. By this time cosmetics had become so commonplace that even schoolgirls wore some makeup. Revlon's massive advertising campaigns for its Paint the Town Pink and Fire and Ice lipsticks and nail polish were wildly successful, so much so that they sparked the seasonal advertising we have grown accustomed to, with new cosmetic colors introduced for spring and fall.

Color even invaded the wardrobe of the conventional male during the 1950s. The colorful shirts of American tourists started a fashion trend internationally, while the intellectuals and artists of London attempted to revive Edwardian fashion. This fad was taken up by British working-class youths who called themselves Teddy boys and dressed in elongated jackets of light blue, silver, or gold lamé with high, stiff velvet collars worn over tight black stovepipe trousers and suede shoes. Soon even conventional male dressers were seen in dinner jackets of dark blue, green, or burgundy velvet.

The craze for rock and roll brought forth full, circular skirts covered with musical motifs such as appliquéd felt records or music notes, barely concealing layers of ruffled petticoats ranging from white to hot pink and, occasionally, rainbow hues.

The Psychedelic Sixties

Taking a bird's-eye view of the first half of the twentieth century, colorists in the sixties might have chosen to revive neutrals as a backlash against the colorful fifties. Instead, they exploded with color in a way never before seen, partly made possible by the new and dramatic range of cotton reactive dyes developed in the previous decade. In combination with the growing range of synthetic drip-dry fabrics, it became possible to color everything—from underwear to plastics—in brilliant hues (Figure 9-10).

While couturiers continued to develop collections in their own color palettes, such as Saint Laurent's muted tones of 1966, the ethnic look overwhelmed fashion and was adopted by hippies as their own (Figure

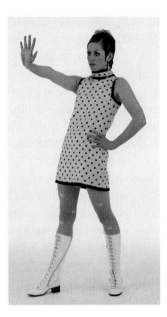

figure 9-10 The 1960s changed everything, including fashion. The miniskirt had never before been seen, and there was a strong "space age" influence in fashion for the first time. © *Dorling Kindersley*

9-11). Young people were trooping off to Nepal and Morocco, bringing back with them colorful fabrics, clothing, and jewelry. Long-haired flower children appeared in brilliantly colored Afghan dresses, Indonesian batik skirts, and caftans. Men wore Nehru jackets, Mao jackets, and Arabic djellabas. Silver jewelry studded with turquoise, coral, and amber was the rage, as were "love beads" worn strand on strand.

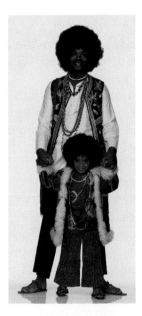

figure 9-11 The Hippie Movement of the 1960s and 1970s caused a revolution in fashion including brightly colored clothing and patterns borrowed from ethnic dress. © *Dorling Kindersley*

Suddenly, bejeweled men appeared in colors that would have been unheard of a few years earlier. Casual sport shirts in dazzlingly colored abstract designs became the norm. In America and then worldwide, blue jeans became a classic.

The drug scene had a great influence on color use as many artists and designers followed Timothy Leary's advice to "turn on, tune in, drop out." Mind-expanding psychedelic drugs inspired a new color awareness popularized by the Beatles' *Yellow Submarine* film of 1968. Peasant skirts richly embroidered in overlaid colors were paired with velvet jackets, tall boots, and body painting (Figure 9-12). Street fashion was "in." British designers such as Mary Quant and Zandra Rhodes interpreted the fads and trends of Swinging London's Carnaby Street for the masses. Courreges introduced a short skirt in 1964. Within two years Mary Quant had reinvented it as the revolutionary miniskirt. Op Art influenced fashion, bringing with it stark black-and-white geometric designs in clothing, shoes, and makeup. Soon, translations into color followed, with double-knit fabrics appearing in combinations of lime with bright pink, orange and purple, or yellow and blue—virtually any imaginable combination of colors. Sixties fashions drew from the past, brought ethnicity to the forefront, and thrust themselves into the space age with an explosive force typical of the decade. Even airlines got the color habit, with Braniff International Airways painting its jets in brightly colored psychedelic patterns.

The only thing pale about the sixties was cosmetics. The sixties' face was radically different from that of the fifties. Fifties makeup focused on red or brightly colored lips with little eye makeup. The sixties borrowed the kohl-rimmed eyes and pale lips of the beatniks and reinterpreted it. Eyes were accentuated with eyeliner, long false eyelashes, and artistically applied powdered eye shadows. Foundation appeared in a very wide range of skin tones, and cosmetics specifically colored for dark skin tones appeared. Lipsticks went very pale or nonexistent, with gloss applied in their place; pale blushers replaced the rouge of earlier decades.

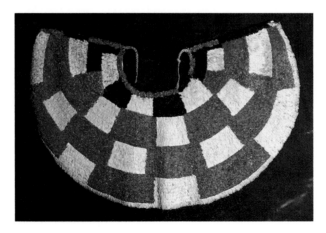

figure 9-12

Many designers of the 1960s were influenced by the geometric patterns and bright colors of ethnic textiles such as this feathered cape. © *Dorling Kindersley*

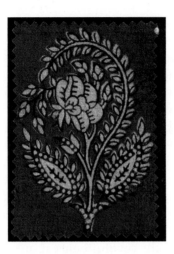

figure 9-13

Indian textiles became highly popular during the 1960s for their vibrant colors combined with geometric and floral designs. © *Dorling Kindersley*

The Unisex Decade

The sixties split convention wide open. By the 1970s anything seemed possible and acceptable—even unisex clothing (Figure 9-13). Men and women wearing the same clothing was high fashion then. Color continued in favor into the seventies, although the psychedelic colors, miniskirts, and ethnic look were becoming passé. Green was popular, as were yellow and cream. There were dusty pinks and blues, ochres, sage, and a greenish beige called "greige." People seemed jaded, constantly looking for something more shocking than the topless bathing suits and miniskirts of the sixties. Then came hot pants. The very short shorts appeared briefly in 1971 but were not readily accepted, although they caused a sensation and much controversy as they began to appear in the workplace. London again set the trends with a revival of the 1930s popularized by the Biba boutique. Peach, beige, and chocolate brown satins and crepes were worn with felt hats and ostrich feathers. Laura Ashley's nineteenth-century pastels and prints were made into smocks and long dresses that established a look that lasted through most of the decade. The natural look prevailed in cosmetics, with eye shadows and lipsticks in brown and terra cotta, pink and yellow, or colorless gloss.

In the 1970s colors were worn layered, and so were patterns (Figure 9-14). Suddenly it was okay to mix and match small checks, large squares, and stripes, all in the same outfit. Beginning in the late seventies, the backlash against color came in the form of the black leather and chains of the punk movement, although color remained in their hair, which was dyed bright blue, green, red, orange, or violet, sometimes in stripes or tufts. The disco fad brought its own form of glitter and color in changing the naturals to bright red, royal blue, yellow, turquoise, and acid green. Suddenly, daywear glittered with sequins and rhinestones previously reserved for the evening, as the disco crowd's influence was felt. Stretch fabrics and the ubiquitous polyester shirt for men became trademarks of the period, as popularized by John Travolta in the film *Saturday Night Fever*. Cosmetics gleamed with gold, silver, and copper, for both day and evening. By the late seventies colors were becoming somber, and earth tones, russets, and dark browns prevailed.

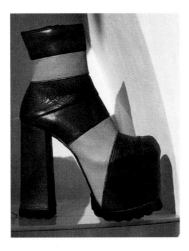

figure 9-14

Platform shoes in bright colors starred in the 1970s. Some of the more extreme styles had platform soles five or six inches high. © *Dorling Kindersley*

The Extravagant Eighties

The summer of 1979 brought a brief revival of bright, acid colors (Figure 9-15), but it was short-lived and adopted by only a few fashion victims. The eighties saw a return to classicism and elegance in fashion. Ralph Lauren became emperor with his brilliant marketing ploy of selling an image—that of old money, security, wealth without a hint of trendiness. Colors followed: rich burgundy, forest green, saturated navy, black, and white (Figure 9-16). Perry Ellis reinterpreted the twenties and thirties in longer skirts with belted jackets and fine detailing. Gone was the "make the world a better place" attitude of the sixties; gone was the dance-crazed gaiety of the seventies. The eighties were about affluence, serious affluence. It became essential to flaunt one's wealth or to invent it. The "me generation" found solace in spas that catered to every whim and in new cosmetics that promised youth and beauty through the latest technological innovations.

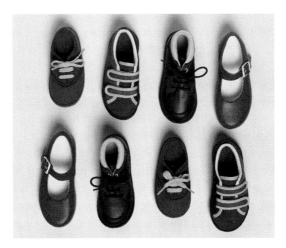

figure 9-15

Color in fashion continued into the 1980s, as shown in these brightly colored children's shoes. © *Dorling Kindersley*

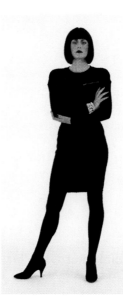

figure 9-16

The end of the twentieth century returned to black in a big way not seen since the Victorian age, almost as if mourning its own passing. Suddenly black became de rigueur, artsy, and very desirable, changing its image from one of mourning to one of chic. © *Dorling Kindersley*

The Nineties and Beyond

Like the sixties' fashions of three decades earlier, designers in the 1990s were influenced by the street. Black dominated the clothing of young people for much of the decade, while the rest of the population appeared to be in search of an identifying "look." If pressed to define the general image of the decade perhaps the word "casual" is the common denominator, dominated by Nike sportswear. Denim jeans and cargo pants were also very popular with their wide leg and large pockets partway down the leg. They were available in blue, black, whitish, beige, and khaki. Adidas windpants, which made noises every time you moved, became commonplace. They came in many colors with either a black or white tuxedo stripe down the side. Baggy clothes were the signature of the young, usually worn many sizes too large to get the desired effect. In the early nineties, baseball caps worn backward made a fashion statement, but mostly among young men. Footwear for both young men and women tended toward dark, heavy boots with thick soles, and later in the decade high platform soles made a comeback for women. Lightweight and warm polar fleece fabric appeared in everything from hats to gloves and a wide range of outerwear, often in bright colors.

Perhaps the most unexpected trend of the nineties was a very new use of color in fashion—that of using the International Safety Colors in commonplace attire. These startlingly bright, highly visible colors were developed to catch attention primarily in industrial or potentially hazardous environments. International Safety Colors are so powerful that they are visible even in glare or hazardous weather conditions. Although these colors are far brighter than most people would feel comfortable wearing in business clothing, they have been used successfully in high fashion lines and in sports clothing lines. Because of their high visibility, safety colors have become quite common in high activity sports such as bike racing, climbing, and skiing as well as in team sport uniforms.

Athletic shoes, particularly sneakers, are commonly found in safety colors. Zebra patterns of black and white from traffic signs, safety orange most often seen in construction cones, safety yellow of caution signs, and safety blue of handicapped signage have all found their way into footwear. It is interesting to note that people (particularly men) who often shy away from strong color in their attire have embraced these fantastically vibrant colors in sports gear to the extent that it is now widely accepted as casual street wear.

Another trend of the nineties, both for men and women, was the return to the earlier practices of tattoos and body piercings. Originating in the twentieth century with gang members, jailbirds, and other rebels, tattoos became so common late in the century that young people in the mainstream now have them. You used to get a tattoo to stand out, now you get one to blend in. While small, discreet tattoos began the trend with perhaps a flower or a butterfly, by the end of the decade young people often sported elaborately colored designs on limbs, on shaved heads, on backs, and sometimes over most of the body that harken back to primitive times when body painting was the norm.

As we enter the twenty-first century, the only thing that we can be assured of is that there will be change. New technologies will create new opportunities and new problems. Color selection may stem from a return to older times, or technological developments may propel color into new areas that we are incapable of imagining now. One such trend are products variously called *smart textiles*, *e-textiles*, *wearable computers*, or *intelligent textiles*. Whatever you call them, these textiles are taking us into a whole new world. Artists now create interactive wall hangings of fabric interlaced with electronics and special dyes so that colors change in programmed sequence. New technology is part of the emerging wave of weaving intelligence into textiles, including the ability to detect dangerous chemicals, the ability to sanitize themselves, and the ability to serve as a communication network. Potential applications run the gamut from health and sporting goods to combat uniforms. In the not too distant future, our clothing may take the place of cell phone, medical monitor, and chemical protectant. It is quite likely that this new technology will propel textiles forward because of its diverse applications.

Whatever the future holds there will always be people who are style setters rather than followers. It is our belief that each of us would do best to select styles and colors that we feel best represent us. To achieve that, each of us can begin by developing a personal color plan.

Color Selection in Apparel

Each of us has a color or colors in which we think we look best. When shopping, you might think, "That's my color" or "That's not my color." A person's ideal color is usually based somewhat on color bias, as we discussed in Chapter 3, such as the associations we make with a color, whether we feel good or bad when wearing that color, and what compliments we may have received while wearing a specific color or colors. Most people have a basic, intuitive understanding both of what works best with their particular hair, eye, and complexion color and of what color message they are portraying either consciously or unconsciously.

Teenagers are masters at using color to shock their elders, either by their methods of combining colors or by choosing to ignore color altogether and arriving at a wild mélange. Choosing drab combinations of neutrals is another way teenagers have of establishing their own turf and breaking with the concepts of the previous generation. In 1925 undergraduates at Oxford University shocked their elders by wearing lavender, cinnamon, mauve, and green pants with legs more than forty inches wide, known as "Oxford bags." Color selection in clothing often has hidden, symbolic meanings. For example, girls may wear black, hoping to appear older; mature women may wear black to look sophisticated and elegant at black-tie events; black may be selected for anything from an evening at the opera to a funeral. The red dress has connotations that go far back into history, from the "scarlet woman" of Puritan times to the woman wanting to stand out in a crowd.

Although much more color has been permitted in the workplace in recent years, the general trend still seems to be one of conservatism and formality at higher income levels. Instead of adding color to the workforce, women have chosen to copy the somber, dark tones of men's dress at the office. In an attempt to be recognized for her professional skills rather than her looks, the professional woman has traded some of her color freedom for the color uniformity allotted to men. A look into today's office usually presents one with a blur of neutrals.

Even people who choose to wear a lot of color in their everyday lives usually have an intuitive sense of sobriety in color selection when faced with important events such as a court date, a visit with a loan officer, or a job interview. At these times even the most colorful dresser usually opts for more neutralized hues.

Prior to the nineteenth century, both men and women wore colorful clothing. Beau Brummel, the nineteenth-century English dandy, is credited with creating the drab, neutralized look for men. He believed that refinement is best expressed in subdued colors and elegance of cut. Soon society followed, and men are still stuck with his ideas today. Colorful male dress is usually found only on young men in the arts or other fields not needing to promote a stable impression.

Color in clothing must always be considered in context with accessories as well as hair, eye, and complexion color. Color will reflect against your skin. If, for example, the main fashion color being promoted is a chartreuse that makes your skin look sickly yellow, you can still be in fashion if you choose the color in an article of clothing that is worn away from the face, such as pants or a skirt. A red sweater or scarf may cast a rosy glow on your face, while deep blue may appear either chilling or fresh, depending on your skin tone.

Creating a Personal Color Palette

No matter what fashion dictates, when it comes to personal color selection it is best to use your own coloring as a guide. You may age, your hair may turn gray, but the basic underlying colors of your complexion and eyes will not change (Figure 9-17). These are the foundations of your personal color plan in clothing and accessories. No matter whether you have very dark or very light skin, all complexions can be broken down into two color bases: yellow-based and blue-based. We are not implying that you have blue skin; we are referring to the subtle undertones that

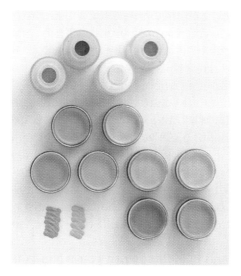

figure 9-17

Genetics dictate your skin tone, hair color, and eye color. Whether you are very pale or very dark, you have either a blue-based or yellow-based skin tone. © *Dorling Kindersley*

dictate which color group you belong to. Before a child's sense of color is influenced by family and education, the child invariably has a sense of what colors work best. You might begin there, by recalling what your favorite colors were when you were a child. Chances are they are also your best colors to wear today. When you are wearing your best colors, you look radiant! Your skin glows, your eyes gleam, and your hair creates a halo effect around your face. Wearing colors that are inappropriate for you results in a tired, faded look at best, and sometimes you just look downright sick.

Genetics dictate your skin tone and hair and eye color. Whether you are very pale or very dark, you still fall into the category of either a blue-based or yellow-based skin tone. If you acquire a tan, your basic skin tone remains the same. As you age and your hair turns gray, it retains the correct tint of gray for you unless you dye or tint your hair. If you do choose to change the color of your hair, you need to be sure that the color you select is in harmony with your skin and eye color in order to look your best. The blue-based complexion looks best in blue-based colors such as blues, bluish greens, bluish pinks and reds, black, white, and charcoal gray and in accessories with a silver hue. You can adjust the lightness or darkness of the color based on how light or dark your skin tone is. Usually, lighter skin tones look best in the lighter, more pastel tints of a color, while darker skin tones can carry the brighter, more color-saturated hues. Yellow-based skin tones look best in autumn colors that are also yellow-based, such as yellow-golds, pumpkin, terra cotta, camel, warm browns, turquoise, yellow-greens such as chartreuse or lime, and accessories with a golden hue.

How to Determine Your Color Base

You can determine what your best personal colors are by first determining your own color base. An easy way to do this is to purchase a package of multicolored construction paper that contains a range of both blue-based and yellow-based colors: red, orange, yellow, green, blue, violet, white, black, a bluish gray, a brownish gray, and the lighter tints of pink and aqua. If you want to invest a little more money, you can buy one-yard lengths of fabric in the same colors and neutral range. Locate a really good natural light source. The light from a north-facing window is ideal. Set up a mirror so that you are facing the light and can easily see your reflection. If you dye or bleach your hair, pull it back and cover it so that its color will not lead you astray. If your hair is its natural color, you can leave it alone. As you put each of the colors up to your face, you will notice some remarkable differences. Some colors will make your skin glow; others will make you look worn or tired (Figure 9-18). Note which colors look best on you. This will determine whether you are blue-based or yellow-based. You can then concentrate on weeding clothing from your wardrobe that does not fit into your "best colors" category. It is also a good idea to cut little clips from your "best colors" construction paper or fabrics and take them with you when you go shopping. That way you can select only colors that you know will look good on you.

If you have pants or skirts that are not in your best colors, you can continue to wear them by adding a shirt or sweater in one of your best colors so that the color near your face will keep you looking good. If you wear cosmetics, make sure that you select only foundation, eyeshadow, blusher, and lipstick colors that represent your best color group. No matter what fashion dictates for a particular season, there are always yellow-based and blue-based cosmetics options available. Even when neutral brown cosmetics are in vogue, they still appear in these two basic undertone categories. You may have to experiment a bit with store samples to find the best colors for you, but it is well worth it. There are some cosmetic lines now, including Prescriptives and Cover Girl, that guide you in breaking down their cosmetics into "warm" or "cool" categories. If you are blue-based, you will look best in "cool" colors. If you are yellow-based, select the "warm" colors. It's really that simple, and it will make a tremendous difference in your appearance.

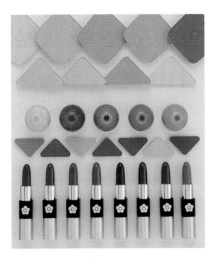

figure 9-18

This range of cosmetics shows both blue-based and yellow-based colors. Wearing the proper color suited to your color base can make you look brighter, fresher, and healthier. © *Dorling Kindersley*

Hair color can also be categorized as yellow-based or blue-based. Nature never makes mistakes in combining hair and complexion colors, but if you color your hair, you may have made an inappropriate choice. Platinum blond, blue-black, white or silver, salt-and-pepper, or ash brown hair are in the blue-based group. Golden blond, black with reddish lights, brown-gold, auburn, red, and gray with highlights (as when red hair goes gray) are yellow-based shades. To look your best, your hair should always complement your natural complexion color.

If you wear eyeglasses, they, too, should blend in with your basic color group. If you are in the yellow-based category, the following colors will look best on you: polished gold, copper, bronze, antique gold, camel, dark brown, golden brown, khaki, beige, off-white, coral, peach, orange, orange-red, yellow-green, blond tortoise, or light tortoise. If you are in the blue-based category wear pewter, graphite, silver, chrome, antique silver, rose gold, black, rose brown, taupe, cocoa, medium or light gray, pearl or snow white, blue-gray, pink, magenta, plum, blue-violet, blue, emerald green, or cool-based tortoise.

Always remember that the intensity of a color has an effect. If you are a paler type, you will look best in pastels, while more vivid complexion, hair, and eye colors can carry off the brighter colors. Whether you are male or female, when you wear your best colors, you will always look great.

Color in Cosmetics

The use of cosmetics to enhance or alter appearance is nothing new. Body painting and self-decoration are found in most tribal communities (Figure 9-19). Leaves, shells, feathers, tattoos, scars, and colored paint have all been used to this end. Anthropologists have discovered that in tribal societies members of the group carried a precise record of their relation to the society on the surface of their bodies (Figure 9-20). The

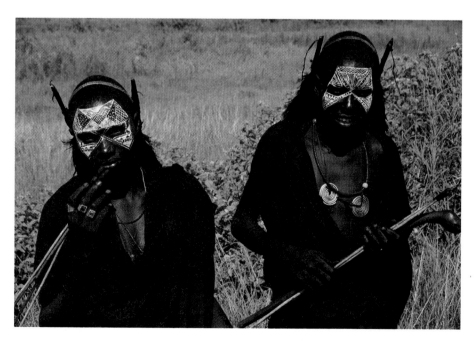

figure 9-19

Self-decoration through cosmetics is nothing new. Body and face painting is found in most tribal communities. © *Dorling Kindersley*

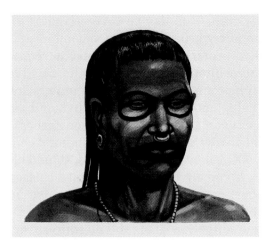

figure 9-20

Anthropologists have discovered that tribal society members carried a precise record of their relation to the society on the surface of their bodies. Body paints became cosmetics when ancient peoples began to use them for decorative purposes. © *Dorling Kindersley*

famous Maori tattoos represent the notion that a face is not a face at all until it is painted. An unpainted face is considered a "dumb" face by them. In Maori belief, a painted face confers human dignity and spiritual significance. It is seen quite literally as a mask that defines social role and individual identity.

Body paints became cosmetics when ancient peoples began to use them for decorative purposes. The Egyptians are known for using traditional green malachite, gray and black kohl, and red ochre to emphasize the eyes and redden the lips, palms, and fingernails (Figure 9-21). Women tinted their bodies with dilute yellow ochre and gilded their nipples, and both sexes wore dyed red or black wigs on their carefully shorn heads. In our choice of cosmetics and dress, we express our affinity with or separation from a particular group. Team uniforms, school colors, gang dress codes, and religious habits are all examples.

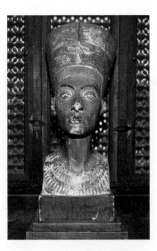

figure 9-21

As this image of Nefertiti shows, the Egyptians were well known for using traditional green malachite, gray and black kohl, and red ochre to emphasize the eyes and redden lips, palms, and fingernails. © *Dorling Kindersley*

Greek women wore little makeup, but the courtesans and harlots throughout the ages painted themselves lavishly. Rouges made from vegetable dyes, white lead to lighten the complexion, and kohl to line the eyes were commonplace. Roman women tinted their hair with dyes made from tree bark, beechwood ashes, and goat tallow. Early Christians considered cosmetics vain, and eventually the expression "painted woman" came to mean a prostitute or at least a woman of questionable virtue. Japanese women traditionally masked the face with pink and white rice powders, vermilion rouge, and black eye and eyebrow coloring, all still seen on today's geisha. Indian women rouged the lips, feet, and fingertips with lac dye, saffron, or henna. The body was often covered with a colored sandalwood paste.

Because Queen Elizabeth I of England wore cosmetics, English women soon followed suit. By 1558, makeup had spread northward from Italy. White lead was used to coat the face. Calcined in vinegar, it was beaten into flakes and then ground into a powder. As might be expected, it ruined the health of many manufacturers as well as wearers. Rouge was made from red ochre or cinnabar, and lip color came from crayons of ground alabaster and cochineal. The whole face was often varnished with an egg-white glaze and had to be protected outdoors with a mask to prevent melting. It was fashionable to lighten hair with chamomile or to dye it red with henna. An engraving of Elizabeth shows her embracing the practice of painting blue veins on the forehead to simulate the translucent look of youth.

The prevalence of smallpox scars led to a fad of wearing tiny black or scarlet patches on the face during the seventeenth and eighteenth centuries. Smallpox left faces pitted and scarred for life. The disfiguring effects of this disease were instrumental in originating the fashion of applying patches to the face as an ideal camouflage for pock marks. The patch or *mouche* was commonly used in the eighteenth century. They were cut of silk, taffeta, or leather and variously shaped and colored. Black was popular, as was bright scarlet. In fact, the scarring of the population was so great and the fashion of wearing mouches so popular that some people may have resembled Dalmatians.

Overdone or not, the eighteenth-century population must have been grateful for this fashion, as most skins were severely blemished by pock marks. The only women reputed to retain a perfect complexion were milkmaids, who were thought to be immunized from smallpox by catching a mild form of the disease from cattle. By Victorian times, a more natural look was adopted. The Victorian notion of innocent beauty meant that women must use makeup either not at all or so discreetly as to make it undetectable.

Today, most cosmetics are made from synthetic pigments, although there is currently a rebirth of natural cosmetics. Pigments are considered too bright for use in their pure form, so they are generally muted with white titanium dioxide, which is also a natural sunscreen. About forty organic and twenty inorganic pigments are used to create the hundreds of colors available in today's market.

Color in Textiles

We usually differentiate textile uses into upholstery fabric, drapery fabric, and apparel fabric, although there are still some crossovers. While today we often use different textiles for interiors than we do for clothing,

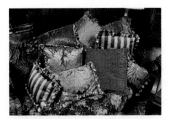

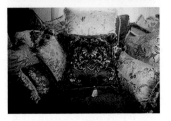

figure 9-22

This group of pillows made from antique fabrics shows a variety of fabric styles and surface treatments, including brocade, jacquard weaves, tapestry, and embroidery. *Pillows designed by Fehrman & Fehrman*

historically this was not the case. Early in American history the same wool used for a woman's skirt might also keep drafts away when used as window curtains. In Europe the same elaborate cut velvets and brocades might be used as a gentleman's vest, a woman's dress, bedcovers and draperies, and upholstery on a chair or settee. Then as now, textiles often provided the major source of color in the decoration of a room or in garments (Figures 9-22 and 9-23). For example, people are often much more comfortable using strong color in fabrics for upholstery, pillows, or

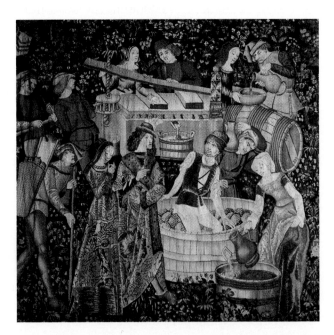

figure 9-23

Early tapestries were woven by hand with naturally dyed yarns. They were often used to record historical events and to keep out the cold in drafty castles. *© Dorling Kindersley, Musee des thermes et de l'hotel de Cluny, Paris*

draperies than they are using it in large expanses on walls as paint or wallpaper. Color is more universally accepted in apparel design than in interior design, but this may be attributed to the fact that it is easier and less costly to change a garment than to change the color scheme of a room. While historically the fabric of a man's suit might also cover the family sofa, the introduction of flammability codes for public spaces did much to change the kind of textiles we use for personal and home fashions. Fabrics specified for public spaces must meet flammability standards. A few fibers such as olefins, polyesters, and glass fibers are inherently flame-resistant, so they captured the market for interior textiles. Since the 1980s, manufactured fibers have also been used extensively in apparel design, although natural fibers such as wool, silk, cashmere, and linen are still considered luxury textiles.

To fully understand the impact of color in personal or home fashion, it is important to have at least a basic understanding of color's effect in the textile industry. Any discussion of color in textiles is complicated by the texture, weave, or pattern of the fabric. The impact of textiles without pattern depends on two factors—color and texture (Figure 9-24). Light, of course, comes into play whenever texture is considered because textured surfaces can be exploited for their relationship to light. For example, if a silk taffeta is used vertically with some gathering (as in draperies or a skirt), light from one side will highlight the top of the folds and create deep, shadowed areas between them. This can add an aura of extreme richness to a garment. Ridges and dotted textures will be highlighted if a light source is angled across them. The weave of the textile can also influence how a color appears because different textures or woven patterns affect the density of the dye. For example, a heavy ribbed cotton twill will look different from a fine silk, even if they are colored with exactly the same dye batch (Figures 9-25 and 9-26). In general, it is rare to find a printed cloth that has the depth and beauty of a textile in which the weave creates the pattern. Shiny fabrics appear lighter in color than matte surface fabrics even if they have been colored with exactly

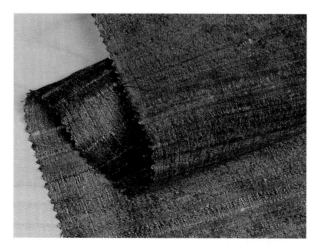

figure 9-24

Natural silk has a sheen like no other and creates beautiful color effects in different lighting conditions. *Used with permission of Tapestria*

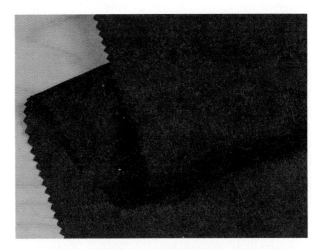

figure 9-25

This red silk appears quite different from the red knitting wool in Figure 9-26 because different textures affect the density of the dye. *Used with permission of Tapestria*

the same dye. A third category that affects the color of textiles is pile—the raised dimension of textiles such as velvet, terrycloth, corduroy, chenille, and velour. It is common to see an almost two-tone effect in older velvets or crushed velvets because the subtle aging and wearing of the pile creates a beautiful mottled effect when light strikes the surface.

Color Dyeing

The primary factor in the color of textiles is, of course, dye. The concept of dyeing is nothing new. Tribal humans dyed their skin with various natural pigments derived from plants or minerals. Rubbing mineral pigments such as manganese, hematite, ochre, or clay directly into the fabric is the simplest dyeing method. This method is still used in many tribal communities today (Figure 9-27).

As technology developed, people learned ways of crushing and heating plants to produce dyes. The berries, fruits, leaves, and roots of many plants yield colored juices suitable for dyeing fabrics. For example, safflower

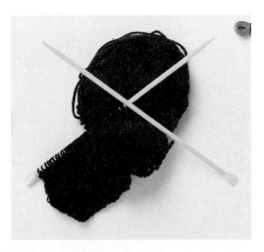

figure 9-26

When compared with the red silk in Figure 9-25, this knitting wool shows how different textures affect the appearance of color. *© Dorling Kindersley*

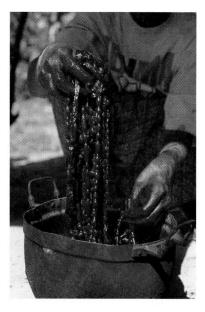

figure 9-27

Primitive dyeing method similar to that used for centuries by tribal peoples as a colorant. © *Dorling Kindersley*

petals produce a yellow dye when steeped in water. Aster flowers produce a rose-pink. The barks of many common trees supply coloring materials for yarns and cloth. Black oak is a powerful natural dye, producing light tan to brown. White ash, madrone, silver maple, willow oak, and sweetgum barks also provide dyes in the brown tones. On wool, apple bark gives a dark yellow-tan or brass color. Chamomile flowers give a buff to yellow color that becomes brighter after washing in soap. Privet leaves produce a good gold. Cochineal dye is prepared from a dried insect found in Mexico and Central America. It produces colors that have good fastness to light and washing. Cochineal produces a bluish red to rose-pink. Even common coffee beans produce a dark yellow-tan with good color fastness. Recently, tea-dyed cloth has come back into fashion, particularly tea-dyed chintz that has an older, faded look. One of the first dyes was derived from indigo (the color of blue jeans) and was probably first used in India or Egypt. Indigo was introduced into Europe during the sixteenth century. It met with great opposition from the producers of a similarly colored dye, woad, which was used by the early Britons to dye their skin blue to appear fiercer in battle.

To fully appreciate color in the textiles medium, it helps to understand how color becomes bonded to fibers. Many natural dyes fade or bleed badly unless the yarn or fabric is first treated with a chemical called a **mordant**, which helps fix the color to the fiber. The mordants commonly used with natural dyes are alum, potassium dichromate, ferrous sulfate, and tannic acid or some other source of tannin, such as oak galls or sumac leaves. Almost all plant dyes require mordants as fixatives, but a mordant will work on some fabrics and not on others. Different mordants produce entirely different colors from the same dyes. Commercial dyers rely on oils and chemicals for mordanting. Mordants do more than just fix dye to the fiber; they also alter the color produced. By using different mordants, a variety of shades and colors can be obtained from one dye. For example, on wool, dahlia flowers used with potassium dichromate mordant give an orange color. If used with alum, a light yellow is produced. Cochineal mordanted with alum produces red. If mordanted with potassium dichromate, cochineal produces purple.

Both wool and silk have the property of holding chemicals in their fibers. When wool is boiled in a solution of the potassium dichromate mordant, a certain amount of it is held in the fiber, and the dye then combines with this mordanted wool to form a permanent color. Cotton and other vegetable fibers do not absorb the metallic mordants as readily as wool. They combine best with tannic acid, which is used either as a mordant itself or as an agent for fixing metallic mordants in the fibers. Within the tribal context, textiles were often symbols associated with rituals or with religious or social customs. In one Balinese community, the dye colors of ikat textiles are an essential part of their rituals, requiring a series of dye baths lasting six to eight years. Whenever tribes attached ritual significance to color, they often attempted to bind dyes to fabric with blood, saliva, tree resin, egg albumen, or the juice of lemons or limes.

Until the 1860s, the few hundred dyes commonly used were derived from the same insects, shells, and plants as those used by earlier people. Then everything changed. In 1856 William Henry Perkin was a student at London's Royal College of Chemistry. He was attempting to synthesize quinine, used to control malaria. Instead of his intended potion, he obtained only a black sludge but, rather than throwing it away, he tried diluting it in alcohol and came up with a purple solution. He went on to discover that it would dye silk and was resistant to both washing and the fading effects of light. Perkin borrowed his father's life savings to put his new commercial dye into production. The French christened the new color *mauve* after the delicate purple of the mallow flower, and for the next decade mauve was the rage, so much so that the period became known as the Mauve Decade. Queen Victoria wore a mauve dress to the Great Exhibition of 1862, a penny stamp was printed in mauve, and mauve was eventually accepted as the color for half-mourning. The novelty of mauve soon gave way to new synthetic dyes. Fuchsine, a brilliant bluish red, was discovered in France in 1859 and became known in English as magenta. Perkin's teacher, August Hofmann, developed Hofmann's violet. New dyes flooded the market, including aniline black, methyl violet, malachite green, and Congo red. Suddenly it was possible to create commercial dyes in a laboratory that were cheaper, more varied, and more reliable than natural dyes. In 1868 two German chemists synthesized alizarin, the red color of one of the world's most desirable dyes, madder.

Another breakthrough led to the production of the azo dyes that were more resistant to fading. Indigo was the first to be synthesized, which eventually destroyed the livelihood of the Indian peasants who had farmed the indigo plants. By the 1920s new acetate dyes were being discovered that would color the new synthetic fibers. The 1950s saw the development of dramatic new dyes, the ICI Procions. These dyes were able to bond with cellulose fibers in an entirely new way. The Procions were brightly colored, cheap to produce, and colorfast, and they spurred the color revolution of the 1960s. By 1980 the number of dyes had reached the three million mark, with about two new dyes appearing each week.

Gradually, the infatuation with synthetic dyes began to fade and the natural dyes once again became intriguing. They were not as colorfast, but they faded with a beautiful natural sheen, particularly notable in handmade oriental carpets. In some instances, natural fading is preferred to the tireless brightness of synthetic dyes. We wanted our blue jeans to fade naturally the way they had when natural indigo dyes were used, but no matter how hard manufacturers tried, they could not create natural-looking faded blue jeans. Classic blue jeans have to be bought in pristine dark indigo and gradually faded with washing and wear. There is considerable difference in appearance between the classics and the stonewashed, pre-faded type.

Several different methods of dyeing are commonly practiced. **Stock-dyeing** is a process of dipping the raw fibers in a vat of dye before the thread is spun. **Yarn-dyeing** is dipping the yarns before weaving. **Cross-dyeing** is a process in which one fiber in a fiber-blend textile will absorb one type of dye while the second or a third fiber will absorb only the dye of a different chemical formula (Figure 9-28). In this way a woven textile can be dyed two or more colors or two or more shades of the same color by dipping the woven textile into two or more dye baths (Figure 9-29).

Textile designs are usually produced in three or more color ways to appeal to different color preferences. The color of the foreground design may change while the background color remains the same, or both background and design may have different colors. In all cases, the visual effect will be radically different. It is possible to find the same pattern both appealing and awful, depending on the colors selected. This was first noted during the eighteenth century, when textile printing was in its infancy. A color often appeared to change in transition from small-scale design to printed fabric. For example, a green pattern in a blue field might look yellowish; black against red might appear green. Chevreul's investigation of these effects led him to the conclusion that they were caused by the influence of one color on another. This is known as **simultaneous contrast** and is evident in afterimage effects. Textile designers need a thorough knowledge of color combinations in context in order to

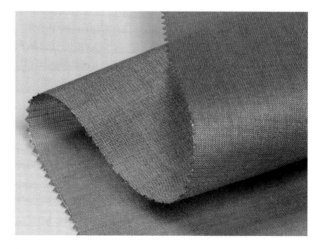

figure 9-28

In cross-dyeing, one fiber will absorb one type of dye while a different fiber absorbs a different dye, resulting in a textile that can be dyed two or more colors. *Used with permission of Tapestria*

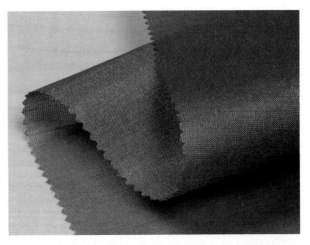

figure 9-29

Another example of dual-toned fabric. *Used with permission of Tapestria*

create successfully designed and marketable fabrics. For example, a textile designer may want to produce a red and blue fabric, and that seems like a reasonably simple task. However, red and blue are colors that **flicker** when seen together. If both colors have the same value and saturation, they seem to flash when seen together. Flicker is an attention-getting color device that is often used in advertising, packaging, or signage, but it is very irritating and unsuitable in textile, fashion, or interior design unless a particularly irritating effect is desired. Some color pairs exhibit this effect more intensely than others. Red and green and cyan and orange have the same brilliance when at their most saturated. Blue is darker than its complementary color, yellow, even at its most saturated, so these colors will not seem to flicker as much. Flicker often depends on proportion for its effect. For example, the flickering effect of red and green is most vivid when the two colors occupy an area of equal size. An entirely different effect is created when the proportions of the colors change.

Exploring color contrasts is the basis of designing with color. In printed textiles, the way the color is applied to the fabric can have an effect on how the color is observed. In the **direct printing** method, the color is applied directly to the cloth by hand with pen or brush or with wooden blocks, each of which prints one color and a certain section of the design (this is known as block printing). Designs are now etched on copper rollers, one roller for each color and part of a pattern. An old method of producing patterned fabrics is the process known as **resist dyeing**. In this method a pattern was formed by coating portions of the fabric with wax or clay. The entire fabric was then dyed, but where the coating had been applied it "resisted" penetration of the dye. When the clay or wax was removed, the pattern of the fabric was visible. Today a version of this method is still in use and is known as **extract printing**. After the fabric has been dyed, a chemical is applied to certain portions that removes the background color and forms the desired pattern. **Stencil printing** is sometimes used to color textiles. When the stencil or screen pattern is placed on the cloth in proper relation to the pattern, the dye is pressed through the opening by means of a rubber squeegee. The stencil is then moved to the next position, and the process is repeated until all the cloth is covered with the desired pattern. If the pattern is elaborate, many stencils are required, making the process very slow and costly. A similar but cheaper process was invented at the beginning of the twentieth century. It is called **screen printing**. In this process the stencil consists of a large sheet of fine silk or dacron fabric stretched and mounted on a frame that is the same dimension as the pattern repeat and width of the fabric. The yardage is laid flat and the color is brushed or squeezed through the screen to produce the pattern.

The period since World War II has been a time of great exploration and experimentation in the fashion and design industries. With regard to textiles, one of the greatest innovators was Eszter Harastzy, who became the director of Knoll Textiles in 1949. She was to have a marked effect on contemporary fabrics and the use of color. She introduced the Knoll stripe (now in the Museum of Modern Art's design collection) and transportation cloth, which she described as "the first industrial fabric, the first one that stood all the tests. It was used widely by Detroit ... the first pure linen in the American (industrial) market. It was my greatest design success." Harastzy was also a brilliant colorist who introduced the then-startling combination of orange and pink in patterned textiles. The proliferation of synthetically manufactured fibers during the last half of the twentieth century caused a revolution in the textiles industry that has affected both personal and home fashions.

To summarize, the only constant about color in fashion is that it is always changing. What is the height of fashion in one decade is often the laughingstock of the next. Fashions have a tendency to reappear every twenty to thirty years, when they may seem fresh again. The colors of fashion mirror the spirit of their time. Fashion reflects the changing influences at work on society. Colors come in and out of fashion, as does clothing. For decades Paris was the undisputed leader in Western fashion, but gradually the glamour of the Hollywood movie stars weaned away some of fashion's followers to be influenced by U.S. tastes. From Jean Harlow's platinum blond hair to James Dean's black leather jacket, the movies have influenced the way we dress and the way we choose to present ourselves to the world.

The colors we choose to wear project an immediate and lasting image that affects the way others relate to us. In fashion and industry, color selection is determined by color consultants through groups such as the Color Marketing Group and the British Colour Council, who decide two or three years in advance on color palettes that are then adopted by industry. Clothing is dependent on textiles, so to fully understand color in fashion it is desirable to have at least a basic understanding of color's effect on the textile industry. Color in textiles is dependent on the dyeing process. Initially, textiles were colored with pigments derived from natural sources. In the late nineteenth century, dyes were synthesized, revolutionizing the textile and fashion industries. We now take for granted the more than three million colors available to us that had their beginnings in the simple pigments of the earth.

REFERENCES

Adrosko, R. J., *Natural Dyes and Home Dyeing*, Dover Publications, 1971.

Angeloglou, M., *A History of Makeup*, Studio Vista, 1970.

Anquetil, J., *Silk*, Flammarion, 1998.

Arnold, J. A., *A Handbook of Costume*, Macmillan, 1973.

Battersby, M., *Art Deco Fashion*, Academy Editions, St. Martin's Press, 1974.

Chambers, B. G., *Colour and Design in Men's and Women's Clothes and Home Furnishings*, Prentice Hall, 1951.

Corson, R., *Fashions in Makeup from Ancient to Modern Times*, Peter Owen, 1972.

Dormer, J., *Fashion in the 1920s and 30s*, Ian Allen, 1973.

Garland, M., *The Changing Face of Beauty*, Weidenfeld & Nicholson, 1957.

Ginsburg, M., ed., *The Illustrated History of Textiles*, Studio Editions, 1991.

Gunn, F., *The Artificial Face: A History of Cosmetics*, Hippocrene Books, 1983.

Larrabee, E., Vignelli, M., *Knoll Design*, Harry N. Abrams, 1981.

Schoeser, M., Rufey, C., *English and American Textiles from 1970 to the Present*, Thames and Hudson, 1989.

Taylor, E. S., Wallace, W. J., *Mohave Tatooing and Face-Painting*, Los Angeles South West Museum, 1947.

Thurman, C. C. M., *Textiles*, Art Institute of Chicago, 1992.

Chapter ten

Color in culture and society

The Color Link

No matter what our cultural background or cultural differences—color links us all. For centuries tribal and city people alike depended on natural earth-derived pigments for coloring agents. So even though patterns and designs may have varied dramatically from one culture to another, there was a color link between cultures. When Western technology introduced new and inexpensive means of coloring to the world, there came a sudden rift that turned conventional ideas about color upside down. In a few short years, the indigenous earth-toned palette of tribal societies disappeared, to be replaced by the insatiable need for bright colors, the gaudier the better. At the same time the West, wearied of intense, synthetic dyes, showed a preference for a return to natural hues derived from earth pigments, although these are now becoming quite rare in the commercial marketplace.

The use of color in ancient and tribal civilizations arose not so much out of aesthetics but out of pigment availability, religion, and superstition. Color use was functional and practical in that it was symbolic. The common cultural palette was simple: red, yellow, green, blue, purple (if available), and a range of neutral browns, white, and black. In religion, early civilizations combined philosophy and science. The great principles of nature and the vital forces of the universe were personified by gods, goddesses, and their symbolic colors. The foremost leaders of the day—teachers, scientists, philosophers, priests—were also mystics who guided the people, regulated affairs of war, peace, commerce, and industry, and formed the backbone of the culture.

To early cultures the sun often played a pivotal role. God was an entity often associated with light, and his bounty was represented by the rainbow and its dazzling display of spectral color. Today we still become excited by the appearance of a rainbow in the sky. Imagine how much more significant this phenomenon must have seemed to early cultures who had no exposure to artificial lighting, film, television, and computers. All of the spectral colors—red, yellow, orange, green, blue, and violet—emanated from the rainbow and became symbolic of divine forces (Figure 10-1).

In Mongolia, the earth was conceived of as a high mountain called Sumur. The four sides of the mountain were colored. To the north was yellow, to the south was blue, to the east white, and to the west red. In China, color has always been woven into the culture. The points of the compass were identified by color: black for the north, red for the south, green for the east, white for the west. This association of color with the four corners of the world has also been found in the early cultures of Ireland and the Indians of North America.

The Chinese had five primary colors: red, yellow, black, white, and green-blue (Figure 10-2). These colors were related to the five Chinese elements (fire, metal, wood, earth, and water) and to the five happinesses, the five virtues, the five vices, and the five precepts of faith. Dynasties were known by hues: brown for the Sung Dynasty, green for the Ming, yellow for the Ching. The emperor wore blue when he worshiped the sky and yellow when he worshiped the earth. All edicts from the emperor were signed with vermilion ink. The emperor's grandchildren rode in purple sedans, while his higher officials rode in blue vehicles and his lower officials in green ones. In the Chinese theater, the sacred person was indicated by a red face; the color of the villain was

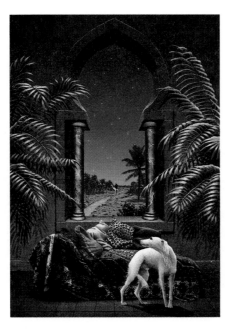

white. These colors were so ingrained in the society that they were equally understood by all, whether peasant or noble, elder or child.

In India, there were originally four castes, each symbolized by color (Figure 10-3). The Brahmans were symbolized by white. They were supposed to study, teach, and be priests to others. They were the privileged and sacred class. The Kshatriyas were symbolized by red. They were meant to study but not to teach, to sacrifice for themselves but not to officiate as priests. Their class was militant; they governed and fought the wars. The Vaisyas were symbolized by yellow. They were of the merchant class. They cultivated the fields, bred cattle, traded, and were money lenders. Finally, the Sudras were symbolized by black. They were the servile class and earned their living by laboring for others. They were allowed to practice the useful arts, but they were not permitted to study the holy Vedas.

Ancient Chinese, Hindu, and Egyptian ways were known to the later Greek and Roman cultures, and many earlier color symbols were adopted along with other traditions. The old gods were given new names, but color symbolism remained. Athena was adorned with a yellow robe. Red was sacred to Ceres and Dionysus. A white robe symbolized purity, a red robe was symbolic of sacrifice and love, and a blue robe represented altruism and integrity. Purple became the imperial color in ancient Rome, and Caesar wore it to personify Jupiter.

Greek artists also gave symbolism to color. Mythology told of the four ages of humanity as gold, silver, copper, and iron. Blue was used to symbolize earth, red was for fire, green for water, and yellow for air. Josephus

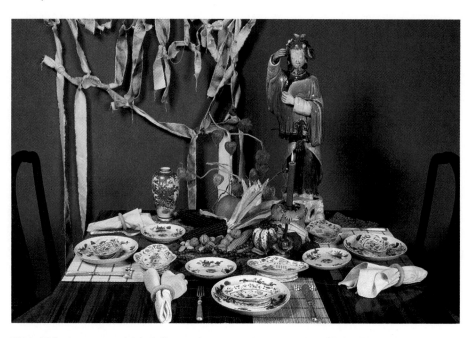

figure 10-2

The Chinese recognized five primary colors—red, yellow, black, white, and green-blue—as shown in this table setting using Qing Dynasty porcelain and roof tile statue. *Interior design by Fehrman & Fehrman, authors' collection.*

in the first century spoke of white earth, red fire, purple water, and blue air. Da Vinci in the fifteenth century related yellow to earth, red to fire, green to water, and blue to air. People were composed of colors and elements, with flesh and bones considered blue, body heat represented by red, blood and bodily fluids by green, and internal gases by yellow.

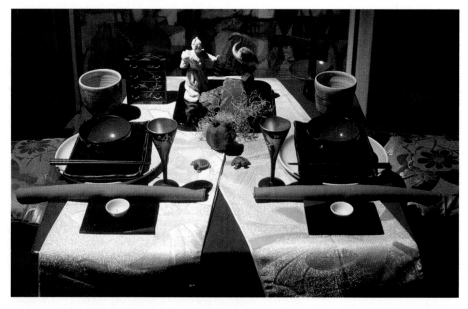

figure 10-3

This table setting utilizes Japanese elements and colors, including red and black lacquer, turquoise raku tea bowls, an antique silver and white obi used as a table runner, and seat cushions of antique brocade in orange, blue, and gold. *Interior design by Fehrman & Fehrman, authors' collection*

From birth to death, color played an important role in the life of primitive and ancient people. In all lands and nations, color was one of our first blessings and part of the last sacred act performed on the corpse. As children grew into adulthood, they were protected by sacred amulets of magical colors. Color was also used to protect the home from evil spirits' entry. Early people witnessed the red of blood during birth or battle and both feared and revered it. Women were often covered with red pigment, buried in the ground, or secluded in a cave or hut during their menstrual periods.

Color and Weddings

Weddings are full of tradition and ancient color symbolism (Figure 10-4). Some tribes painted women's faces red and white at marriage ceremonies and fertility rites to prevent the birth of monsters. Among the ancient Jews, the marriage ceremony was performed under the Talis, a golden silk robe supported by four pillars. Around this the bride walked seven times in memory of the siege of Jericho. In India red paint and even blood were used as wedding symbols. Six days before her wedding, the Hindu bride wore old, tattered yellow garments to drive away evil spirits. Her clothing at the ceremony was yellow, as were the robes of the priest. Once married, the wife wore yellow whenever her husband returned from a long journey. In China brides wore red embroidered with dragons. The bride was carried in a red marriage chair adorned with lanterns inscribed with the groom's family name in red. She carried a red parasol, and red firecrackers were exploded on her behalf. During the marriage ceremony, the bride and bridegroom drank a pledge of wine and honey from two cups that were tied together by a red cord.

In Japan it was believed that the daughter of a man who fed a thousand white hares in his house would marry a prince. In the Dutch East Indies, red or yellow rice was sprinkled over the bridegroom to keep his soul from flying away. Red was also the color of love potions. It was

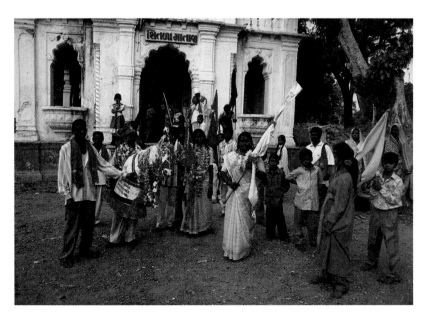

figure 10-4

In the West we have come to associate white with the bride's wedding gown, but other cultures symbolize marriage with different colors, as in this wedding in Rajahstan. © *Dorling Kindersley*

believed that if the names of a man and woman were written on white paper with the blood of a red hen, the woman would become infatuated when touched by it.

Red and yellow were, and continue to be, the marriage hues of Egypt, Asia, Russia, and the Balkans. In Western countries white is most often used for bridal gowns, and we still adhere to the old English rhyme, "Something old, something new; something borrowed, something blue."

Color and Death Rituals

Whatever our culture, most of us respond in the same way to death: sometimes with shock or disbelief, but always with grief. Reverence for the dead is practiced in most cultures. The dead must be disposed of and the family must prepare the shroud and equip the burial place in accordance with their beliefs. Red, black, and white are almost universally accepted in death rituals and associations (Figure 10-5).

When a Nandi tribesman of East Africa killed a member of another tribe, he painted one side of his body, spear, and sword red and the other side white to protect him from the ghost of his victim. In South Africa the lion killer painted his body white, went into seclusion for four days, then returned to the village with his skin coated in red. Fiji natives who killed another man were smeared with red from head to foot by the chief of the tribe.

With a few exceptions, black is the universal symbol of death among Western peoples. In nineteenth-century England, black attained its highest sense of symbolism during the reign of Queen Victoria. She wore black as a symbol of mourning for decades after the death of her beloved husband, Prince Albert. Black combined with white is often used in England to denote death. White announcement cards edged in black, a black wreath at the door, black armbands, or black-and-white clothing for the widow are common. During Victoria's day, servants in mourning for their masters were dressed completely in black, even down to the buttons on their clothes, while a state of half-mourning was represented by mauve. Certain primitive tribes even dyed their teeth black after the

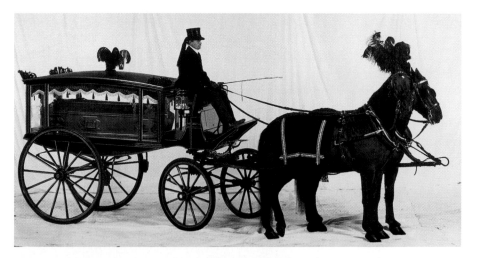

figure 10-5

Black is the universal symbol of death among nearly all Western people. In nineteenth-century England, black attained its highest sense of symbolism during the reign of Queen Victoria as seen in this hearse dating form the mid-1800s. © *Dorling Kindersley*

passing of a relative. Only in Egypt did black represent life, as a symbol of the fertile Nile mud.

Color and Religion

A respect for color can be traced to virtually all races throughout the world. In earlier times, philosophy and science were incorporated into religion (Figure 10-6). The great principles of nature and the vital forces of the universe were personified by gods and goddesses. Religion influenced not only spiritual life but also every institution of government. The true leaders of ancient times were the mystics who guided the rise and fall of empires and regulated the affairs of the society by such means as divination and reading the symbols of color. Because the sun was considered the ultimate goodness, providing warmth and sustaining life, yellow and gold were highly significant colors in many cultures, including ancient Egypt. God was (and in many cultures still is) considered the supreme deity associated with light. The golden ornaments of priests and the crowns of kings referred to the sun and God's symbolic link to light. The spectral colors—red, yellow, orange, green, blue, and violet—seen in a rainbow reminded people in many cultures of the powers of God on earth. The Druids of England used green, blue, and white in their rituals.

For Egyptians, the color red represented humans. Green represented the eternity of nature. Purple or black represented earth. The blue of the sky was linked with justice and worn on the breastplates of Egyptian priests to indicate the holiness of their judgments. Osiris was symbolized by green. His son, Horus, was symbolized by white. Set, the evil

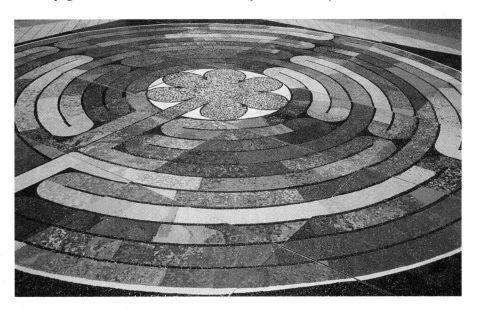

figure 10-6

This Prismatic Labyrinth, measuring 20 × 20 feet, is the collaborative effort of more than 170 students of diverse backgrounds under the direction of Kenneth Fehrman. It was created in a Color and Design class from thousands of pieces of colored paper torn from recycled magazines, which were then affixed in a mosaic pattern to form the spectrally colored labyrinth. The colors represent diversity. The center is a combination of all colors, representing unity. The Prismatic Labyrinth is portable and travels to various sites where it is used as a meditation and focus tool. © *Copyrighted 1998 by Kenneth and Cherie Fehrman*

deity, was black. Amen, the god of life and reproduction, was blue. Color was used with precision to denote specific religious meanings through symbolism.

In some civilizations, humans were sacrificed in a red temple draped with red hangings. The elements were thought to be controlled through incantations and rites involving color imagery. The ceremonies of birth, circumcision, puberty, marriage, and death were rich in color associations. Amulets and charms in appropriate colors protected the wearer from the evil eye and disease. In many Middle Eastern countries, blue is viewed as a color of protection. Front doors are painted blue to ward off evil spirits. Symbolically, color can have the same meaning cross-culturally. In the U.S. Southeast, front porch ceilings were painted blue to keep ghosts from entering and haunting the premises, while in the Southwest many Native Americans paint their doors blue to keep the bad spirits away. In Asia similar color symbolism prevailed. Gods were identified with colors. In India Brahma was yellow; Siva, the destroyer, was black. Yellow was sacred to Buddha and Confucius. While yellow is the color most associated with Buddha, he was sometimes depicted in red when he meditated. Green was sacred to Muhammad (being thought to be the color of the Prophet's cloak), and its use was saved for those who had made pilgrimages to Mecca.

There are many color references in the Judeo-Christian Bible. Colors are described in relation to the Tabernacle in the Wilderness, which was to have linen curtains in blue, purple, and scarlet. When the Lord spoke with Moses, he said, "And this is the offering ye shall take of them: gold, and silver and brass. And blue, and purple, and scarlet and fine linen." According to Exodus, God's color was depicted as blue, "and there was under his feet as it were a paved work of sapphire stone."

Legend has it that the Ten Commandments were inscribed on blue sapphire and that a red carbuncle (garnet) was at the prow of Noah's ark. In ancient times without the benefit of gemology, people sometimes confused sapphire with lapis lazuli because of its color. It is therefore possible, and more likely, that the Ten Commandments may have been inscribed on lapis since it is a rock. Green emerald is sometimes associated with Christ. St. John the Divine said, "And there was a rainbow around the throne, in sight like unto an emerald."

As Christianity developed, color began to lose its symbolic importance—but not entirely. Both Jewish and Christian color symbolism still exist. In synagogues and churches, stained-glass windows and clerical vestments were colored in deference to the old color symbolism. Green often represented the awakening of life in spring; autumn harvests were symbolized by golden hues. To this day the Roman Catholic church uses color to symbolize different religious events: white and gold represent Christmas and Easter, while red is worn at Pentecost and on the feasts of the martyrs. The red hats of cardinals are a reminder that they should defend the church even to the point of shedding blood like the martyrs. Green vestments appear at the birth of a new year, after Epiphany until Septuagesima, signifying God's provision for human needs. Purple, the color of Passiontide, represents the penance of the individual sinner and the sufferings of Christ. It was the most sacred color from early times, in part because it was so costly and difficult to obtain.

Color in Ancient Healing Techniques

In virtually all early cultures, the priests were also the healers. Being the spokespersons for the gods, they alone knew the secrets of survival. A study of Tibetan medicine reveals that many of the early traditions are continued today, particularly with respect to color and healing. Color plays an important role in Tibetan medicine. The color of bodily fluids is utilized as a diagnostic tool. The differentiation of colors and degree of transparency in urine samples are very detailed in Tibetan medicine and require a trained, skilled physician to interpret. Unlike Western medicine that relies on laboratory tests to determine a medical condition, physicians in Tibetan medicine are trained to observe and differentiate between colors as one of their diagnostic tools. When a urinalysis is done, the urine is placed most often in a plain white porcelain cup so that the color of the container will not affect the appearance of the urine's color. It is believed that the absence or presence of albumin in urine combined with an assessment of its color is an important aid in diagnosing illness. According to Tibetan medical doctrine, in a healthy person the color of urine is described as a bright, cheerful yellow, as of the butter on top of milk. The urine of a person with health problems may appear light blue in color and transparent, yellowish to orange, or pale, whitish, and milky. Urine that appears rust in color indicates a lymph disorder. If urine is yellow like mustard oil, it can indicate a bile disorder and contagious disease. If the urine is generally dark but has a spectrum of color like a rainbow, this indicates poisoning. Examining the color of the skin, eyes, and tongue is also a valuable tool of the practitioner of Tibetan medicine.

Another ancient form of healing is reading the color of a person's aura and making necessary adjustments based on that (Figure 10-7). Many cultures, including the Chinese, believe strongly that the proper orientation of buildings and homes to the earth's north-south axis is vital for

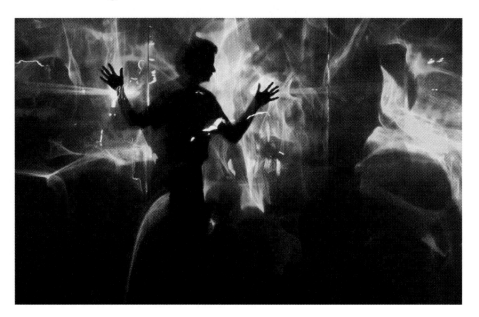

figure 10-7

An ancient form of healing is reading the color of a person's aura and making necessary adjustments based on that. Some psychics say they can see the auras that surround living beings, as this photo simulates. *Reprinted with permission of Exploratorium, www.exploratorium.edu*

health and well-being. This is based on the existence of magnetic sensitivity, which also plays a role in the detection of auras. We have been able to measure the brain's electrical activity for many years with devices such as the EEG (electroencephalograph). But a relatively new device called the SQUID (superconducting quantum interference device) used by researchers at New York University can measure extremely fine electrical activity in the brain from just above the scalp. Shifts in brain activity that result from different types of thought can be recorded and mapped with this instrument. This suggests that the activity of the brain may actually project out beyond the scalp. In addition to whatever our body and facial language does to reflect our thoughts, the brain itself may be signaling its thoughts to the outside world. It is postulated that these signals are what some people are able to detect as "auras," or fields of electrical activity that are displayed in a variety of colors. There are people who claim to be able to see auras around people, animals, and plants, and their color descriptions are similar from person to person. Aura readers have associated certain colors with various emotional or physical states.

Red is considered a very active color, showing vitality and physical energy. Burning red or scarlet around someone's body shows irritation, inflammation, or someone who's angry. When aura readers see someone who is angry, they say the red shoots blotches or sparks around the person. It is not just a field. A bright, vibrant green is considered a healing color, and it is also associated with the heart. If there is a murky green around someone, it indicates some imbalance in the physical body. Green is related to physical emotions.

Orange around someone is considered a very special color. A lot of actors have orange around them, as do people involved in public relations. Orange is considered an outgoing energy. Orange shows a lot of nervous energy and can be overstimulating. Yellow around someone is seen as an intellectual color, related to the third chakra, and represents reasoning ability or writing ability. (A chakra is considered to be an energy center that keeps the body in balance.) Sky blue is the color of the throat chakra and represents creativity, musical ability, ability to communicate, or creative energy. Blue is seen around teachers, counselors, psychologists, and people who talk or use their voices for some type of healing.

Indigo is a deep blue that shows intuition—psychic ability, intuitive ability, the ability to simply know things and not know where they come from. Deep indigo blue to violet is the shade seen around spiritual masters and teachers who are teaching on a spiritual level. The crown chakra at the top of the head is represented by violet, which symbolizes total cosmic awareness or total bliss. Aura readers say violet shows that a person is on a path of service, but it also shows around creative artists and schizophrenics. Violet is thought to be a healing color for the nervous system.

Many aura readers believe these colors have universal meanings (Figure 10-8). One person we interviewed said, "Color is just light radiating at the particular vibration level. When you look at it, it goes through your eyes and affects a part of the nervous system responsive to that particular vibration—it brings out a chemical reaction in the endocrine glands. It's like there's a web, a field of energy. Colors affect the subtle energy field which then has a stimulating effect on the body's

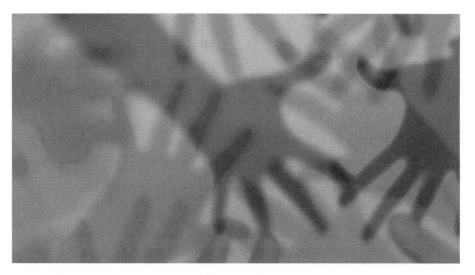

figure 10-8

Many aura readers believe colors have universal meanings. Indigo shows intuition and psychic ability, orange is considered outgoing energy, red is considered an active color showing vitality and physical energy, and intense burning red or scarlet indicates irritation or inflammation. *Reprinted with permission of Exploratorium, www.exploratorium.edu*

physical energy field. Seeing something green affects the thymus—it's a rejuvenating or balancing force that acts in the middle of the body. Yellow would affect the solar plexus and adrenal glands. Black is a neutralizer somehow; after a while you'd probably get really drained if you saw black all the time. Blue affects the thyroid. Violet affects the pituitary gland. Deeper blue affects the pineal gland. Red affects the plexus of nerves at the base of the spine—an activating color."

(It should be noted that the foregoing discussion of auras is based on the personal impressions of aura readers. Future color and energy research may prove or disprove these claims.)

Color and Amulets

Most tribal cultures have associations with talismans and amulets to protect them from evil or to make them stronger in battle. A talisman may include colored stones considered to have exceptional powers, crystals, or transparent golden amber, which represented the sun falling to earth. The Australian Aborigines regarded quartz crystals as power-bearers of rich symbolic significance and called them "wild stones" that were said to embody the Great Spirit himself. These quartz crystals were supposed to have fallen from heaven to earth as "solidified light." To the Aborigines there were only four sacred colors that could be used in ritual cave painting: red, yellow, white, and black. The colors were taken from the earth pigments: red and yellow ochre, white pipe clay, and black charcoal. The Taoists regarded jade as a powerful medicine and protectant. In the fourth century A.D. white jade was regarded so highly that it was believed those who ingested it would have life without end. Ground up into a powder and mixed with water, jade was supposed to confer immortality.

The ancient Babylonians and Assyrians used cylinder-seal amulets of agate, purple amethyst, red carnelian, clear crystal, emerald, bloodstone, green jade, red jasper, blue lapis lazuli, and golden topaz to protect them

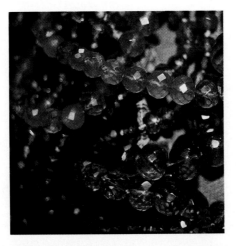

figure 10-9

Amber has long been considered an amulet. Ornaments made of golden amber were worn in the earliest periods of Asia, Africa, and Europe. Amber represented the sun and became a powerful tool for warding off evil spirits. Beads made of amber were thought to preserve the wearer against rheumatism, toothache, headache, jaundice, and every other kind of internal ailment. *Authors' collection*

(Figure 10-9). They believed the blue of lapis lazuli possessed the spirits of the gods; and that a seal made of clear rock crystal would extend the possessions of and bring auspicious events to the wearer. Red jasper guaranteed the protection of the gods.

The ancient Egyptians were noted for their amulets. They placed them under and in their houses and tombs, wore them while living, and placed them on the bodies of the dead. Egyptian amulets were made of many different stones and gems, wood, gold, copper, silver and gold combined, ivory, bone, shell, wax, and faience. The common word for amulet in the dynastic period was *mk-t*, which meant protector, the thing that keeps one safe or strong.

The scarab is one of Egypt's most recognizable amulets. It represents the dung beetle, and from earliest times the Egyptians associated this beetle with the god of creation and its egg-ball with the sun. The god was believed to roll the ball of the sun across the sky as the beetle rolled its dung ball over the ground. The Egyptians wore models of the beetle to give them the life and strength of the god of creation. They placed in their mummies amulets of green stone, black basalt, hematite, or bloodstone to effect the resurrection of the dead. Colossal models of the scarab were set up on pedestals in the temples, and scarab amulets of turquoise blue faience or deep blue lapis lazuli were also used as seals.

The *tjet* was associated with the genital organs of the goddess Isis and was supposed to bring to the wearer the virtue of the blood of Isis. It was commonly made of some red substance such as red jasper, red glass, red wood, red porphyry, red porcelain, carnelian, or reddish agate. The *urs* or headrest pillow amulet was usually made of red hematite or bloodstone. When it was intended for use as a funerary article, it was made of wood, ivory, or stone. These large pillows were placed under the necks of mummies to lift up their heads into the other world.

The *ab* or heart amulet was made of many kinds of red stones, red jasper, red glass, red porcelain, red paste, and red wax. It was inscribed in the breast of the mummy in place of the heart, which was mummified separately. The vulture amulet was constructed in the color gold to give the deceased the strength and fierceness of the goddess Isis when she wandered about in the papyrus swamps in the form of a vulture. The papyrus scepter or *uadj* was made of emerald green and gave the deceased renewed youth and vitality and all the qualities of the growing papyrus plant. The *udjat* (eye) amulet typified good health, soundness, safe protection, and physical comfort and well-being. *Udjats* were made of blue lapis lazuli, carnelian, gold, silver, copper, or various colors of precious and semiprecious stones or faience. The *nefer* amulet was frequently made of red carnelian or some other red stone. It was believed to bring the wearer youth, joy, strength, and happiness. The word *nefer* means good, beautiful, gracious, and pleasant. The *sma* amulet was buried in the folds of the mummy's wrappings to impart the power to breathe. It was made of dark basalt or some other brownish-black stone. The serpent's head amulet was made of red stone, red glass, or red faience and was thought to protect the wearer against the bite of the cobra or other venomous snakes. These are just a few of the many amulets the Egyptians utilized, but it is interesting to note that red and black appear again and again as symbols of power and strength in this culture. Even in the West today, these colors are still linked with those attributes.

Sometimes the amulet's written symbols in conjunction with its color combined to form its strength. At other times, the color of the stone or material used was sufficient to bring the desired power. Red agate, sometimes called blood agate, protected the warrior against poisonous reptiles, gave a lover favor in the sight of the beloved, and brought riches, happiness, health, and long life. It was also thought to increase intelligence. It Italy and Persia it protected the wearer against the evil eye. It was believed that if a woman drank the water in which a green agate had been washed, she would remain fertile. Moss agate, with its beautiful markings resembling trees and vegetation, was much prized and promised an abundant harvest. Ornaments made of golden amber were worn in the earliest periods in the history of many of the peoples of Asia, Africa, and Europe. When ancient peoples discovered its electrical properties combined with its beautiful golden color representing the sun, amber became a powerful tool for warding off the evils of the unknown. Beads made of amber preserved the wearer against rheumatism, toothache, headache, jaundice, and every other kind of internal ailment. Amber was believed to prevent excessive bleeding and was used in circumcision rituals for this purpose. In many European countries, amber was worn as a protection against witches and warlocks.

Purple amethyst was greatly prized as an amulet. Because it represented the color of wine, it was thought to protect the wearer from drunkenness. When placed under the pillow, it was supposed to give the wearer pleasant dreams and improve memory. Worn around the neck, it protected against poison. Its presence in bishop's rings was supposed to help the wearer to become gentle, amiable, and free of temper and anger. Emerald protected the wearer from diseases of the eye and from liver problems. Emerald supposedly struck such terror into the viper and cobra that their eyes leaped out of their heads. Clear crystal was sometimes considered petrified ice. Little balls of crystal set in metal bands were found all over Europe and in England and Ireland, where they were used as amulets. The early Christians regarded crystal as a symbol of the Immaculate Conception because of its association with purity. The Scots thought crystal was the stone of victory. Deep red garnet protected the wearer from nightmares and skin disease. It also assured the wearer love, faithfulness, and freedom from wounds.

For thousands of years, jade has held a special place as an amulet and healing stone. Jade amulets assisted women in childbirth. Jade brought rain and drove away evil beasts and spirits. It made a warrior victorious in battle, protected wearers from lightning, and relieved palpitations of the heart. Jade as an amulet in western Asia dates from the fourth millennium B.C. and was prized among the Turks, Arabs, and Armenians. In China jade was a sacred stone. White nephrite jade was used by the emperor to converse with heaven, and the lore of jade continues to be linked to Chinese culture. The Maoris of New Zealand wear figures of their ancestral gods in nephrite suspended from their necks. (It should be noted here that jade is really two categories of stone: nephrite, which is the toughest stone on earth, and jadeite, which is more fragile. Whenever ancient texts refer to jade, they usually mean nephrite. Jadeite was not discovered until the eighteenth century.)

Another prized amulet was the beautiful blue of lapis lazuli. The earliest inhabitants of India, Persia (Iran), and Mesopotamia used it for official seals and as an amulet for the ruling class. The Egyptians distinguished two kinds of lapis lazuli—the genuine and a paste artificially created from the powdered stone. The real lapis was used for making scarabs and figures of gods; the artificial blue paste was used for beads. The Sumerians believed that the wearer of lapis carried the presence of a god. In its powdered form, it was administered to patients suffering from gallstones, depression, sleeplessness, and fever. In Macedonia, lapis amulets were supposed to prevent miscarriage and abortion and to ward off tragic influences.

Green malachite amulets were common in both Asia and Europe and were attached to the necks of children to protect them from the evil eye and prevent pain during teething. The Italians believed green malachite cured diseases of the eye. White, translucent moonstone amulets protected against epilepsy and guaranteed a good harvest. Yellowish-green peridot was called topaz in ancient writings. When worn on the left arm, it protected the wearer against the evil eye and was regarded as a preventive measure against diseases of the liver. It was also supposed to rid the mind of envious thoughts. Ruby was a very powerful amulet that protected against witchcraft of all kinds, as well as plague, pestilence, and famine. Turquoise is an ancient and much-loved amulet. It was highly prized all over Asia and in many parts of Africa for its prophylactic and therapeutic qualities. The Arabs called it "the lucky stone." In many cultures, from the Tibetan to the Native American, it is mounted in rings, necklaces, earrings, and head ornaments. As an amulet it protects the wearer from poison, venomous snake bites, and eye disease. It was also believed to warn the wearer of approaching death by changing color.

The Vedic System

One of the most fascinating and oldest associations with color in relation to gemstone amulets is found in the ancient Vedic texts of India, where it is believed that natural gemstones transmit astral powers like radio crystals transmit sound. The practice of *jyotish* has been in continuous use for thousands of years and links the colors transmitted to health and personal happiness. Fine gems promote good fortune while poor-quality gems bring sickness and cause bad influences. In the Vedic system the power of gems emanates from nine cosmic bodies: ruby or red stones for the sun; pearl or moonstone for the moon; yellow stones for Jupiter; hessonite (a form of orange garnet) for Rahu (the ascending node of the moon); emerald or green stones for Mercury; diamond for Venus; cat's eye for Ketu (the descending node of the moon); blue sapphire for Saturn; and coral for Mars. The Vedas tell us that these cosmic bodies influence different aspects of life and, being luminous bodies, also radiate specific cosmic colors. According to these ancient beliefs, the colors radiated by these cosmic bodies are identical to the cosmic colors of the different gemstones.

In the Vedic system, gemstones help by adding cosmic color to one's own aura or by astrologically enhancing one's life, as well as by attracting the power and protection of their ruling deities—the sun spirit, the moon spirit, and so on. The color hue of each gem fits into one of the four designated socioeconomic and intellectual categories (*varnas*): the ruling class, warriors, farmers and merchants, and servants. One of the most fascinating aspects of this system is the way it classifies the cosmic color of gemstones, although sometimes these colors are a little hard to comprehend. For example, while red is the cosmic color of rubies, orange is considered the cosmic color of pearls and moonstone. Ultraviolet is the cosmic color of hessonite and orange gems, green is the cosmic color of emeralds and green gems, indigo is the color transmitted by diamonds and colorless gems, infrared is the cosmic color of cat's-eye gems, violet is the cosmic color of blue sapphire and blue, yellow is the cosmic color transmitted by coral, and light blue is the cosmic color of natural yellow gems. It is intriguing to consider that although the Vedas date back thousands of years, their authors appeared to know about ultraviolet and infrared radiation. It should be noted that the Vedic system is very elaborate and complex and only touched on briefly here.

Gradually, over time, many of these different ancient beliefs merged, and we began to associate color with the planets and signs of the zodiac. By the nineteenth century, gold represented the sun and silver the moon; green was linked with Venus, red with Mars, blue with Jupiter, and black with Saturn. In the signs of the zodiac, fire red symbolized the ram (Aries); dark green the bull (Taurus); chestnut the twins (Gemini); silver represented Cancer; gold defined Leo, the lion; purple symbolized Virgo; aquamarine symbolized the scales (Libra); vermilion was the scorpion (Scorpio); black was for the goat (Capricorn); gray symbolized Aquarius; and sea blue represented the fish (Pisces), as well as Saggitarius.

The Importance of Color in Amulets

While the shape and form of amulets is of great importance, color was equally important in making sure the amulet contained sufficient power to do its job as a prophylactic and therapeutic aid. Most cultures associated similar symbolism with specific colors. Green stones such as nephrite jade, emeralds, and malachite were symbolically linked with luxurious vegetation, rain, and fertility. By association, the color green became linked with fertility and virility. Yellow stones were almost universally associated with jaundice and were believed to help in curing diseases of the liver. Red stones were used in bleeding disorders and wounds and to protect wearers from fire and lightning. Black stones were a protection against the evil eye. White stones not only protected against the evil eye but also brought the protection of heaven. Particularly prized were stones that sparkled. The quality of light inherent in such transparent stones seemed a magical link with the cosmos, heaven, and gods in general. Transparent rock crystal defeated every kind of witchcraft and was considered extremely powerful.

If individual colored stones were powerful, then worn in combination the powers must be even greater. For this reason amulets made of stone combinations were believed to hold even greater power. The breastplate of Aaron contained a number of colored stones, believed to be carnelian (brownish-red), peridot or topaz (yellowish-green), emerald, ruby or garnet, blue sapphire or lapis lazuli, jacinth (orangish), agate (color unknown), amethyst (purple), heliodor (yellow), chrysolite (green), and jasper (color unknown). Since agate and jasper come in a multitude of colors, it is not possible to determine which colors specifically were used by Aaron. On each stone was engraved the name of one of the tribes of Israel; this was believed to add to the powers of the stone.

While diverse cultures used color in different ways to protect them in battle, heal them from sickness, and allay their fears, the use of color as an integral part of cultural and societal systems dates back so far in human history that it is impossible to date it with certainty (Figure 10-10). Early humans lived days of difficulty and dark nights of anxiety and fear of the unknown. The magic of light and the color of rainbows gave them hope, and the powers attributed to color and amulets gave them support (Figure

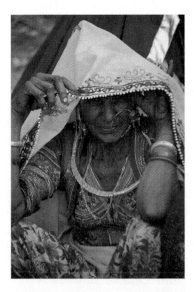

figure 10-10

Color as an integral part of cultural and societal systems dates back so far in human history that it is impossible to date it with certainty, yet it links all cultures with its universal importance. © *Dorling Kindersley*

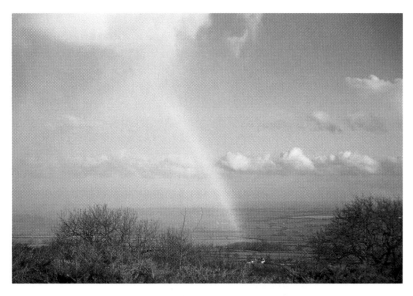

figure 10-11

The magic of light and the color of rainbows gave ancient humans hope, and the power attributed to color gave them support. © *Dorling Kindersley*

10-11). Most early texts (the Vedas being an exception) did not understand that color is an energy wave that has an effect for scientific reasons. They merely believed that it gave them an edge as a powerful survival tool. The physical difficulties they faced were so incomprehensible that early people invented devils, demons, and evil spirits to blame for their misfortunes. Once they had established a system of color-linked amulets to defeat these evil demons, they had found a way to alleviate stress, to heal, to survive, and to pay homage to their gods. This was the role of color in early cultures. Color has been and is used universally for these reasons. Even though today we consider ourselves modern and scientific in our approach, we are still influenced by our cultural associations with color, its ancient roots inextricably entwined with the very survival of humans on earth.

Color and Feng Shui

Feng shui (pronounced *fung shway*) is an ancient Chinese method of creating harmony and balance between the workings of the universe and nature. Feng shui literally translates to "wind and water." It is the Chinese art of balancing and enhancing the environment through placement. In this belief system, all permutations, from cosmic to atomic, from macro to micro, resonate within each of us. The force that links humans to their surroundings is called *chi* and can be roughly related to an energy field that infuses and integrates all things. The point of feng shui is to harness and enhance environmental *chi* to improve the flow of *chi* within our bodies, resulting in improved health and welfare. Feng shui is a very complex process, and a complete discussion of it is beyond the scope of this book. Here we present a brief overview of the interaction of color in the feng shui process.

To understand the process of feng shui, we must set aside linear thinking and consider the multitude of factors and dimensions that affect our *chi* and our lives. The feng shui system is based on the premise that all things are interlaced, so everything has an effect on something else. For example, the universe and the movement and position of the sun, moon, stars, and planets; weather patterns, tides, atmospheric conditions; political, geographic, and economic situations; customs; and even the position of one's bed within the bedroom or the colors we choose can affect our *chi*, thereby affecting all aspects of our lives. According to feng shui, the closer the environmental factor is, the greater influence it possesses. Because color is something all of us interact with every day, it is thought to have a great influence.

In feng shui colors can be applied to areas in a room or a building to enhance aspects of one's life. The Chinese consider certain colors more auspicious than others. For example, black is the color of the water element, which symbolizes wealth, but black also signifies loss of light and is therefore often avoided. Red is a very auspicious color that is often used in celebrations. Yellow, the color of the sun, represents longevity. Green, the color of spring, symbolizes growth, freshness, and tranquility. Blue is considered an ambiguous color, representing sky but also death. In feng shui colors can be used to adjust the *chi* of a home or office. The five colors in relation to the five elements can be used to enhance health, career, family life, knowledge, and so on. Family is represented by green; wealth is part green, part red; marriage is part red, part white; children are represented by white; helpful people are represented by part white, part black; career is black; knowledge is part black, part green. Yellow represents the earth and the center. So, according to feng shui, red and green together encourage wealth; green, red, and yellow used together bring fame; red and white used together enhance marriage; yellow, white, and black encourage children; black and white bring helpful people; white, black, and green help careers; black and green deepen knowledge; and black, green, and red help the family.

Color Vocabulary

It is not known how precise color terms develop, but environment, culture, and economic growth undoubtedly play a large part. The basic color vocabulary of even the richest languages is fewer than a dozen words. All other color terms are a matter of qualifying a basic word, such as light blue or dark green. Sometimes the name of an object is used as a color—gold or silver, for example. Sometimes color names occur when major events are linked with technology. For example, magenta is the name of a dye invented in 1859. The name was derived from the Battle of Magenta, which was fought that year in northern Italy. During the evolution of the English language, the Anglo-Saxon word *wann* has no modern equivalent and referred to such diverse things as the gloss on a raven's wing, the light that dances on a dark wave, and the rippling sheen on dark chain mail. Desert dwellers have a large range of words for yellows and browns. Eskimos possess a wide vocabulary to differentiate various colors and conditions of ice and snow; the Maoris have more than a hundred terms to cover what we call red. The Maoris also have color words for the ages and stages of plant growth that we would describe in terms of time or size. They also have forty color words to distinguish one cloud formation from another. Many African tribes have extensive color vocabularies to describe their most treasured possessions such as cattle, just as the old Germanic peoples had a great many words to describe horses. This tradition has passed into English, which possesses a large number of horse color words: roan, strawberry roan, bay, chestnut, gray, piebald, skewbald, and so on. English speakers also possess a surprisingly large number of color words for hair: blond, grizzled, mousy, auburn, chestnut.

As color language evolved with the culture, sophisticated languages required an ever-increasing number of words to make precise color definitions clear. These were borrowed from almost any source, especially those applying to the blue-violet end of the spectrum that occurs rarely in nature. Some of the descriptive color words are taken directly from the object itself: amethyst, peacock blue, violet, emerald, ruby, and so on. Ultramarine meant that the color came from overseas. Azure comes from the Persian *lazhward*, meaning blue stone, lapis lazuli. Puce is the shade of a flea's belly, from the Latin word *pulex*, a flea; mauve is the color of the wood mallow, whose botanical name is *Malva*. Purple comes from the Greek *porphyra*, taken from the sea creature from which Tyrian purple is made. The Chinese characters for red, green, and purple all contain the root character for silk, suggesting that colors were originally those of silk dyes. Light green is called kingfisher color and deep green is jade color; ash color is gray. Neither the Chinese nor Japanese have a word for brown, although the Japanese have a number of descriptive terms such as tea color, fox color, and kite color. The Chinese do not use the terms light or dark when describing colors. Instead, they use the water images, shallow and deep.

In 1969 two American anthropologists, Brent Berlin and Paul Kay, made an exhaustive study of color terms in ninety-eight different languages and discovered that universal basic color terms do exist, but there are no more than eleven of them in any one language. Berlin and Kay's second startling discovery was that if a language has fewer than eleven basic color terms, there are such strict limitations on which they are based that out of 2,048 possible combinations, only 22 are found. Their study revealed the following:

1. No language has only one color term; they all have at least two.
2. If there are three terms, the third is always red.
3. If there are four terms, green or yellow is added.
4. If there are five terms, green and yellow are added.
5. If there are six terms, blue is added.
6. If there are seven terms, brown is added.
7. If there are eight or more terms, purple, pink, orange, and gray are always added, but they can occur in any order or combination.

Berlin and Kay's findings suggested that languages acquire color terms in a chronological order that can be interpreted as a sequence of evolutionary stages. It would seem that at the beginning of human communication, there were only two terms: black and white. Gradually, a name for red came into use. In languages that have reached stage four (those using five basic color terms), there is still a certain amount of confusion in color language. For example, some of the people studied may use the same word for blue and green. Melanesian, Welsh, Eskimo, and Tamil do not contain a word for brown at all, while Thais and Lapps call it black-red; neither ancient Greek nor modern Greek-Cypriot has any word for brown. In Japan the word for blue appears to be older than the word for green. If this proves true, it would be an exception to the usual evolutionary order. This research has opened up a fascinating branch of study relating to color and culture.

REFERENCES

Berlin, B., Kay, P., *Basic Color Terms: Their Universality and Evolution*, University of California Press, 1969.

Birren, F., *Color and Human Response*, Van Nostrand Reinhold, 1978.

Brown, R. S., *Astrological Gemstone Talisman*, Bangkok, Thailand, 1988.

Budge, E. A. W., *Amulets and Superstitions*, Dover Publications, 1978.

Cowan, J., *Mysteries of the Dream-Time: The Spiritual Life of Australian Aborigines*, Avery Publishing Group, 1989.

Donden, Y., *Health through Balance: An Introduction to Tibetan Medicine*, Snow Lion Publications, 1986.

Kunzang, J., Rinpoche, R., *Tibetan Medicine*, University of California Press, 1976.

Landsdowne, Z. F., *The Chakras and Esoteric Healing*, Samuel Weiser, 1986.

Rivlin, R., Gravelle, K., *Deciphering the Senses*, Simon and Schuster, 1984.

Chapter eleven

Color order systems

Why Do We Measure Color?

The human eye can differentiate between more than ten million colors, yet only a fraction of these colors are selected for inclusion in the range of products available to the consumer. Producing colors is a costly business, and mass production of a limited color range keeps prices low. Manufacturers build their color ranges on a nucleus of best-selling colors, around which fashion and industry orbit.

So, while you may be able to choose from fifty eye shadow colors, thirty colors of bed sheets, and five colors of plastic kitchenware, manufacturers are faced with a bewildering array of possibilities. Because consumers are accustomed to picking out the exact colors presented in fashion or home furnishings magazines, a single shade or tint can mean the difference between a satisfied or dissatisfied consumer, a sale or lost business. Yet, how do you describe that perfect color of sweater to go with your trousers? Is it sky blue? That opens up literally hundreds of possibilities. Is it the blue of the sky on a sunny day or when it's just getting cloudy? Is it a greenish blue or a true blue? Or is it more of a turquoise? If so, American turquoise, Persian turquoise, or Himalayan turquoise, all of which vary in color? You can see how complex and ridiculous it can be to try to describe color succinctly, and when millions of dollars in industry depend on that description, it had better be accurate. From this need, color order systems grew.

If you were asked to categorize a stack of colors, where do you begin? This is a problem that artists, mathematicians, and philosophers have been dealing with since Newton first dispersed light into its constituent wavelengths during the seventeenth century (Figure 11-1). Each color of the spectrum—red, orange, yellow, green, blue, and violet—and all the intermediate hues that range between them can be bright and intense or pale. **All colors have three dimensions: hue, saturation, and value (lightness or darkness).** To place colors in order, these three dimensions must be taken into account. Color theorists have tried many geometric shapes to accomplish this, but to arrange the thousands of colors available to industry today, a simple and convenient color order system had to be derived (Figure 11-2). Color/light is such a complex phenomenon

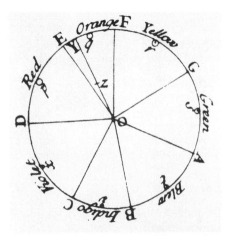

figure 11-1

This original drawing by Newton of his color wheel relates colors to notes of the musical scale, a concept followed by others, as discussed previously in this book. © *Dorling Kindersley*

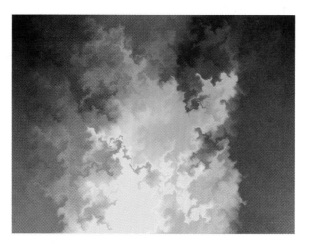

figure 11-2

Color theorists have tried many shapes to accomplish color measuring systems. This computer-generated image renders the color spectrum in a way that makes it appear kinetic and flowing. *Reproduced with permission of Edward S. May*

that this task has not been easy. Through false starts and trial and error, we have arrived at color theories that enable us to attempt an explanation of color. We have developed color order systems that allow us to communicate color to each other fairly accurately. However, we are far from having a complete and true grasp of the nature of color/light. Even at the end of his life, after dedicating years to trying to explain light, Einstein said he felt no closer to understanding it than he had at the beginning. Within these pages, we offer a sampling of the many attempts humans have made to capture and communicate this color/light phenomenon.

The physical aspects of color are not the only criteria being measured. Sometimes color systems are used to measure the psychological effects of color. Some of these include the Rorschach Inkblot Method, the Lüscher Color Test, the Color Pyramid Test, and the perplexing Retinex Theory, as discussed in Chapter 5. **One very important thing to remember when considering psychological color studies is that color is often used only as a code marker.** For example, a recently published work on personality defines personality profiles in terms of color. A person may be a "red," a "blue," and so on. However, these profiles have nothing to do with the specific color. The colors have merely been used as tags and could easily be replaced with a numerical or other tag code such as a, b, and c or 1, 2, and 3.

Visual color organization is easily expressed in graphics. One of the first widely recognized charts or graphs is that of Hofler, dating back to 1897. It consists of a double pyramid. At the top apex is the white, with black at the bottom. Between black and white is a scale of neutral grays. On the four corners of the central connecting base are red, yellow, green, and blue. All colors seen by the eye lie within the outer boundaries of the pyramid. This schematic concept of representing color was followed by others, including Wilhelm Ostwald, who developed a double cone rather than a double pyramid, and Albert Munsell, who visualized a sphere or "tree."

Since no two of us see color in exactly the same way, two people can look at the same sweater and each sees a slightly different color. While this individual color distinction is part of what makes people unique, industry needs something more practical. Manufacturers need a common language to discuss color and color variation. This common language is provided by color-analysis instruments such as **spectrophotometers, densitometers**, and **colorimeters**, which quantify a color's hue, chroma, and saturation or value.

A spectrophotometer measures individual wavelengths and then calculates a variety of values from this information. Spectrophotometers can measure in all standard illuminants, including daylight, incandescent, and fluorescent.

Densitometers measure density of ink films by using one or more filter. Densitometers do not give complete color information but are useful for specification and control of printed colors, particularly when standard process inks are used.

Colorimeters measure color by using three or four filters that match the human color receptors. Colorimeters can measure in only one light source.

Despite their technological advancement, color-analysis instruments still cannot measure color in the same way that people see it. For example, manufacturers have found that when different textures are introduced, spectrophotometers do not yield accurate results because they operate on the principle of reflected light. Different surfaces and textures reflect the same visual color differently. This means that a color measurement instrument generates two different results for two surfaces that are the same color. For this reason, major manufacturers still depend on human vision to augment spectrophotometrical analysis. The bottom line is that colors need to look good to the human eye, regardless of what a machine says. In the future, color measurement devices may be developed that render accurate color analysis under a variety of textural and surface conditions. But, as of this writing, color measurement instruments have limitations.

Of the color order systems currently in use, two of the most commonly used by manufacturers are the Hunter L, a, b and CIE LAB. Hunter L, a, b was developed by the founder of Hunter Associates Laboratory Inc., in Reston, Virginia, and completed in 1958. The CIE of CIE LAB stands for Commission Internationale de l'Eclairage (International Commission on Illumination), which was developed by the French. Both scales operate on the principles of opposite colors:

1. Some colors are darker than others.
2. Green and red are opposite, not typically combined colors.
3. Blue and yellow are opposite colors.

These scales also build upon the Munsell system, developed in the early 1900s. The Munsell system is considered visually uniform because adjacent samples represent equal intervals of visual perception. Munsell takes hue, value, and chroma into account. The tristimulus values (X, Y, Z) developed in the 1930s also do this but do not make the communication of color any easier than the Munsell system did. Hunter L, a, b and CIE LAB quantify and communicate color, but they also have their limitations. In choosing a color order or measurement system, the most important factor is that all parties involved are using the same system.

This is currently the best way to ensure valid comparisons and avoid the pitfalls of comparing apples to oranges.

Goethe's Color System

In 1790, about sixty years after the death of Sir Isaac Newton, Johann Wolfgang von Goethe attempted to replicate Newton's experiment (Figure 11-3). He looked at a white wall through a prism. He expected to see the whole wall burst into spectral colors but was amazed to find that the wall remained white: "I immediately spoke out loud to myself, through instinct, that Newtonian theory was erroneous." Goethe may have been a bit hasty in his conclusions, but it provided him with sufficient impetus to spend the next twenty years experimenting with color, culminating in *Color Theory*, published in 1810, which he considered his greatest work.

To Goethe's poetic mind, Newton's explanation of color/light was as about as accurate and exciting as describing a flower as a collection of uniformly gray subatomic particles. It tried to explain by fragmentation rather than by looking at the whole picture. To Goethe, Newton's abstract mathematics of optics failed to do justice to the experience of color in everyday life. Goethe wanted to classify the different conditions under which color is produced and to assess their reality in terms of ordinary experience.

Goethe denigrated Newton's attempt to explain light, which he believed had a flawed experimental base. In order to break down light and examine its constituent parts, Newton used the artificial conditions of a dark room, an aperture, and prisms, through which he had a beam of light pass. Goethe thought this procedure totally missed the point. To begin with, light should not be broken down but considered as a totality. Second, the colors light produced should be studied in their natural habitat. Therefore, the natural environment became Goethe's laboratory, and he set out to refute Newton's views. Goethe theorized that if colors

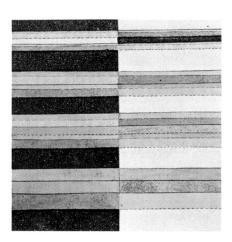
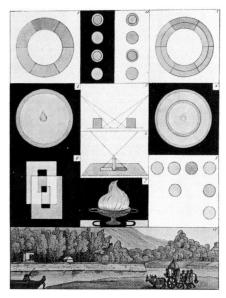

figure 11-3

These images show Goethe's early experiments with the color wheel.
© Dorling Kindersley

were no more than the components of white light entering the eye in different wavelengths, it would be impossible to distinguish among a colored lamp, a dull object seen in a bright light, and a bright object in shadow. He believed seeing depended on perception of the light reflected from an object in relation to the light that falls on it. And, of course, he was right. If we are uncertain about the light source, we cannot be certain about the color or even the nature of the object.

If we take the example of a sunset, the accepted scientific description says that as the sun's light passes through the more or less opaque medium of the atmosphere, the shorter wavelengths are scattered while the longer, yellow-red ones are transmitted. This process causes the colors that appear at sunset. Goethe was not concerned with the ultimate cause of color, only its effects on the eye and mind of the observer. Goethe explained color in terms of pairs. Yellow and blue are the two poles of a whole system of color pairs, each of which has opposing qualities, plus-minus, warm-cool, active-passive. Other pairs are red-green and orange-violet. Arranged in a circle, the six colors of Goethe's spectrum express a system of harmony or contrast, depending on whether they are viewed from the left or right sides of the circle. Blue harmonizes with its neighbors, green and violet, and contrasts with or complements its opposite, orange. This grouping of colors in pairs was a crucial innovation, in comparison with the conventional seven-color Newtonian wheel.

Who was right, Newton or Goethe? This tough question is still controversial today. There are those who believe only in Newton's way of breaking things into fragments to study them, and there are those who believe that to truly understand anything, we must observe it in its relational entirety. Since color/light is such an elusive phenomenon, it is no wonder that we are still trying to come to grips with fully understanding and explaining it.

The Munsell System

Albert H. Munsell is one of the most famous American colorists and can be considered the founding father of modern color order. His color sphere, first developed at the end of the nineteenth century, has since been improved by scientists and today is one of the most widely used systems of color (Figure 11-4). Munsell became frustrated with the ambiguity and limitations of color names like "plum" (which can range from green through purple) and "smoke gray," which do not classify colors in relation to each other and give only a vague indication of identity. He sought to rectify "the incongruous and bizarre nature of our present color names . . . with an appropriate system based on the hue, value and chroma of our sensations." In his system, these three dimensions (chroma = saturation) are measured against a defined scale.

Remember that Munsell was a child of his generation, in this case the Victorian era, and that his color theories developed from his own color bias. (This comment is not intended as a disparaging remark about Munsell, but a reminder that we all have learned color biases.) His comments such as "the use of strongest colors only fatigues the eyes; beginners should avoid strong color; and quiet color is the mark of good taste" clearly establish his strong color bias. This, and his tendency to make laws of color harmony rather than encouraging freedom and

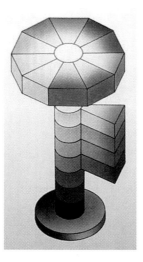

figure 11-4

A version of Munsell's color model. © *Dorling Kindersley*

creativity are serious flaws in the Munsell system. However, since common ground for color discussion is needed, his system has long-established roots, and his system continues to be taught in many schools today.

Essentially, the Munsell system can be broken down into eight categories.

1. Munsell favors colors that have medium value (brightness) and medium saturation or chroma (a term he invented). Within a scale of nine gray steps, a combination of steps 1 (black), 5 (medium gray), and 9 (white) would be considered ideal. So would steps 3, 5, and 7 or steps 4, 5, and 6, with 5 always a point of balance. Value 5 is considered the fulcrum with light or dark accents.
2. Monochromatic harmonies involving one key color should also follow this principle, according to Munsell. The ideal would be a color of medium 5 value and medium 5 chroma, combined either with 3 or 7 or 4 or 6 value of the same color with 3 or 7 or 2 or 8 chromas. Diagonal monochromatic harmonies could also be arranged but again with the 5-5 formula as the key fulcrum.
3. Complementary colors were considered harmonious but with reservations. Fore example, a red of 5 value could be combined harmoniously with a blue-green of 5 value or a value 5 gray. Other complements of equal value would be considered equally harmonious.
4. Munsell believed that balance was the key to harmonious color. For example, a red of 3 chroma would need a blue-green of 3 chroma to balance it. If the red had a 6 chroma, a blue-green twice the size would be necessary for balance. If different values were involved, any stronger chroma should occupy less area than a weaker chroma.
5. Different chromas and different values could be neatly arranged, as in category 4, as long as the measured result used value 5 as the fulcrum.

6. Neighboring hues could be combined with split complements but, again, must be balanced.
7. Diminishing sequences from light to dark values and from pure to weak chromas could be plotted throughout the solid.
8. Complicated elliptical paths could be arranged that, while beautiful, always resulted in the muted and grayed combinations that Munsell preferred and did not permit bright hues.

A complete Munsell system with glossy-finish chips includes more than 1,500 colors. Color standards can be readily notated with a few letters and numbers. Scientists have measured all Munsell notations and given them technical identification in what are known as CIE XYZ terms. In 1955 the National Bureau of Standards (Department of Commerce) issued *The Inter-Society Color Council–National Bureau of Standards* (ISCC-NBS) *Method of Designating Colors and a Dictionary of Color Names*. It resulted from a series of conferences sponsored by the ISCC and was based largely on the Munsell color system, which had been scientifically renotated by a group of experts. A language of color was developed that used everyday English words to describe blocks that corresponded to sections of individual Munsell charts. For example, the following Munsell notations are paired with their plain English translations:

5R 4/14, strong red

5R 8/4, moderate pink

5R 2/6, very dark red

5R 5/2, grayish red

This early publication gave color names to 31 key Munsell charts with 267 blocks devoted to the charts, each containing descriptive terms. These descriptive terms were adopted to describe colors included in other systems. More than 10,000 names are alphabetically arranged and approximate their visual appearance in Munsell colors.

In 1965 the Centroid Color Charts were produced, further refining the Munsell system. There are eighteen charts that contain 267 mounted chips. These chips are directly related to the previously mentioned 267 blocks and have been given numbers from 1 to 267. The blocks are plotted against the charts of the Munsell system. To identify a specimen of paint, textile, plastic, or paper you need only locate it exactly or approximately in the Munsell book of color and note the Munsell designation, such as 5R 4/14 described previously. Then, referring to the color names dictionary or the synonymous list of the color names dictionary, you would find that 5R 4/14, described as strong red, is on block twelve of the Centroid Color Charts, which lists ninety-three names.

Even with scientific categorization methods, it is still very difficult to accurately communicate about color.

The Ostwald System

Wilhelm Ostwald won the Nobel Prize for chemistry in 1909. He took an interest in the problems of color organization, creating an original concept of color order attributed at least in part to the work of Ewald Hering, a German psychologist, and gained a worldwide fame as an authority on color. Ostwald's *Die Farbenfibel* was published in 1916, running into 15 editions. The 1969 English translation, *The Color Primer*, added a history of color systems.

While Munsell emphasized value and chroma, Ostwald dealt with qualities of whiteness and blackness in color. His rational form for color was the triangle, with pure hue (C) on one angle, white (W) on the second, and black (B) on the third. All possible variations of a given hue could be plotted within this triangle, for example, C + W + B = 1.

Ostwald's theories of color harmony basically state that any colors that have the same hue, white content, and black content will be harmonious, regardless of value differences. Color scales parallel to CW have equal black content, showing the deeper tone to be pure and the lighter tone weak. Color scales parallel to CB have equal white content, and with them the lighter tone will be pure and the deeper tone dull. Color scales parallel to WB (vertical scales) were great favorites of Ostwald. He called them the "shadow series" and likened them to the chiaroscuro modeling of the Renaissance painters. These scales had an apparent equal hue content. More complex were "ring-star" harmonies, which, like the diminishing sequences and elliptical paths of Munsell, plotted concordant steps within the color solid but with careful respect for balance of white, black, or hue content.

Swedish Natural Color System

The Swedish Natural Color System (NCS) is based on the study of color perception conducted by Ewald Hering in the early nineteenth century. It defines six natural color sensations that are called red, yellow, green, blue, black, and white. The chromatic hues are arranged in a circle, with nine intermediate steps between each, totaling 54 hues. Then, for each hue, a triangular chart is developed, showing the pure hue and its relationship to white and black. Many study materials are available from the Swedish Standards Institution of Stockholm that can be helpful aids to those wishing to test or train their color perception skills.

Pantone Color Institute

The Pantone Color Institute, located in Carlstadt, New Jersey, is a non-profit organization sponsored by Pantone, Inc., the developers of international color communication systems. The institute was created to conduct color research and to study and report on the psychology of color, color preferences, and professional color applications. It conducts a consumer color preference study and, while the results are strictly subjective, they may show trends in color preference among consumers that can benefit marketing strategies. The study was developed to determine color preferences for a wide range of products in the apparel, home furnishings, and automotive industries, decorative accessories, active wear, and lingerie. Questions range from what colors of particular products the respondents own to their future purchasing plans in specific color ranges. Subjective questions such as "What colors do you choose to make a statement?" or "What colors do you use to set the mood of your home?" rely on conditioned responses based on our ingrained color myth and biases. While these responses may act as predictors in consumer spending, they should not be considered scientific data. Unfortunately, the two often are confused when results are reported.

The Roper/Pantone Consumer Color Preference Study asked 2,000 men and women eighteen and older to select their colors from a wide range in the Pantone Textile Color System. Responses were categorized by age, sex, occupation, education, household income, geographic area, and market size. (It is not known if the lighting conditions differed for each person or under what type of lighting the colors were selected. Since this variable might prove problematic in terms of keeping tight control of the study's responses, the findings may be considered anecdotal rather than strictly scientific.) The study found that blue is the favorite color in the United States, with 35 percent of those polled selecting it as their favorite color. Green was the second favorite, with 16 percent. Green is favored by a demographic group called influentials, who are considered opinion-leaders—the very vocal 10 percent of the population considered trendsetters. Purple was the third favorite, slightly above red by only 1 percent.

The Roper/Pantone Study found that a preference for red was linked to the most economically stable segment of society. Black was considered mysterious, powerful, and sophisticated among wealthy, achievement-oriented women, but it is still associated with mourning among blue-collar people and middle-aged women and men. The two colors selected as the most cheerful were pink and yellow, with pink the more popular of the two. Bright orange was the least favored color overall, but it has the highest acceptance rate among adolescents. The second most disliked color among adults was a strong yellow-green, a color that was favored by the youth market.

Color Forecasting

One of the oldest organizations in the field of color forecasting is the Color Association of the United States (CAUS). It is the successor to the Textile Color Card Association of America, which was established during World War I. At that time, textile manufacturers, cut off by the war from their sources of German dyes and French fashion trends, needed color predictions so that they could match dyes and fabrics with consumer trends, so they formed the association to fill in the gaps. CAUS forecasts for four industries: interior/environment, women's fashions, men's clothing and children's clothing. The trends are determined by a consensus of committees.

The Color Council in New York City is another influential voice in color forecasting. Its advisory board is seventeen experts from all aspects of interior design: floor covering, wallcovering, tabletop, furniture, accessories, and so on. They meet every other month to discuss what each person is designing and developing and to track product trends. The results are the basis for the forecast, which is supplemented with information on what has been successful in the previous market. Results are published yearly in *The Color Palette* and twice yearly in the council's *Trend Folio*, which are supplied to the council's client list. The council's directional information helps manufacturers coordinate color palettes between industries.

As color trends change, new colors are often introduced as accents, and as they become more familiar and more acceptable to the consumer, they are used more broadly or toned down to meet consumer needs. For example, if bright lime green and orange become popular accent colors, they may be toned down to a soft sage green and a soft melon for furniture, which must have more enduring color traits than an accent piece.

Naming Color

Reading the last paragraph, you noted the descriptions "soft sage green" and "soft melon." The first term may be universal to all who know that sage is a plant with grayish green leaves, but what about that "soft melon"? Does it mean the furniture will be the color of a honeydew melon (pale green) or the color of a cantaloupe (a pale orange) or one of those new yellowish hybrids, or how about watermelon with its reddish pink flesh—or those white watermelons that are inside more of a pale gold? You can easily see how difficult it is to talk about color and be sure everyone concerned is talking about the same thing. Because of this difficulty, it became essential for professionals working in color to have some common ground for communications.

It would be so nice if we had a universal color language, but then we would all need to have the same cultural background, the same color associations, and the same visual systems. Of course, the names of colors have more to do with language than with color. When ready-made paints first became available in the eighteenth century, their names were simple and descriptive: "lead color" and "pearl color" were two examples offered by British dealer, Alexander Emerton. By the mid-nineteenth century, names had become more exotic, such as "rose Magdala" and "Lyons blue." By the mid-twentieth century, popular names such as "calypso" and "fire and ice" are immediately identifiable with the fifties, while "kinky pink," "tequila sunrise," and "kosmic blue" proclaim the sixties. You can often date yourself by the name you select to describe a color. Here are a few examples of how the same color has different names at different times.

Red color	Eighteenth century
Congo red	Nineteenth century
Hot pink	1950s
Candy apple red	1960s
Rhubarb	1970s
Red Sea	1980s
Lemon color	Eighteenth century
Canary yellow	Nineteenth century
Harvest gold	1950s
Mellow yellow	1960s
Pure cream	1970s
Yellow bamboo	1980s
Olive color	Eighteenth century
Malachite green	Nineteenth century
Pistachio	1950s
Magic dragon	1960s
Avocado	1970s
Lacquer green	1980s
Sky blue color	Eighteenth century
Lafayette blue	Nineteenth century
Ice blue	1950s
Kozmic blue	1960s
Watercolor	1970s
Faience	1980s

As you can see from this list, color names appear to stray further and further from being truly descriptive the more we move away from the eighteenth century. Even though we are saddled with a very difficult task when we try to communicate color, there are some popularly accepted color names that mean pretty much the same to most of us. If you select salmon, paprika, pippin apple green, and caramel, you may wonder if you are choosing paint or ordering lunch, but most of us would be visualizing approximately the same color. Rose, primrose, and violet mean pink, yellow, and purple to most people, although all three flowers really come in a wide range of colors. The dye names of colors such as indigo, madder, alizarin, cyan, and magenta would probably have been better understood in the nineteenth century as dark blue, brownish rose, crimson, blue-green, and red-violet, as those terms are not in common use today. Artists are familiar with the names of specific pigment colors, such as vermilion, umber, cobalt, ultramarine, cadmium, and viridian, but if you said you wanted to put a cadmium sofa on a viridian carpet, the average person would not know whether you mean yellow or red or green. If you feel ready to scream in confusion at this point, you have a good idea of how color professionals felt before color order systems were devised.

The most advanced color order systems are based not just on the appearance of colors as samples are matched against each other but on **colorimetry**, the identification and matching of colors by precise measurement. Colors can be matched by tristimulus colorimeters, machines based on three colored filters, the light primaries, red, green, and blue. These colors are mixed in different proportions until the resulting mixture matches the color of a chip or swatch. Still more advanced is the spectrophotometer, which measures the amount of light reflected or transmitted by a sample at each wavelength in turn throughout the visible spectrum. A curve plotted from the results can be converted into tristimulus values to show exactly how any given color is built up in terms of its wavelength measurements.

The CIE System

The Commission Internationale de l'Eclairage (CIE) is an international body that specifies methods of measuring color. They devised a color order system based on spectrophotometric measurements of color samples illuminated by specific types of lighting and related to the visual response of a "standard observer." For example, a sample may reflect green light and look green under a northern skylight, but under artificial light it may appear slightly more yellow. CIE specifications are presented in mathematical form. They do not show what colors look like, so reference has to be made to color samples built up from the coordinates. So, although the CIE system is extremely accurate, it is of less value to most people than systems that can be matched visually. However, the CIE system can be cross-referenced with the Munsell system, which has notations based on both instrumental measurement and actual color samples.

Color designation is becoming a more important issue as more consumers are purchasing goods from catalogs and Internet shopping malls. In the case of print media and web sites, color rendition is often inexact. If you are trying to purchase an item whose success depends heavily on its color—say, an article of clothing—then you really need to know what the catalog or Web site is offering. Giving the article a name such as oyster really doesn't mean much if you can't get a good idea what the color looks like. It would all be so much easier if consumers were educated like color professional to recognize colors by their designated numbers, but then we'd all have to be using the same color order system as well.

The Gerritsen System

Frans Gerritsen's 1975 *Theory and Practice of Color* proposed a color theory based on the ability of the retina to distinguish red, green, and blue. He designated these colors as primaries and considered yellow, cyan, and magenta (colors used in the printing process) to be secondaries. His theory is based on using the colors of light rather than pigment, leading to the unusual pairing of complements blue-yellow, green-magenta, and red-cyan.

The Küppers System

Harold Küppers wrote *Color: Origin, Systems, Uses* in 1972 and made use of a color circle of six primaries: red, yellow, green, cyan, blue, and magenta. The introduction of the dye names *cyan*, which is a greenish-blue, and *magenta*, which is a red-violet, relates to the inks of the printing process. The fact that the appearance of virtually any color can be generated by the ink colors yellow, cyan, and magenta creates the basis for Küppers's system. Since it deals primarily with additive color, it has particular usefulness to the color lighting and color printing industries.

With all the attempts at arriving at a simple, universal way to communicate about color, where are we today? The fact is that no system is universal, and it is still very difficult to find a way to effectively communicate specifically detailed color information. Within a given system, if both parties are using the same system, reasonably accurate color communication may be expected. But if we step outside a particular system, we may not even be able to agree on what the primary colors are. Most design schools, at least in the United States, have adopted the Munsell system as the most practical, but maybe it is so practical because most people use it. Munsell's numerical notation system is perhaps both its strength and its weakness. It is certainly precise to designate a color by number, but it is much easier to remember Moroccan moss as a color name than as a string of numbers. A good compromise is using the accepted color name, such as red, blue, or green, and then adding a modifier to form light green, dark red, or orangey-pink. This is the simplest way to describe color in everyday life, leaving the more complex notation systems to technology and industry.

REFERENCES

Albers, J. *Interaction of Color*, Yale University Press, 1971.

Eiseman, L., Herberg, L. *The Pantone Book of Color*, Harry N. Abrams, 1990.

Gerritsen, F. *Theory and Practice of Color*, Van Nostrand Reinhold, 1975.

Küppers, H. *Color: Origin, Systems, Uses*, Van Nostrand Reinhold, 1973.

Munsell, A. H., *The Munsell Book of Color: Munsell's Color Notations*, Kollmorgan Corp., 1976.

Munsell, A. H., *A Color Notation*, Munsell Color Company, 1929.

Ostwald, W. *The Color Primer*, Van Nostrand Reinhold, 1969.

Von Goethe, J. W., *Color Theory*, MIT Press, 1970.

Wright, W. D., *The Measurement of Color*, Van Nostrand Reinhold, 1969.

Chapter twelve

Color: Pushing the envelope

In this chapter we explore the far reaches of color and extrapolate on where color discoveries may take us (Figure 12-1). In this new century and new millennium, we can only guess at the marvels that may lie ahead in the field of color study. In the following pages, we present some of the directions color research is currently taking and the paths down which it may lead us. We also present theories and insights, old and new, fascinating and often controversial, about this complex phenomenon called color.

Color and Light in Space

The National Aeronautics and Space Agency (NASA) has made significant strides in studying the most efficient uses of color in space stations and possible extraterrestrial habitats, as well as color usage in spacecraft. Early research work in spacecraft design focused more on the survival of crew members, but as space travel has become more commonplace, the importance of color in this area is being considered.

Only a small number of articles deal with color perception in relation to weightlessness or the use of color in spacecraft interiors. Most of these studies are Russian, and many were not well controlled or designed. However, they are worth citing for general interest. In 1967 and again in 1972, Kitayev-Smyk conducted perceptual experiments in short-term weightlessness via parabolic trajectory. He noted that subjects reported, at the onset of weightlessness, illusions of varying duration that often consisted of a change in color intensity. Some subjects reported a decrease in brightness during weightlessness. White (1965) observed a similar phenomenon and attributed it to an exaggerated motion of retinal image. Kitayev-Smyk's 1972 study reported that highly saturated yellow and red were perceived as brighter, while blue was seen as less bright during short periods of weightlessness. He also noted that a matching task performed during weightlessness resulted in a mixed green (yellow/blue) being matched to yellow. These findings suggest that some visual processing differences may occur during initial periods of weightlessness. The duration of the differences has yet to be determined.

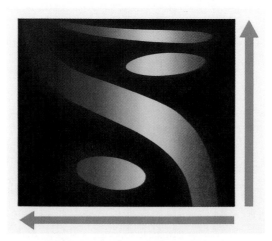

figure 12-1

The Hertzsprung-Russell Diagram, pioneered independently by Ejnar Hertzsprung and Henry Norris Russell, plots luminosity as a function of temperature for stars. © Dorling Kindersley

In 1979 Kitayev-Smyk continued his color studies by examining the effects of color on motion sickness, particularly nausea. During this study, subjects underwent periods of prolonged rotation that lasted at least eleven days while they were exposed to fields of colored light, although the means of production of the colored light and the duration of exposure were not reported. The results indicated that yellow and brown increased the sensation of nausea, causing many subjects to vomit, while blue light somewhat lessened the sensation of nausea. These findings are the basis of avoiding the color yellow in space station interiors.

Another series of studies has implications for lighting recommendations in space environments. Gurovskiy, Kosmolinskiy, and Melnikov (1981) noted that as the length of a mission increased, astronauts desired higher levels of illumination in their environment. Under various working conditions, they needed increased ambient light as fatigue increased. When they worked under conditions of both intense visual and monotonous auditory stimulation, even higher levels of light were required. From these findings, Gurovskiy and associates concluded that a varied and individualized lighting plan was desirable in a space environment so that each person could control his or her own lighting needs.

Color in Space Stations

These and a few other studies were the basis for coloring the interiors of space station habitats, at least by the Russians. For Salyut 6, a team of psychologists selected an interior color scheme of soft pastels in an attempt to provide a homey atmosphere. Salyut 7 tried something new by painting one wall an apple green and the opposing wall beige (Konovalov, 1982). Further studies of interior colors in space environments indicate a strong reliance on preferred colors in the following order: blue, red, green, violet, orange, yellow. Attempts have been made to duplicate the natural surroundings of earth and overcome the monotony of space travel by using a series of color slides or filmstrips with strong natural and landscape elements. A study of astronauts sleep reveals dream content mostly of woods, rivers, and blue skies, indicating a strong need to replace monotony with the familiar dynamics of a constantly changing environment.

To date, the use of color in American spacecraft has been limited. Comments from the inhabitants of Skylab suggest that livelier color schemes such as blue or green may have been preferable to the tan and brown used. Astronauts reported problems with visually losing small objects in the monotonous background, which indicates that surface contrasts and color identification should be introduced. Cooper reported that the window in Skylab was the most popular place to spend limited recreational time. The window in Skylab served as a means of introducing dynamic color into the setting since the view of the earth was constantly changing in both light and color. Current and former astronauts have expressed a desire for increased variety and color in clothing, and since color is one of the easiest ways to introduce variety, it seems to be a good way to remedy the monotony of space.

The concept of introducing color into spacecraft is not as simple as it may at first seem. In small, compacted interior spaces, too many different colors can cause a chaotic feeling. The low illumination levels of the interiors suggest a need for light-colored surfaces to avoid a potentially depressing cavelike feeling. Also, any items used in the interiors must meet stringent safety requirements and receive space certification. Many surface materials offgas in weightlessness and would be unsuitable. (Offgassing is the process whereby chemicals contained in manufactured products such as paint or carpeting are released into the air. It is a primarily cause of sick building syndrome, in which the interior environment can actually cause illness.) Maintainability and cleanability standards can also affect the choice and range of colors used. Since the concept of space travel is still in its infancy, the topic of color and light use in spacecraft and extraterrestrial environments poses exciting possibilities for the future.

The Strange Case of Eyeless Sight

Color is electromagnetic radiation of a certain narrow band of frequencies that is registered by the eye and interpreted by the brain. In studies of the visual process, it has already been shown that color/light influences chemical reactions in the body and that reactions to different colors differ. We are also sensitive to electromagnetic radiation outside the range of visible light, as evidenced by sunburn, which is caused by ultraviolet light that is invisible to us. Humans react to many forms of equally "invisible" electromagnetic energy. Microwaves and radio frequency (rf) radiation that is used to transmit radio and television signals are absorbed by the body and cause our cells to react. One question under study by photobiologists is whether additional biochemical reactions happen simultaneously with color vision, reactions that may have extremely powerful effects on human physiology and behavior.

The eye need not be involved in such color reactions. Color, like microwave or rf radiation, may also be sensed by a totally separate process, such as through the skin. Keep in mind the remarkable study mentioned in Chapter 4. The school environment of a group of children was changed from orange and white to gray and royal blue. The children in the class responded with a drop in blood pressure averaging 17 percent—yet all the children were blind!

The ability of the body to detect color separately from vision seems to be nothing short of phenomenal. To say that sight is not essential to detect color is a controversial statement, yet one generation's heresy is often another generation's science. Sightless seeing, or **dermo-optic vision**, enables us to differentiate between the color of energy waves through the skin (Figure 12-2). While very little experimentation has been done on alternative methods of color reception in the United States, Russian studies on the topic are fascinating.

In the early 1960s, a girl named Rosa Kuleshova lived in a small town in the Ural Mountains. She was an ordinary girl with nothing exceptional at all about her, and she filled her free time by leading a small drama group. A few members of her own large family were blind, so she had learned to read braille. Gradually, Rosa began to wonder if she could help the blind to be more aware of their surroundings by using some of the techniques employed in drama. Somewhere during this process, Rosa developed the dream to teach the blind to see color, see pictures, or even read without braille. She began by training her fingers to distinguish between colors—red, green, light blue, orange—then moved on to newspapers, magazines, and books. Gradually, she became able to detect the outlines of black letters on a page with just her fingers. Word of Rosa's remarkable ability soon spread and attracted the attention of a neuropathologist, Joseph Goldberg. He tested her ability by blindfolding her tightly and was shocked to dis-

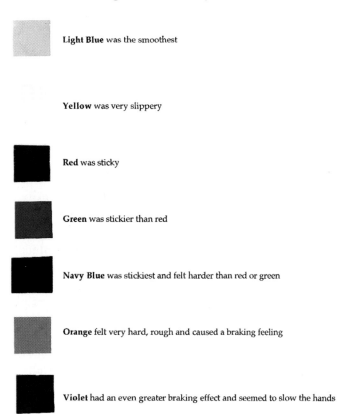

Light Blue was the smoothest

Yellow was very slippery

Red was sticky

Green was stickier than red

Navy Blue was stickiest and felt harder than red or green

Orange felt very hard, rough and caused a braking feeling

Violet had an even greater braking effect and seemed to slow the hands

figure 12-2

THE FEEL OF COLOR IN A DERMO-OPTIC VISION EXPERIMENT
This chart shows the results of an experiment in dermo-optic vision. Blindfolded students attempted to distinguish the difference between colored paper with only their fingertips.

cover that she could actually differentiate between colors and even read, just by running her fingers across a page. It had taken Rosa six years of practice, several hours a day, to get to that point.

Goldberg checked and rechecked Rosa, trying to discover some explanation for her ability. Finally, he took her to a regional conference of the Society of Psychologists in the fall of 1962. Rosa was heavily swathed with bandages and blindfolds, but she was still able to distinguish people in photographs, the color of the scientists' clothing, and the shapes of objects taken out of their pockets to test her. During the next few years, Rosa was subjected to all manner of controlled studies to determine if her ability was real or an elaborate hoax. Finally, she was taken before the prestigious Biophysics Institute of the Soviet Academy of Sciences in Moscow. There she was subjected to a vigorous round of controlled experiments in their labs. It was finally determined that Rosa Kuleshova could, indeed, read a text by touching it and identify color and light with her hands without benefit of vision.

By this time, Rosa's hands had become so skilled at dermo-optic vision that she could distinguish the colors of even tiny patterns on a tile or a slight gradations of colors on a flower. She could even pick out earrings on a woman in a photograph. Researchers were beginning to wonder if they had a one-shot phenomenon on their hands or if others could train themselves to do what Rosa did. To answer this question, Dr. Novomeisky of the Nizhni Tigil Pedagogical Institute began a study with eighty graphic arts students. He found that about one in six could distinguish the difference between two colors of paper after trying for about half an hour. The experiment resulted in general agreement by subjects on the feel of color. Light blue seemed the smoothest; yellow is very slippery; red, green, and dark blue feel sticky; and green is stickier than red but not as coarse. Navy blue was thought to be the stickiest and felt harder than red or green. Orange felt very hard and rough and caused a braking feeling. Violet gave an even greater braking effect that seemed to slow their hands. Experimental observers noted that the fingers of trained students actually did move with greater difficulty over the braking violet and sticky red than over the slippery yellow.

The first time we encountered this research study we were very skeptical. To satisfy our own curiosity, we decided to try it out ourselves. We acquired construction paper of the same brand and texture in several colors. Then, with tight blindfolds in place, we tried to distinguish first between red and green. After about twenty minutes, a difference between them became evident. We both found the green to be slightly smoother and cooler and the red to feel slightly rougher and warmer. We practiced this for several weeks and became fairly adept at distinguishing between red, green, blue, yellow, black, and white construction paper. Unfortunately, other commitments prevented us from continuing the process for the length of time it might have taken us to distinguish print on a page, but we satisfied ourselves that it was possible to distinguish colors with our fingers alone. Experimenting on friends and volunteers convinced us even further. Considering that each color is really a representation of a different energy wavelength, it is not far-fetched to think that sensors in the skin are able to detect the difference.

It is an interesting experiment to try on yourself. It can make the point of how much color affects us much better than any number of words. If you decide to try it, make sure that the construction paper you purchase (from any art supply store) is the same brand and texture for each color to prevent variables from confusing the issue.

To explain dermo-optic vision, several possibilities have been considered. Is the skin picking up the energy field of the color? Is the energy field of the skin reflecting back on itself? Is some interaction of fields taking place? Several studies were undertaken, with an interesting discovery. It was noted that, like regular sight, dermo-optic vision declines in twilight and ceases in total darkness. Under intense red light, subjects were not able to identify color any better with their skin sensors than sighted people are able to do under red light. Through further studies, it was theorized that the color of the light in a room makes a difference to the outcome. Like heightens like. For example, blue is easier to identify under blue illumination, yellow under yellow, and so on.

It was then suggested that if certain critical objects such as doorknobs, faucets, telephones, and some portable objects were colored the same color as the light in the room (green objects under green light, for example), then the blind might be trained to "see" with their skin as easily as sighted people are able to locate things. It is certainly a provocative concept and one that seems well worth pursuing.

Another instance of dermo-optic vision took place in Vermont, where work was done with a girl born without any eyes. She learned to perceive color through its feel. She found red to be a "hot" color, but blue was "cool." The blind girl worked with red and blue paper identical except for their inks. She learned how to identify colors by touch and to distinguish the color of clothes someone was wearing. When you consider that color is really just an energy wave, it is not that difficult to understand how this phenomenon can occur.

Jacob Liberman has some fascinating views about the process of sight, seeing, light, and the relationship to overall well-being. Liberman is an optometrist with a doctorate in vision sciences who is the director of the Aspen Center for Energy Medicine. He is a pioneer in the therapeutic use of light/color in the art of mind-body integration. As we learned early in this book, each of us creates the world we see. As Liberman states "You don't really see what's truly going on; you just make of it some distorted things based on your own experience. . . . I was always led to believe that the way our vision worked was that light entered the eye, and then all this stuff happens. But something else is going on. You see, light affects the body, but consciousness determines how we take light in and what portion we take in. We have this field of energy we live in, and the field is a big radar screen that picks up information before our senses pick it up. . . . Our relationship with light is very crucial to our evolution."

Regarding blindness, Liberman said, "First of all, there are no blind people. There are people who do not see the same way as we see, but they are not blind at all. In fact, most of them are very sighted. Spend some time with Ray Charles. What's he seeing that we're not? . . . We're not totally seeing from our eyes, and we are not only hearing with our ears either. We'll probably find that the areas of mind-body medicine and quantum physics will prove this in the next few years."

He went on to say, "What are we actually seeing? We have this illusion that when we look out there, we see something out there. But what's "out there" is just some dynamically moving little bits of energy that come into existence; they move around, and then they disappear. And my sensors pick up that moving energy and send that energy to somewhere in my computer. Then my computer says, 'That particular movement of energy means this to me.' Next, I take that information and I project it out through this particular projector onto an invisible screen, and I think that it's out there. But you're not seeing me, you're seeing you; you're not even hearing me. This information, this vibration coming out of my mouth, is stimulating your eardrum; the information is going into your computer, and somewhere in your computer it's saying, 'That particular movement of molecules means this . . . to me.' Then I project it out and I'm fooled because I think you're saying it, but what you're hearing is yourself and what you're seeing is yourself. So when you talk about someone who has a limitation in sight, then you have to take a look at who's doing the seeing."

In an interview, Liberman was asked if there had been any research on the effect of light with specific diseases such as multiple sclerosis, Parkinson's, or amyotropic lateral sclerosis (ALS). He replied, "Remember, you're not dealing with diseases; you're dealing with people. You can call it anything you want; it doesn't really make a difference; it's affecting every cell in the body. You can call it any number of different names. When you're right on the money, you'll notice that every single function in the individual will open up simultaneously; everything just opens right up! So, the way I approach it is, I don't care to have a name for it. It doesn't make any difference anymore. That's more limiting than it is helpful." This response may seem bizarre because we have been taught to think of ourselves as a set of symptoms, a list of diseases, a separation of mind and body. What current research is showing is that true healing can occur spontaneously and completely when we consider the entire person and that person's relationship to the whole environment and when we realize that our health and wellness are much more in our own hands than in those of an outside practitioner.

Looking Forward, Going Back

Each scientific generation seems to think it is the most advanced, with the most likely answers to a series of complex questions. Often, however, research questions tackled decades earlier resulted in very interesting conclusions that may have been abandoned because of new developments in technology. A case in point is that of Edwin D. Babbitt, a nineteenth-century self-proclaimed magnetist and psychophysician. He spent years writing *The Principles of Light and Color*, which was published in 1878. It catapulted him to prominence, and soon he headed the New York College of Magnetics. The nineteenth century was a time of snake oil salesmen and unproven medical miracles. However, if any real truth is to be discovered, we must approach a subject with an open mind free of prejudice, and we continue the discussion of Edwin D. Babbitt in that spirit.

Babbitt went into the business of color therapy and sold books, "chromo disks," and "chromo flasks," which were intended to supply the color/light deemed essential to healing a particular ailment. He also designed the "chromalume," a 57-inch by 21-inch stained-glass window to be placed within a house facing south. When sunlight passed through the glass, it was believed to provide healing treatments for those sitting beneath it. Babbitt theorized an amazing series of relationships between color and elements and between color and minerals and spoke of "thermal colors" and "electric colors." In his own words:

There is a trianal series of graduations in the peculiar potencies of colors, the center and climax of electrical action, which cools the nerves, being in violet; the climax of electrical action, which is soothing to the vascular system, being in blue; the climax of luminosity being in yellow; and the climax of thermism or heat being in red. This is not an imaginary division of qualities, but a real one, the flame-red color having a principle of warmth in itself; the blue and violet, a principle of cold and electricity. Thus we have many styles of chromatic action, including progression of hues, of lights and shades, of fineness and coarseness, of electrical power, luminous power, thermal power, etc.

Babbitt's quotes on color therapy are equally intriguing. He wrote, "Red light, like red drugs, is the warming element of sunlight, with an especially rousing effect upon the blood and to some extent upon the nerves, especially as strained through some grades of red glass which will admit not only the red but the yellow rays, and thus prove valuable in paralysis and other dormant and chronic conditions."

He believed yellow stimulated the nerves: "Yellow is the central principle of nerve stimulus as well as the exciting principle of the brain which is the foundation head of the nerves." He considered yellow a laxative, an emetic, and a purgative, and he used it to treat constipation, bronchial problems, and hemorrhoids. Yellow mixed with considerable red was used as a diuretic. Yellow with a little red added was a cerebral stimulant. Equal parts of yellow and red were considered a tonic that helped the human system in general.

Babbitt considered blue and violet "cold, electrical and contracting potencies." These colors were considered soothing to all systems in which inflammatory and nervous conditions predominated, such as sciatica, hemorrhage of the lungs, cerebrospinal meningitis, neuralgic headache, nervousness, sunstroke, and nervous irritability. Blue and white were considered particularly effective for sciatica, rheumatism, nervous prostration, and concussion. Babbitt's theories never cease to amaze. Just when you think he's an archaic charlatan, he indicates remarkable prescience, as in the following statement describing atomic fission (Figure 12-3) (remember that he lived in the nineteenth century before atomic power was discovered): "If such an atom should be set in the midst of New York City, it must create such a whirlwind that all its palatial structures, ships, bridges and surrounding cities, with nearly two millions of people, would be swept into fragments and carried into the sky."

Was Babbitt a charlatan or a gifted healer who found a way to utilize color/light to do what the medical profession was unable to do? Perhaps we will never know. The antibacterial effects of sunlight were recognized during the nineteenth century and used to treat tuberculosis, strep and staph infections, and other diseases. Those nineteenth-century medical practitioners who chose to use chromotherapy (treatment with color) or phototherapy (treatment with light) reported some remarkable results. Unfortunately, with the invention of antibiotics in the twentieth century, color/light therapy research virtually came to a halt. Following is a series of case histories of patients treated by Edwin Babbitt with color/light therapy in the late nineteenth century, when many of today's medical treatments were unavailable. These case histories are not reported here with the intention of replacing conventional medical treatments, but as an illustration of the healing potential of color/light.

Case 1: The patient had difficulty breathing because of a bronchial condition that had not responded to conventional treatment. Bronchial difficulty was relieved by exposing the patient to sunlight treatments filtered through yellow glass, fifteen minutes per day for one week.

figure 12-3

The atom as conceived by Edwin S. Babbitt during the nineteenth century. Decades before atomic energy was discovered, he envisioned its destructive power, saying, "If such an atom should be set in the midst of New York City, it must create such a whirlwind that all its palatial structures, ships, ridges and surrounding cities with nearly two millions of people, would be swept into fragments and carried into the sky." *Authors' collection*

Case 2: A woman suffered from sciatica and inflammation of the knee, ankle, and foot, which were swollen to twice their size. Three panes of blue glass were inserted in a west window of her home, and she was treated to sunbaths of the afflicted areas. After the first treatment, which lasted approximately two hours, it was reported that a large purplish lump the size of a hen's egg on her ankle entirely disappeared, as did the pain and soreness.

Case 3: The patient suffered from incapacitating migraine headaches. After sitting in sunlight filtered through blue glass for thirty minutes, all symptoms were relieved.

Case 4: An infant was found to have a hard tumor about the size of a robin's egg on its left side. The child was treated to sunbaths through blue glass for one hour a day. At the end of forty days, the tumor had disappeared. Seven months later, no sign of the tumor had reappeared.

Case 5: A deeply depressed mental patient who had refused all food for days became cheerful and asked for food after spending three hours in a red room.

Case 6: An eighteen-month old infant suffered from an extreme case of cholera that had not responded to conventional treatments. Little hope was held for his survival. Finally, the blue light treatment was used. Within two months, the child was completely well.

Case 7: The patient was extremely nervous and suffered from irritability, insomnia, nightmares, loss of appetite, frequent headaches, and periods of depression. Five blue light treatments later, his health was restored, and all symptoms had disappeared.

Case 8: An eighteen-month-old boy had been unable to properly use his legs since birth, so that he could not even crawl. After a few days of treatment under the blue glass sun therapy, he showed a marked improvement in the strength of his limbs. Within a few weeks, he was able to stand with the help of a chair and began crawling.

Case 9: A thirty-five-year-old woman suffered from an advanced state of tuberculosis in both lungs. After three weeks of treatment with red light therapy, her condition began to improve. After two and a half months, she recovered completely. She remained well for nearly three years but then caught a severe cold, which developed into a fatal case of pneumonia.

Case 10: After an attack of diptheria, an eight-year-old boy became completely paralyzed. He could not walk and could stand only when supported. After treatment with red light therapy for a period of one hour per treatment for a duration of three weeks, he was able to stand unaided and take feeble steps. By the end of two months, he was completely well.

What can we say about these case histories and their remarkable responses? Chicanery? Coincidence? Mind over matter? A real hope for the future? The results may seem downright bizarre because we have grown so accustomed to taking drugs for illnesses. To this day, more than a hundred years later, the chromotherapy of Edwin D. Babbitt still survives and continues to be practiced. Books founded on his principles are still published. Courses, lectures, meetings, and schools of color can all be traced to Babbitt. While his beliefs and treatments were outlawed in the United States, chromotherapy is still practiced in England and other countries. A spin-off of Babbitt's work called the spectro-chrome system was developed by Dinshah Ghadiali in the United States in the 1920s. He was also labeled a charlatan and banned from practicing his healing techniques. However, a current version of his Circle of Color Projector System is now available, sold without medical claims and only as an educational and investigative device for exploring alternative research and theories on the use and structure of color. Perhaps we should be looking toward the possibilities of treating illness with color/light as an alternative or adjunct to conventional medicine. There is no question that much research in this area is needed, but with current trends in photobiological research showing such promise (see Chapter 4) we may one day be able to reach for color/light treatment rather than a medicine bottle. Color/light therapy is not far-fetched when you consider the findings of the International Commission on Illumination: "The action of ultraviolet radiation intensifies enzymatic processes of metabolism, increases the activity of the endocrine system, promotes the immunobiological responsiveness of the body and improves the tone of the central nervous and muscular systems." We know the potential is there; we just need to investigate this potential and learn to harness it.

Coco, A Personal Case Study

We had occasion to personally test Babbitt's theories, and we were astounded by the results. One of our dogs, Coco, a German Shepherd/Whippet cross, became very ill suddenly and without warning. One morning she simply could not move. Her muscles had atrophied, literally overnight, and she had become completely unable to move or to even stand on her own if we tried to assist her into a standing position. We rushed her to the vet, only to find that our worst fears had been realized. She was pronounced paralyzed and in total kidney failure. She was not interested in food, and any food we could coax her to take was vomited back up. She was incontinent, having completely lost bladder control. After many tests and attempted treatments by several specialists, we were urged to euthanize her, as there was no hope for recovery.

We were not quite ready to give up on Coco, although she was past eleven years old at the time. Since there was nothing to lose and everything to gain, we decided to give Babbitt's theories a try. We purchased a piece of cobalt blue glass that had been made to Babbitt's specifications by a local stained-glass maker. We then found a low, glass-topped table in a thrift store and had the cobalt blue glass installed in place of the clear glass. We moved Coco outside in the natural daylight and placed her underneath the blue glass for thirty minutes at high noon.

After the first treatment, she seemed brighter and more energetic. We weren't sure if it was reality or wishful thinking. However, that evening she did eat a little food without coaxing, and she was able to keep it down. The next day we did another blue light treatment for thirty minutes; in fact, we did it every day for five days. After each treatment, she improved a little, so that by the end of the fifth day she was eating well again. On the sixth day she was able to stand on her own if we helped her into a standing position, and her muscles felt less like gelatin.

We continued the treatments every day for thirty minutes according to Babbitt's directions, knowing that more than thirty minutes might be too much and cause a reversal of her progress. By the end of ten days, she was able to get up on her own and take a few faltering steps. At this point, her incontinence had resolved and she now had bladder control again. Each day she grew stronger, and her health improved. After blue light treatments for one month, she was so improved that we were able to walk her five blocks from our home to our vet. When the vet saw her walk into his clinic, he shook his head and said, "Why did I go to vet school?" Coco's recovery mystified everyone who had come in contact with her, and we could only assume that the light treatments had been her salvation.

We continued her light treatments every day for the next two months and then began to taper off to every other day. She still continued in an excellent state of health, although tests indicated that she was still in total kidney failure. Once again, the vets could not understand how she could continue to function in such good health with her kidneys in total failure. As long as we continued the light treatments, she continued to remain stable. Ten months passed, and as far as we could tell, Coco was healed again and in perfect health. She ate well, she moved well, and she played with the other dogs and the new puppy as if she were a pup herself instead of a twelve-year-old. Then we made a fatal mistake. We tapered off the light treatments to just twice a week, and even with that she was doing well, so we discontinued the treatments completely. After one week without the light treatments, she died.

We have chastised ourselves ever since for discontinuing the light treatments, but we were working blind, not knowing what was really happening or what to expect. We try to make ourselves feel a little better by knowing that she had nearly an extra year of excellent health, but we can't help wondering if she would still be with us if we had continued her treatments.

The blue light therapy has now been tried on several other dogs in kidney failure who had no hope of survival, and each one has lived for at

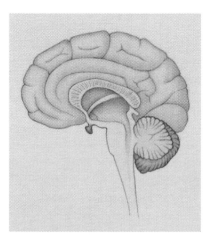

figure 12-4

The pineal gland may be of great importance in the sensing of color separate from our visual systems. In Eastern religions, the pineal is considered a true "third eye" by which the inner self sees the true world.
© Dorling Kindersley

least a year in fine health as long as the treatments are continued. Neither our vet nor we know why this works. We can only make an educated guess that it might be similar to the cases of neonatal jaundice cured as the blue light rays from the sun transform the molecules of toxic bilirubin into an excretable form. Perhaps the toxins were purged from Coco and the other dogs, even though their kidneys could not do the job. All we can say with certainty is what we have reported here, and we hope that others will be encouraged to seriously investigate the potential of healing with light.

The Pineal Connection

The pineal gland (Figure 12-4) has been suggested to be of great importance in the sensing of color separate from our visual systems. In Eastern religions, the pineal is considered a true "third eye," by which the inner self sees the true world (Figures 12-5 and 12-6). For more than

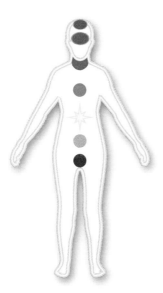

figure 12-5

THE *CHAKRA* SYSTEM

For more than 4000 years, the yoga system has maintained practitioners at peak health. Yoga divides the body into *chakras* or energy centers and assigns a symbolic color to each. *Chakras* link nerve centers and endocrine glands, which produce hormones that affect and control the body. Note that the colors form the spectrum.

VIOLET represents the crown *chakra*, related to the upper brain.

INDIGO represents the forehead or eye *chakra*, related to the lower brain, ears, nose, and nervous system, and is thought to be the controller of the pineal gland or "third eye."

BLUE represents the throat *chakra*, related to the thyroid, lungs, and bronchial and vocal apparatus.

GREEN represents the heart *chakra*, related to the heart, blood, and the circulatory system.

YELLOW represents the solar plexus *chakra*, related to the stomach, liver, nervous system, and gall bladder.

ORANGE represents the sacral or pelvic *chakra*, related to the reproductive system.

RED represents the base or root *chakra*, related to kidneys and the spinal column.

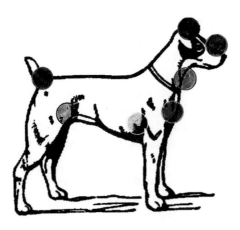

figure 12-6

LOCATION OF ANIMAL *CHAKRAS*
Like humans, animals also have *chakras*. While this image is of a dog, *chakra* placement is universal to all animals, and the same colors relate as in the human *chakra* system. Alternative medicine utilizing *chakra* balancing has helped many pets to better health.

4,000 years, the system of hatha yoga has maintained its practitioners at the peak of health and vitality. Yoga has specific exercises to stimulate the pineal gland. One exercise is to close your eyes and hold a finger about half an inch away from the middle of your forehead. Some people see a bright area of light, indicating that the pineal has been stimulated. Yoga, like many Eastern philosophies and practices, attributes certain colors to certain states of awareness. The yoga system divides the body into chakras (energy centers) and assigns a symbolic color to each.

The pineal gland may play an important role in health functions not now fully understood in its relation to the light-dark cycle. Richard Wurtman's photobiological studies have, among other things, studied the effects of the light-dark cycle on fundamental biochemical and hormonal rhythms of the body, which are synchronized directly or indirectly by the daily cycle of light and dark. This light-dark cycle is another variant of the intricate color complex that must be taken into consideration for a complete understanding of light/color in relation to humans. Wurtman has found that the light-dark cycle particularly affects the rate at which normal human subjects excrete melatonin, a hormone synthesized by the pineal organ of the brain. Melatonin induces sleep, inhibits ovulation, and modifies the secretion of other hormones.

Because of these and related studies, the pineal gland is being considered more seriously as playing a major role in maintaining optimum functioning of the human body. The pineal gland may prove to have even more influence on humans than is currently thought, as we compare its influence in other vertebrates. In some animals, the pineal gland is as important as eyes are in humans, since it provides a steady stream of information about the environment that we humans are not even consciously aware of.

The pineal gland is an outgrowth of the brain, located in most species in the area between the eyes. Until recently, its function was ignored, misunderstood, or considered a useless remnant of mysticism and "third eye" quackery. While there is still much to learn about the function of the pineal gland, we do have some rudimentary information. It is the only organ in the brain that is asymmetrical. It does not conform to the laws of bilateral symmetry, perhaps because it is one of evolution's oldest organs and may stem from a time before the origins of bilateral symmetry.

The strangeness of the pineal gland lies in the contrast between its enormous importance to the survival of many species and the fact that only very recently has its function been understood. The pineal gland is the nonvisual photoreceptor of an independent sensory system. It is not connected to the eyes or to any other sense organ. For many species, the ability of the pineal to detect the position of the sun is essential to survival. Lizards, for example, must keep accurate track of the sun's position to regulate activities needed to keep them warm, such as basking, and to help them seek shade to prevent overheating.

The pineal gland synchronizes internal rhythms with those in the external environment so that activities correspond with the natural cycles of light and dark and the seasons. This is accepted in relation to animals, and it is likely that further studies will prove the same to be true of humans, who have fully functional pineal glands. What happens if the pineal gland is destroyed or made nonfunctional?

In an attempt to answer that question, a research study was devised in which several animals were captured, their pineal glands were blocked, and they were released. A year later they were recaptured for study. Several major changes had taken place in these animals. For one, there were marked changes in their reproductive cycles, as if their breeding activity had suddenly been dramatically speeded up. The animals also showed signs of displacement and were less able to find their way back to their normal territories. These disturbances were probably due to confusion over the position of the sun and its angle and polarization of rays. Animals whose pineal glands are blocked have their photoreceptor mechanisms disturbed and become out of phase with their natural surroundings. There may be implications for human beings who live within the unnatural color and lighting conditions created in indoor environments.

Studies at the University of Texas Medical School on the relationship of alcoholism to the function of the pineal gland and the light-dark cycle have shown some interesting results. Experimental animals drank more alcohol after exposure to darkness over the weekends, when the lab was kept in darkness. Nobel Prize winner Julius Axelrod found that the pineal gland produces more of the enzyme melatonin during dark periods. When Kenneth Blum discovered that subjects that were kept on a regular light-dark cycle and were injected with melatonin became alcoholic, there appeared to be a connection. It therefore seems possible that alteration of the light-dark cycle can influence alcoholism in humans.

Photobiologists do not relate to just the light-dark cycle but to specific narrow bands of wavelengths within the spectrum. If these specific wavelengths are missing, as in an artificial light source, then this lighting is the equivalent of darkness to our photoreceptor mechanisms, even though we visually see light. Keeping in mind that different wavelengths translate to different colors, the connection between color/light and the regulation of biological systems becomes obvious.

The pineal gland may prove vitally important to human health because of its ability to regulate our responses to the light-dark cycle. Melatonin, the hormone produced by the pineal gland, is synthesized from serotonin (the same neural transmitter that is involved in the body's internal pain-killing system). The conversion of serotonin into melatonin depends on the production in the pineal gland of an enzyme named *N*-acetyltransferase. This is the key to the interaction of the regulation of daily activities (circadian rhythms) and the rhythms of the sun. Although the production of these chemicals by the pineal gland appears to follow circadian patterns, it is strongly stimulated by darkness and inhibited by light. When it is light, the enzyme is not produced; when it is dark, melatonin production is increased. Melatonin plays a major role in regulating sexual activity, primarily by inhibiting activity in the sex organs during periods of low illumination. The studies underway on the interactions between the light-dark cycle and the human body's natural circadian rhythms indicate that lengthy exposure to an imbalanced color/light condition (such as the extended periods we all spend under artificial light) can cause upheaval in human biological systems. Why haven't we realized this before? One reason is that researchers thought that lighting levels of at least 2,000 lux were necessary to have any photobiological effect. Recently, however, a study conducted at Harvard Medical School demonstrated that significant changes in the body can occur at lighting levels as low as 180 lux, which is within the range of normal interior lighting.

Another recent study has shown that night lights can have a marked effect on our biology. We are rapidly becoming a twenty-four-hour society, with people working shifts around the clock. Anyone who has worked the "graveyard" shift from midnight to eight A.M. knows how difficult it can be on the body. You are trying to stay awake when your body wants you to be asleep. Rapidly adjusting the sleep-wake cycle at the start and end of night shifts by using light to gradually shift the phase of the worker's circadian rhythms can alleviate this problem. Light exposure enables a worker's waking period to adjust more quickly to the nighttime start of the new work shift and then rapidly reverses the situation when needed. Studies have also shown that exposure to bright light can increase productivity and performance in night workers.

The light-dark cycle may also have dramatic effects on the elderly, who often complain of disrupted sleep patterns and an inability to sleep the same number of hours they did when they were young. This may be partly due to chemical changes induced by the aging process, but there is also a light-dark connection. Findings reported by R. J. Cole in the *Journal of Biological Rhythms* indicate that many older people do not stay outdoors for long periods and, because their living environments are poorly lit, they have little exposure to bright lighting levels. This study indicates that exposure to bright light in the evening and to natural daylight outdoors on a regular basis would adjust the sleep-wake circadian rhythm of these people and enable them to have more regular sleep patterns.

Alzheimer's patients in particular have very irregular periods of rest and activity. This is a real problem for their caregivers, who often have their sleep interrupted and develop sleep deprivation and stress.

Research by A. Satlin published in the *American Journal of Psychiatry* and another study by E. J. W. Van Someren published in *Sleep Research Abstracts* indicate that providing higher illumination in places where Alzheimer's patients are cared for made their rest-activity cycles more regular and made caring for them easier on the caregivers.

The SAD Syndrome

The importance of color/light in relation to the cycle of light and darkness cannot be overemphasized with regard to human health. Sufferers of the seasonal affective disorder (SAD) syndrome would be quick to agree. SAD is a serious depression whose cyclic onset appears curiously linked to the changing length of the day.

Let's consider the case of Robert, a SAD sufferer. For Robert, life was a series of tranquilizers, antidepressant drugs, psychotherapy, and shock treatments. Every winter he was so fatigued that he could barely move at all. He described his life as "pure hell." He couldn't even handle small problems and became increasingly unable to tolerate color. Even the red and green traffic lights were unbearable to him. His life gradually went from bad to worse. He lost his job and then his wife and family. Finally, he encountered a physician who thought there might be a connection between Robert's condition and the changing seasons. The physician was aware of research at the Sleep and Mood Disorders Laboratory at Oregon Health Sciences University. Alfred Lewy, director of the lab, was working on a study of seasonally depressed patients. Lewy classifies SAD patients as "phase delayed," meaning that their circadian body rhythms run behind schedule. They need morning light to put them back on track. Lewy has found that certain wavelengths, such as blue-green, are the most effective in lifting the depression. Based on Lewy's work, Robert's doctor thought light therapy might help. He suggested that Robert get up at sunrise and go for a walk. Robert thought the idea was far-fetched but reluctantly gave it a try. After five mornings of walks, Robert suddenly experienced a flood of energy. Almost miraculously, he was able to tolerate color again.

Realizing that Robert could be helped by exposure to appropriate wavelength bands of light, his doctor prescribed a treatment of full-spectrum lighting and encouraged Robert to experiment with the lighting to set his own length of day. Within a few weeks, Robert had worked out a schedule that suited him. By turning on the full-spectrum lighting at intervals that duplicated summertime natural lighting conditions, he was able to keep his depression at bay. Within a remarkably short time, Robert was back at work and free of drugs, with a new life ahead of him.

By the mid-1980s, phototherapy had become the treatment of choice for SAD. Initial phototherapy of SAD patients required them to sit in appropriate lighting conditions for approximately four hours each day, two hours in the morning and two hours in the evening. The time commitment was a major issue. Michael Terman of the Light Therapy Unit at Columbia Presbyterian Medical Center in New York City determined in additional studies that morning-only light sessions were sufficient, which cut the therapy time in half. The time was cut further by increasing the brightness of the treatment lights. Light intensity is measured in lux units. The typical home is illuminated at a level of about

200 to 250 lux. Early light boxes for phototherapy emitted 2,500 lux. This may sound bright, but compared with daylight on a summer day, which is about 120,000 lux, it really isn't. Terman's studies led him to conclude that 10,000-lux phototherapy enabled people with SAD to obtain effective relief with daily exposure of just thirty minutes. People with this condition are encouraged to use phototherapy from October through April, since symptoms recur once the light treatments are discontinued.

The SAD syndrome has only recently been identified and named, but its presence nay have been with us since we moved indoors and began altering the natural light-dark cycle that controls our biological rhythms. More than 10 million Americans are thought to suffer from SAD, and more than 25 million more people are susceptible to it. We have only just begun to identify health problems associated with the alteration of our exposure to natural lighting conditions. For this reason, until the connection between color/light and health is thoroughly understood, we recommend avoiding some of the more novel light sources, particularly fluorescent, and instead use full-spectrum lighting to better simulate natural light conditions. Even full-spectrum fluorescents continue to have a strobing effect, which causes the pupil of the eye to constantly expand and contributes to fatigue, headaches, and eyestrain.

The Future of Color/Light

What might we expect in the future of color? From a technological viewpoint, colorists predict that holographic, refractive, and luminescent colors will continue to rise in popularity across industries. Holographic packaging that seems to twinkle at the viewer and change colors depending on perspective is being considered for a line of low-fat snack foods. A California company, Spectratek Technologies, has developed a holographic pigment that changes from violet to green to red, depending on

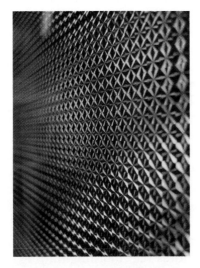

figure 12-7

This example of holographic packaging material incorporates spectral colors that change, depending on the angle of the viewer. *Reproduced with permission of Spectratek Technologies, Inc.*

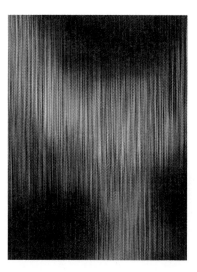

figure 12-8

Another holographic packaging option, which gives the impression of colored rain. *Reproduced with permission of Spectratek Technologies, Inc.*

then angle of the viewer (Figures 12-7, 12-8, and 12-9). Some examples of new color effects are refractures (a translucent, multisurface patterning that contrasts with the color underneath it), multiplicity (a thin film containing holographic chips layered over color for a glittering effect), unobtanium (a liquid silver designed to simulate the brilliance of metallic leafing), sheer layering (multiple layers in a variety of sheer colors), and optic shift (a high-tech, chameleon-like surface that displays multiple colors.) Geometric Pigment (Figure 12-10) by Spectratek Technologies is widely used as an additive in automotive paints, powder coating processes, consumer coatings and packaging, molded plastic items, printing inks for paper and fabric appliqué, and the magic

figure 12-9

"Galaxy," a shimmering, attention-getting holographic material, provides packaging options unheard of just a few years ago. *Reproduced with permission of Spectratek Technologies, Inc.*

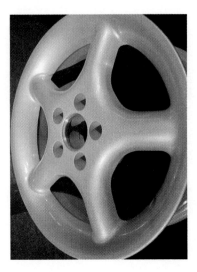

figure 12-10

This wheel is an example of Geometric Pigment, developed by Spectratek Technologies, Inc., which can be used for applications that require high-temperature processing or long-term immersion durability in solvents and resins. Geometric Pigment is widely used as an additive in automotive paints, a wide range of consumer items and packaging, printing inks, and the magic glittering component in cosmetic lines such as Urban Decay and Girl. *Reproduced with permission of Spectratek Technologies, Inc.*

glittering component in cosmetic lines such as Urban Decay and Girl (Figures 12-11 and 12-12). Geometric Pigment has a high heat tolerance of 400 degrees Fahrenheit and excellent optical clarity. Such new concepts will result in an extremely complex consumer reaction to color, which leads back to the original question we asked at the beginning of this book: What is color, really? Because color is a complex interaction of light, eye, and brain, technology could change the very way we think about color (Figure 12-13).

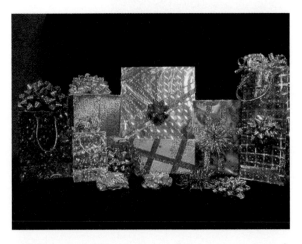

figure 12-11

This display shows some of the many options available to consumers in holographic packaging. *Reproduced with permission of Spectratek Technologies, Inc.*

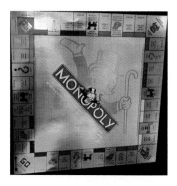
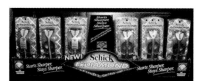
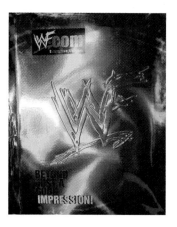

figure 12-12

Such new concepts as holographic packaging, which displays the entire range of the spectrum simultaneously, will result in an extremely complex consumer reaction to color. *Reproduced with permission of Spectratek Technologies, Inc.*

The photobiological effects of light are only now beginning to get the attention they deserve. There is much to be learned and much more to be studied if we are to define the risks associated with artificial lighting. As for other areas color research may uncover, we can only imagine. We believe the future of medicine will involve an increasing understanding and use of color/light in a therapeutic way. Reality tells us that color/light research will be seriously funded only if drug companies can find a way to market it. However, this may happen as we come to understand more about the interactions of light with photosensitizing chemicals in therapy, as discussed in Chapter 4. Whenever humans venture into the unknown, we always have fear, uncertainty, and a reluctance to accept new ideas. Color/light research

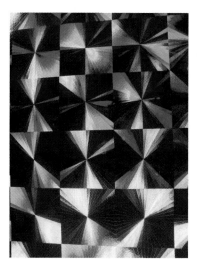

figure 12-13

The exciting technology that developed holographic packaging materials and pigments could change the very way we think about color and will undoubtedly continue to revolutionize the way products are presented to the consumer. *Reproduced with permission of Spectratek Technologies, Inc.*

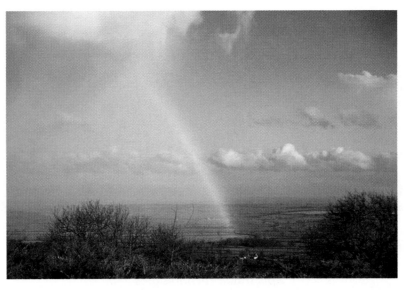

figure 12-14

As we continue in our attempts to understand color, we may find that it contains the very meaning of life itself. © *Dorling Kindersley*

is in the gestation stages; it has not even reached infancy. Intensive research is needed to understand and apply its potential to preventive and therapeutic health care. We know the impact of color/light is far-reaching, but perhaps it holds secrets beyond our imagination. As we continue to grope and probe our way toward understanding, we may find it contains the very meaning of life itself. Whatever the future holds, one thing is certain: There is much more to color than meets the eye (Figure 12-14).

REFERENCES

Babbitt, E. D., *The Principles of Light and Color*, University Books, 1967 (reprint).

Binkley, S., "A Timekeeping Enzyme in the Pineal Gland," *Scientific American* 240, 1979, 66–71.

Bluth, B. J., *Soviet Space Stations as Analogs*, NASA, 1986.

Bongard, N. M., Smirnov, M. A., "About the Dermal Vision of R. Kuleshova," *Biophysics* 1, 1965.

Connor, M. M., Harrison, A. A., Akin, F. R., *Living Aloft: Human Requirements for Extended Spaceflight*, NASA, 1985.

Cooper, H. S. F., Jr., "A Reporter at Large: Life in a Space Station I and II," *New Yorker*, August 30 and September 6, 1976.

Edelson, R. L., "Light Activated Drugs," *Scientific American*, August 1988, 68–75.

Friedman, A. H., Walker, C. A., "Circadian Rhythms II: Rat Midbrain and Caudate Nucleus Biogenic Amine Levels," *Journal of Physiology* 197, 1968, 77–85.

Geller, I., "Ethanol Preference in the Rat as a Function of Photoperiod," *Science* 173, 1971, 456–458.

Gurovskiy, N. N., Kosmolinskiy, F. P., Melnikov, L. N., *Designing the Living and Working Conditions of Cosmonauts*, NASA, 1981.

Haines, R. F., "Color Design for Habitability," in E. C. Wortz and M. R. Gauert, eds., *Proceedings of the 28th Annual Conference CCAIA*, 1973, 84–106.

Holodov, U. A., "Man in a Magnetic Web," *Znanie-Sila* 7, 1965.

Kaufman, L., Williamson, S., "The Evoked Magnetic Field of the Human Brain," *Annals of the New York Academy of Sciences* 340, 1980, 45–65.

Kitayev-Smyk, L. A., "Optical Illusions in People in Weightlessness and with the Combined Effect of Weightlessness, Angular and Coriollis Accelerations," *Problems of Space Biology* 7, 1967, 180–186.

Kitayev-Smyk, L. A., "The Question of Adaptation in Weightlessness," in B. N. Petrov, B. F. Lomonov, and N. D. Samsonov, eds., *Psychological Problems of Space Flight*, NASA, 1979, 204–233.

Kitayev-Smyk, L. A., "Study of Achromatic and Chromatic Visual Sensitivity during Short Periods of Weightlessness," *Problems of Physiological Optics* 15, 1972, 55–159.

Konovalov, B., *New Features of Salyut 7 Station*, USSR report 17, 1982.

Novomeisky, A., "Nature of Dermo-Optic Sense," *International Journal of Parapsychology* 7, 1965, 4.

Novomeisky, A., "The Role of the Dermo-Optic Sense in Cognition," *Questions of Philosophy*, July 1963.

Novomeisky, A., "Again about the Nizhni-Tagil Riddle," *Science and Life*, February 1963.

Novomeisky, A., "Changes in Dermo-Optics Sensitivity in Various Conditions of Illumination," in *Questions of Complex Research on Dermo-Optics*, Pedagogical Institute (Sverdlovsk), 1968.

Petrov, Y. A., "Habitability of Spacecraft," in M. Calvin and O. G. Gazekno, eds., *Foundations of Space Biology and Medicine*, Vol. III, NASA Scientific and Technical Information Office, 1975, 157–192.

Rivlin, R., Gravelle, K., *Deciphering the Senses*, Simon and Schuster, 1984.

Rogers, J., "Environmental Needs of Individuals and Groups," in E. C. Wortz and M. R. Guert, eds., *Proceedings of the 28th Annual Conference CCAIA*, 1973, 54–62.

White, W. J., "Effects of Transient Weightlessness on Brightness Discrimination," *Aerospace Medicine* April, 1965, 327–331.

Wilson, P., "Induction of Alcohol Selection in Laboratory Rats by Ultraviolet Light," *Journal of Studies on Alcohol*, November 7, 1976.

Wutman, R. J., "The Effects of Light on the Human Body," *Scientific American*, July 1975.

Index

Color
The Secret Influence
WORKBOOK

IMPORTANT—READ ME FIRST!

In today's competitive marketplace, a designer must have more than just the basic tools to survive. Savvy consumers want to get the most for their money. It is with this in mind that *Color: The Secret Influence* was written. It is not enough to simply know the color basics. The inseparable combination of color/light affects every aspect of life, from your health to your choice of laundry detergent. In our experience, even artists and designers who have spent years working directly with color/light rarely know just how much it affects us.

Color: The Secret Influence is written for both students of color/light and general readers using the aligned learning method (ALM). What does that mean? ALM means we present the material that is to be learned, we provide you with assignments that reinforce the information that has been presented, and then we test you on only that information. We don't trick you. We don't give you information on one thing and then test you on something else. The purpose of ALM is to **learn** and **retain** a specific body of knowledge. If you just want to know general information about how to use color/light more effectively in your life, you may not want to bother with this workbook section. If, however, you are a student of color/light, then the exercises, assignments, and tests in this workbook will help you become proficient. If this book is being used in a classroom situation, the instructor can choose from the extensive assignments included. A separate *Instructor's Manual* is available from the publisher.

Einstein said that the only way to truly understand a subject is to experience it. **Empirical knowledge that is gained by doing is the only true knowledge.** Experiential learning is the basis for ALM. The things you learn through ALM will stay with you throughout your life because you don't just read about topics, you actually experience them. By doing the assignments and exercises in this workbook in conjunction with reading the text, the concepts will be reinforced and retained, and you will receive a thorough grounding in the topic of color/light.

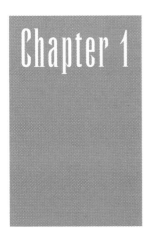

Chapter 1

The Color Connection: Basic Color Instruction Unit

Before proceeding with this section, the student should have read and gained a basic understanding of the concepts laid out in the text of Chapter 1, the Color Connection.

INSTRUCTIONAL FOUNDATIONS

Color is an essential tool of the designer or artist. To create a functional and aesthetically appealing design, a student needs a thorough understanding of color, its properties, its uses, and its relationship to light. This learning module on color is geared to that purpose. It is a lecture format supplemented by studio projects. The pre-test has been designed to ascertain how much basic color information each student entering the program has prior to instruction.

Terminal Objectives

At the end of this instructional unit, the student will be able to:

1. identify the properties of color
2. define how the human eye sees color
3. demonstrate competency in the vocabulary of color
4. do basic color mixing and neutralization

Student Name:

Course:

Instructor:

Date:

BASIC COLOR PRE-TEST

Circle the correct answer from the choices given below. Then remove this page and give it to your instructor.

1. The primary colors of light are:

a. red   f. green
b. brown   g. gray
c. orange   h. violet
d. yellow   i. magenta
e. blue   j. cyan

2. The primary colors of pigment are:

a. red   f. green
b. brown   g. gray
c. orange   h. violet
d. yellow   i. magenta
e. blue   j. cyan

3. Select the color below that results from mixing red and blue light.

a. yellow   d. violet
b. cyan   e. orange
c. magenta

4. Select the color below that results from mixing green and red light.

a. blue   d. orange
b. yellow   e. violet
c. cyan

5. Select the color below that results from mixing green and blue light.

a. magenta   c. yellow
b. cyan

6. Select the letter that correctly defines the word *tint*.

a. a color or pigment containing a large amount of white
b. the vividness of a hue
c. the color obtained by mixing two or more primary colors
d. a color obtained by mixing a hue with gray or black

7. Select the letter that correctly defines the word *shade*.

a. a color that appears on the spectrum of light
b. a synonym for lightness
c. a color obtained by mixing a hue with black
d. a synonym for saturation

8. Select the letter that correctly defines the word *hue*.

a. the separation of light into colors by refraction
b. the attribute of a color by which it is distinguished from another
c. the interplay of colors with change of position
d. intensity of color

9. Select the letter that correctly defines the word *value*.

a. the estimated lightness of a surface color
b. colors opposite on the color wheel
c. a quantum of light energy
d. light having a narrow wavelength

10. Select the letter that correctly defines the word *saturation*.

a. a color differing from a specified hue
b. the vividness or intensity of a hue
c. the measurable brightness of a light source
d. a form of electromagnetic radiation

11. Select the neutrals from the choices listed below.

a. red   h. brown
b. yellow   i. green
c. gray   j. black
d. violet   k. magenta
e. white   l. cyan
f. pink
g. orange

Student Name:

Course:

Instructor:

Date:

CHAPTER 1: HUMAN COLOR VISION CURRICULUM-RELATED TEST

Circle the correct answer from the choices given below. Then remove this page and give it to your instructor.

1. Between five and ten photons of light are sufficient to produce the sensation of light in the human eye.   True   False

2. Rhodopsin is the pigment contained in cones.   True   False

3. It takes twenty minutes for the human eye to regenerate rhodopsin.   True   False

4. There are five types of cones.   True   False

5. The pupil is black because most of the light entering the eye is absorbed.   True   False

6. The retina contains 120 million rods and 6 million cones.   True   False

7. Only when the light and color signals from the eye reach the visual cortex of the brain do we see color.   True   False

8. The rhodopsin molecule is closely related to vitamin A.   True   False

Student Name:

Course:

Instructor:

Date:

CHAPTER 1: VOCABULARY OF COLOR
CURRICULUM-RELATED TEST

Circle the correct answer from the choices given below. Then remove this page and give it to your instructor.

1. Hue is another word for color.   True   False

2. The basic hues of the spectrum are red, orange,
   yellow, green, blue, and violet.   True   False

3. A shade is the result of mixing pure color with
   white.   True   False

4. Value is the lightness or darkness of a color.   True   False

5. When all the primaries are mixed together, black
   is the result.   True   False

6. The additive secondaries are yellow, magenta, and
   cyan.   True   False

7. The subtractive primaries are red, green, and blue.   True   False

8. Pigment colors that appear opposite each other on
   a color wheel are traditionally called
   complementary colors.   True   False

COLOR MIXING ASSIGNMENTS

Title: | **Secondary Pigment Colors Derived from Mixing Primaries**

Objective: This simple exercise is sufficient to determine basic color-mixing knowledge.

Materials: Primary colors of water-based paint, brushes, a water container, and white paper.

Description: Each student will mix a palette of secondary colors from the existing primary colors.

Title: | **Graded Color Scale**

Objective: To train the eye to variations in color.

Materials: Red, green, yellow, black, and white water-based paint, brushes, white paper, water containers, and glue stick.

Description: Given paint, brushes, water containers, and paper, the students will mix a twenty-three-step graded scale for each of the hues red, green, and yellow at the center point and the neutrals black at the right and white at the left.

There will be ten steps between the center hue (red, green, or yellow) and the neutral black. There will be ten steps between the center hue and the neutral white. Each of the steps should be one inch by two inches in size, and the color variations must touch or overlap.

Students should mix the paint on paper. When the paint is dry, the colors can be cut apart and applied to another piece of white paper to form the graded scale.

White   Red, Green, or Yellow   Black

(10 tints)   (10 shades)

Time Frame: One class period.

Title: | **Color Neutralizing Exercise**

Objective: To neutralize one primary color with black and white.

Materials: Poster paints in black, white, and one primary; brushes; papers; and containers for mixing paint.

Description: Take one primary color and neutralize it with black and white by mixing the color with black and then by mixing the color with white. Using the color and the two neutralized colors, create a design in geometric patterns.

Time Frame: Forty-five minutes to one hour.

Title: **Found Object Color Wheel Assignment**

Objective: The purpose of this assignment is to encourage the students to observe their environments and focus on color. They then take the colors that have been selected and arrange them in a color wheel that reflects their observations and unique perspectives on color.

Materials: Found objects, twelve-inch by twelve-inch white cardboard, glue, and tape.

Description: Each student will create a color wheel representing the basic color spectrum from found objects brought to class. Students are not permitted to purchase items for this project. The objects are to be found within the environment and may be flowers, foods, paper products, plastic, wood, metal, textiles, string, yarn, and the like. These objects are then to be arranged during a class period in a circle on the cardboard, beginning at the top with red, red-orange, orange, yellow-orange, yellow, yellow-green, green, blue-green, blue, blue-violet, violet, and red-violet. The objects are to touch or overlap, with no white showing between them. The students are required to bring to class something to adhere the objects to the boards.

Time Frame: Forty-five minutes to one hour.

Title: **Differences in Color Neutralization Exercise**

Objective: To train the eye to see differences in color and practice color neutralization.

Materials: Water-based paint in the six spectral colors (red, orange, yellow, green, blue, violet) plus black and white, brushes, water container, and white paper.

Description: Mix together the following colors of paint. Paint a sample swatch of each result on white paper. Note the different tonal values of the resulting mixture.

> 1 part yellow + 1 part violet
> 1 part red-yellow + 1 part violet + 6 parts white

> 1 part red + 1 part green
> 1 part red + 1 part green + 6 parts white
>
> 1 part orange + 1 part blue
> 1 part orange + 1 part blue + 6 parts white

Time Frame: One or more class periods.

Title: **Color Neutralization Exercise (Shade)**

Objective: To train the eye to see differences in color and practice color neutralization.

Tutorial: To darken a color, the first instinct is to add black, but this may have a graying effect on the color, making it look dirty and losing its true hue. Red, blue, green, and brown can be successfully darkened by adding a little black, but to prevent the hue from changing, add a touch of a darker shade of the color being darkened. For example, add a touch of a dark red to red. Do not add black to light colors. Black added to yellow makes it turn green. Instead, add a touch of red and blue. To darken colors, try adding a small quantity of the strongest hue in the range nearest the color you are aiming for. This may cause a slight change in hue as a result of the type of pigment used. To maintain the apparent hue of a red, add a touch of yellow; when working with blue, add a touch of green. To darken a color, **always add dark to light**. Now, try the following exercise.

Materials: Water-based paint in the six spectral colors (red, orange, yellow, green, blue, violet) plus black and white paint, brushes, water container, and white paper.

Description: Mix together the following colors of paint. Paint a sample swatch of each result on white paper. Note the different tonal values of the resulting mixture.

> 4 parts red + 1 part black
> 4 parts red + 1 part dark red*
> 4 parts red + 1 part dark red* + a small amount of yellow

*(Create dark red by adding a drop or two of black to red.)

This process may be repeated with the other spectral colors.

Time Frame: At least one class period or more, at the discretion of the instructor.

Title: **Color Neutralization Exercise (Tint)**

Objective: To train the eye to see differences in color.

Tutorial:

To lighten a color, the rule is: Add the color to white. However, the addition of white often changes the hue. For example, adding crimson to white results in a bluish pink. The hue can be maintained by adding a touch of yellow to the pink. Yellow can be used to lighten colors, but it will also change the hue slightly. To lighten orange with yellow, add a touch of red. Yellow and orange can be used to lighten burnt sienna. Light yellow can be used to lighten orange and green. **The light color must be in the same family as the color being lightened.** If not, color changes will occur. For example, yellow will turn blue to green, and green added to blue will change it to turquoise. **Always add colors to white. Never add white to colors.** It takes a lot of white to lighten a color even slightly. Now, try the following exercise.

Description:

Mix together the following colors of paint. Paint a sample swatch of each result on white paper. Note the different tonal values of the resulting mixture.

> 4 parts red + 1 part white
> 1 part red + 4 parts white
> 1 part red + 4 parts white + a small amount of yellow.

Time Frame:

At least one class period or more, at the discretion of the instructor.

Title:

Color Series Mixing

Objective:

Additional training of the eye to see the differences when pigment colors are mixed together.

Materials:

Water-based paint in the six spectral colors (red, orange, yellow, green, blue, violet) plus black and white paint, brushes, water container, and white paper.

Description:

1. Take each of the six spectral colors and mix together related color pairs in equal proportions as follows:

> yellow + red
> red + violet
> blue + green
> green + yellow

Paint a sample swatch of each result on white paper. Note the different tonal values of the resulting mixture.

2. Take the same set of colors and mix them together in different proportions. Paint a sample swatch of each result on white paper. Note the different tonal values of the resulting mixture.

3. Mix together the following combinations, paint each as a sample swatch, and note the results.

2 parts yellow + 1 part black
1 part yellow + 2 parts black
1 part yellow + 3 parts black

Repeat with:

2 parts red + 1 part black
1 part red + 2 parts black
1 part red + 3 parts black

Repeat with:

2 parts blue + 1 part black
1 part blue + 2 parts black
1 part blue + 3 parts black

Compare the results of this mixing exercise.

4. Keep the results of this exercise and observe them at different times of the day and under different lighting conditions. Note the differences.

Time Frame: One or several class periods, at the instructor's discretion.

Title:	**Making Gray**
Objective:	To develop an eye for the variations of neutralization.
Materials:	Water-based spectral paint colors plus black and white, brushes, water container, and white paper.
Description:	Do the following mixing exercises and paint a sample swatch of each result on white paper. Observe and compare the results.

1. Mix together 3 parts white + 1 part black.

2. Mix together 3 parts white + 3 parts red + 3 parts blue + 1 part yellow.

3. Mix together 3 parts white + 2 parts red + 3 parts blue + 1 part yellow.

Time Frame: One or several class periods, at the instructor's discretion.

Title:	**Creating Tints Exercise**
Objective:	To train the eye in the observation of pastels.
Description:	Create a range of pastels by adding each of the six basic spectral hues to white in the proportion 1:15. Next, vary the pastels as follows:

1. Mix 15 parts white + 1 part red + a small amount of yellow. Show the result.

2. Mix together equal quantities of pastel yellow (white and yellow) and pastel pink (white and red). Show the result.

3. Mix together pastel blue (white and blue) and a small amount of pastel yellow (white and yellow). Show the result.

Time Frame:

At least one class period. May be repeated for practice at the instructor's discretion.

Student Name:

Course:

Instructor:

Date:

CHAPTER 1: BASIC COLOR POSTTEST

This test is designed to assess the student's knowledge of basic color after studying the basic color unit. Competency should be shown before the student moves to the next unit on basic lighting.

Circle the correct answer from the choices given below. Then tear out this page and give it to your instructor.

1. The primary colors in light are:

a. red	e. blue	h. violet
b. brown	f. green	i. magenta
c. orange	g. gray	j. cyan
d. yellow		

2. Select the color below that results from mixing red and blue light.

a. yellow	d. violet
b. cyan	e. orange
c. magenta	

3. The primary pigment colors are:

a. red	e. blue	h. violet
b. brown	f. green	i. magenta
c. orange	g. gray	j. cyan
d. yellow		

4. Select the color from the choices listed below that results from mixing green and red light.

a. blue	d. orange
b. yellow	e. violet
c. cyan	

5. Select the letter that correctly defines the word *value*.

a. the estimated lightness of a surface color
b. colors opposite on the color wheel
c. a quantum of light energy
d. light that has a narrow wavelength

6. Select the letter that correctly defines the word *saturation*.

a. a color differing from a specified hue
b. the vividness or intensity of a hue
c. the measurable brightness of a light source
d. a form of electromagnetic radiation

7. Select the letter that correctly defines the word *shade*.

    a. a color that appears on the spectrum of light
    b. a synonym for lightness
    c. a color obtained by mixing a hue with gray or black
    d. a synonym for saturation

8. The neutrals are gray, white, black, brown.   True   False

9. Color exists without light.   True   False

10. Rhodopsin is the pigment contained in cones.   True   False

11. Black, white, and gray are not colors.   True   False

12. Light can be both a particle and a wave.   True   False

13. There are five types of cones in the human eye.   True   False

14. The rhodopsin molecule is closely related to vitamin A.   True   False

15. Fluorescence is the phenomenon of converting high-frequency radiation into visible light at a lower frequency.   True   False

16. The retina contains about 120 million cones and about 6 million rods.   True   False

17. Hue and color are synonymous.   True   False

18. When all the primaries are mixed together, black is the result.   True   False

19. The additive secondaries are yellow, magenta, and cyan.   True   False

20. The subtractive primaries are red, green, and blue.   True   False

21. The basic hues of the spectrum are red, orange, yellow, green, blue, and violet.   True   False

22. Fluorescent tubes are available that render true color reproduction.   True   False

23. Metamerism is the capacity of colors to change under different lighting conditions.   True   False

24. Aesthetic considerations are as important as illumination in regard to artificial lighting.   True   False

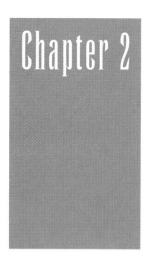

Chapter 2

Color: Pigment and Light
Basic Lighting
Instruction Unit

Before proceeding with this section, the student should have read and gained a basic understanding of the concepts laid out in the text of Chapter 2, Color: Pigment and Light, and shown competency in the previous unit, Basic Color Instruction.

INSTRUCTIONAL FOUNDATIONS

A student successfully completing this unit in conjunction with the text reading will have gained a basic understanding of the concepts and techniques used in the area of basic lighting. With increased skill, the student will gain a strong foundation for further study at higher levels of difficulty in this area. The study of basic lighting techniques involves the study of the whole human being in relation to the natural and artificial environment. Effective lighting of interior spaces can improve the physiological and psychological health of the populace.

With the completion of this unit, students will be able to assess and design lighting plans. Additionally, students will have gained a better understanding of their relationship to the environment and will have begun to develop an understanding of the psychological and physiological effects of lighting on the human body. Thus, the student will have gained an increased awareness of self in relation to society as a whole.

Terminal Objectives

At the end of this unit, students will be able to execute or critique an effective lighting plan for a space of their choice from the following list:

- product design
- theater design
- display and marketing
- interior design: commercial and residential
- closed environments, such as schools, prisons, and hospitals
- television and film
- public spaces, such as streets, parks, parking lots
- security lighting
- airport lighting

Student Name:

Course:

Instructor:

Date:

CHAPTER 2: LIGHTING BASICS CURRICULUM-RELATED TEST

Circle the correct answer from the choices given below. Then remove this page and turn it in to your instructor.

1. A prime function of light is disclosure.   True   False

2. Light can make an object appear more valuable.   True   False

3. The difference between glare and sparkle is the
    degree of brightness.   True   False

4. The eye automatically seeks out the brightest
    object in its field.   True   False

5. Given the list of terms below, circle the six main concepts to consider when you begin to design a lighting plan for an interior space.
    a. visibility   g. review and correction
    b. atmosphere   h. spatial environment
    c. composition   i. interior color
    d. object appearance   j. fenestration
    e. mechanical development
    f. brightness

Student Name:

Course:

Instructor:

Date:

CHAPTER 2: LIGHT SOURCES CURRICULUM-RELATED TEST

Circle the correct answer from the choices given below. Then remove this page and give it to your instructor.

1. Daylight is a major factor to consider in any lighting plan.　　　　　True　　False

2. The color of daylight changes according to the composition of the atmosphere.　　　　　True　　False

3. The proper term for any artificial light source is lamp.　　　　　True　　False

4. The sun and the incandescent lamp both create light by heating materials until they glow.　　　　　True　　False

5. Incandescent lighting is the least like the sun's light.　　　　　True　　False

6. General service lamps are the most commonly used lighting devices.　　　　　True　　False

7. Tungsten-halogen lamps are a form of electric discharge lighting.　　　　　True　　False

8. Reflectorized lamps are fully enclosed lighting instruments in their own right.　　　　　True　　False

9. Flame-shaped lamps fall into the decorative lamp category.　　　　　True　　False

10. Dichroic filters produce very transparent and sparkling colors.　　　　　True　　False

11. There is only one base size for incandescent lamps.　　　　　True　　False

12. There are two types of electric discharge lamps, low-intensity discharge and high-intensity discharge.　　　　　True　　False

13. All electric discharge lamps must be used with a
    ballast.   True   False

14. Electric discharge lamps may be used in any
    household socket.   True   False

15. Ill effects on the human body from exposure to
    fluorescent light are unheard of.   True   False

Student Name:

Course:

Instructor:

Date:

CHAPTER 2: LIGHT MEASUREMENT AND CONTROL CURRICULUM-RELATED TEST

Circle the correct answer from the choices given below. Then remove this page and give it to your instructor.

1. Lumen refers to the quantity of light that is given off in all directions by the lamp itself.   True   False

2. Lumens are never compared to watts.   True   False

3. Candlepower describes the amount of light given off in a particular direction.   True   False

4. Candela is the measurement applied to the light issuing from a lighting fixture.   True   False

5. The light falling on a target is called incident light.   True   False

6. Foot-candles measure incident light.   True   False

7. Light that is reflected from an object is measured in footlamberts.   True   False

8. Extreme contrasts in brightness can cause temporary eyestrain.   True   False

9. Contrasts in brightness are not essential to the process of seeing.   True   False

10. When contrast in brightness is so great that it causes loss in visual performance, it is called glare.   True   False

11. Direct glare is caused by poorly shielded light sources.   True   False

12. Reflected glare results from disturbing reflections off mirror-like surfaces.   True   False

13. Discomfort glare occurs when reflected glare is
irritating.　　　　　　　　　　　　　　　　　　True　False

14. Veiling glare is the same as disability glare.　　True　False

Student Name:

Course:

Instructor:

Date:

CHAPTER 2: LUMINAIRES FOR INTERIOR LIGHTING CURRICULUM-RELATED TEST

Circle the correct answer from the choices given below. Then remove this page and give it to your instructor.

1. Luminaire is the synonymous term for lighting fixture.   True   False

2. A recessed fixture uses a general service lamp in a polished metal reflector.   True   False

3. The reflector downlight is not as effective as the open reflector.   True   False

4. The low cost of can luminaries is offset by the fact that they require the use of expensive reflectorized lamps.   True   False

5. Wall washers are designed to coat a wall evenly with light.   True   False

6. The chandelier and sconce are not decorative luminaires.   True   False

BASIC LIGHTING ASSIGNMENTS

Title:	**Lighting Plan Assessment**
Objective:	To determine knowledge of interior lighting.
Materials:	Students will be provided with a floorplan or photograph of an office or residence.
Description:	**Option 1:** Students will write an assessment of the lighting plan, offering criticism and alternatives as considered necessary. **Option 2:** Given an office floorplan and the functions of the office, the student will design an effective lighting plan for that space to the satisfaction of the instructor. (This may be modified to suit specific needs, such as lighting for a fashion show and lighting for a landscape plan.)
Time Frame:	One or more class periods at the instructor's discretion or as a homework assignment.
Alternative Assignments:	1. The student will design or write a critique of the lighting or the set of a theatrical production. 2. The student will design or write a critique of a lighting plan for a fashion show. 3. The student will design or write a critique of an outdoor lighting plan for a landscaped garden. 4. The student will design or write a critique of a lighting plan relating to product design.

Title:	**Commercial Spaces Observation**
Objective:	To focus the students' attention on the color, lighting, and design used in the selected spaces.
Description:	Students will select three commercial spaces, such as banks, restaurants, theaters, shopping malls, boutiques, or department stores. These can be places they have previously visited or new places. They will observe the use of color within these spaces, not the use of the neutrals black, white, gray, and brown. Students will write a narrative describing the color, its use, and the effect it has on them. 　　For example, *Commercial Space: XYZ department store* *Location: 123 Maple Drive, City*

Type of merchandise or business:
Colors used in space:
Student response to colors used:

Time Frame: Homework and in-class assignment.

Chapter 3 Color Myths and Biases

Before proceeding with this section, the student should have read and gained a basic understanding of the concepts laid out in the text of Chapter 3, Color Myths and Biases.

INSTRUCTIONAL FOUNDATIONS

Each of us, no matter our age, race, gender, or culture, carries color biases that were learned from the cradle. Some of our color biases develop as a result of culturally induced superstitions or old beliefs that are carried into the present. Also, the color conditioning involved in language plays a part in determining our color biases. Unless we identify and understand our color biases, we will continue to be controlled by them. Within this section are exercises to aid in the identification of personal color biases.

Terminal Objective

At the end of this instructional unit, the student will be able to:

1. identify personal color biases

2. identify cultural color biases

3. begin to separate our color myths from color facts

4. demonstrate a basic knowledge of the origins of color myths

ASSIGNMENTS

Title:	**Personal Color Preferences**
Objective:	To define color preferences and their associations.
Materials:	Writing implements.
Description:	Make a list of your three favorite colors. Make a list of your three least favorite colors. For each list, write down your first thought or memory associated with that color. Note the correlation between happy memories and favorite colors and vice versa.
Time Frame:	This can be done as a homework assignment to be discussed in the next class meeting.

Title:	**Color Response Exercise**
Objective:	To investigate perceptions of color.
Materials:	A pack of variously colored construction paper.
Description:	The instructor will hold up one color of construction paper and, moving around the room, ask the students to describe the color in one word. For example, while holding up pink, you may receive responses such as "cotton candy," "eraser," "baby," "girl," "valentines," and "bubble gum." Using these responses, the instructor can initiate discussion around how people respond to a specific color.
Time Frame:	One class period.

Title:	**Color in Relationship to Attitude**
Objective:	To get people to see how color affects attitudes toward individuals.
Materials:	None.
Description:	The instructor gives the following scenarios:

1. A woman is standing in a red minidress on the street corner under a lamp post at midnight. What is your perception of her? Does color have an effect on your perception?

2. You meet an individual on the street who is pushing a baby carriage. The baby is dressed all in blue. What is your perception of the baby?

3. A young man is dressed in a pink shirt and pants. What is your perception of him?

4. An old woman is dressed all in the neutral black. What is your perception of her?

5. A young woman is dressed all in the neutral black. What is your perception of her?

Time Frame:	One or more class periods, at the instructor's discretion.

Student Name:

Course:

Instructor:

Date:

CHAPTER 3: COLOR MYTHS AND BIASES
CURRICULUM-RELATED TEST

Circle the correct answer from the choices given below. Then remove this page and give it to your instructor.

1. In heraldry, the symbolic meaning for red was:
   a. loyalty
   b. bravery
   c. purity
   d. honesty

2. In heraldry, the symbolic color associated with loyalty was:
   a. blue
   b. red
   c. white
   d. yellow

3. What is the best-selling paint?
   a. red
   b. blue
   c. beige
   d. white

4. What represents the negation of color?
   a. white
   b. indigo
   c. black
   d. gray

5. Which of the following is most associated with technology?
   a. gray
   b. black
   c. white
   d. blue

6. What color is most often associated with passion?
   a. violet
   b. red
   c. orange
   d. pink

7. In nature, what color signals danger?
   a. red
   b. yellow
   c. orange
   d. green

8. What color is most associated with jealousy?
   a. red
   b. violet
   c. green
   d. orange

9. What is the most favored color in the United States?

    a. blue   c. red

    b. green   d. yellow

10. What color is associated with England's Knights of the Garter?

    a. red   c. purple

    b. blue   d. yellow

11. What color is most often associated with royalty?

    a. purple   c. green

    b. scarlet   d. blue

12. Climate plays a role in defining color biases.   True   False

13. The favorite color of most Germans is green.   True   False

Chapter 4 Color and Health

Before proceeding with this section, the student should have read and gained a basic understanding of the concepts laid out in the text of Chapter 4, Color and Health.

INSTRUCTIONAL FOUNDATIONS

Photobiology is the branch of science that studies the effects of light/color on human biology and health. Although photobiology is in its infancy, we already know that the effects of color/light on human health are far-reaching. In the text, we have described some of the many ways that life on earth is affected by light and color. Future research will undoubtedly add to this knowledge base. However, the effects of light/color are so provocative and extensive that all color practitioners should be well versed in their application.

Terminal Objective

At the end of this instructional unit, the student will be able to:

1. identify the relationship between light/color and the human condition.

ASSIGNMENTS

Title: **Effects of Color/Light**

Objective: To understand the effects of color/light on humans.

Materials: The lighting system used in the classroom setting. (In most cases, this will probably be fluorescent light.)

Description: Have the students do a color mixing assignment. You could use one of those outlined in Chapter 1. About halfway through the class, make sure that all the window coverings are opened to admit natural light and turn off the fluorescent lights. The immediate response from the students will be that the space is too dark, no matter how bright it is outside. Tell them to wait a minute to allow their eyes to adjust to the new lighting level. Ask the students to continue with the color mixing project. Compare the results of the mixing done under the different lighting conditions. What are the results? Discuss whether colors are brighter, cleaner, and purer. Also, ask the students immediately upon turning the lights off if they notice a difference in their vision. Some of the responses you may receive are: "My eyes feel softer." "There's not as much tension around my eyes." You can then reiterate to them how the subliminal strobing of fluorescent light causes the pupil to constantly expand and contract and fatigues the eye. (Refer to Chapter 2 for additional information if needed.) This is a very simple but dramatic exercise in explaining how color and light affect the human system. (If you do not have fluorescent light in your classroom, consider yourself very lucky!)

Time Frame: One class period.

Title: **Effects of Color/Light on the Human System**

Objective: To dramatically show how color affects the human system.

Materials: Bubblegum pink and baby blue construction paper large enough to surround a person's field of vision.

Description: Select a subject (selecting the largest male in the class makes the effect more dramatic). Have the selected individual stand in front of the class with hands clasped together and arms extended at a ninety-degree angle to the body. Press down on the subject's hands while instructing him or her to resist. In most cases, the subject can resist your pressure. Select an assistant from the class to position behind the subject and hold the pink construction paper to surround the subject's field of vision. Make sure the peripheral vision is included. Allow the subject to view the pink construction paper for a few seconds. With her or his arms again extended in front, ask the subject to resist your pressure once again. The result will be that the subject is unable to resist your pressure and his or her arms will drop or fall. Have the assistant remove the pink construction paper from the field of vision. Allow the subject's arms to rest for a moment. Ask if the subject would like her or his strength back. Then repeat the process, using the blue construction paper in the same manner. Almost magically, the subject's strength will be restored.

This is an extremely dramatic way to show people how color affects them without their knowledge.

Time Frame: Approximately fifteen to twenty minutes to open a discussion on how color affects us physiologically.

Student Name:

Course:

Instructor:

Date:

CHAPTER 4: COLOR AND HEALTH CURRICULUM-RELATED TEST

Circle the correct answer from the choices given below. Then remove this page and give it to your instructor.

1. Photomedicine studies the effects of light on disease. True False

2. The use of light-based techniques to treat tumors and HIV is being explored. True False

3. Light exposure can affect the immune system. True False

4. Mammalian cells grown in the laboratory are mutated by fluorescent room light. True False

5. Animals and plants have the ability to distinguish time of day without reference to external light or darkness. True False

6. Seasonal affective disorder is a depression linked to the lack of light brought on by shorter days. True False

7. The perception of light by receptors other than true eyes is not possible. True False

8. Current research indicates that light can penetrate and affect the human body by means other than through the eyes. True False

9. Studies have found that people become much more fatigued in rooms lighted by fluorescent light than by rooms with full-spectrum lighting. True False

10. Visible light is able to penetrate mammalian tissues. True False

Chapter 5

Color and Psychology

Before proceeding with this section, the student should have read and gained a basic understanding of the concepts laid out in the text of Chapter 5, Color and Psychology.

INSTRUCTIONAL FOUNDATIONS

Although much has been written about the relationship of color to psychology, psychological measurements are often highly subjective and open to individual interpretation, and the color/light interactions are so complex that dogmatic statements should be viewed with suspicion. Although color preference has been widely studied, early research was often poorly controlled and led to inadequately investigated conclusions that were adopted by the popular press and formed the basis for many of our current misconceptions about color.

Terminal Objective

At the end of this unit, the student will be able:

1. to understand that statistics can be manipulated to suit the study

2. to understand the need to review original source material and determine what the sample for that study was and how the statistics were reported

ASSIGNMENTS

Title:	**Color/Light Research**
Objective:	To secure an article about color/light and psychology from a periodical or journal and backtrack it to its original source.
Materials:	An article about color/light and psychology from a periodical or journal.
Description:	The student will select an article on color/light from a periodical or journal and trace the footnotes back to their original sources to determine the size of the sample, the types of statistics used and how they were run, the population, and how the variables were or were not controlled to determine if the data are consistent with the original article selected.

| Time Frame: | Homework assignment to be discussed and critiqued during one or more class periods. |

Title:	**Color/Light in the Popular Media**
Description:	Replicate the previous assignment with an article selected from the popular media, such as design articles in local newspapers and articles on the Internet about color/light.
Time Frame:	Homework assignment to be discussed and critiqued during one or more class periods.

Title:	**Color and Perception**
Objective:	To determine the correlation between color and the perception of size, space, and/or weight.
Materials:	Cardboard, paint, brushes, tape, and glue.
Description:	Have each student in the class create a package of the same size, approximately a six-inch cube. Depending on the size of the class, each student can select a different color, or groups of students can select the same color. Be sure that all the colors in the spectrum are represented, as well as at least one package in black and one in white. Paint the packages in the colors selected. Place the packages on a table, and ask the students to give their perception of the size, weight, and amount of space taken up by each package.
	Then take these packages and have the students add a pattern to the packages in another color. See if their perceptions of size, weight, and space change.
Time Frame:	At least two class periods.

Student Name:

Course:

Instructor:

Date:

CHAPTER 5: COLOR AND PSYCHOLOGY CURRICULUM-RELATED TEST

Circle the correct answer from the choices given below. Then remove this page and give it to your instructor.

1. Psychological measurements are often highly subjective and open to individual interpretation.   True   False

2. Outcomes of psychological color/light studies are often contradictory.   True   False

3. Red is the most common signal color in nature.   True   False

4. Color preference is the product of cultural norms and subjective color bias.   True   False

5. The intensity of color appears to be of greater significance than the color itself with regard to excitement or arousal.   True   False

6. The association of color with mood is a learned behavior.   True   False

7. In understanding color, it is important to differentiate between culturally learned color associations and true biological responses.   True   False

8. Most people avoid blue food.   True   False

9. Perception of spaciousness is attributed to the brightness or darkness of a color rather than to specific colors.   True   False

10. Spatial impressions are highly influenced by contrast effects, particularly brightness differences between objects and backgrounds.   True   False

11. We see what we expect to see.   True   False

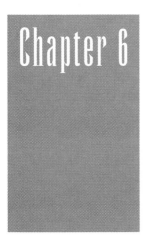

Chapter 6

Color and Interior Environments

Before proceeding with this section, the student should have read and gained a basic understanding of the concepts laid out in the text of Chapter 6, Color and Interior Environments. It will also be helpful for the student to have a good understanding of the concepts outlined in Chapter 4, Color and Health.

INSTRUCTIONAL FOUNDATIONS

Color/light in interior environments has a profound effect on human health. This fact is often overlooked or misunderstood, yet it is an essential part of a healthful environment that promotes physical and mental well-being. The average person does not consider for a moment how the color or light selected for an interior space will affect mood, physical well-being, or productivity. Improper use of color/light can be detrimental; proper use can promote optimal well-being. The assignments in this section should be done with a consideration of aesthetics and function, as well as the importance of color/light in the interior environment.

Terminal Objective

A student who has completed this section will have:

1. a basic understanding of the use of color in interior environments

2. a basic understanding of how to use color/light for optimum health in an interior environment

ASSIGNMENT

Title:	**Color Plan Assignment**
Objective:	To familiarize the student with various color choices in interiors.
Materials:	The floorplan can be prepared either manually or by CAD. Students will need paint color samples, fabric samples, carpet samples, wallpaper samples, and examples of furniture and accessories that show their color.

Description:

The student will conceptualize and prepare three interior color plans, including walls, flooring, ceiling, furnishings, window treatments, and accessories, and provide a rationale for each choice. The finished projects should be mounted on appropriately sized boards with a key describing the colors and where they are to be applied. The student should also be prepared to give a verbal explanation of color choices and why they were selected.

Time Frame:

Homework assignments to be discussed in the following class. This should be distributed over a three-class time frame.

If the institution has a lighting lab available, it will be appropriate for the instructor to show objects under various lighting conditions. For example, how does red light appear on red carpeting? How does pink light affect skin tones?

Student Name:

Course:

Instructor:

Date:

CHAPTER 6: COLOR AND INTERIOR ENVIRONMENTS CURRICULUM-RELATED TEST

Circle the correct answer from the choices given below. Then remove this page and give it to your instructor.

1. The emotional effects of color have a great impact on a living space.　　True　False

2. Aesthetic and health considerations are as important as illumination in artificial lighting.　　True　False

3. Low-pressure sodium lamps render true color reproduction.　　True　False

4. Incandescent light radiates a broad spectrum closest to sunlight.　　True　False

5. Incandescent lamps render color on the warm side of natural.　　True　False

6. Fluorescent tubes are available that render true color reproduction.　　True　False

7. Metamerism is the capacity of colors to change under different lighting conditions.　　True　False

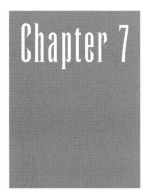

Chapter 7

Color in Architecture and Landscape Design

Before proceeding with this section, the student should have read and gained a basic understanding of the concepts laid out in the text of Chapter 7, Color in Architecture and Landscape Design.

INSTRUCTIONAL FOUNDATIONS

While we have come to accept the lack of color in our public buildings, the prototypes of all Western neoclassical architecture were the brightly colored temples of ancient civilizations. Centuries of weathering transformed these edifices into the neutrals we have come to associate with classical architecture. A basic understanding of the historical applications of color is essential for the designer and desirable for anyone interested in using color to its fullest. The selection of color for architectural applications requires knowledge and consideration of the same confines that affect all color selection: lighting and context. These same criteria are the basis for all effective architectural and landscape designs.

Terminal Objective

A student who has completed this section will have:

1. a basic understanding of the historical uses of color in architecture and landscape design

2. an ability to create efficient color plans for each

ASSIGNMENTS

Title:	**Architectural Exterior Tonal Variance Exercise**
Objective:	To train the eye to see the differences that tonalities can make to building exteriors.
Material:	Line drawings of building exteriors. A selection of black and a range of gray pencils or markers.
Description:	Select a line drawing of a building exterior. Make a series of ten photocopies. Create a pattern on each building by applying black, various grays, or white to each photocopy. Alter the pattern for each photocopy.

Compare the results. How does the difference in black, grays, and white change the appearance of the structure?

Time Frame:

Two or more class periods or homework assignment.

Note to the Instructor: *The completed assignments should be posted in the room so that all the students can see the range of variations achieved.*

Title:

Architectural Exterior Coloration Exercise

Objective:

To train the eye to see the differences that color can make to building exteriors.

Materials:

Photocopies of photographs of building exteriors. Colored markers or pencils.

Description:

Select a photograph of a building exterior. Make ten black-and-white photocopies of this photograph. Using the colored markers or pencils, create ten color plans, one for each photocopy. Compare the results.

Time Frame:

Two or more class periods or homework assignment.

Note to the Instructor: *The completed assignments should be posted in the room so that all the students can see the range of variations achieved. It will be beneficial to compare the results from the foregoing neutral and color exterior exercises.*

Title:

Landscape Color Exercise

Objective:

To expose the students to a variety of color usage in landscaping.

Materials:

Photographs of gardens or landscapes from magazines or newspapers.

Description:

The students are to locate photographs of gardens or landscapes in magazines or newspapers that show the use of color. Students should be looking for use of complementary, analogous, or monochromatic color schemes. How does the use of color change the appearance of the landscape or garden? Students should be prepared to discuss these issues in class.

Time Frame:

Homework assignment to be discussed in class.

Student Name:

Course:

Instructor:

Date:

CHAPTER 7: COLOR IN ARCHITECTURE AND LANDSCAPE DESIGN CURRICULUM-RELATED TEST

Circle the correct answer from the choices given below. Then remove this page and give it to your instructor.

1. Early use of color in architecture glorified the gods.   True   False

2. What were the prototypes of all Western neoclassical architecture?
  a. Greek temples   d. all of the above
  b. ziggurats   e. none of the above
  c. cathedrals

3. The Parthenon was originally colored in bright
green, red, and blue.   True   False

4. Ancient marble statues were originally brightly
colored.   True   False

5. Ancient Greek architecture may have served as
giant billboards on which color played a strong
symbolic role.   True   False

6. In ancient Greece, which color represented truth and integrity?
  a. blue   d. purple
  b. red   e. yellow
  c. green

7. Which color has played the most significant role in the emergence
of architectural color?
  a. green   d. blue
  b. red   e. yellow
  c. purple

8. In China's Forbidden City, what color represents the positive
essence?
  a. red   d. yellow
  b. green   e. blue
  c. purple

9. In China's Forbidden City, what color represents the negative essence?

    a. red   d. yellow
    b. green   e. blue
    c. purple

10. Constructivism used color to emphasize function.   True   False

11. Cities have their own defining colors.   True   False

12. Color selection for architecture should be selected under

    a. natural daylight   d. halogen light
    b. fluorescent light   e. laboratory lighting
    c. incandescent light

13. The smaller the area of color, the greater the visible saturation.   True   False

14. Background color may influence judgment of a color sample.   True   False

15. Effectively colored architectural facades always consider the neighboring natural and built environment.   True   False

16. What is the best clue to selecting colors for a building exterior?

    a. the sky   c. soil and plant colors
    b. owner preference   d. availability of paint

17. Color selection in architecture can be used to conserve energy.   True   False

18. In landscape design, the shape and scent of plants are secondary to the initial visual impact of color.   True   False

19. The gradually changing emphasis on different parts of the spectral range that will create distinctive atmospheres at different times of the day is called:

    a. verdigris phenomenon   c. daylight shift
    b. Purkinje shift   d. saturation system

20. Mosquitoes alight most frequently on dark blue, red, and brown.   True   False

21. To avoid mosquitoes, hikers should dress in yellow, orange, or white.   True   False

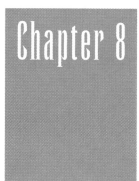

Chapter 8

Color in Advertising and Marketing

Before proceeding with this section, the student should have read and gained a basic understanding of the concepts laid out in the text of Chapter 8, Color in Advertising and Marketing.

INSTRUCTIONAL FOUNDATIONS

Color is the first thing noticed, and it carries an immediate message. Lasting impressions are made within the first ninety seconds, and color accounts for 69 percent of the acceptance or rejection of an object or person. Decisions about color are critical factors in the success or failure of an encounter or sale. Color is an extremely effective medium for consumer manipulation. Knowing how color is used to market and advertise products enables us to make informed decisions.

Terminal Objective

The student who completes this section will be able to analyze the use of color in products, advertising, and marketing and its effect on the consumer.

ASSIGNMENTS

Title:	**Color Impression**
Objective:	To understand how color affects product choice.
Materials:	Each student will select a product such as a toothpaste tube, detergent box, or candy wrapper and bring it to class. Students should also bring to class drawing materials and colors, brushes, and paper.
Description:	Using the selected product as a sample, render it on a piece of paper and change the color of packaging. Compare it with the original and solicit responses from class members as to their impressions of the original and altered package colors.
Time Frame:	One or more class periods.

Title:	**Packaging Exercise**
Objective:	The student will directly experience creating a product package with an ultimate consumer in mind.
Materials:	Drawing equipment, colors, brushes, and paper.
Description:	Each student will create a series of packages, each with an ultimate consumer in mind as follows:

1. fragrance for women

2. fragrance for men

3. dishwashing liquid

4. laxative

5. breakfast cereal

6. soft drink

Results should be compared and discussed in class.

Time Frame:	One or more class periods. Assignment may also be given as homework to be discussed in class.

Student Name:

Course:

Instructor:

Date:

CHAPTER 8: COLOR IN ADVERTISING AND MARKETING CURRICULUM-RELATED TEST

Circle the correct answer from the choices given below. Then remove this page and give it to your instructor.

1. Marketing psychologists say a lasting impression is made within
   a. thirty seconds
   b. sixty seconds
   c. ninety seconds
   d. ten seconds
   e. one minute

2. Color accounts for what percentage of the acceptance or rejection of an object?
   a. 10
   b. 30
   c. 50
   d. 60
   e. 90

3. Color sends a subliminal message that plays a critical role in success or failure.   True   False

4. Color does not play a large role in the transmission of advertising messages.   True   False

5. Which of the following colors are used to stimulate our salivary glands?
   a. pale brown
   b. purple
   c. blue
   d. black
   e. white

6. What color is used in advertising to express motherly love?
   a. red
   b. baby blue
   c. yellow
   d. pink
   e. violet

7. What color is used in advertising to symbolize eroticism?
   a. red
   b. baby blue
   c. yellow
   d. pink
   e. violet

8. What color is used in advertising to express prestige?

    a. red   d. pink
    b. baby blue   e. violet
    c. yellow

9. In advertising and marketing, which color is used to attract attention?

    a. red   d. pink
    b. baby blue   e. violet
    c. yellow

10. What is the most readable color combination?

    a. black on yellow   d. white on black
    b. black on white
    c. yellow on black

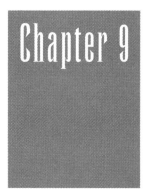

Chapter 9

Color in Fashion and Textile Design

Before proceeding with this section, the student should have read and gained a basic understanding of the concepts laid out in the text of Chapter 9, Color in Fashion and Textile Design.

INSTRUCTIONAL FOUNDATIONS

The clothes we choose to wear make an immediate impression about us. An understanding of fashion concepts enables us to be sure that the image we project is the image we intend to project.

Terminal Objective

A student who completes this section will have gained a better understanding of how apparel creates an image and the relationship of textiles to fashion.

ASSIGNMENTS

Title:	**Fabric Design**
Objective:	To design a length of fabric that can be manipulated to create a garment.
Materials:	A three-yard length of white cotton fabric and a variety of tools to apply design to the fabric, such as brushes for paint, outlines for stenciling, colored markers, wood block or potato block printing, or any other method desired.
Description:	Apply a design of your own choice and creation to the fabric. Using the finished product, design and produce a garment you can wear. It does not have to be sewn; it can simply be wrapped, stapled, lashed, taped, or attached with Velcro or any other method desired. In class, students should model their finished garments.
Time Frame:	Three to four class meetings.

Title:	**Headdress Project**
Objective:	To select a period of history and create a headdress faithful to the period and colors of the period.
Materials:	This project should be constructed completely from paper and materials such as glue and tape for attaching parts together.
Description:	Select a period of history—Renaissance, Roaring Twenties, Sixties—for either gender and construct a headdress of that period true to the style and colors of the period.
Time Frame:	Three class meetings.

Student Name:

Course:

Instructor:

Date:

CHAPTER 9: COLOR IN FASHION AND TEXTILE DESIGN CURRICULUM-RELATED TEST

Circle the correct answer from the choices given below. Then remove this page and give it to your instructor.

1. What is the most costly pigment?
   a. cobalt blue
   b. green
   c. brown
   d. red
   e. yellow

2. What is the first thing to capture a shopper's attention?
   a. lighting
   b. display
   c. color
   d. price
   e. size

3. A personal color plan should be based on:
   a. age
   b. size
   c. complexion
   d. gender
   e. preference

4. There are only two basic complexion categories. True False

5. Paler skin tones look best in pastels. True False

6. White lead pigment was once used in cosmetics. True False

7. Simultaneous contrast is the influence of one color on another. True False

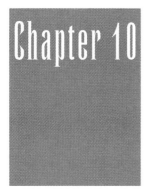

Chapter 10

Color in Culture and Society

Before proceeding with this section, the student should have read and gained a basic understanding of the concepts laid out in the text of Chapter 10, Color in Culture and Society.

INSTRUCTIONAL FOUNDATIONS

The use of color links all cultures and societies, although the meanings attached to a color may vary from culture to culture. Color and language are linked. An understanding of the relationship of color to language and culture furthers the understanding of human communication.

Terminal Objective

The student who completes this section will gain a basic understanding of the uses of color in various cultures.

ASSIGNMENTS

Title:	**Color and Language Exercise**
Objective:	To gain a better understanding of the cultural aspects of color.
Description:	Conduct an interview with a person from a different culture or ethnic background than your own to determine her or his cultural uses of color. Write up the results in a brief essay or in note form that can be shared with the class.
Time Frame:	Homework assignment, plus in-class discussion time.

Student Name:

Course:

Instructor:

Date:

CHAPTER 10: COLOR IN CULTURE AND SOCIETY CURRICULUM-RELATED TEST

Circle the correct answer from the choices given below. Then remove this page and give it to your instructor.

1. The use of color in ancient civilizations was primarily based on availability.　　　　True　False

2. Which of the following was not one of the ancient Chinese primary colors?
   a. red
   b. yellow
   c. black
   d. white
   e. green-blue
   f. orange

3. In India, there were originally four castes, each symbolized by a color.　　　　True　False

4. What color is associated with Hindu weddings?
   a. yellow
   b. white
   c. red
   d. blue
   e. green

5. Symbolic color often has cross-cultural meanings.　　　　True　False

6. Environment, culture, and economic growth play a part in the development of color terms.　　　　True　False

Chapter 11 — Color Order Systems

Before proceeding with this section, the student should have read and gained a basic understanding of the concepts laid out in the text of Chapter 11, Color Order Systems.

INSTRUCTIONAL FOUNDATIONS

Producing colors for industry is a costly business. A single shade or tint can mean the difference between a sale and loss of business. Color order systems grew in an attempt to categorize color and communicate about color accurately.

Terminal Objective

A student who completes this section will have a basic understanding of color order systems.

ASSIGNMENTS

Title:	**Color Comparison Exercise**
Objective:	To determine the effect of texture on color.
Materials:	Water-based paints in matte and gloss finishes, a variety of different textures of paper from smooth to rough, brushes, water container, and water.
Description:	Select a color in a **matte finish**, and paint the same color on each of the different paper textures. Does the color appear different from one texture to the next? Select a color in a **gloss finish**, and paint the same color on each of the different paper textures. Compare the gloss and matte finishes. How do the texture and surface finish affect the color? (At the instructor's discretion, this exercise can be repeated for each of the spectral hues.)
Time Frame:	One or more class periods.

Title:	**What Do We See When We See Color?**
Objective:	To compare how different people see color.
Materials:	Each student will need paint chips or small squares of colored paper for five different shades and tints of each of the spectral colors (red, orange, yellow, green, blue, and violet), totaling thirty squares or chips. All students should be using the same brand of paint chips or paper. A piece of white paper or board large enough to accommodate all the color chips will also be needed for each student.
Description:	Each student will arrange the color chips, ranked in order from light to dark, on a white paper or board. Compare the students' work and discuss the similarities and differences in color vision. (Note: Students may attach the chips to the paper with a temporary medium, but the chips should not be permanently affixed as they will be used in other exercises.)
Time Frame:	One or more class periods at the instructor's discretion.

Title:	**Hue Family Exercise**
Objective:	To train the eye to see the differences and similarities in hue families.
Materials:	Each student will utilize the color chips described in the last exercise.
Description:	1. Each student will identify a true green chip and place it in the middle of the white paper or board. On one side of it, arrange the colors of yellow with a green undertone. On the other side of it, arrange the colors of blue with a green undertone.
	2. Repeat this exercise with true red as the center chip. On one side, arrange the color violet with a reddish undertone. On the other side, arrange the color violet with a bluish undertone.
	3. Repeat this exercise using true yellow as the center chip. On one side, arrange red with a yellow undertone. On the other side, arrange red with an orange undertone.
Time Frame:	One or more class periods at the instructor's discretion.

Student Name:

Course:

Instructor:

Date:

CHAPTER 11: COLOR ORDER SYSTEMS
CURRICULUM-RELATED TEST

Circle the correct answer from the choices given below. Then remove this page and give it to your instructor.

1. The three dimensions of color are hue, saturation, and value.   True   False

2. Goethe's color theory was based on a holistic model.   True   False

3. What is the most commonly used color order system in the United States?
   a. Goethe   d. Ostwald
   b. Munsell   e. NCS
   c. Newton

4. According to the Roper/Pantone study, what is the favorite color in the United States?
   a. red   d. orange
   b. blue   e. yellow
   c. green

5. The names we give to colors help to date them.   True   False

6. Colorimetry is the identification and matching of colors by precise measurement.   True   False

7. There is a universal color order system.   True   False

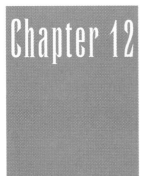

Chapter 12

Color: Pushing the Envelope

Before proceeding with this section, the student should have read and gained a basic understanding of the concepts laid out in the text of Chapter 12, Color: Pushing the Envelope.

INSTRUCTIONAL FOUNDATIONS

As the study of color moves into the new millennium, we can expect to see many discoveries and changes in relation to color. Studies of color in space travel have already uncovered some interesting possibilities. Much more study of the effects of color is needed, and we hope that these studies will explore the full ramifications of color's effect.

Terminal Objective

A student who has completed this section will have gained an understanding of some of the far-reaching possibilities of color.

ASSIGNMENTS

Title:	**Dermo-Optic Vision Exercise**
Objective:	To personally determine if color can be perceived without vision.
Materials:	A variety of colored construction paper at least eight by ten inches in size and a blindfold.
Description:	While blindfolded, run your fingers over each of the different colors of construction paper in turn. Do you sense a difference? Next, select one color and spend several minutes running your fingers over it while concentrating on the sensations you feel in your skin. Do this with a second color. After fifteen minutes or so of practicing with these colors, see if you can detect the difference between the two. Over time, begin adding more colors in pairs, first learning to distinguish between the pair. At the end of several weeks or months, you should be able to distinguish specific colors from the group.
Time Frame:	This can be done at home or in class at the instructor's discretion. This exercise usually works most effectively if it is done gradually over a

week or more. (It is interesting to introduce this exercise early in the semester and ask students to practice on their own, giving them an opportunity to compare their progress after several months of practice.)

Title:	**Color Box**
Objective:	To experience color through alternative sensory means other than vision.
Materials:	Each student will need a shoe box plus tape, glue, and an assortment of found objects to be determined by the student. Cut a hole in one end of the shoe box large enough to allow a hand to pass through into the box.
Description:	Imagine that you must describe the concept of color to a person who was born without sight. Select a color of the spectrum, (red, orange, yellow, green, blue, violet) and make a tactile assemblage of found objects to describe the color. Place that assemblage in the box and secure the objects by glue or tape, making sure that the observer will not be able to touch the mechanism by which the objects have been attached. (You want the observer to be able to feel only the objects, not the fixative.) Print the name of the color you have selected somewhere inside the box. Cover the shoe box and tape the lid shut. The box should be brought to class without telling either the instructor or the other students what the color selection is. During class time, have each student experience other students' color boxes by placing their hand inside the box and describing the color that they feel is represented. The instructor should tally the results of each student's perception.
Time Frame:	Homework assignment to be brought in and discussed during one or more class periods at the instructor's discretion.

Final Unit

FINAL PROJECT

In addition to the written final examination provided next, we suggest that students complete a final project, selected to be most pertinent to the class. For example:

Interior Design Course:	Students will prepare a complete interior color plan, including sample and color boards.
Landscape Design Course:	Students will prepare a landscape plan showing how color will be used.
Fashion Design Course:	Students will design a color plan for a collection of garments.
Graphic Design Course:	Students will prepare a poster incorporating color that is easy to read and effective as a marketing tool.
Advertising or Marketing Course:	Students will prepare a color plan to sell a specific product, such as an automobile, dishwashing liquid, or nail polish.

Student Name:

Course:

Instructor:

Date:

FINAL EXAMINATION

Circle the correct answer from the choices given below. Then remove this page and give it to your instructor.

1. Circle the primary colors of light.
   - a. red
   - b. brown
   - c. orange
   - d. yellow
   - e. blue
   - f. green
   - g. gray
   - h. violet
   - i. magenta
   - j. cyan

2. Circle the primary pigment colors.
   - a. red
   - b. brown
   - c. orange
   - d. yellow
   - e. blue
   - f. green
   - g. gray
   - h. violet
   - i. magenta
   - j. cyan

3. Select the answer that correctly defines the word *shade*.
   - a. a color that appears on the spectrum of light
   - b. a synonym for lightness
   - c. a color obtained by mixing a hue with black
   - d. a synonym for saturation

4. Select the answer that correctly defines the word *value*.
   - a. the estimated lightness of a surface color
   - b. colors opposite on the color wheel
   - c. a quantum of light energy
   - d. light having a narrow wavelength

5. There are five types of cones.   True   False

6. The retina contains 120 million rods and 6 million cones.   True   False

7. Pigment colors that appear opposite each other on a color wheel are traditionally called complementary colors.   True   False

8. Given the list of terms below, circle the six main concepts to be considered in designing a lighting plan for an interior space.

a. visibility
b. atmosphere
c. composition
d. object appearance
e. mechanical development

f. brightness
g. review and correction
h. spatial environment
i. interior color
j. fenestration

9. Daylight is a major factor to be considered in any lighting plan.

True   False

10. The color of daylight changes according to the composition of the atmosphere.

True   False

11. Tungsten-halogen lamps are a form of electric discharge lighting.

True   False

12. Electric discharge lamps may be used in any household socket.

True   False

13. Ill effects on the human body from fluorescent light are unheard of.

True   False

14. Lumen refers to the quantity of light that is given off in all directions by the lamp itself.

True   False

15. Candlepower describes the amount of light given off in a particular direction.

True   False

16. Veiling glare is the same as disability glare.

True   False

17. Luminaire is the synonymous term for lighting fixture.

True   False

18. In heraldry, the symbolic meaning for red was

a. loyalty
b. bravery

c. purity
d. honesty

19. In nature, what color signals danger?

a. red
b. yellow

c. orange
d. green

20. Climate plays a role in defining color biases.

True   False

21. Light exposure can affect the immune system.

True   False

22. Mammalian cells grown in the laboratory are mutated by fluorescent light.

True   False

23. Seasonal affective disorder (SAD) is a depression linked to the lack of light brought about by the shorter days of winter. True False

24. The perception of light by receptors other than true eyes is not possible. True False

25. Current research indicates that light can penetrate and affect the human body by means other than through the eyes. True False

26. Visible light can penetrate mammalian tissues. True False

27. Psychological measurements are often highly subjective and open to individual interpretation. True False

28. Red is the most common signal color in nature. True False

29. Color preference is the product of cultural norms and subjective color bias. True False

30. The intensity of color appears to be more significant than the color itself with regard to excitement or arousal. True False

31. The association of color with mood is learned. True False

32. Spatial impressions are highly influenced by contrast effects. True False

33. We see what we expect to see. True False

34. The gradually changing emphasis on different parts of the spectral range that will create distinctive atmospheres at different times of the day is called
a. verdigris phenomenon   c. daylight shift
b. Purkinje shift   d. saturation system

35. Color sends a subliminal message that plays a critical role in the success or failure of a product. True False

36. What is the most costly pigment?
a. cobalt blue   d. red
b. green   e. yellow
c. brown

37. What is the first thing to capture a shopper's attention?
a. lighting   d. price
b. display   e. size
c. color

38. Simultaneous contrast is the influence of one color on another.   True   False

39. The three dimensions of color are hue, saturation, and value.   True   False

40. There is a universal color order system.   True   False